Blurbs

Don't underestimate the power of youth ministry! A thriving youth ministry wins souls and edifies the whole body. *In Christ's Image* is a comprehensive one-volume youth minister's library, providing decades of experience and spiritual insights from seasoned, successful youth ministers. I know most of these contributors personally and admire them as some of the greats in ministry today. What an opportunity to learn from all of them in one volume!

— David Shannon, President Freed-Hardeman University, Henderson, Tennessee

In Christ's Image: A Guide to Youth and Family Ministry is such a valuable "go to" book packed with favorite authors. This will be a read & re-read resource for many in the brotherhood. I look forward to encouraging the youth ministers at the Nashville L2L Convention with this needed book. Dr. Kirk Brothers's leadership at HCU is such a blessing to the Lord's work. His dedication leading HCU is top shelf! 1968, was a very good year. L2L and HCU both began that year and praise God for that blessing!

— Rhonda Zorn Fernandez, L2L Board of Directors

In Christ's Image: A Guide to Youth Ministry is a comprehensive and insightful exploration of the dynamic field of youth ministry. Edited by Dr. Kirk Brothers, President and Professor of Leadership and Ministry at Heritage Christian University, this volume brings together a distinguished group of authors who are considered "giants" within Christian ministry.

In Christ's Image offers a well-rounded perspective on the multifaceted challenges and opportunities inherent in ministering to young people. Each chapter delves deep into the various aspects of youth ministry, providing readers with a robust and detailed understanding of this vital area of Christian service.

For quite some time, the need for a definitive youth ministry "textbook" has been evident, and *In Christ's Image* stands to fill this void. This book has the potential to transform the way we approach and implement youth ministry, equipping practitioners with the knowledge, tools, and inspiration to better serve the next generation of believers.

Whether you are a seasoned youth worker or a newcomer to the field, *In Christ's Image* is a must-read resource that will challenge, enlighten, and empower you to deepen your impact on the lives of young people. With its comprehensive coverage and the collective wisdom of its experienced contributors, this book is poised to become a seminal work in the field of youth ministry.

— Hunter Puckett, Youth Minister, Flint Church of Christ, Decatur, Alabama

"Youth and Family Ministry sometimes gets lumped into a second tier (or even third tier!) of kingdom work. It's not unusual for a youth minister to be referred to as a "junior minister," or hear words like, "You'll make a fine preacher someday." However, we at M2Y believe that working with our young people is one of the most invaluable ministries in all of the church. To that end, we recommend *In Christ's Image: A Guide to Youth and Family Ministry* as a great tool for anyone working with youth, from the seasoned youth ministry veteran to the newly-minted, fresh-out-of-school rookie minister.

The church has long needed a book to fill the gap on all things related to youth and family ministry. Kirk Brothers has compiled this valuable resource with wisdom from seasoned youth ministers, pulpit ministers, elders, and counselors. You'll see chapters written by Phillip Jenkins, Chad Landman, Reed Swindle, Lonnie Jones, and many more. There are also chapters from M2Y board members Ben Hayes, Justin Morton, and the late Jarrod Bailey. We look forward to seeing the spiritual fruits that will surely come from this treasure trove of knowledge. May God bless the readers and hearers of this book who help young souls become an "image" of Christ!

— Aaron Dodson, For the Ministering to Youth (M2Y) Conference Board

Many books have been written in the youth ministry category over my over forty years of serving as a youth minister. *In Christ's Image* is the most concise effort I have read covering all aspects of youth work within the church. While all of the topics are current and relevant, what makes this book effective is the experience of the individual contributors. I am personal friends with many of the writers and have seen their effective work within the church. A special thanks to Kirk Brothers, who is a true visionary and servant to the Lord's church and who wants the best for all ministers. *In Christ's Image* is not just another tool; it is a manual of instruction, encouragement, and love, helping to build better youth ministers now and in the future!

— Jerry Elder, Youth Minister, Spring Meadows Church of Christ, Spring Hill, Tennessee

They are only young and trainable once. Adults become set in their ways. So, our emphasis needs to be on training our youth. They are the future leaders in the home, church, and society. We need godly leaders. This book is packed with valuable information on how to build an intergenerational youth ministry with purpose.

— Dr. Roy Johnson, Lads to Leaders

In Christ's Image: A Guide to Youth and Family Ministry is such a valuable "go to" book packed with favorite authors. This will be a read & re-read resource for many in the brotherhood. I look forward to encouraging the youth ministers at the Nashville L2L Convention with this needed book. Dr. Kirk Brothers's leadership at HCU is such a blessing to the Lord's work. His dedication leading HCU is top shelf! 1968, was a very good year. L2L and HCU both began that year and praise God for that blessing!

— Rhonda Zorn Fernandez, L2L Board of Directors

In Christ's Image

A Guide to Youth and Family Ministry

Heritage Christian Leadership Institute

Edited by
W. Kirk Brothers

In Christ's Image: A Guide to Youth and Family Ministry

Copyright © 2024 by W. Kirk Brothers

Manufactured in the United States

Cataloging-in-Publication Data

In Christ's Image: A Guide to Youth and Family Ministry / edited by W. Kirk Brothers

Heritage Christian Leadership Institute series

p. cm.

ISBN: 978-1-956811-71-1 (hdbk); 978-1-956811-72-8 (ebook)

1. Church work with teenagers. 2. Church work with families. I. Brothers, W. Kirk (Wilburn Kirk)–1965. II. Title. III. Series.

259.23 DDC20

Library of Congress Control Number: 2024944409

Unless otherwise noted, all Scripture quotations are from the English Standard Version, 2001, Crossway.

Scripture quotations are from the ESV® Bible (The Holy Bible, English Standard Version®), © 2001 by Crossway, a publishing ministry of Good News Publishers. Used by permission. All rights reserved. The ESV text may not be quoted in any publication made available to the public by a Creative Commons license. The ESV may not be translated in whole or in part into any other language.

Cover design by Brad McKinnon and Brittany Vander Maas

All rights reserved.

No part of this book may be reproduced in any form or by any electronic or mechanical means, including information storage and retrieval systems, without written permission from the author, except for the use of brief quotations in a book review.

For information:

Heritage Christian University Press
3625 Helton Drive
PO Box HCU
Florence, AL 35630
www.hcu.edu

Heritage Christian Leadership Institute

The Mission of the Heritage Christian Leadership Institute is to provide workshops, seminars, and resources that train godly servant leaders who can serve in congregations, families, and communities with an emphasis on training elders and deacons.

A Heritage Christian Leadership Institute resource in cooperation with Heritage Christian University Press

Contents

Preface	xix
Introduction	xxi
Reasons for Youth and Family Ministry	1
1. A THEOLOGY OF YOUTH AND FAMILY MINISTRY W. Kirk Brothers	2
2. A PHILOSOPHY OF YOUTH AND FAMILY MINISTRY W. Kirk Brothers	12
3. MINISTERS ON A MISSION Philip Jenkins	24
4. FAMILIES MATTER Tim Frizzell	33
Relationships in Youth and Family Ministry	43
5. CONNECTING TO GOD Bill Bagents	44
6. CONNECTING TO FAMILY *Singleness, Marriage, and Ministry* Craig Evans	54
7. CONNECTING TO A CONGREGATION *Resumes, Interviews, and First Steps* Chad Landman and Ben Coleman	63
8. CONNECTING WITH ELDERS, DEACONS, AND CO-WORKERS Matt Heupel	73
9. CONNECTING WITH PARENTS Reed Swindle	82
10. CONNECTING PARENTS, CHILDREN, AND YOUTH MINISTRY *Parent-Child Relationships* Steve Wages	90

11. CONNECTING DIFFERENT RACES AND
    ETHNICITIES   105
    Zack Martin

12. CONNECTING THE GENERATIONS, PART 1   113
    Intergenerational Ministry
    W. Kirk Brothers

13. CONNECTING THE GENERATIONS, PART 2   128
    Understanding the Generations
    W. Kirk Brothers

14. CONNECTING THE GENERATIONS, PART 3   145
    Generations Y & Z
    W. Kirk Brothers

15. CONNECTING CONGREGATIONS   165
    Teamwork Among Youth Ministers
    Will Myhan and Patrick Kershaw

Recovery in Youth and Family Ministry   174

16. COUNSELING TIPS FOR YOUTH MINISTERS   175
    Ben Hayes

17. HELPING TEENS DEAL WITH ADDICTIONS   184
    Ryan N. Fraser

18. HELPING TEENS DEAL WITH DEATH   198
    Bill McDonald

19. HELPING TEENS DEAL WITH DEPRESSION   209
    Jeremy Hinote

20. CONFLICT MANAGEMENT   219
    Rosemary Snodgrass

Real-World Ministry of Youth and Families   229
Youth Ministry Nuts and Bolts

21. THE YOUTH MINISTER AS A LEADER   230
    Jim Martin

22. THE BALANCING ACT   238
    Managing Your Personal and Daily Calendar
    Carter Hoover

23. YOUTH MINISTRY BUDGETS AND CALENDAR
    PLANNING   249
    Richard Turner and Jordan Abrams

24. YOUTH MINISTRY ON THE ROAD   259
    Michael Deese

25. PLANNING CAMPS AND RETREATS 272
    Jarrod Bailey

26. PLANNING SPECIAL EVENTS 281
    Larry Davenport

27. MINISTRY TO YOUTH OUTSIDE THE US 292
    Paul Spurlin, Jeff Johnson, W. Kirk Brothers

28. YOUTH MINISTRY INTERNSHIPS 307
    Bryan LeMasters and Blaine McKinney

29. CHILDREN'S MINISTRY 101 316
    Thad Looser

30. COLLEGE AND YOUNG PROFESSIONAL
    MINISTRY 101 326
    Will Sharp

31. MINISTRY TO SPECIAL NEEDS CHILDREN
    AND FAMILIES 336
    Justin and Tiffany Guin

32. AFTER THE YOUTH GROUP 346
    Preparing Students for Sustained Faithfulness
    Andrew Kingsley

33. YOUTH MINISTRY IN MINORITY
    COMMUNITIES 355
    Native American and Black
    Josh Austin and DeWayne Tapscott

34. YOUTH MINISTRY IN MINORITY
    COMMUNITIES 365
    Hispanic
    Hector Cruz, Justo Dorantes, Jesus Gallardo, and Beto Huamani

35. TAX AND FINANCIAL TIPS FOR YOUTH
    MINISTERS 373
    Brandon Lanciloti

    Real-World Ministry to Youth and Families 388
    The Youth Minister as Teacher

36. ESSENTIAL ELEMENTS OF YOUTH MINISTRY . . 389
    Luke Dockery

37. ADOLESCENT DEVELOPMENT, PART 1 405
    Principles of Human Development in the Context of Youth Ministry
    James C. Guy

38. ADOLESCENT DEVELOPMENT, PART 2   419
Moral Development and Decision-Making Processes
James C. Guy

39. ADOLESCENT SPIRITUAL DEVELOPMENT   431
Justin Morton

40. DEVELOPMENT AND DISCIPLESHIP   441
W. Kirk Brothers

41. EVANGELISM 101   453
Rob Whitacre

42. TEEN EVANGELISM   467
Philip Jenkins

43. EVANGELIZING COLLEGE-AGE YOUNG ADULTS   477
Colt Mahana and Jody Apple

44. BASIC BIBLE STUDY TIPS   490
Properly Handling God's Word
Ryan Gallagher

45. THE YOUTH MINISTER AS THEOLOGIAN AND SCHOLAR   498
Nathan Daily and Ed Gallagher

46. TIPS FOR TEACHING TEENAGERS   508
Jeremy Gargis and Joey Barrier

47. PREACHING AND SONGLEADING TIPS FOR YOUTH MINISTERS   516
Andrew Philips

48. WRITING AND PUBLISHING FOR CHILDREN/TEENS   525
Jeremy Pate

49. TEACHING CHRISTIAN EVIDENCES TO TEENAGERS   538
Kyle Butt

50. TEACHING TEENAGE WOMEN   548
Lori Boyd

51. TEACHING IN THE CHILDREN'S CLASSROOM AND VBS PLANNING   557
Lauren Moss

52. CURRICULUM DEVELOPMENT FOR TEACHING TEENS Billy Bearden	566
53. AT-RISK SPIRITUALITY Lonnie Jones	577
54. TRAINING TEENS TO LEAD J. D. Schwartz	593
55. INTRODUCING TEENS TO MISSIONS Austin Fowler	602
56. TECHNOLOGY IN MINISTRY Jason Helton	613
57. POWERPOINT USAGE 101 W. Kirk Brothers	620
58. EQUIPPING PARENTS FOR DIGITAL PARENTING Chad Landman	633
Remaining Strong in Youth Ministry	639
59. WHAT I HAVE LEARNED IN YOUTH MINISTRY Chase Surrell	640
60. DON'T QUIT Dale Jenkins	648
Appendix 1—Camp Medical Release Form	656
Appendix 2—Youth Ministry Protocol List	657
Appendix 3—Curriculum Development—Student Learning Objectives handout	658
Contributors	659
Heritage Christian Leadership Institute Series	665
Heritage Christian University Press	667

Dedication

To the congregations, camps, and parents who allowed us to work with young people.

To all the amazing young people whom the authors in this book have had the privilege of working with. You inspired us far more than we could ever have inspired you!

To all those who dedicated their lives to helping to shape young people into the Image of Christ. You are our heroes!

To our friend Jarrod Bailey, who loved young people with all his heart and turned his chapter in a few weeks before his sudden death.

Preface

I was training to be a preacher. I went on a spring break mission trip to Auburn, Indiana in the spring of 1985. The leadership of the congregation mentioned that they would like for one of the college students to work with their young people that summer. I decided to do it. Though I was a pretty lousy intern, it changed the course of my life. The congregation back in my hometown of Elizabethtown, Kentucky asked if I would be their youth intern the next summer, and at the end of the summer, the elders asked if I would come on as the full-time youth minister when I graduated (1987). I am grateful to these churches as well as the Hill Grove church of Christ in Kentucky which first allowed me to plan youth activities and lead VBS and the Rivergate church of Christ in Tennessee which allowed me to teach the junior high class when I was a freshman in college. They instilled in me a love for working with young people that would later lead to training youth ministers at the college level.

I am grateful to Chuck Morris for dreaming of this book with me. I am indebted to the Heritage Christian Univeristy Press Committee, who did much to make this book possible. I am grateful to my Executive Assistant, Melissa McFerrin for her editorial work (especially on my chapters) and for the financial donations of my friend, and Heritage Christian University Board member, Boyd Pate, which made this book possible. I appreciate all the authors who have poured their lives into young people and shared their experiences in this text. Most of all, I am grateful to our awesome God who is shaping each of us into the image of His Son and gives so many of us the blessing of being tools in His hand as He shapes young people into the same Image. To Him be glory in Christ Jesus, His church, and this book! KB

Introduction

King Solomon wrote these words to his son: "The way of a fool is right in his own eyes, but a wise man listens to advice" (Prov 12:15). As a young man, I found myself making many "foolish" mistakes as I began my ministry with young people. Consider this work before you a compilation of wisdom and advice collected from over 60 authors with many years of experience and a wide variety of expertise.

Dr. Kirk Brothers and I began dreaming about this work in the fall of 2010. Having both taught courses on Youth Ministry, we realized that there was no work that sought to utilize the collective wisdom of many and to emphasize the great importance of youth and family ministry in the church. In this book, we have professors from four brotherhood universities, youth ministers, preachers, counselors, and elders who have contributed their wisdom in order to bless your ministry. *In Christ's Image: A Guide to Youth and Family Ministry* is focused on the importance of shaping young people and families into the image of Christ. It is our prayer that it will not only help you to disciple students and parents but that it will strengthen your life as well.

May God bless you as you continue to serve Him,

Chuck Morris

In Christ's Image

Reasons for Youth and Family Ministry

Chapter 1
A Theology of Youth and Family Ministry
W. Kirk Brothers

Introduction

I had been preaching every Sunday since I was sixteen, so I went to a brotherhood school upon graduation with the intention of preaching. God had some other plans. He does that sometimes. My journey to youth ministry started while on a stateside mission trip in Indiana during a college spring break. The church in Auburn, Indiana asked if any of the college students would come and work with their young people in the summer. Though I do not believe I was a great youth intern, that request changed my life. I worked with that congregation during the summer, and then my home congregation in Elizabethtown, Kentucky asked me to do the same thing the next summer. After graduation, E-town hired me to work with the teens on a full-time basis.

I had no formal training in youth ministry. (There was little available at the time.) I jumped in and learned as I went. I listened to experienced youth ministers and started attending youth worker conferences each year. Later, ironically after accepting a preaching position at another congregation, I took some graduate courses in youth and family ministry. In my first pulpit work, I worked with the teens as well. I served as a college minister while teaching at a brotherhood school. God has allowed me to work with leadership and ministry training camps for young people for over thirty years in twelve different countries (and counting). I have also had the privilege of training youth ministers at two of our brotherhood universities and one foreign preaching school for many years now.

The point is that I have worked with young people for most of my life. I love them and those who work with them. One thing I have learned very clearly over the last forty years is that if we have not wrestled with what God is doing in the world and in the lives of young people and have not attempted to articulate what we should be seeking to accomplish and why, we may well do more harm than good. Thus, I want to begin this book by exploring the theological basis, or lack thereof, for youth and family ministry.

What does Scripture say about youth and family ministry? Can it be found in God's word? Is it an unbiblical, modern invention? Do we have examples in the New Testament of individuals who minister to young people and are financially supported by believers? I will seek to answer these questions by focusing on God's mission in the world and how faith was formed in the lives of believers in Israel and in the early church, and by considering examples of adult Christians in the New Testament who ministered to young people.

The Father's Focus

Let us begin with the big picture of what God is doing in the world. The story of the Bible can be summed up in the phrase, "God so loved the world" (John 3:16). Love is part of the nature of God (1 John 4:7–10). Love creates. Loving beings seek others to love. The God of love created a world filled with beings with whom He could have a relationship. For this relationship to be deep and meaningful, He created beings with free will, not robots or slaves. He created Adam and Eve in His image to live as His images in the world (Gen 1–2). The first human beings abused this gift and sinned against God (Gen 3). Thus began a downward spiral from the garden of Eden to the tower of Babel in Genesis 11. Human beings did the opposite of what God commanded (cf. Gen 1:27–31; 11:3–4). They chose to live in their own image instead of God's. Humanity has continued this practice ever since (Rom 2:23).

Holiness is the other side of God's divine nature (Lev 11:45). I would contend that everything God does flows out of His nature of love, His nature of holiness, or both (cf. "the kindness and the severity of God" in Rom 11:22). God's holiness must judge us, but God's love seeks to save us. His love did not leave us in our sins and brokenness: "For God so loved the world, that he gave his only Son" (John 3:16). Christ was sent into the world as God's representative to die on the cross and restore the broken relationship between God and humanity (Luke 19:10; Heb 1:1–4). Thus, God's holiness (justice) and love meet in Jesus. The Savior came to portray God's presence and love (John 1:14–18), to proclaim God's kingdom (Luke 4:42–44), and to provide salvation for humanity by dying on the cross (Luke 22:20–21; Rom 5:6–11).

The church is described as the body of Christ (Eph 1:22–23). It is a body made up of people in Christ who are guided by the will and mission of Christ, the Head (1 Pet 2:9). Todd Bolsinger has a powerful quote from Christopher Wright in his book *Canoeing the Mountains*: "It is not so much that God has a mission for His church in the world, but that God has a church for His mission in the world" (2018, 30). We, the people of God, are to continue the work of God and of Christ in the world. To do so, each Christian should be in the process of being transformed into the image of Christ so he or she can participate as part of the body of Christ and minister in His name to build up His church and fulfill His mission (Eph 4:12–16). Simply put, God wants us to be like Jesus and to carry on His Son's work to the ultimate glory of Himself.

Faith Formation

Every Christian is a work in progress. As Paul put it, we "are being transformed into the same image from one degree of glory to another." (2 Cor 3:18). Babies are not born full-grown. Neither are Christians. They transform into the likeness of Christ over the course of their lives. In this section, I want to take a moment to look at key influences in the process of faith formation.

Faith Forms in Family

Scripture is clear on the role of parents and family. We see this in both the Old and New Testaments. Deuteronomy 6 calls on Israel to love God with heart, soul, and might; to keep God's commandments in their hearts; and to "teach them diligently to your children" (Deut 6:7). In Ephesians 6, Paul challenges children to honor and obey their parents, and he challenges fathers to bring up their children "in the discipline and instruction of the Lord" (Eph 6:4). In addition to Scripture, countless research studies reveal that family is the primary factor in faith formation. Landmark research by Christian Smith and his team is an example of this:

> Contrary to popular misguided cultural stereotypes and frequent parental misperceptions, we believe that the evidence clearly shows that the single most important social influence on the religious and spiritual lives of adolescents is their parents (2005, 260).

My dissertation also supports this reality. It focused on "factors motivating church of Christ ministry students to enter ministry." I interviewed Bible majors from eleven brotherhood schools in the U.S. and found that family had a greater influence on the decision to train for ministry in the church than any other influencers (youth ministers, preachers, Bible class teachers, peers, etc.) (2010, 115, 122).

Faith Forms in Fellowship

Thus, we begin with the realization that family is to be the primary place of faith formation. It is not, however, the only place.

The community-oriented nation of Israel would have understood Deuteronomy 6 as a national responsibility as well as a family responsibility. In the New Testament, we see evidence that fellowship and interaction with other Christians is a part of faith formation. In fact, there is evidence of specific individuals being commanded to assist with faith formation.

For example, Paul commanded the older women to "train the young women to love their husbands and children" (Titus 2:3–4). It is worth noting that Jewish girls tended to marry in their early to mid-teens (Keener, 2010, "Marriage," 2.1). The older women would likely be ministering to teens. In addition, some of the most important verses on leadership in the early church are in Ephesians 4:11–16. Paul explains the purposes of apostles, prophets, evangelists, pastors, and teachers. The purposes are to assist with unity in faith and knowledge, to help other Christians mature into the likeness of Christ, and to help other Christians find ways to minister for the benefit of the body of Christ. This work would have included working with teenagers. It is also worth noting that many of those in these leadership positions were financially supported by the church (cf. 1 Tim 5:17–18). The biblical model is for adult Christians to help new and younger Christians to mature in the faith. Adult Christians who are mentoring and ministering to teenagers follow a biblical pattern.

This is also consistent with the research into adolescent development. Smith states,

> Much existing research has suggested the crucial importance in adolescents' lives of meaningful relational ties to parents and nonparent adults—grown-up friends, teachers, mentors, coaches, and other parents—who can help watch over, care for, and provide resources to teens (2005, 226).

Faith Formers

Thus far we have seen that faith forms in family and that faith forms in fellowship and mentoring by non-family adults. Now let us look at some specific examples of spiritual leaders who worked with young people.

Jesus and the Apostles

Many of Jesus's followers traveled with Him (cf. Luke 10 and the seventy-two that He sent out). Jesus chose a group of twelve, from His disciples, who came to be known as "apostles" or simply "the twelve" (cf. Luke 6:12–16). Luke tells us that Jesus "when he began his ministry, was about thirty years of age" (Luke 3:23). While it is possible that some were older than Him, it is also likely that most were younger than Him. Howard Vos states the following:

> A high infant mortality rate, death in childbirth, a high mortality rate in accidents, and much else kept life expectancy short in Jesus' day. If it was only 35 in the United States at the time of the Civil War or during the Golden Age of Athens in the fifth century B.C. (as is sometimes stated)—perhaps it was not much different in the Roman world during the New Testament times (1999, 454).

James and John were young enough that not only was their father still living when Jesus's ministry began, but Zebedee was young enough that he was still working in the family fishing business with them (Matt 4:21). Jewish men tended to marry in their late teens or early twenties (Keener, 2000, "Marriage," 2.1). The best estimates for the death of Jesus are between AD 28 and AD 30. That puts His ministry as beginning around AD 26–28. If John the apostle died around AD 95–96, as many suspect, then he would have been ninety years old if he was twenty when Jesus's ministry began. The point of all of this is that Jesus likely mentored and trained young men in their teens and twenties. By the way, Jesus was financially supported in this work (Luke 8:1–4).

Timothy and His Mentors

Next, let us think of the influences in the life of Timothy. He was shaped by his family (mother and grandmother; 2 Tim 1:5), a Christian mentor (Paul; 2 Tim 3:10–11), the brethren in his local community ("well spoken of by the brothers"; Acts 16:2), and a group of elders (1 Tim 4:14). Paul came through Timothy's hometown of Lystra on his first missionary journey. When he came back through on the second journey, Timothy was already a Christian. Paul called Timothy, "my true child in the faith" (1 Tim 1:2). This likely means that Paul converted him to Christ. Timothy did not have a godly father. Paul stepped into that void. Paul referred to Timothy as a "youth" in 1 Timothy 4:12. Kenneth L. Barker and John R. Kohlenberger III observe, "A person could be a 'young man' until his fortieth year. Timothy was probably about thirty years old at this time" (1994, 1 Tim 4:12). William Mounce puts Timothy's age from his late twenties to mid-thirties at the time 1 Timothy was written (2000, 1 Tim 4:12). Thus, Timothy was likely a teenager when converted by Paul and in his late teens to early twenties when he started traveling with Paul and being mentored by him. Paul ministered to youth.

Is there biblical evidence for individuals, other than parents and family, who played a role in mentoring teenagers in their faith? Yes. Is there biblical evidence for individuals being financially supported as they ministered to and mentored young people? Yes. Is there a biblical foundation for youth and family ministry? Yes. A youth minister is anyone who ministers to young people by assisting them in their faith development. Biblically, sometimes these individuals who mentored teenagers were financially supported and sometimes they were not.

Let me conclude this section with some thoughts by Ron Belsterling from his book *A Defense of Youth Ministry*. He states,

I'd like to end this section with a brief outline validating why we do youth ministry, why the church needs youth ministry, why our communities need youth ministry, and why I believe that youth ministry can be understood to be the arm of Christ:

1. Jesus himself modeled a youth ministry approach. All but one of his disciples were teenagers.

2. Most people are most responsive to the gospel and decide to accept an invitation into a relationship with Christ prior to the age of eighteen. Half of the world's population is under the age of twenty.

3. Relative to developmental attributes and Systems Theory considerations, adolescents are the strongest age group of change agents in family, community, and society.

4. According to Steinberg and Monahan (2007), susceptibility to peer influence peaks at the age of fourteen, at which point, teens become more adept at resisting peer pressure a little more every year thereafter until the age of eighteen.

5. The forging of one's identity and the last developmental chance at a major overhaul of one's internal perceptions of self (worth, esteem, and efficacy) occur during adolescence. Adolescents are the most likely to watch and imitate role models, literally, neurologically adjusting, with the intent to be like the role models....

6. The combination of not yet repressed spiritual inclinations, rebellious cravings, and emotional volatility, and impulsiveness make adolescents susceptible to spiritual influences, good and bad.

7. Political, academic, and entertainment industries are increasing attention on and mimicking youth ministry approaches to adolescents specifically (2019, 15–16).

I included his thoughts because I want to challenge us to consider that there are not only theological, but also developmental and societal bases for youth and family ministry.

Conclusion

Some would question the biblical legitimacy of youth and family ministers who are supported by the church. We have demonstrated that God's will is to save the world and that each saved person be transformed into the image of Christ so that he or she may minister in the name of Jesus and carry on God's work in the world. We have observed that faith develops in family and in fellowship with other Christians. We have seen examples of godly mentors outside the family who assisted in the faith formation of teenagers and twentysomethings. We have also noted that some of these were financially supported for their ministry. Thus, there is a biblical foundation for youth and family ministry (and also college ministry). Yet, Scripture is clear in its emphasis on the home as the first factory for faith formation!

Discussion Questions

1. How does reflecting on God's work in the world impact your understanding of the church and youth and family ministry?
2. What stood out to you in the "Faith Forms in Family" and "Faith Forms in Fellowship" sections?
3. Had you ever considered the age of the apostles or Timothy when their journeys of faith began? How did reflecting on these things impact you?
4. Do you believe a valid case was made in this chapter for having youth ministers who are financially supported by the church? Explain your answer.

Bibliography

Barker, Kenneth L. and John R. Kohlenberger III. *Expositor's Bible Commentary*. Abridged ed. Grand Rapids, MI: Zondervan, 1994.

Accordance Software. Version. 13.1.2. Oaktree Software, Inc., 1994–2020.

Belsterling, Ron. *A Defense of Youth Ministry*. Eugene, OR: Wipf and Stock, 2019.

Bolsinger, Todd. *Canoeing the Mountains*. Downers Grove, IL: InterVarsity Press, 2018.

Brothers, Kirk. "A Cross-Cultural Study of Factors Motivating Church of Christ Ministry Students to Enter Ministry." PhD diss., The Southern Baptist Theological Seminary, 2010.

Keener, Craig. "Marriage." In *Dictionary of New Testament Background*. Downers Grove, IL: InterVarsity Press, 2000. *Accordance Software*. Version. 13.1.2. Oaktree Software, Inc., 1994–2020.

Mounce, William. *Word Biblical Commentary on the Pastoral Epistles*. Vol. 46. Nashville, TN: Nelson, 2000. *Accordance Software*. Version. 13.1.2. Oaktree Software, Inc., 1994–2020.

Smith, Christian. *Soul Searching*. New York, NY: Oxford University Press, 2005.

Vos, Howard. *Nelson's New Illustrated Bible Manners and Customs*. Nashville, TN: Nelson, 1999.

Chapter 2
A Philosophy of Youth and Family Ministry
W. Kirk Brothers

Introduction

Much to the chagrin of many of my university students, I had several professors in graduate school who liked philosophy papers: *A Philosophy of Ministry*, *A Philosophy of Leadership*, *A Philosophy of Education*, etc. I found them to be some of the most profitable assignments I was ever given. As a result, I require students in my *Fundamentals of Youth and Family Ministry* class and in my *Biblical Leadership* class to write philosophy papers. Philosophy papers are self-evaluations that require us to think about what we do and why. They challenge us to reflect on everything we have learned from Scripture and the statements and writings of others, to consider our personal experiences and practices, and then, based on these things, to articulate what we do or should be doing in a particular area. Thus, based on the theological foundation that faith is formed in family and fellowship, I would like to propose a simple philosophy for how we should approach ministry to teenagers and their families. I will focus on three key areas.

Minister on Purpose

Doug Fields asserts, "Far too many youth workers are busy doing programs, but they can't articulate the biblical purpose behind what they are doing" (1998, 44). What is the purpose of youth ministry? In the previous chapter, we wrestled with what God is doing in the world and how the church and the individual Christian fit into that work. Establishing a purpose for youth and family ministry grows out of an understanding of the mission of God, the purposes of Christ's coming to earth, the purposes of the church, and the purposes of the Christian. With that as our background, I propose the following: *The purpose of youth ministry is to assist in the development of mature Christian adults who are shaped into the image of Christ and who are equipped to carry out his mission in the world as active participants in a body of believers.*

Mark Devries elaborates on what a mature Christian adult is as follows: "Mature Christian adults then, are those people who no longer depend on whistles and bells to motivate them to live out their faith" (2004, 28). In other words, they have a personal faith in Christ that motivates them to live out authentic faith without any prompts or coercion from others. It is not our mission to keep young people busy and out of trouble, to make them happy, or to teach them that Christianity is fun. Our mission is to shape them into the image of Christ (which sometimes includes a cross). Considering this, *a youth minister is a designated representative of God and a local congregation whose mission is to share the word of God with adolescents, to serve as a Christian mentor, and to plug other godly mentors into their lives so as to assist in bringing them to Christ, in helping them to mature into the likeness of Christ, and in equipping them to minister as an integrated part of a local body of Christ.* I would recommend three action steps here. It would be very valuable to have youth ministry team retreats to work through these steps together.

Clarify the Mission

First of all, I recommend that congregations work to develop a mission statement for the youth ministry that helps to keep everyone focused on God's purpose. This can be followed up with a list of goals that make the mission statement actionable.

Here is a sample mission statement: *"The aim of this youth and family ministry program is to assist parents and the congregation in mentoring young people to become mature Christian adults."*

Here are some sample program goals (CHRIST):

- **C**ONVERSION to Jesus Christ as Savior and Lord.
- **H**OLDING a personal faith that will endure (not an inherited faith).
- **R**EFLECTION of Jesus's life and love in their daily lives.
- **I**NVOLVEMENT in the worship, work, and fellowship of the congregation.
- **S**ERVING Christ and others with their assets and abilities.
- **T**AKING the message of salvation to their friends and the world.

Defining Maturity

Secondly, I suggest you clarify what a mature Christian adult looks and acts like. When developing curriculum, I encourage youth ministers to think in terms of four categories that describe what a young person will be like when he or she leaves the youth program and moves into young adulthood.

- KNOWLEDGE
- BELIEF
- ATTITUDES/VALUES
- ACTIONS

What facts do they need to know? (the books of the Bible, the 12 tribes of Israel, the 12 apostles, the plan of salvation, etc.)

What do they need to believe in? (God made the world, Jesus rose from the dead, the Bible is God's inspired word, etc.).

What attitudes and values should they have? (love, joy, peace, patience, kindness, goodness, faithfulness, gentleness, self-control, value the spiritual over physical, etc.)

What should they do, not do, or be able to do? (make moral decisions on their own, stay pure until marriage, share Jesus with friends, etc.)

Once you have filled in these categories, you can then plan a curriculum and a youth and family ministry that targets this description. Remember that all the items you list in your four categories need to be covered in classes, retreats, and/or devotionals (and often multiple times). The process of wrestling as a team with what goes in the categories will be valuable to your work.

Identifying Stages

Finally, I suggest you break the maturity process down into stages. Duffy Robbins, for example, uses five stages: 1) Come level, 2) Grow level, 3) Disciple level, 4) Develop level, and 5) Multiply level (1990, figure 1.1). Doug Fields uses these five levels: 1) Community (no connection), 2) Crowd (visitors), 3) Congregation, 4) Committed, and 5) Core (1998, 87). I have known of youth ministers who kept spreadsheets that listed the teens they work with and where they are in the developmental process. This helps youth workers to focus on what each teenager needs at the current stage and what is needed to get to the next level. Another research project is highlighted in the book *3 Big Questions that Change Every Teenager*. The researchers, Kara Powell and Brad Griffin observe, "Every teenager is a walking bundle of questions" (2021, 21). Their research identified three key questions that teenagers are struggling with: Who am I?, Where do I fit?, and What difference can I make? (2021, 35). Helping teens answer these three questions will make a significant difference in their development into the likeness of Christ.

Focus on the Family

The second tenet of my philosophy of youth ministry is that we must focus on the family. Fruedenburg and Lawrence are right when they say, "Parents are the primary youth ministers in the church, and the family and home is the God-ordained 'institution' for faith-building in children and youth and for the passing on of the faith from one generation to the next" (1998, 58). Rick Lawrence observes, "Parents' impact on their teenagers' faith journey will always be stronger than the impact of the best youth ministers in the world" (2015, 153). This statement is consistent with Deuteronomy 6:1–12 and Ephesians 6:1–4. The home was designed by God to be the primary conduit of faith. Despite the wonderful comment quoted above, Fruedenburg and Lawrence make the following statement later in their book, "I would suggest that you avoid seeing parents as threats to your ministry; rather, see them as your well-trained assistants who have great power to influence young people" (1998, 76).

Parents are Primary

The quote above illustrates part of the problem with some youth ministries. Parents are either viewed as the enemy or as the youth ministers' assistants. Both are unbiblical views (though I do not believe that was the intention of the above-mentioned authors). God created parents before He created preachers and He created moms before he created financially supported ministers. God did not say, "Youth ministers bring up our children in the nurture and admonition of the Lord" (cf. Eph. 6.4). Doug Fields was right when he said, "A youth ministry that excludes parents is about as effective as a Band-Aid on a hemorrhage" (1998, 251). The youth ministers are the well-trained assistants to the parents (not vice versa).

I wish I had understood this when I started out in youth ministry. Congregational youth ministers serve as teachers and mentors to the teenagers. Their goal is not to replace the parents but to work with the parents to help teens transform into the likeness of Christ. Some parents will not accept their responsibility and thus other mentors may play a bigger role (like Paul did in the life of Timothy). Yet, God's plan was for parents to be the primary youth ministers. Remember that Ephesians 4:12 tells us that one purpose of church leaders and teaching ministers is to "equip the saints for works of ministry." Congregational youth ministers need to realize that they are called to be equippers. Thus, they need to invest themselves in encouraging and providing resources to help the parents. That does not mean we tell them how to parent (especially if they have never raised faithful Christian children to adulthood). It just means we share information, resources, and experienced mentors that can help them.

Partnering with Parents

If parents and youth ministers can learn to work together then great things can happen. The parents know and love their children. They are also often older and have more life experiences. Youth ministers, on the other hand, often know how to relate to teenagers, know characteristics of youth culture, and know how to study and teach God's word. There is much that parents and youth ministers can learn from each other. If parents and youth workers stand united, then our teens are less likely to fall. The second philosophical key to my view of youth ministry, then, is that youth programs should supplement and support the home, not replace it. We have intentionally put "Youth and Family Ministry" into the title of this book. To truly minister to youth is to minister to the whole family. They are not two different things.

Connect them to the Body

The final area of consideration in my philosophy of ministry involves connecting the teens to the congregation as a whole. Chap Clark is right when he says,

> Youth ministry, then, is not an appendage of the body, it is rather an expression of the *whole* body caring for a specific group. Adolescents need an adult community who will love them appropriately and with great care. This is the call of the church. Young adolescents need several second families, and middle adolescents need a safe place to explore peer relationships *while* knowing that there are many others in the wings committed and available to them. Older adolescents need to know that they matter to the other adults in the community. Youth ministry is everybody's job! (2001, 61).

The youth program must not become a church unto itself or a separate entity that is only loosely connected to the congregation. This is what the old-timers used to call "The One-Eared Mickey Mouse Model."

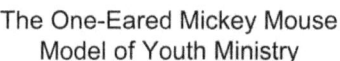

We noted in the previous chapter that research supports the value of adult connections. Wesley Black, in an article in the *Christian Education Journal*, adds evidence to this assertion: "Young adults who did not have close adult mentors during their teenage years seem to drop out more than those who did. Those with two or less older adult friends attend church less often in their adult years" (2008, 42). Much of the current research on young people and their faith is being done out of Fuller Seminary in California. Some of this research is highlighted in the book, *Sticky Faith*. The authors note, "Involvement in all-church worship during high school is more consistently linked with mature faith both in high school and college than any other form of church participation" (Powell and Clark 2011, 75).

The evidence is overwhelming that many churches are aging out. In other words, they are increasingly growing older with fewer and fewer young adults. Kara Powell, Jake Molder, and Brad Griffin highlight their four-year study of churches going in the opposite direction in their book, *Growing Young*. Their results highlight "the core commitments of churches that are not aging or shrinking but growing young" (2016, 20).

They discovered ten qualities that churches *do not need* in order to grow young:

1. A precise size.
2. A trendy location or region.
3. An exact age.
4. A popular denomination…or lack of denomination.
5. An off-the-charts cool quotient.
6. A big, modern building.
7. A big budget.
8. A "contemporary" worship service.
9. A watered-down teaching style.
10. A hyper-entertaining ministry program (2016, 25–27).

They also identified six core commitments for churches to grow young:

1. Unlock the keychain leadership. Instead of centralizing authority, empower others—especially young people.

2. Empathize with today's young people. Instead of judging or criticizing, step into the shoes of this generation.
3. Take Jesus's message seriously. Focus less on the gospel as "sin management" and focus more on transformation into the likeness of Jesus.
4. Fuel a warm community. Instead of focusing on cool worship or programs, aim for warm peer and intergenerational friendships.
5. Prioritize young people (and families) everywhere. Instead of giving lip service to how young people matter, look for creative ways to tangibly support, resource, and involve them in all facets of your congregation,
6. Be the best neighbors. Instead of condemning the world outside your walls, enable young people to neighbor well locally and globally (2016, 43).

David Fraze of Oklahoma Christian University worked with Tyler Greenway of the Fuller Youth Institute to conduct research based on the core commitments listed above. The results of their research were published in the fall 2022 *Journal of Youth Ministry*. They used an online Growing Young Assessment tool developed by Fuller. Over two thousand different Christian religious groups have completed the assessment. Fraze wanted to focus on how congregations of the churches of Christ would respond to the assessment. Thirty-seven congregations yielding 3,551 participants participated in his study (2022, 11). The researchers compared the findings among churches of Christ with other religious groups. They found that churches of Christ scored above average on Neighbor Commitment, and slightly above average on Empathy and Priority Commitments. The thirty-seven churches that participated scored below average in Keychain, Jesus, and Warmth Commitments (2022, 27). This is just a small sampling of the nearly 12,000 congregations of the churches of Christ in the U.S. and there is little evidence of significant numbers of participating congregations coming from the southeast where most congregations are located

(2022, 11). Yet, the research by Fraze and Greenway, as well as Fuller Institute can challenge congregations to consider whether they are growing young and can provide six core commitments that can help with that process. Also, while acknowledging that I have not read the 60 questions in the assessment, the Growing Young Assessment might provide a tool for wrestling with this. (There is a charge to complete the assessment.)

The point of Scripture and recent research is that teenagers need to be around mature Christian adults if they are going to become mature Christian adults. This does not mean they cannot have activities with those in their peer group (understanding cognitive and personality development reveals the value of age-appropriate learning and interaction). It just means that to be spiritually healthy, much of their time needs to be spent interacting with the entire congregation and multiple generations. As Mark DeVries stated, "When we separate an appendage from the body, both die." (2004, 43). Let us not separate teens from the body of Christ that they need to survive.

Conclusion

I am a firm believer in youth ministry. Are there problems and needs for improvement? Absolutely! Yet, for many young people, youth ministers are among the few who are standing in the gap and engaging in their lives. I have seen many youth ministers who are among the most devoted and hardworking ministers in the Lord's church. They pour their lives into young people and their families. My goal in these first two chapters and indeed in this book, is to refocus our efforts. I have attempted to begin laying out a theological-based philosophy that can aid us in keeping our young people faithful and helping them to mature into the likeness of Christ. The specifics of how this philosophy plays out will be different for each individual congregation. If any youth ministry focuses on shaping children into the likeness of Christ; will understand that its mission is to assist, not replace, the parents; and will integrate the teens and their families into the life and work of the congregation then it can accomplish great things for the cause of Christ. Jesus said, "Let the little children come to me" (Matt. 19:14). A biblically based youth and family ministry can help this request to become a reality.

Discussion Questions

1. Does the youth program in your congregation have a mission statement? If not, why not? If it does, how has it helped the youth program?
2. What are some possible resources that might be helpful to parents?
3. Give a few examples of what teens need to know, believe, value, and do when they graduate from the youth program.
4. Is the youth program connected to the rest of the congregation or is it disconnected? Elaborate on your answer.

Bibliography

Brothers, Kirk. "A Cross-Cultural Study of Factors Motivating Church of Christ Ministry Students to Enter Ministry." PhD diss., The Southern Baptist Theological Seminary, 2010.

Black, Wesley. "Stopping the Dropouts: Guiding Adolescents Toward a Lasting Faith Following High School Graduation." *Christian Education Journal* 3.5 (2008): 28–46.

Clark, Chap. *Starting Right: Thinking Theologically About Youth Ministry*. Grand Rapids, MI: Youth Specialties, 2001.

DeVries, Mark. *Family-Based Youth Ministry*. 2nd ed. Downers Grove, IL: InterVarsity Press, 2004.

Fraze, David W., and Tyler S. Greenway. "Growing Young in the Churches of Christ: Exploratory Analysis Across Churches Within a Denomination and Denominational Comparisons." *The Journal of Youth Ministry* 2:20 (Fall 2022): 9–30.

Freudenburg, Ben and Rick Lawrence. *The Family Friendly Church*. Loveland, CO: Vital Ministry, 1998.

Fields, Doug. *Purpose Driven Youth Ministry*. Grand Rapids, MI: Zondervan, 1998.

Lawrence, Rick. *Youth Ministry for the 21st Century*. Grand Rapids, MI: Baker Books, 2015.

Powell, Kara, and Chap Clark. *Sticky Faith*. Grand Rapids, MI: Zondervan, 2011.

Powell, Kara, and Brad Griffin. *3 Big Questions*. Grand Rapids, MI: Baker, 2021.

Powell, Kara, Jake Mulder, and Brad Griffin. *Growing Young: 6 Essential Strategies to Help Young People Discover and Love Your Church*. Grand Rapids, MI: Baker, 2016.

Robbins, Duffy. *The Ministry of Nurture*. Grand Rapids, MI: Zondervan, 1990.

Smith, Christian. *Soul Searching*. New York: Oxford University Press, 2005.

Chapter 3
Ministers on a Mission
Philip Jenkins

Button Pushing

I don't know if you loved, hated, or have even heard of the TV show "Lost," but it's my favorite show of all time. Basically (although there's nothing basic about the show!) the survivors of Oceanic Flight 815 crash land on a mysterious island somewhere in the South Pacific, and all kinds of incredibly strange events begin to unfold. For starters, the island has polar bears, some sort of roaring monster that kills people, and I'll stop there for spoilers' sake.

For illustration's sake, I'll share one more mystery: in season two they discover a computer connected to all sorts of important-looking equipment, and they are told that every 108 minutes, they must input the numbers "4 8 15 16 23 42" into the computer. A failure to do so, they are told, will cause the world to come to an end.

Well, not everyone on the island is convinced. After all, the menial task of pressing a button every 108 minutes sounds less like a world-saving tactic and more like a sadistic psychological experiment in human behavior. Then again, is it really that far-fetched for an island with polar bears and monsters to feature a computer of this caliber? What if pressing the button really is that important? What if the fate of the entire world really does depend on them pushing that button?

So they push the button. The timer resets. The timer runs down. An alarm goes off. They input the numbers. They push the button. The timer resets. The timer runs down. An alarm goes off. They push the button. Over and over and over again. It's a frustrating, mind-numbing, insanity-inducing process. Why? Because they're not even sure if what they are doing, this button-pushing, really even matters, if it's important, if it even makes a difference.

There are probably going to be times when you feel like you are "pushing a button" in ministry. "What am I doing here? Does this even matter? Is what I'm doing really important? Is this really the best way to spend my time? My budget? Am I making a difference? Is what I'm doing really accomplishing anything?"

Get the Picture

Believe it or not, those "What am I doing here and why am I doing it?" moments are actually healthy because they cause us to look at the big picture and wonder how the little things—the details, the events, the communication, the buttons—fit in ... or don't. Imagine dumping a 5,000-piece puzzle onto a table. The only way to see how all those little details fit together is to look closely at the picture on the box, for it is the picture that serves as a reminder of what it is you are trying to build.

If we want to see a picture of what a successful ministry looks like, all we really need to do is look to Jesus (Heb 12:1–2). How did He do ministry, and what was it that made Him so effective? I think if we boiled it all down to one simple idea it's that *Jesus had a clear understanding of His purpose.* He knew *exactly* what He was supposed to do and accomplish. He said things like this ...

> Did you not know that I must be about my Father's house? ("Fa-

ther's business" in NKJV) (Luke 2:49, remember he said this at age 12!).

For the Son of Man came to seek and to save the lost (Luke 19:10).

For I have come down from heaven, not to do my own will but the will of him who sent me (John 6:38).

For even the Son of Man came not to be served but to serve, and to give his life as a ransom for many (Mark 10:45).

He came to fulfill the Scriptures. In Matthew 5:17 He says, Do not think that I have come to abolish the Law or the Prophets; I have not come to abolish them but to fulfill them.

The thief comes only to steal and kill and destroy. I came that they may have life and have it abundantly (John 10:10)

Do not think that I have come to bring peace to the earth. I have not come to bring peace, but a sword. For I have come to set a man against his father, and a daughter against her mother, and a daughter-in-law against her mother-in-law (Matt 10:34–35)

Look at those "purpose statements." Jesus made it His aim to do His Father's work, to do His Father's will, to seek and save the lost, to serve, to give Himself up, to fulfill the Scriptures, to give life, and to cause people to make a tough choice to follow Him.

Know Purpose

Once we are able to understand and articulate our purpose, some wonderful things happen.

1. Knowing your purpose points you in a direction.
2. Knowing your purpose governs your schedule.

3. Knowing your purpose helps you say yes to things and no to things.
4. Knowing your purpose gives you a to-do list.
5. Knowing your purpose causes you to evaluate who you are and what you're doing, and respond accordingly.

Those concepts all ring true in the life of Jesus, too, aren't they?

Knowing His Purpose Pointed Him in a Direction

When you read the Gospel accounts, you don't get the feeling Jesus spent time sitting inside an office wondering what to do. Instead, He is intentional about where He went, even when He went, rising early in the morning to spend time on the mountain in prayer, purposefully visiting a well in a Samaritan village at noon, "setting His face toward Jerusalem," and so on. Knowing His purpose gave Him direction and caused Him to be proactive.

Knowing His Purpose Governed His Schedule

Don't forget the context of the great purpose statement: "For the Son of Man came to seek and save the lost" (Luke 19:10). These are actually the words Jesus spoke at the end of the story of Zacchaeus. "...when they saw it [the way Jesus treated Zacchaeus], they all grumbled, 'He has gone in to be the guest of a man who is a sinner'" (Luke 19:7). In essence, Jesus says, "Exactly! My purpose is to seek and save lost people!" No wonder Zacchaeus fit into Jesus's schedule!

Knowing His Purpose Helped Him Say "Yes" and "No" to Things

On one occasion the people wanted to take Jesus by force and make Him their king (John 6:15). There was just one problem: where did being an earthly king fit into His purpose? It didn't, so Jesus didn't allow it.

Knowing His Purpose Gave Him a To-Do List

I wonder if Jesus ever used His divine foreknowledge to look into the events of the day before they happened, or if He positioned Himself in such a way that He was ready for whatever His day brought (or maybe a combination of both?). At any rate, we know that Jesus's to-do list consisted of serving, healing, teaching, feeding, praying, and spending time with individuals.

Knowing His purpose Caused Him to Evaluate

I cannot help but think of the time when we read about Jesus being tempted in the wilderness. When you stop and think about it, so much of what Satan set out to attack about Jesus was His purpose (cf. "If you are the Son of God," Matt 4:3, 6). Satan thought if he could distract Jesus from His purpose if he could make Him forget who He was and what He was sent here to do, he could win! Of course, Jesus did not fall for it: not only did He know His purpose, but He knew Satan's, too!

Back to the Youthiverse

Look again at the five statements above, and consider how helpful it is when you know your purpose in your ministry.

1. Knowing your purpose points you in a direction.
2. Knowing your purpose governs your schedule.
3. Knowing your purpose helps you say yes to things and no to things.
4. Knowing your purpose gives you a to-do list.
5. Knowing your purpose causes you to evaluate who you are and what you're doing, and respond accordingly.

If you are ADD, and you've been lulled to sleep on this whole "purpose" discourse, let me bring it back to the "youthiverse":

running your programs, events, calendars, crazy ideas, and creativity through a "purpose-filter" will help keep you from button-pushing.

If you know exactly what you want to accomplish (your purpose), you don't sit around wondering how to spend your Sunday-Saturday. You won't get bored. You find things to do inside the office and things to do outside the office. You get a better feel for what kinds of youth events belong on the calendar and what kinds of youth events don't. (Hint: the ones that help you accomplish your purpose stay and the ones that do not go!). So, enough with the philosophical stuff! Let's get to the fun part. In the section below, pay close attention to the sometimes unseen, always important influence of purpose.

Purpose at Work

I was overwhelmed. I had not been at Mt. Juliet long, but it did not take long to realize how big the job was. There were nearly 100 students in the youth program, and to complicate things, Laura and I learned our first child was expected in July. How was I going to be an amazing dad, husband, and youth minister all at the same time? How could I meet the needs of 100 students, plus the needs of my growing family?

Thankfully I was not dumb enough to believe that I could. The odds of one person meeting the diverse needs of 100 diverse people are laughable. Instead, we began to imagine what would it look like to build a team.... So, we made a list of 28 of some of the most amazing adults we knew in the church and invited them to join us for a devotional. We asked them to consider who it was that showed up for them when they were young, asked them to consider being that person for the students in the youth group, and asked them to take a couple of weeks to pray about it before saying "yes."

To our wonderful surprise, 27 out of the 28 adults said "yes" to the adventure, and our newly formed team began meeting on Sunday afternoons to scheme, dream, pray, and study a book about youth ministry (*Sustainable Youth Ministry* by Mark DeVries). And so in 2012, with a team in place and a whole lot of exciting questions we did not quite know the answers to, we launched "Cocoons": small spaces (groups) meant for great transformation. The idea was to take our large group and make it smaller to help us better see our students and their needs. Cocoons meet on Wednesday nights. We have separate guys and girls Cacoons for each grade and each Cocoon has two leaders who have made a commitment to invest in their students from 6th grade through graduation.

Where do you see purpose at work in this tale?

Six Words — In 2014, I read the book, *Purpose-Driven Youth Ministry*, and took our Cocoon Leaders on a retreat. The entire weekend centered around one word ... you guessed it, *purpose*.

When you stop to think about it, a Cocoon Leaders Retreat features grown-up versions of what we hope our students will be: lifelong disciples of Christ. In a way our question became, "How can we cultivate students who become Cocoon Leaders?" As you can imagine, that led to some valuable discussion! Here are the questions we asked ...

- *What does a strong, healthy, youth ministry look like?*
- *What are the things that have helped you sustain your faith over the years?*
- *What things would you want every one of our students to have done or experienced by the time they leave the youth program?*
- *Hannah is your new sister in Christ. She is 16 years old, and her parents are not Christians. Her home life isn't great. Her dad has been in prison and her stepmom, to quote Hannah, "hates" her. Imagine that you have the opportunity to sit down with Hannah to talk about her new walk with God. You want to help her grow in every way you can. What would you share with Hannah in that meeting?*

Again, talk about valuable discussion! Their answers led us to identify six words (purposes!) that laid the foundation for what we're striving to do in our ministry: commit, connect, grow, serve, tell, and thrive.

These words became the bull's eyes for our youth ministry. Here is what we had in mind for each one:

- Commit: We want our students to commit to coming every Sunday and Wednesday.
- Connect: We want our students to make seven meaningful connections in the church.
- Grow: We want our students to grow in their relationship with God.
- Serve: We want our students to find a place to serve in the Body.
- Tell: We want our students to tell people about the Lord and His church.
- Thrive: We want our students to develop a faith that thrives into their college years and beyond.

Basically, everything we do fits into one of those categories (remember that bit about purpose helping you decide what you do and what you don't?). New ministries and events go through the "six words" filter, too.

Having a purpose is cute and all, but the real power and beauty is that all six of those words are rooted in God's Word. When you think about it, they are really God's expectations for His people. He wants us to be committed (Matt 6:33), connected (1 Cor 12), growing (2 Pet 1:5–8), serving (1 Pet 4:10), telling (Matt 28:19–20), and thriving (Phil 1:9–11).

People, Not Computers

I've gotten pretty good at running a youth program. I mean, if you do something for 17 years, you ought to be pretty good at it! But you know what else is good at running programs? Computers.

Computers run programs. So you can run a youth program? So what?!! People are not programs, and that's who we've been called to serve. When ministry stops being about people, it becomes about something else. You are not a youth programmer. You are a youth (watch this word) minister and minister means servant. So get out there and do things that matter, and minister with purpose.

Discussion Questions

1. What are some youth ministry activities and responsibilities that make us feel like we are just punching numbers, similar to the characters in "Lost?"
2. What stood out the most to you as you read over the purpose statements related to Jesus?
3. Explore the six words we use in our program. What would you add, subtract, or combine and why?
4. What are some ways in which we can make youth ministry more about people than programming?

Chapter 4
Families Matter
Tim Frizzell

Introduction

Families *do* matter. When my generation started in youth ministry in the early 1980s, we were just expected to work with teenagers, not with parents. We did not think our role was to work with families. Honestly, most of us probably avoided the parents because we were young and related better to the teenagers. In time it became clear that the best thing we could do for the teens was to help their families.

If we could choose one thing to do for our youth group that would provide a spiritual blessing for their lives, there would be many possibilities. Mission experiences are remembered for a lifetime. A week of Bible camp is a spiritual mountain-top opportunity. A youth retreat or spiritual leadership weekend with hundreds of Christian teenagers can provide inspiration that changes the direction of their lives.

But there is something else we can do for our youth group which is "the gift that keeps on giving." It involves helping their families to grow strong spiritually and to become the godly anchors the Lord intended them to be. Even when teens are highly involved in youth group activities, the influence and time investment of the home far surpasses that of the youth minister and youth sponsors.[1]

When the teenager graduates from high school, it is the teen's family that continues to have that constant influence for a lifetime unless there is a disconnect. By working with the teenager and the teen's family, we have a double impact that gives a lifelong blessing.

We often advise young people who are contemplating marriage to also consider the family of the one they want to marry. The same advice applies to youth ministers. When we decide to work with teenagers, we better pay attention to their families because it is a package deal. It is healthy to recognize that in youth ministry, families matter.[2]

Biblical Foundations of Youth *and* Family Ministry

Before we consider the aims of youth *and* family ministry, let us first notice some biblical principles that guide us in helping the homes of our teenagers.

Ephesians 6:1–3: Honor Parents

In keeping with this passage, youth ministers must encourage youth to show honor and respect for their parents even when they think their parents are wrong. We must also show honor to the teens' parents. We honor them by being humble and being slow to offer parenting advice. We do better to provide resources and encouragement. Parents appreciate good news reports and respond better to suggestions when they know we are on their team.

Philippians 2:3–4: Consider the Parents' Viewpoint

As youth ministers, if we are parents ourselves, we must make parenting a priority. This gives us credibility in the parents' eyes. If we are not parents yet, we need to try to think like a parent. Parents will pick up on this and appreciate it. No matter what our age, we are to show maturity in thought, speech, and behavior. Parents look for this type of maturity in the one who is in charge of their children's activities. We can't believe everything the teens tell us about their parents. When there is a conflict, we must be sure to get the parent's side of the argument as well as the teen's viewpoint before we form opinions.

Deuteronomy 6:6–9: Support the Home as Headquarters for Spiritual Training

Youth ministers must remind the parents that we are simply supplementing the spiritual instruction they are giving in the home. We are not able to provide sufficient spiritual nourishment for their children, but we can provide valuable assistance. We must be careful not to dominate the teens' schedule which would cause the home to no longer be the center of their lives. When recruiting volunteers, we should make it a priority to recruit parents, especially those who can lead spiritual growth activities. Some parents will need both encouragement and training to know how to lead spiritually in the home. The emphasis should always be on sharing genuine faith over leading a perfectly crafted devotional that has little application or meaning to the family.

Malachi 4:6; Ephesians 6:4: Encourage and Equip Fathers as Spiritual Leaders in the Home

In many cases, it seems that moms are more tuned in when it comes to the spiritual nurturing of their children. Dads tend to need more encouragement and training. Many men did not have a father who showed them how to be a spiritual leader at home. How important is this? In Search Institute's nationwide study of 11,000 teens from 561 congregations across 6 denominations, 12% of youth have a regular dialogue with their mom on faith or life issues. In other words, just one out of 8 kids talk with their mom about faith. It's far lower with their dad. One out of 20 kids or 5% have regular faith or life conversations with their dad.³ In the book *Families and Faith*, Vern Bengtson reports that in evangelical Christian families, 71 percent of children who have a close relationship with their dads will remain faithful, while just 46 percent of children with a weak relationship with their father will remain faithful.⁴ The father's role is critical for "sticky faith" (a term used by the research team at Fuller Youth Institute). Therefore, we need to take a special interest in fathers. Give them the resources and encouragement they need to lead spiritually at home and maintain a close relationship.

Psalm 68:5; Psalm 82:3: Be a Father to the Fatherless and Point Them to the Father of All

Not all teens will have spiritual parents. We must not leave these spiritual orphans to Satan. We need to stress to them the Fatherhood of God and show them examples like Timothy whose father was not a believer. In his book *Adoptive Youth Ministry*, Chap Clark summarizes one of the tenets of sticky faith by saying that the long-term faith of a teen is positively impacted when that teen believes "that he or she is known, valued, actively engaged, and proactively loved within a community (usually described as being composed of at least five nonparental Christian adults)."⁵ While youth ministers cannot adopt every spiritually neglected youth, we can be godly influences and recruit other adults to be spiritual mentors.

Psalm 78:1–8: Take the Long View—Train the Youth of Today for Spiritual Parenthood

When some parents refuse to become spiritual leaders, do not despair. Take this as motivation to start now to train the teens to be spiritual parents when their time comes. We need to lengthen our focus and peer into the future. Consider the influence we can have on the children and grandchildren of our current youth group members. We need to help our teens establish their goals to be spiritual parents and grandparents and that preparation begins now. If this generation is not firmly rooted and grounded in the truth of God, the next generation will suffer.

Aims of Youth *and* Family Ministry

With the biblical principles from the previous section in mind, let us explore some aims of youth *and* family ministry.

The Priority of Being Added to God's Family

No matter what kind of ministry, the priority is saving souls and that means being a member of the family of God, the church! We are missing the main point if we think youth and family ministry is simply teaching life skills that will help families get along well in this world. Those skills can be learned at any number of community centers. There are many good, loving, functional families who are lost spiritually and not in God's family. Let's not get so wrapped up in teaching parenting techniques and marriage enrichment that we neglect the number one priority: bringing lost souls into God's family, the church. In 1 Corinthians 15:19, we learn that if our ministry and teachings are dealing strictly with matters of life in this world, "we are of all people most to be pitied." As followers of Jesus, we need to remember that Christ himself said in Luke 19:10 that He came to this world "to seek and to save the lost." It is easy to get so focused on doing a good thing that we forget to do the best thing. This can happen in youth and family ministry as well. We certainly need to help families survive and thrive in this world but most importantly, we need to help these families to go to heaven!

Ministry to Our Own Families

Another crucial aim of youth and family ministry is ministry to our own families. One of Satan's favorite traps is to get us so wrapped up in helping other families that we neglect our own families. 1 Timothy 5:8 shows us how serious it is to God when we neglect to give our own families the physical necessities of life. This passage tells us that such neglect is a denial of the faith and makes us worse than an unbeliever. If God feels this strongly about our neglect of the physical provision for our families, how much worse would it be in His view to neglect our personal families spiritually? Other families are watching to see if we practice what we preach. While the people we serve can be very demanding of our time, they really need a family to look to for a spiritual example. The faith lived out in our personal families gives credibility to our youth and family ministry within the congregation. On the other hand, if we neglect our own families, our teaching about family will sound hollow.

Ministry to the Teens' Parents

We can certainly stay plenty busy working with the teens in our youth group, but we have established in this chapter that helping their homes become strong spiritual headquarters is the gift that keeps on giving. We need to take to heart one of the purposes of John the Baptist's ministry that was prophesied in Malachi 4:5–6 and described in Luke 1:16–17: to "turn the hearts of fathers to their children and the hearts of children to their fathers." Perhaps we work too hard to turn the hearts of teenagers to us instead of to their parents. Is there truly a need to help parents to become spiritual leaders in their homes? In his book *Family Ministry Field Guide*, Timothy Paul Jones cites the FamilyLife survey of nearly 40,000 Christian parents that provided a snapshot of what is and what is not happening in Christian homes in North America. Those surveyed were involved, church attendees. More than half of these parents said their families never or rarely engaged in any sort of family devotional time. Nearly one-fourth never or rarely prayed with their children.[6] What a difference youth ministers can make by simply helping families establish healthy spiritual disciplines in their homes.

Ministry to the Church Family

When we read descriptions of the church in the New Testament, we do not see the isolation of age groups that is so often the case in modern ministry approaches. 1 Timothy 5:1–2 urges us to encourage older men as fathers, younger men as brothers, older women as mothers, and younger women as sisters. How can we carry out the instruction of this verse if these age groups are constantly separated and isolated from each other? It is a beautiful thing to develop love in the hearts of our teens for the elderly in the congregation. It is touching to see our teens serve and care for the little children in the congregation. Our teens need the experience of interacting with all age groups in the congregation and other age groups receive great blessings when they spend time with the teens. One of the core reasons for congregations showing growth, outreach to youth, and spiritual health reported in the book *Growing Young,* was aiming for warm peer and intergenerational friendships instead of focusing on cool worship or programs.[7]

Practical Suggestions

There are so many things we can do to help families. Let's consider four: Promotion of Relationships, Preparation for Crucial Transitions, Prevention of Crises, and Prescription for Problems. In this section, practical suggestions will be offered as examples of what we can do to help families and the church family.

1 Promotion of Relationships

- Intergenerational "Family Night" meals for the congregation or selected age groups in the congregation. Programming can range from discussion of family topics to tech assistance for senior members provided by teens.

- Big brother/little brother; big sister/little sister pairings for activities at camp or some other event. Mentoring relationships are formed that bless for years to come.
- Teen-sponsored game night with the Primetimer or Golden Group of the congregation (Senior Saints). Pick games that the seniors can teach the teens.
- Teen-sponsored children's activity. This could be a movie night or a picnic.
- Visiting projects can combine the teens and children to visit the older members in their homes or a care facility.
- Parent-Teen activities, retreats, classes.

2 Preparation for Crucial Transitions

- Examples of life transitions include young adult/college, newly married, birth of children, parenting at various age levels, empty nest, and golden years.
- The life transitions can be addressed through classes, retreats, family night discussions, or care groups.
- There are also major spiritual growth transitions that deserve attention and preparation. Examples would include: becoming a Christian, a Bible class teacher, a leader in the church, a spiritual mentor, and a mission team member.
- The spiritual life and leadership transitions take preparation that can be offered through classes, training sessions, retreats, and resources.

3 Prevention of Crises

- Some crises can be prevented with adequate preparation.
- Marriage mentoring, enrichment retreats, and classes can help avoid the heartbreak of serious conflict and divorce.

- Parenting classes, retreats, and counseling can give parents the solutions they need to avoid family dysfunction.
- Training to detect and deflect peer pressure can give youth the strategy needed to make wise choices.
- Provide parent-teen or intergenerational discussion nights that feature someone who has survived poor choices and is willing to give pointers on taking a better path in life.

4 Prescription for Problems

- Sometimes despite our best efforts to prevent problems, a crisis will happen. The church is a great place to provide healing and help to those in pain.
- Provide support groups for grief recovery, job seekers, addiction recovery, caregivers, and specific illnesses.
- Develop a list of mentors or resource people who can help with issues such as financial struggles, the death of a child, the death of a mate, miscarriage, addictions, specific illnesses or disabilities, and rebellious children.
- Develop a list of professional counselors who are trusted and capable of assisting with mental and emotional struggles, addictions, marriage, and parenting conflicts.

Conclusion

When we invest in parents, we bless teenagers. When we bring together the various generations in a congregation, we strengthen the spiritual family. When we focus on our own families, we set an example for the believers. When we combine youth *and* family ministry, we send a message that families matter.

Discussion Questions

1. Why is it so important for youth and family ministers to have an impact on parents?
2. What benefits come to teenagers when their home is a headquarters for spiritual growth and training?

Notes

[1] Jim Burns and Mike DeVries, *Partnering With Parents In Youth Ministry* (Minneapolis, MN: Bethany House, 2003), 41.

[2] Doug Fields, *Purpose Driven Youth Ministry* (Grand Rapids, MI: Zondervan Publishing House, 1998), 251. Fields says "A youth ministry that excludes parents is about as effective as a Band-Aid on a hemorrhage."

[3] Search Institute's Report: *Effective Christian Education: A National Study of Protestant Congregations, 1990.* https://www.search-institute.org/wp-content/uploads/2018/02/six_denominations.pdf

[4] Vern L. Bengtson, Norella M. Putney, and Susan Harris, *Families and Faith: How Religion is Passed Down Across Generations* (New York, NY: Oxford University Press, 2013), 78.

[5] Chap Clark, "Introduction – Reenvisioning Youth Ministry and the Family of God," in *Adoptive Youth Ministry*, ed. Chap Clark (Grand Rapids, MI: Baker Academic, 2016), 7.

[6] Timothy Paul Jones, *Family Ministry Field Guide* (Indianapolis, IN: Wesleyan Publishing House, 2011), 27.

[7] Kara Powell, Jake Mulder, and Brad Griffin, *Growing Young, Six Essential Strategies To Help Young People Discover And Love Your Church* (Grand Rapids, MI: Baker Books, 2016), 43.

Relationships in Youth and Family Ministry

Chapter 5

Connecting to God
Bill Bagents

Introduction

Youth and family ministers are often quite young—at least as they begin their official roles. Frequently, they are perceived as even greener than they are. They are stunningly wise to take 1 Timothy 4:12–5:2 to heart. Even 2,000 years ago, some older believers tended to question the wisdom, stability, and spirituality of young ministers. We know this trend did not start in the New Testament era. Though God rejected his excuse, Jeremiah recognized that young people who speak for God often serve from a deficit of respect and gravitas (Jer 1:6).

Centuries before the church was born, Solomon (and others) authored an entire inspired book offering wisdom, blessing, instruction, protection, and understanding to the young man who would hear his father's instruction and "forsake not your mother's teaching" (Prov 1:1–9). He nailed the point emphasized in this chapter: everything good starts and ends in connection to God. "The fear of the Lord is the beginning of knowledge" (Prov 1:7), and "The fear of the Lord is the beginning of wisdom, and the knowledge of the Holy One is insight" (Prov 9:10). And the earlier we build a solid connection to God, the better (Eccl 12:1–7).

Paul addressed the matter beautifully with Timothy. Show the brethren your connection with and commitment to God. Do not give them a reason to doubt or question. "[S]et the believers an example in speech, in conduct, in love, in faith, in purity" (1 Tim 4:12). Give them reason to respect your work. And here's how you do that:

> Devote yourself to the public reading of Scripture, to exhortation, to teaching. Do not neglect the gift you have, which was given you by prophecy when the council of elders laid their hands on you. Practice these things, immerse yourself in them, so that all may see your progress. Keep a close watch on yourself and on the teaching. Persist in this, for by so doing you will save both yourself and your hearers (1 Tim 4:13–16).

God's help is essential to those lofty spiritual goals. Without a solid, dynamic, and growing relationship with God, what Paul commanded cannot happen. The importance of a deep relationship with God is strongly implied by the emphasis on right relationships with older men, younger men, older women, younger women, widows, elders, and erring brethren. First Timothy 5–6 are a clinic on right relationships. Paul couched his first letter to Timothy in the context of his grace-given right relationship with God (1 Tim 1:12–17). He strongly warned against the false ministries of those who made shipwreck of their faith (1 Tim 1:18–20). He condemned those who tried to substitute the keeping of self-invented rules for true connection to God (1 Tim 4:1–5). Only true godliness informs and enables true ministry (1 Tim 4:6–10).

Those who serve in youth and family ministry strategically embrace the sacred responsibility of helping parents bring up their children "in the discipline and instruction of the Lord" (Eph 6:4). We hold ourselves to the highest of human standards. We know God holds us to an even higher standard (Jas 3:1–2). We cannot honor God's call without deep and abiding personal knowledge of the Lord. And no matter how well we currently know Him, the biblical call is ever upward (2 Pet 1:2–11; Phil 3:12–16; Eph 3:14–21).

All we assert below is predicated upon having obeyed the gospel and choosing to live in Christ (Gal 3:26–27; Rom 6:1–4; Matt 28:18–20). Without biblical faith in the redeeming blood of Jesus Christ, there can be no saving connection to God. Without being born again of water and the Spirit, we have no access to God's spiritual blessings (John 3; 2 Pet 1:1–4).

Essential 1: Assessment

Logically, we know that personal spiritual assessment makes sense. There are numerous spiritual inventories, both online and in print, but the following ten questions have served so well.

- To what degree am I currently connected to God (Gal 3:25–29; 1 John 1:5–2:2; Phil 2:5–8)?
- Am I "walking worthy" of God's call (Eph 4:1; Col 1:10; 1 Thess 2:12)?
- Do I live the reality of Matthew 5:3–12?
- Is the word of Christ dwelling in me richly (Col 3:16–17)?
- Do I practice love as described in 1 Corinthians 13:4–8?
- Am I putting to death the sins of the flesh and manifesting the fruit of the Spirit in ever-increasing measure (Gal 5:16–26)?
- Am I personally practicing 2 Corinthians 13:5?
- Am I consistently growing in the Christian virtues of 2 Peter 1?
- Is there any sense in which I'm claiming to know God but denying Him by my works—including my words (Titus 1:16)?
- Do I courageously and consistently help those around me ask and benefit from these questions?

Our most godly friends—and sometimes even our critics—will help us stay real with these questions.

Paul offers an important caveat in 1 Corinthians 4:1–5. Humble, measured, and biblical self-assessment stands wise. But there is no wisdom in graceless self-condemnation or in prideful pronouncements of self-righteousness. God's guidance is key. God's word is the standard, but godly mentors often help us stay real and balanced. None of us are as bad as we think on our worst day or as good as we think on our best. We want to practice ongoing assessment that's fair, paying strong attention to directionality. God does so much to help those who are moving toward Him.

Essential 2: Biblical Understandings

If we think of connection with God under the heading of "spirituality," much caution is in order. I collect definitions of spirituality, both good and terrible. Until you have read and carefully considered, it is very difficult to know what any author means by "spirituality." The word is frequently used differentially (sometimes even in contradictory manners) within a single publication. Usages/definitions range from the mystical and esoteric to checklists—simplistic claims that if you manifest all these behaviors, then you are spiritual. Let the reader beware; there is much that has been written that is not in step with divine revelation. Below is the best we know to say about spirituality in terms of connection to God. It's the current edition of an outline that has been developed over several years as part of a graduate course on spiritual formation.

Defining Christian Spirituality

Christian spirituality is loving God with all our heart, soul, mind, and strength and showing that love by embodying the gospel of Jesus Christ (Matt 22:36–39; 2 Cor 5:17; Gal 2:20; Col 3).

Corollaries:

1. Those who are spiritual think as Jesus thought.

- Purposefully and joyfully seeking the mind of Christ (Phil 2:5-11; Rom12:1-2; 1 Cor 2:16; 1 Pet 4:1).
- Adopting the attitudes/mindset of Christ (Matt 5-7).
- Embracing Christ's understanding of the truth of God and the nature of reality (Eph 4:11-16; Matt 4:1-10, 19:4-5, 25:31-46).

2. Those who are spiritual teach as Jesus taught.

- Lovingly (Mark 10:21; John 8:1-12).
- Passionately (Matt 7:28-29; 23:37-39).
- Consistently (Matt 5-8).
- Clearly (John 8:31-32; Mark 10:17-21).
- Faithfully (Matt 5:17-20; John 7:16; 2 John 9).

3 Those who are spiritual live as Jesus lived.

- Walking as Jesus walked (1 John 2:6; Eph 5:1-2).
- Loving as Jesus loved (Mark 6:34; Luke 23:34; Eph 5:25; 1 John 3:16; 2 John 6).
- Suffering without retaliating as Jesus did (1 Pet 2:21-23; Phil 3:7-11).
- Growing as Jesus grew (Luke 2:52; Heb 5:8).
- Embracing the same purpose—honoring God the Father (John 8:29; Matt 26:39-24).
- Embracing the same mission—seeking and saving souls (Matt 20:27-28).
- Living up to the same holy and selfless ethics (Matt 5-8; John 9:4).
- Choosing the same life of service (John 13:1-14).
- Showing the same submission to God (Luke 2:51; Matt 26:39-42).
- Manifesting the same heart of sacrifice (John 10:14-18, 15:12-14; 1 John 3:16).

- Showing the same love for the church (Matt 16:13–19; Eph 5:22–32).
- Honoring the same commitment to prayer and worship (Mark 1:35; Luke 4:16, 5:16).
- Showing the same concern for the outcast and powerless (Matt 19:3–15; Luke 4:16–19, 5:27–32, 7:36–50; John 4).
- Showing the same respect for marriage, parenting, and family (Matt 12:46–50, 19:1–9; Luke 2:51; John 2:1–12, 19:25–27).
- Living the same trust in and respect for the word of God (Matt 4:1–17, 5:17–18, 19:16–22, 23:1–3).

Essential 3: Practicing the Spiritual Disciplines

It's virtually impossible to lead others where we have never been. It never works to call others to practice disciplines that we omit. The classic spiritual disciplines as identified by Richard Foster (Foster, *Celebration of Discipline*, 2018) are prayer (Matt 6:9–13), meditation (Ps 1:2), contemplation (Ps 78, 119:9–16), study (Luke 2:46–47), fasting (Matt 6:16–18), simplicity (Matt 6:19–24; Luke 12:15), submission (1 Pet 2:13, 18, 3:1, 5:5–7), service (Matt 20:25–28), solitude (Matt 6:6; 14:23), confession (Jas 5:16), guidance (Phil 2:1–4; 2 Tim 2:2), worship (John 4:23–24; Heb 10:24–25), and celebration (Phil 4:4). Each discipline is broadly supported within Scripture; none flows from a single verse or passage.

While we find Foster's book most helpful, we offer two caveats. While the practice of fasting is strongly assumed, it is never commanded in Scripture (Matt 6:16–18). However, finding ways to deny the flesh in service to spiritual growth is biblically mandated (1 John 2:15–17, 1 Cor 9:24–27). Secondly, each of the disciplines comes in forms strongly supported by Scripture, but both unscriptural and ascriptural forms also exist. We strongly promote doing Bible things in Bible ways. Counterfeit versions—for example, meditation as emptying the mind to find answers from within or celebration that focuses on exalting self rather than edifying others and expressing thanks to God—would harm, rather than foster, connection to God. We're wise to identify and reject false versions. We're just as wise to avoid letting the prevalence of false practices scare us away from tools that can bless us.

Purposefully building stronger connection to God through practicing spiritual disciplines functions best under the following conditions:

- Always guided by Scripture
- Practiced within biblical balance—never taken to unbiblical extremes
- Practiced with pure motives—never to be praised by others or seeking to earn special status before God
- Practiced prayerfully
- Practiced with the support and accountability of faithful friends; think elders, senior ministers, fellow youth ministers, and parents of youth group members
- Practiced with joy and thanksgiving. All progress is from God
- Practiced with the appropriate balance of hiddenness and transparency
- Practiced with a continual commitment to use what we are learning to honor God and bless others

Bibliography

For several years, I have taught a graduate course, Spiritual Development of the Minister. Below are select works that have helped that course. Please remember the fish/bones principle. The Bible is authoritative and God-breathed. Whatever accords with the Bible is fish; what does not is discarded as bones. Foster's books and the works by Dallas Willard have been particularly helpful. Steve Williams's "A Brief Guide to Devotional Reading" is outstanding.

Alerlund, Truls. "'To Live Lives Worthy of God': Leadership and

Spiritual Formation in 1 Thessalonians 2:1–12." *Journal of Spiritual Formation and Soul Care.* 9.1 (2016): 18–34.

Chandler, Diane J. *Christian Spiritual Formation: An Integrated Approach for Personal and Relational Wholeness.* Downers Grove, IL: InterVarsity Press, 2014.

Chung, Michael. "A Pauline Definition of Spiritual Formation." *Studies in Spirituality* 27 (2017): 237–256.

Foster, Richard. *Freedom of Simplicity.* San Francisco, CA: Harper and Row, 1981.

_____. *Life with God: Reading the Bible for Spiritual Formation.* New York, NY: HarperOne, 2008.

_____. *The Celebration of Discipline: The Path to Spiritual Growth.* Special Anniversary ed. New York, NY: HarperOne, 2018. (1st ed. 1978).

Gunnells, Timothy C. "Spiritual Formation: Process and Praxis." Pages 97–118 in *Living and Active Word: A Symposium by the Faculty of the Turner School of Theology Amridge University.* Fletcher, Daniel H., David Musgrave, and John Young, eds. Montgomery, AL: Amridge University Press, 2020.

Guy, Cynthia. "Spiritual Disciplines: A Means Toward Christian Maturity." Pages 119–138 in *Living and Active Word: A Symposium by the Faculty of the Turner School of Theology Amridge University.* Fletcher, Daniel H., David Musgrave, and John Young, eds. Montgomery, AL: Amridge University Press, 2020.

Hall, Elizabeth L. "Suffering in God's Presence: The Role of Lament in Transformation." *Journal of Spiritual Formation and Soul Care.* 9.2 (2016): 219–232.

Hindmarsh, D. Bruce. "Contours of Evangelical Spirituality." *Journal of Spiritual Formation and Soul Care.* 10.2 (2017): 195–206).

Howard, Evan B. "Contributions to Evangelical Spirituality." *Journal of Spiritual Formation and Soul Care.* 10.2 (2017): 237–247.

Macchia, Stephen A. *Broken and Whole: A Leader's Path to Spiritual Transformation.* Downers Grove, IL: InterVarsity Press, 2015.

McClendon, Adam. "Defining the Role of the Bible in Spirituality." *Journal of Spiritual Formation and Soul Care.* 5.2 (2012): 207–225.

Nouwen, Henri. *Making All Things New: An Invitation to the Spiritual Life*. San Francisco, CA: Harper and Row, 1981.

_____. *Life in the Beloved*. New York, NY: Crossroad, 1992.

Sheldrake, Philip F. *Spirituality: A Brief History*. 2nd ed. Malden, MA: Wiley-Blackwell: 2013.

Smith, Gordon T. "Inter-Generationality and Spiritual Formation in Christian Community." *Journal of Spiritual Formation and Soul Care*. 10.2 (2017): 182–193.

Stenschke, Christoph W. "Spiritual Formation and Leadership in Paul's Address to the Ephesian Elders (Acts 20:17–35)." *Southeastern Theological Review*. 5.1 (2014): 83–95.

Vanhoozer, Kevin J. "Putting on Christ: Spiritual Formation and the Drama of Discipleship." *Journal of Spiritual Formation and Soul Care*. 8.2 (2015): 147–171.

Willard, Dallas. *The Spirit of the Disciplines: Understanding How God Changes Lives*. New York, NY: Harper and Row, 1988.

_____. *Renovation of the Heart: Putting on the Character of Christ*. Colorado Springs, CO: NavPress, 2002.

Williams, Joel Steven. "A Brief Guide to Devotional Reading." Pages 175–186 in *Living and Active Word: A Symposium by the Faculty of the Turner School of Theology Amridge University*. Fletcher, Daniel H., David Musgrave, and John Young, eds. Montgomery, AL: Amridge University Press, 2020.

Questions for Discussion

1. If a youth and family minister lacked a strong connection to God, how would you know? What would be the key indicators?
2. If a youth and family minister lacked a strong connection to God, how would that impair his ministry? What damage and deficiencies would you expect to see?
3. What are the advantages of a strong connection to God?

What blessings, opportunities, and protections flow from strong trust in and reliance on the Almighty?
4. How might youth and family ministry best encourage youth and families to build strong connection to God? What would biblical intentionality look like attitudinally? Structurally? Relationally?
5. What are the major indicators that a youth and family minister—or ministry—is strongly connected to God?

Chapter 6
Connecting to Family
Singleness, Marriage, and Ministry
Craig Evans

A Heart for Ministry

For most of my life, I have wanted to be a minister. My parents were both ministers, but not in a professional way. They were and still are good to people. They cooked and took food, helped people move, opened their home to those who needed a place to stay, watched others' children, mentored people, checked in on the elderly, and found ways to serve others. They truly had hearts for other people. They were also good to preachers and their families. My family practiced hospitality, and we had ministers and college students preparing to be ministers in our home often for meals. When I was about twelve years old, Fred House, the evangelist for the Parsons Church of Christ, asked me if I would be interested in learning how to preach. He worked with several young men training us to deliver God's word. We practiced weekly and preached often as he encouraged us. The thought was planted to serve the church as a youth minister after college.

After finishing Freed-Hardeman University I found it difficult to find a church that would hire me to be their youth minister. The answer was consistent, we want someone who is married. I was sad and angry, wondering, " Why would congregations not allow me to serve as their minister?" I constantly heard we need more ministers, I had several good internships, I had been told I was gifted for ministry, and had a page full of references for any group of elders to check, but I was repeatedly met with rejection.

Some of the reasons I was given for why congregations only wanted a married minister:

- Married people are more stable than single people.
- Married people are more responsible than single people.
- Married people are more mature than single people.
- Married people are more moral than single people.
- They expected the youth minister's wife to be a minister to the girls (albeit unpaid).

Each of these reasons is subjective, and I could find examples disproving these reasons. I eventually reasoned none of the congregations would have hired Jesus or Paul either if marriage was the deciding factor. After a year of teaching school, I was blessed with a job as a minister. The position was unique in that the expectations involved the work of a youth minister and associate minister, and to date, I have spent about twenty-five years in full-time ministry. For most of those years, I was single, but now I am married and have a child. I have been asked to offer my perspective on ministry and how it may change with marital and family status.

What is the Purpose of Ministry?

What is the purpose of youth ministry? That may be a loaded question, but it is a question we all must answer if we are to be effective ministers for Jesus. Some want youth ministry to be about events that provide opportunities to be together. Some want the kids to have fun. Some do not want their kids to be bored. Some want their kids to have so many opportunities for involvement they do not have time to get into trouble. Some want youth ministry to be a surrogate parent and teach things that used to be taught at home. None of these are the true purpose of ministry. The purpose of ministry must be to connect people to Jesus and encourage them to take His word seriously.

Jesus compels us to make disciples of Him, not us. I heard a speaker years ago talk about a family tradition (Disclaimer: this would not be a good youth group event or an exciting intro to a devotional. Do not do this!). He said every year his family would gather for a family reunion at the family homeplace which happened to be a farm. He said the day would be filled with amazing food, games, and fellowship, but the day would not be complete until the family carried out a particular tradition: grabbing hold of an electric fence.

I know this sounds shocking (pun intended). The family would all get in a line and hold hands and one of the crazy uncles (most of us have one) would grab the fence and everyone would receive a little jolt of electricity. The truth is when the uncle let go of the fence no one received the electric shock anymore, because your connection to the electricity was based on your connection to someone else. If God is an electric fence, then our goal in ministry is for everyone to grab Him for themselves and not let go.

The purpose of ministry does not change regardless of the marital status, family situation, or even the age of the minister. But there are inherent realities to each one of these situations that we must be aware of to help us to minister to our fullest.

Paul addressed one of these realities in his first letter to Timothy. Paul, a single minister, gave inspired advice to Timothy, a single minister, in 1 Timothy 4:12–16:

> Let no one despise you for your youth, but set the believers an example in speech, in conduct, in love, in faith, in purity. Until I come, devote yourself to the public reading of Scripture, to exhortation, to teaching. Do not neglect the gift you have, which was given you by prophecy when the council of elders laid their hands on you. Practice these things, immerse yourself in them, so that all

may see your progress. Keep a close watch on yourself and on the teaching. Persist in this, for by so doing you will save both yourself and your hearers.

Scripture does not tell us Timothy's age. The word "youth" used here includes all men forty and under. For some, the word youth could carry the connotation of inexperience and immaturity. Paul shows Timothy the potential pitfall, then gives him a clear path to showing those to whom he is ministering that he is a mature and faithful servant to Jesus Christ. Timothy's example of speech, conduct, love, faith, and purity would give him credibility in the eyes of those around him so he could minister most effectively to those around him.

What if we replaced the phrase "despise your youth" with "despise your singleness," or "despise your marriage and family?" Paul does not want our ministry to be negated by the way we live regardless of our age, marital status, or whether we have children or not. There are blessings and challenges to each stage of ministry.

The Blessing and Challenge of Singleness in Ministry

Paul considered it a blessing to be single in ministry (1 Cor 7:6–7). He was able to do ministry at his own pace without being concerned about the God-given responsibilities husbands and fathers have to wives and children. The challenges of Paul's missionary journeys, suffering persecution, and spending time in prison would have increased exponentially if he were married and even more so if he had children. There is definitely room in the kingdom for single ministers, and they can be effective, but there are potential pitfalls.

Sometimes ministers feel the need to be everywhere so they can show the youth and their families they are loved and valued. Attending athletic events, recitals, band competitions, or whatever activities the youth have can be good, but it can also be overwhelming. There is also a tendency to fill up the youth calendar, with few breaks, to keep everyone busy so that no parent or leader accuses you of being lazy and none of the youth ever cry out "I'm bored."

I personally did this in my ministry. I felt guilty if I was not able to attend everything or had something constantly scheduled. At times I did not take off all the time I was allotted weekly and did not take the allotted vacation times. I felt that is what was required because I was single and didn't have a family (This is what I expected of myself, not necessarily what was expected by the elders). I had heard the way you help people to know they are loved is through giving your time to them. The desire to try to help everyone know they are loved and significant can lead to our unlimited availability. This unlimited availability is not healthy for us or them. Teens texting at two a.m. to discuss the meaning of life because they are bored is not best. The parents should have taken the teen's phones before bedtime, but that is another chapter for another day.

There are different reasons and circumstances for being single. Some have chosen not to marry, and some have not yet found the person they want to marry. For those who want to be married, it is important to know ministry will change when you are married and again when you have children.

I distinctly remember a time when two of my friends who were youth ministers were going through divorces. It bothered me and shook me. I traveled to visit my dad and told him about my friends. After I told him about the two situations, he told me if you were married and tried to keep the same schedule you keep, you might be going through a divorce also. This shocked me. He was not saying this is the reason for these divorces he was commenting to me on my schedule and my life. This conversation impacted me deeply.

As a married minister, I knew I could not keep that same kind of schedule because it would not be healthy, and there is a realization: It was never healthy in the first place. Single ministers need good boundaries and healthy schedules as much as any minister.

Things to consider as a single minister:

- Prioritize your relationship with God.
- Cultivate a devotional life saturated with Bible study, prayer, and worship.
- Set good boundaries.
- Find mentors.
- Take your time off.
- Involve other adults in your ministry.
- Remember busyness does not equal a strong relationship with God or a healthy ministry.
- Plan and schedule with purpose.
- Form relationships with other adults in the congregation.
- Your job is not to connect people to you but to Jesus.

The Married Minister

I want to begin this section with a disclaimer. I am now married and have a child. There are many things in this life I am not sure of, but there are two things I am sure of 1) I never knew more about being married than when I was single, and 2) I never knew more about parenting than before I had a child. I was correct in believing that being married and having children would change my ministry, but I had no idea how much.

After being single for so long in ministry, I became the guy who would speak at churches, lectureships, and workshops on how the church can minister to singles. Then God blessed me with an amazing Christian wife and now a wonderful little boy. Ministry does not look the same going from single to married. My first priority is still God, but I made a vow to God and my wife to prioritize her above my job whatever job that is. Whether I am a youth minister or President of the United States, my first priority is God, my second is my wife, and my third is my child or children.

The schedule of youth ministry is a demanding one, and it is important to discuss your schedule with your wife. The summer schedule is especially crazy. From camps to VBS, to mission trips, to summer youth series, to whatever else is on your schedule. If you show up at every kid's activity but never eat supper with your wife and children, you will have problems. I have seen married ministers keep their same schedules once they marry, and I have seen some who try to stop doing everything. I heard of a youth minister who erased most of his calendar trying to please his wife, and while trying to please his wife he upset the church. There must be a balance.

Things to consider as a married minister:

- Prioritize your relationship with God.
- Cultivate a devotional life saturated with Bible study, prayer, and worship.
- Take care of your family.
- Set good boundaries.
- Find mentors.
- Take your time off.
- Involve other adults in your ministry.
- Unless the elders specifically put your wife on the payroll, the elders should not expect her to be the youth minister to the girls in the group. Her level of involvement should be up to her. Be an advocate for her.
- Remember busyness does not equal a strong relationship with God.
- Plan and schedule with purpose.
- Form relationships with other adults in the congregation.
- Your job is not to connect people to you but to Jesus.

You will see the list for single and married ministers is not much different. I would add a couple of things worth thinking about, especially as a married minister. Try to only work during two parts of the day. Years ago, I heard a minister say he divided up the day as the morning, afternoon, and evening, and with the exception of trips or camps, he would only work two parts of that day. If he had an event at night, he would stay home with his family in the morning or come home in the afternoon. Also, when you take trips or have camps/retreats, take off the next Monday and/or Tuesday to not only rest up but to spend time with your family. All of these things would need to be discussed and explained to your elders, but I believe it would be worth it and would bless you and your family and the church.

Conclusion

Let's end as we began. Paul wrote the following to Timothy in 1 Timothy 4:12–16:

> Let no one despise you for your youth, but set the believers an example in speech, in conduct, in love, in faith, in purity. Until I come, devote yourself to the public reading of Scripture, to exhortation, to teaching. Do not neglect the gift you have, which was given you by prophecy when the council of elders laid their hands on you. Practice these things, immerse yourself in them, so that all may see your progress. Keep a close watch on yourself and on the teaching. Persist in this, for by so doing you will save both yourself and your hearers.

Ministry is not for the faint of heart, and I am thankful for your decision to serve Jesus and His church through ministry. May you be blessed and bless others regardless of your age or marital or family status. May we live in a way that our lives do not harm people's faith but that we live where people see Jesus in us, and it will lead to not only our salvation but the salvation of others.

God Bless!

Discussion Questions

1. What is the purpose and job of a youth minister?
2. What would Paul caution Timothy to not let anyone despise his youth?
3. What areas of Timothy's life was he to set an example in? Why?
4. How does this apply if you changed "despise your youth" to "despise your singleness" or "despise your marital and family status"?
5. What are the blessings and challenges of ministry as a single person?
6. How would your ministry change as a married person, and if you had children?
7. How can we make sure we connect people to Jesus instead of us?

Chapter 7
Connecting to a Congregation
Resumes, Interviews, and First Steps
Chad Landman and Ben Coleman

Connecting to a Congregation

Years of prayer, biblical and academic study, and hard work have led you to this point in your life. It is time to find a congregation and get to work, professionally, for the Lord. It is exciting and nerve-racking all at the same time. Where do you begin to connect with a congregation? In a sense this question can be posed, "How can I market myself to a congregation?"[1] Brian Tracy, a world-renowned marketing consultant, defines this aspect of marketing as the promotion of the product. This requires you to answer the questions, "Who is the customer?," "What does the customer value?," and "What does my product provide to my customer?"[2] The analogy to ministry is straightforward, "Who is the congregation?" "What does the congregation value and need?," and "What can I provide in this congregational context?" Help answering the last question will be provided later in this chapter. Our attention here is given to the former questions.

Who is the Congregation?

Where do I find a congregation looking to hire a new minister? You could open a newspaper or the latest issue of the *Christian Chronicle*, but research reveals word-of-mouth advertising is by far the most effective way to sell a product. Therefore, start with those you know and trust. Lean on your network. Your network is made up of those individuals who you have interconnected yourself with your whole life. This network includes former and current ministers; area ministers you interfaced with at area events; individuals from camps, conferences, and seminars; professors; and mentors. Every chance you have to increase your network, do so! Call these individuals you know, love, and trust for guidance in finding a congregation. Second, participate in as many internships as possible. Internships provide you with mentored experience, qualified references, and meaningful congregational connections. Lastly, use resources available to you through colleges, universities, and other institutions to find job listings and make "cold calls (or emails)" to these congregations.

What Does the Congregation Value and Need?

The second question of importance is understanding the congregation's values and needs. This step is crucial and should be completed before sending a cover letter and resumé to congregational leaders. Researching the congregation is often referred to as "doing your homework." This process should begin with the congregation's website and social media outlets. Pay careful attention to the details you find, taking notes of both the positives and negatives (if any) you discover. Remember, they will be doing the same research on you. Think about what you have posted on Facebook, LinkedIn, Instagram, and the like. Secondly, call a few individuals you trust to discuss the health of the congregation and your potential fit therein. Ask questions concerning needs and how you might help the congregation grow. Finally, when possible, call the former minister(s) at the congregation for more information. After you have completed your homework, you are confidently ready to submit your resumé.

What Can I Provide in this Congregational Context?

Now we turn our attention to the third concept identified in our evaluation of Brian Tracy's thoughts: "What can I provide in the congregational context?" Part of the purpose of resumes and interviews is to help you and the congregation determine how that question applies to you and whether or not your gifts and personality are fit for the needs and personality of the congregation.

Resumés

Every book written about resumés provides a different manual on the art. Here is what you need to know—your resumé should be uniquely crafted to help you land an interview. The resumé should not be designed to "sign the dotted line," but to get you an invitation to the table.

First, I suggest looking at a variety of resumé samples online and from respected peers and mentors. Follow an outline that fits your personality. Second, begin to craft your own resumé, and remember to be concise. The general rule is one page, no more than two. It is beneficial to include the following in your resumé: name, contact information (phone number, email, address), educational information (including coursework relative to the specific ministry position), skills and certifications, relative work experience (internships, full-time work, etc—you might include a few of your responsibilities at each position), and a list of references (make sure you ask them before putting them on your resumé).

Finally, after you have crafted your resumé, submit it to the congregation via email or mail (most do it by email). In either situation, include a cover letter. A cover letter briefly introduces yourself, reveals how you heard about the ministry position, identifies any connections to the congregation, and shares why you are interested in the position. If you are sending an email, the cover letter can be the body of the email. Many today keep an updated resume attached to their LinkedIn account.

Interviews

The interview process can be intimidating, daunting, and exhausting. One thing to keep in mind is that when a congregation's eldership or search committee interviews you, *they want to find a reason to hire you*. The main thing that an eldership wants to do is determine if you are a *fit* for that congregation, and we do not use the word *fit* lightly. Every congregation is different. Even the Apostle Paul knew this. He would write and minister to various congregations differently, but he always spoke the truth in love. Some congregations you will interview will be more laid-back, while others will not. It's important that you do your homework beforehand to figure that out.

One very important thing to do is contact the minister in the position that you are applying for who had the job previously. If you have been contacted for an interview, make sure that you do not miss this step. So many ministers go into interviews blind, not knowing anything about the congregation. That is not advisable. Get in touch with the ministry staff at the congregation for which you are applying. The minister may still be there and is transitioning into another job, or he may have already left. It can be incredibly beneficial but also eye-opening to talk to the person who had the job before you. If it's a new position, call any and all ministers on staff at the congregation. This may be the most important step in the interview process. Remember, you are trying to determine if you *fit* with this congregation as much as they are trying to determine if you *fit* them. *A word of caution*: You need to talk to current and former staff members, but you need to also be aware that church leadership and/or search committee may not be ready for current staff members to know who the candidates are. Be open with the search committee about your desire to talk to current and former staff and work with them on the timetable for having these conversations. Seek to honor their requests but also recognize that if they refuse to let you talk to the staff under any conditions, that is a warning sign.

You may also be under the impression that an interview is one-sided—meaning that the elders or search committee are the only ones asking questions. In that, you would be mistaken. You should have your own list of questions, some of which will be naturally answered during the interview process. You need to make notes to make sure that you are asking pertinent questions related to your job. Do not be afraid to ask potentially difficult questions either because it could end up being a much bigger deal when and if you are hired.

We could go in-depth on any of these questions listed below, but these are just some of the ones that you need to think about asking: What is the compensation for this job? Is medical insurance included—why or why not? What ages does your youth program encompass? What would you say is the "state of your youth or your congregation" right now? Where do you want to see this youth program in five years? What is the current youth budget? What is your policy on office hours? What is your policy on spouse involvement? Do you offer a cell phone plan or pay for my cell phone? Are expenses for events and activities covered for my spouse and me? How often will I be asked to preach? What are some additional duties that will be required of me? How much vacation time is allotted for me per year, and what about sick days? Do I get a day off during the week? How many classes will I teach per week, and do I ever get a break from teaching those classes? Am I responsible for acquiring teachers for other children's classes? How often do I get to meet with the elders? Will I have a youth deacon or youth committee? What is your policy on conferences or workshops– and will I get to attend those without having to take time off? What is your policy on getting advanced degrees (i.e. master's or doctorates)? How do you intend to protect me when I'm attacked (when gossip and rumors fly)? Lastly, what is your termination policy?

Odds are that a good percentage of these questions will come up naturally in the interview and discussion process. Some will not, and you may need to be prepared for some surprising answers. Again, ask what is appropriate and in the appropriate setting. Some of these may not be appropriate for an official interview but may be more appropriate in a personal phone call. You will likely have several discussions before and after an "official" interview with a congregation, even some after a job is offered. Some of these questions will also catch an eldership off-guard, and some of them might be questions they have not even thought about or encountered before. Give them time to think through their responses.

All of these parts of the interview process are not necessarily to determine if you are competent, they are to determine if you are the right *fit*. Likewise, you need to make sure that the congregation you serve *fits* you and your family as much as you *fit* them.

Additional Thoughts for Consideration

It would be a good idea to learn about the local school system/s where your children (if you have children) might be attending. There is also value in knowing the average income of the community. Look into housing costs in the area (purchase and rental). Look at costs in various neighborhoods. You need to consider not only the cost of homes but the neighborhood itself that you will live in and potentially raise a family. It can be helpful to go to the main local supermarket and look at the costs of items you routinely purchase. Finally, look at the local tax structure. How high is the sales tax in the area? How much is property tax? Do they have a state income tax? How does the cost of car tags compare to where you currently live? All of these are important as you consider the cost of living in the area. You can answer most of these questions by internet searches or by visiting the community, without needing to bring them into an interview.

One more thing that can be beneficial is to find out how the congregation treats visitors during a normal service or Bible class. You, your wife, and your children might just drop by on their way somewhere (make sure it is a legitimate trip, do not lie) and see how they are treated when you are not coming to "try out." If you think they would recognize your family, you might ask friends in the area to drop in for a visit and share with you what their experiences were like.

First Steps

Congratulations! You've been hired by a group of men to serve at a local congregation. You have a start date, a key to the building, an office, and a love for God to share, but how do you start? Better yet, where do you start? There is so much you wish to accomplish and pass on in the faith to the next generation. If you do nothing else, start like Jesus! John 1 states, "And the Word became flesh and dwelt among us, and we have seen his glory, glory as of the only Son from the Father, full of grace and truth." Jesus lived among us and like us. As you begin your work, be present among the people. Get to know the youth group students, parents, older adults in the congregation, and most of all the leadership. Spend time sharing meals, being in the homes of members, and serving the needs of church members. It is important to invest time in the students and adults alike. As the old adage goes, "People do not care how much you know until they know how much you care." Conduct yourself with grace and truth.

What do grace and truth look like? Jesus! Especially, this is manifested through servant leadership. Jesus made it explicitly clear by stating that "the Son of Man came not to be served but to serve" (Matt 20:28). He demonstrated it every day of His life, but, in particular, He made sure His disciples did not miss the picture when He washed their feet near the end of His life. He left them pondering His words,

> If I then, your Lord and Teacher, have washed your feet, you also ought to wash one another's feet. For I have given you an example, that you also should do just as I have done to you (John 13:14–15).

Therefore, when you arrive at your new congregational home, be a friend to everyone. Go to the students' sporting events and concerts. Wake up early and pray with the student's dad having a lung removed because of cancer. Sit quietly as the newly widowed lady weeps over the unexpected and untimely death of her husband. Pick up the exercise bike the older lady purchased and could not get into her car. In being present first, you demonstrate your genuine love for Christ and his people displaying a character full of grace and truth.

While you dwell with the congregation, it is also important to surround yourself with the right people. Jesus did this when he selected his apostles (Luke 6:12–16). Jesus trained twelve men for ministry in order to carry his work forward once he ascended back to heaven. The group you surround yourself with will mentor you and also provide you an opportunity to mentor them for lasting ministry. If the congregation does not have a youth committee or group of individuals heavily involved in the youth program, create one or create a circle of individuals you can trust, lean on, and ask for wisdom and guidance. These individuals should be those who are first godly examples for the teens, provide insights into the youth program, and are willing to invest time and energy into the students.

Finally, develop a plan. Barnabas encouraged the church in Antioch "to remain faithful to the Lord with steadfast purpose" (Acts 11:23). Having a plan is biblical and wise. It might begin as a one-year plan, a five-year plan, or a seven-year plan. A plan helps guide your interactions with students, events you lead, events you attend, and the Bible classes you teach. This plan should include a spiritual direction for the youth program and growth goals for students who are discipled through the youth group. If a plan is in place, ministry will become more intentional in the day-to-day.

Conclusion

As we conclude this chapter, we would encourage you to read *Your First Two Years in Youth Ministry* by Doug Fields for a more comprehensive list of do's and don'ts as you enter a new work. We leave you with this encouragement for success—live each day among those you serve by the mantra of Paul, "Be imitators of me, as I am of Christ" (1 Cor 11:1). Do this and your first steps will lead to successive successful steps.

Discussion Questions

1. What would you say is the most important aspect of connecting to a congregation? Why?
2. What can you include in your resumé in order to make yourself more marketable to a congregation?
3. What wisdom did you learn from the "Interview" section above that is especially helpful to you when considering interviewing for a ministry position?
4. Considering the list of questions to ask congregational leadership during the interview process, how might you be better prepared to review and respond to a formal job description?
5. What is the significance of knowing the people you work for and are ministering to at the local congregation?

Notes

[1] Humility must be a significant characteristic in the minister's life. If it is not, the minister cannot be like our Lord who washed the

dirt-road trodden feet of His disciples (John 13) and bore the shame of the cross to usher in historic joy to all humanity (Phil 2:1–10). However, a healthy self-evaluation and promotion of the skill sets and assets you provide to a congregation is essential in order to connect effectively to a congregation for maximum kingdom growth.

[2] Brian Tracy, *Marketing* (New York, NY: American Management Association, 2014), 44.

Chapter 8
Connecting with Elders, Deacons, and Co-Workers
Matt Heupel

Introduction

We had just returned from one of the greatest retreats we have ever had. Several of our teens had responded to the call to improve their relationship with Christ and three had obeyed the Gospel. I was on cloud nine as I arrived back to the church that Sunday evening, anticipating the welcome and celebration we would receive because of all the good news. This high continued through the week as I prepared for the meeting with the elders and deacons concerning the work of the church. I began to imagine all the good compliments and praise that I was about to receive due to our recent success at the last week's retreat. Nothing had prepared me for what happened next. First, I was informed that we had gone over budget for the event. Then I was scolded for all the trash that had been left in the church van. Then I was criticized for my handling of a discipline issue in a recent class. My feelings of excitement and accomplishment quickly turned into feelings of inadequacy and loneliness. Whether it was my shortcomings, or simply my age, I felt like the other men in that room felt as though I did not belong. I had believed I was a valuable member of the ministry team, yet that had left me experiencing a total disconnect from the church leadership. After all, in the grand scheme of things, those were trivial in comparison to the good that had been accomplished. I left that meeting wondering if I was even cut out for ministry.

An Unfortunate Reality

Unfortunately, the above experience is not uncommon for youth ministers. While it is true that one of the greatest blessings of working in ministry is the relationships that we accumulate over time, it is also true that some of these relationships can also be the source of much heartache and pain. Many times, that is the case when it comes to our relationships with our elders, deacons, and church staff. Since we are all Christians, one would think that having a good solid relationship with your church leadership and staff should be normal, but that is not always the case. We must remember that the people involved in our leadership positions are just that, people. People, while they are created in the image of God and called into service as elders or deacons, are still imperfect people. We must remember that anytime we work with people, we will encounter opposing personalities, values, and emotions. That means that it is not only possible that conflict will arise, but probable that it already happened. Whether it is because of an age discrepancy, level of maturity, or even a misunderstanding of individual roles, several youth ministers struggle to have a closeness with their leadership.

However, even though things like this happen to us more often than they should, this does not have to be the case. In his letter to the church at Corinth, Paul wrote "Now you are the body of Christ and individually members of it" (1 Cor 12:27). The job of every individual member of the church is to work together with the other members to be able to function as one single unit of the body of Christ. In fact, the word for "member" is μέλος and it means "a part as member of the whole" (BDAG 628). In the sense specifically here, it implies that "the individual Christians ... together form His body" (BDAG). As individual members, we cannot form His body unless we are joined or connected. This is incredibly true when it comes to a church's ministers, elders, deacons, and staff. They should serve as a pattern of good works so that others can be able to follow their lead. Yet, that is not always the case. While we cannot be completely responsible for that connection, we are responsible for our side of it. In fact, there are some preemptive things that we can do that will help us create an environment that is conducive to us connecting in our relationship with church leadership and staff.

Pray for Them

Any relationship we have should be saturated in prayer. In Paul's first letter to Timothy, he writes "I urge that supplications, prayers, intercessions, and thanksgivings be made for all people ..." (1 Tim 2:1). The Bible is very clear that we should pray for these relationships, but it leaves the "for what" aspect to us. When praying specifically for your elders, pray for a connection with them. Ask God to help you both share the same mission and goals for your ministry. Ask God to help them understand your heart as well as your actions. Pray for their souls, the souls of their families, and the souls of the flock that they oversee. Pray that cooler heads will always prevail when there are disagreements and conflicts. Remember that when we pray, we are praying to God who spoke the universe into being; nothing is beyond His reach.

Pray with Them

While it is important to pray for them, it is also important to pray with them. An article in *Focus on the Family*, concerning what happens when a husband and wife pray together, said "Every time you and your spouse pray separately for one another, great things happen in your relationship." Prayer is truly powerful. But when you pray together, that power increases tremendously, and so do the results.[1] It seems only logical that if praying with your spouse increases your connection in that relationship, then praying with your church leaders will improve your relationship with them as well. Ask them to stop by your office or invite them out for a cup of coffee and share your vision, your goals, and your concerns with them. Then ask them to pray with you. Connie Lee stated,

> ... the act of praying together brings us into God's presence in a fuller dimension than when we pray alone. There's a reason why Jesus compared the kingdom of heaven to a banquet, rather than a table for two! Life's important experiences are meant to be shared.[2]

When you pray for them, you are tilling the soil; when you pray with them you are expecting the fruit.

Establish a Relationship with Them

When it comes to elderships, we are aware of the responsibilities that our elders have to our local congregations. In fact, we are often very critical of their ability to fulfill those responsibilities. We expect them to know us, check on us, pray for us, visit us, and provide us with all the tools we need to succeed spiritually. Yet, what about our responsibilities to them, beyond the submission aspect (Heb 13:17; 1 Pet 5:5). How well do we know them? Do we know their goals, their favorite places to eat, or their favorite sports team? Again, we cannot be completely responsible for a connection, but we are responsible for our side of it. While there may be a stigma concerning having your elder as your friend, remember that they need that brotherly connection just as much as we do. I find that establishing a connection just flows more naturally when we are making a concerted effort to be a part of their lives. The same can be true with the deacons in our congregations.

We cannot allow ourselves to forget that these men who serve as our elders and deacons desire the same type of Christian comradery that we do. The only way we establish this type of relationship is time. There is no substitute for spending quality time with people as a means of getting to know them. It is also important to note that the only place in which this type of relationship cannot be established or sustained is in meeting rooms. A connection like this happens when we take them to lunch, visit their homes, watch a game together, have dinner with their families, or send them a birthday card or a note of appreciation. They may not become your best friend, but this connection will help you build a good rapport with them. Then when problems arise, or people begin to criticize or complain to them about you, they will not see the problem; they will see your heart. The opposite of that should also be true when people complain to you about them (and they will); you will give them the benefit of the doubt because you know their hearts. Not only does their job become easier because the two of you have a relationship outside of the minister/elder or minister/deacon relations, but yours will also.

Become Their Biggest Fan

No one likes to be told how to do their job. In my spare time, I serve as the clockkeeper for my son's high school basketball games. I find that it allows me an opportunity to be a part of the community as well as have a front-row seat to watch my boys do what they love. Most people do not know this, but in basketball, the clockkeeper is considered a designated official. Thankfully, I am not required to wear the referee stripes. What I did not expect was the relationships that I would begin to have with the referees. We talk and cut up before, after, and sometimes even during the games. In case you did not know this, most people hate referees! They are constantly yelled at, criticized, called names, and repeatedly told they are wrong. Fans and coaches are constantly telling the referees how to do their job. It is also contagious. During a game, you will find even the most reserved of people falling into the trap and booing with the crowd. Yet, they continue to do their job, and for the most part, even enjoy it. I have often wondered what it would be like if the referees could go to their jobs and yell at them, call them names, and constantly tell them how to do their job. Could you imagine what would happen if someone came to your job and did that to you?

It pains me to say, but this happens all the time in ministry. As a minister/youth minister, you by default become the face of the congregation. When people think of your church, they automatically think of you. Although, that may not be ideal ... that is just the way it is. When someone has a complaint, rather than follow the guidelines of Matthew 18:15–17, they come to you to express their displeasure about how things are going. It sounds something like this, "You know sister so-in-so has been out sick for three weeks and has not gotten a call from even one of the elders." Or maybe like this, "All of the elders ever do is care about money, they do not really care about souls." Let's not forget the deacons, "Deacon what-is-his-name who is over buildings and grounds has not weeded out the flower bed all summer long." It will not stop there, you will hear, "Why are they going to do that? When is this going to get done? When are they going to put somebody in there that knows what they're doing?" Make no mistake, it will happen. People will believe that they know how to do the jobs of elders, deacons, preachers, and youth ministers better than the elders, deacons, preachers, and youth ministers can. If you want a strong connection with them, back them, support them, and by no means allow yourself to get caught up in the negativity and gossip. Your job is to honor, support, and defend them. In most cases, they are doing the best they can with the tools they have. If you support them, then maybe others will follow your example and support them too. You will find that most of the attacks and criticisms are either untrue or unwarranted. Here is the kicker...don't think that you are exempt from this trap. Chances are some of those same members are going to your elders and deacons and criticizing you as well. If you want them to defend you, you better be defending them. Is not that the way Jesus told us to do it, "So whatever you wish that others would do to you, do also to them…" (Matt 7:12). Paul taught us to "in humility count others more significant than yourselves. Let each of you look not only to his own interests, but also to the interests of others" (Phil 2:3–4).

Develop a Strong Work Ethic

My favorite coach of all time was John Wooden. When seeking to motivate people he said,

> There is no substitute for hard work. If you're looking for the easy way, if you're looking for the trick, you might get by for a while, but you will not be developing the talents that lie within you. There is simply no substitute for work.[3]

Henry Ford II once said, "The first qualification for success in my view is a strong work ethic."[4] Kobe Bryant said this about hard work, "Great things come from hard work and perseverance."[5] No one would ever begin to question the success of these three individuals. People love and respect individuals who have a strong work ethic, and ministry is no different. If you want your eldership and your deacons to appreciate you, show them a strong work ethic. Many church elders and deacons view a youth minister as a Millennial who does not want to grow up or as someone who stays up all night playing Madden and sleeps till noon, wears socks with sandals, wears a beanie on their head in August, lazy, and unprofessional. Yes, that is a complete generalization, but sometimes that is the vibe that Youth Ministers have put out. If you truly want to establish a healthy, productive relationship with your elders and deacons, respect the job. Treat it as a career and not an activity. Show up on time to your meetings and dress appropriately. Show them you are an adult ready to snatch their children out of the grasp of Satan with devotionals, retreats, and pizza. This is especially true for someone who is beginning a new work. Hit the ground running, giving them no reason to question your efforts. The Bible said it this way, "Whatever your hand finds to do, do it with your might ..." (Eccl 9:10). They will respect you, admire you, and appreciate you; all of which will help you connect with them.

Conclusion

It happens to the best of teams. Even the apostles of Jesus had their moments. They argued over who was the greatest (Mark 9:34) and the rest of the group became angry with James and John when their mom asked Jesus (likely her nephew) to give them special places of honor in His kingdom (Matt 20:20–24). Yet, in spite of these setbacks, they pulled together and went on to change the world (cf. Acts 1:9–26). If they did, we can!

Discussion Questions

1. What are some examples of incidents with church leadership that you have experienced that made you feel valuable to the ministry team?
2. What are some ways we can build a bridge between the church membership and the church leadership?
3. Discuss why a strong ethic is so important when it comes to ministry.

Notes

[1] Stormie Ormatrian, "When Two Pray," *Focus on the Family*. https://www.focusonthefamily.com/marriage/when-two-pray/.

[2] Connie Lee, "The Power of Praying Together." https://guideposts.org/faith-prayer-devotions/stories-of-faith-faith-prayer-devotions/the-power-of-praying-together/.

[3] John Wooden, https://www.inspiringquotes.us/author/2524-john-wooden/about-hard-work.

[4] Henry Ford, II, https://www.azquotes.com/quotes/topics/strong-work-ethic.html.

[5] Kobe Bryant, https://loveexpands.com/kobe-bryant-quotes-on-work-ethic/.

Chapter 9
Connecting with Parents
Reed Swindle

Introduction

It was already after midnight and we were trying to find our hotel. I had a bus full of rowdy kids in Atlanta after an extra inning baseball game went much longer than expected. We needed to get them in bed because we were going to Six Flags the next morning. Since this was in the early 2000's we were using printed maps from Mapquest and had just ventured out into using hotels.com to book our reservations. We exited the interstate and drove past some nice hotels, but the step-by-step directions told us to keep going. After leaving the bright portion of the exit with the glow of the lights of civilization about us, we came to a red light in a dark area. "Turn right," the map read.

As we made our way down the dark road there were more glowing lights ahead, but there was a slight problem with these lights. The lights said, "Girls, Girls, Girls." There may or may not have been some employees of this establishment on the side of the road trying to guide us to their parking lot. Due to the lack of clothing needed for their profession, I instructed everyone to look down. I said, "The hotel is up here on the right, just keep your eyes closed!" Directly across from this business was a small, dimly lit hotel. Shady is an understatement for this hotel. One of the chaperones and I went into the office where a very skittish late-night employee who could not speak a lot of English ensured us that this was a safe hotel as long as we kept our doors locked.

We had a decision that needed to be made. When we left Huntsville, Alabama earlier that day, a group of parents watched me drive away with the single most valuable thing they owned. You can mess with people's money, and you can mess with people's jobs, but you better be sure to protect their children. An extremely important part of youth ministry is connecting with the parents. They are the ones who make out the family calendars, bring their kids to worship, and make sure they are at your youth events. They are also the ones who have to help make tough decisions about scheduling conflicts and whether to push the ball tournament or your retreat of the family calendar. Youth ministers need to help make these decisions easier for parents. Let us consider four keys to connecting with parents.

Build Trust

Key number one is understanding parents need to the able to **trust** the youth minister. Read that again. Parents need to know that the person taking their kids on trips is going to protect their most prized possessions. They need to know first, their children will be protected physically. As we walked out of the shady unnamed motel, we decided this was no place for kids. We drove ourselves right back up the road and after contacting an elder, we paid more money to put our kids in a safe hotel. If this had been within the last 5 years, we would have had kids messaging their parents about the situation and my phone would have been blowing up. But since this was BCP (Before Cell Phones), it was the first story told as soon as the bus doors were open. My phone rang, but it was parents thanking me for making sure their kids were safe.

They need to trust you will protect their kids spiritually as well. In Dallas, Texas our group was at an area wide where a blatant misapplication of Scripture was conveyed. It was not purposeful. It was a lack of study on the part of the good-hearted presenter. After our meal and as we drove home, I explained to our group the truth about the situation. We not only talked about the topic addressed, but we also talked about how to handle situations when you disagree. We talked about respect and kindness but also standing for what we believe.

In order to better understand this concept of trust, we have to understand how many parents view the youth minister and his program. There are basically two ways. First, there are parents who view the youth group as an aid to their effort to spiritually mature their family. If these families lived off the grid in a tiny house and hunted bears, they would still worship and their kids would still progress spiritually. These families are far more likely to use your program to help their kids if they know the events you choose are solid events. A pretty strong rule to go by for picking events is as follows: We will not take our youth group to any event that is questionable doctrinally. There are too many great options available with trusted speakers and solid track records to feel like we have to be involved with spiritually unsafe events. Not to mention, if there are no events in the area that meet those standards, we are talented and smart enough to create some.

While some families use the youth program to help them, there are other families that use the youth program for all of the spiritual development of their children. They really do not talk about the Bible a lot at home. These parents do not study Scripture much, but they know their kids need it. So, they send them to your youth events as a part of the growth of their family. On the surface, this does not seem ideal. However, there are situations where this is exactly how they need to view it. This view is helpful for newly converted families who do not know much Bible. This view is helpful for families involved in divorce and have many weekly struggles. They need to trust that you are teaching them the Bible and they are safe physically and spiritually with you. By understanding these two basic ideas, we can help make it easier for families to choose our events. I think it is generally true in my experience that most people want their kids involved in youth activities. Yet, if they do not trust the youth minister, they will not show up much.

Promote Communication

Key number two that helps us connect with the parents is **communication**. When youth ministers get in the habit of throwing youth events together at the last minute, some families already have plans. The numbers at events begin to decrease and the youth minister is discouraged because the parents are taking their kids to other things and not coming to "my" youth events.

Strong families are active in a lot of different activities. We want well-rounded young people, so we love it when they play ball, play a horn, or are in some sort of troop. Coaches, band directors, and troop leaders put calendars together and put them out early. They have matching bags, cleats, jerseys, t-shirts, uniforms, and sashes. When the leaders of those events hand out their schedules, the parents pull out their phones and/or refrigerator calendars and mark every single planned expectation. When youth ministers are late to the communication game, it is easy for a parent to say, "We already have something planned that day." But if youth ministers can get their events together, get a calendar on paper, have a parent meeting, and let parents get the events on the calendar; then it will be easier for them to tell the leaders of other organizations that they already have plans that day.

Keep the parents in the loop. Here is what happens. We have a youth event next month, and we tell the youth group in class on Sunday morning about that event. We tell them on Wednesday night, and then we do it again the next Sunday and Wednesday. Suddenly, the date for the event comes and our numbers are down. Youth ministers feel like they have been talking about this event for a month and are disappointed because they expect more to come. There is a fallacy in thinking everything you tell a teenager is going to get to the parents. Sadly, you can often only be assured that the off-the-wall things are the things that will be communicated at home. Meet regularly with the parents. Create a message group for the parents. We cannot always rely on our good-hearted, responsible, yet short attention-spanned teenagers to convey the information we need parents to know.

Be Organized

Key number three is to be **organized**. I would be a hypocrite if I did not disclose that I am writing this from a desk that has papers, books, workout supplements, and a traffic violation that needs some attention. However, I have learned along the way that organization helps lend credibility to our events. Being organized communicates priority and quality. When work, school, extracurricular activities, and family activities are organized but youth events seem thrown together, parents will find it easier to choose other options.

One of the negatives of youth ministry for a long time has been a perception of laziness. Early in youth ministry, I asked one of our parents who happened to be an elder to teach a class for an upcoming retreat. I gave him a topic, and he asked for some guidance. I was somewhat surprised that an elder was asking for advice on a lesson. I mean, he should be able to work up a lesson pretty quickly on the topic I had provided. But, he asked, so I had to give him something. I walked into my office and grabbed a pen and a Post-it notepad. I wrote the topic on the top and the first 3 or 4 verses that came to my mind. I tore it off and confidently walked up to him and handed him the sloppy Post-it note. "That's it? That's what you have for me?" he asked. Reflecting on this, my perspective on the situation was honestly out of respect for his Bible knowledge. Yet, looking back, I realize that his point of view was probably something along these lines: "We gave you a computer, you have an office, you have plenty of time in the day, and you are the one that put this event together and asked me to speak. I want to make sure I give you what you want for this lesson. You are more in tune with the teenagers than I am. I ask for some help, and you jot down a couple of verses on a little piece of paper and think that is enough?" The gracious man never said those things, but I think if I were in his place now, that is what I would have been thinking. I was wrong. Even if it was with good intentions. I communicated disorganization, lack of quality, and laziness.

Being organized attracts faithfulness and produces trust. If you struggle with organization, seek help. There are plenty of hours in the week for a youth minister to be organized. It needs to be a priority. A charming personality, good speaking ability, and friendliness are very important for this job, but these things can only get you so far. You still have to do some work.

Do Not Cancel

Key number four, **Do not cancel anything!** A friend was struggling in youth work. He could not understand why no one was coming to his events. They were not missing games or practice, but they were missing almost all of his events. His numbers were going down. Even in Bible class, he struggled to get some kids to come. I began to notice his social media posts were filled with cancellations of youth events. Even if they were warranted, there were a lot of them. Cancelations from a parent's perspective are bad!

Here is why. Parents sit down with all their calendars to make sure they know what is coming up. They have the youth calendar, ball schedule, ballet recitals, and archery tournaments all in front of them. On the occasion events overlap, something needs to guide their decision. If a parent looks at a youth calendar and wonders if the event will even happen, it is going to be put at the bottom of the list. It will always go to the bottom of the list because no family wants to be sitting at home or scurrying to change their plans because a youth event was canceled at the last minute. Cancelations bring frustration and lead parents to prioritize other events above youth events.

Bonus Content

We will conclude this chapter with some bonus ideas for connecting with parents. One, go to the kids' events and sit with the parents. They want to introduce you to their friends. It helps parents to have more confidence in the youth minister and it helps them use your program as evangelism.

Two, handle yourself respectfully. Yes, you need to relate to teenagers, but you do not need to be disrespectful to accomplish this. I had just moved to begin a new work. A minor league baseball game had been planned for the congregation and a large group was present. Some of the teenagers that I was trying to get to know were sitting down near the field. I thought as the new guy, I should go down and sit with them. After a little bit, I could tell they enjoyed heckling the players on the field. In an attempt to relate to them, I began yelling at the players on the field as well. I did not take into consideration that a large portion of the congregation was sitting right behind me wondering if I was the worst hire they had ever made! You can be relatable without acting like a fool.

Three, support the family. Always speak highly of parents. Youth ministers should never find themselves being negative about any parents around any youth group member. Encourage fathers to baptize their children. Include the parents who are good role models and teachers in youth trips and Bible classes. Teach lessons on how to be a productive member of a family. Organize family events instead of simply planning youth-only events.

Conclusion

We need parents to be connected with our youth programs. This should motivate youth workers to seek opportunities to connect with parents. Ultimately, it is their responsibility to raise their children. They are honoring us by inviting us to be a part of this process. Let us conduct ourselves in a way that shows respect for their role as parents and that shows appreciation for the fact that they have allowed us to influence the most important people in their lives.

Discussion Questions

1. What struggles do you have with connecting with parents?
2. How can our youth program be more family-friendly?
3. What are some parental perspectives we need to consider?
4. What are some specific things we can start doing to connect better with the parents?

Chapter 10
Connecting Parents, Children, and Youth Ministry
Parent-Child Relationships
Steve Wages

Introduction

In the movie *Parenthood* (Howard, 1989), Gill is highly uncertain of his parenting skills and incredibly anxious that his wife, Karen, is now expecting their fourth child, whom he fears could turn out to be like his brother, Larry. She says, "What do you want me to give you, guarantees? These are kids, not appliances. Life is messy." Gill replies, "I hate messy." Parents and youth ministers must realize that, when it comes to parenting, there are no guarantees. Nothing you can do comes with a guarantee. Parenting and youth ministry are connected by a shared goal, a common purpose, and that is to increase the odds that you can influence children to make counter-cultural commitments as disciples of Christ. "Train up a child in the way he should go; even when he is old he will not depart from it" (Prov 22:6). Outcomes with children demonstrate that this passage is true, yet life shows it to be a probability and not a guarantee. This chapter examines strategies designed to connect parents, children, and youth ministry in a way that increases the odds that you will have an incredible influence on forming the character, competence, and faith of the next generation.

The Changed Landscape of Parenthood

Do you believe parenting is more challenging today than it was nearly a hundred years ago? By connecting the context of parenting in contemporary American society with historical changes in family life, Stephen Glenn and Jane Nelsen (2000) provide valuable insights for parenting and youth ministry today. For example, family interaction was high, and intergenerational bonds were many in 1930, whereas family interaction is low and intergenerational bonds are few today. Most importantly, value systems were similar, and role models were mostly healthy then; however, today's youth are inundated with diverse value systems and unhealthy role models on many fronts. There were significant psychological benefits children derived from their involvement in considerable family work and non-negotiable tasks inherent to the daily routines of life then. Today, youth have far fewer opportunities and expectations for work to help meet the demands of family life. Technology, and all that comes with it, was low in 1930, whereas it monopolizes our lives today. Finally, children were mostly raised in stable family environments before single-parenting and blended families became prevalent. As Glenn and Nelsen describe, childhood in those days was an internship for life. There were many resources to encourage the growth of self-discipline, sound judgment, and accepting responsibility. But there were limitations, too, as technology was primitive and communication was restricted. Children learned life skills because they had meaningful roles to play in the economic lives of their families and because they grew up in stable environments in which they followed well-established value systems.

The seminal work of Glenn and Nelsen describes the changed landscape of parenthood, which is foundational to more recent research findings that highlight the unique features of today's families. Generational expert Hayden Shaw states,

> Raising children is different today than it used to be. Teens spend hours online with fifty friends and have to be forced to go outside.

You know it's a different world when your child wants to watch YouTubers play video games more than they want to play them themselves (17–18).

How parents interact with their children in this environment is of interest. In his book, *Meet Generation Z*, James Emory White states,

One of the marks of Generation Z is that they are being raised, by and large, by Generation X—a generation that was warned repeatedly not to become 'helicopter' parents (i.e., always hovering over their children). As a result, Generation Z has been given more space and more independence than any other generation (51).

He notes that this perspective has led to a phenomenon known as "free-range parenting" in which young people are allowed to be largely self-directed (51). Tim McKnight adds an interesting perspective to this discussion. He states, "The parents of Generation Z are both overengaged and underengaged in their parenting" (37). McKnight notes that parents may micromanage homework, interactions with teachers, and even driving but also "permit freedom and hands off approach in areas where students need parental guidance" related to such things as the use of the internet and cell phones (37).

Thus, many young people need more input in some areas of their lives and room to grow in other areas. This presents a challenge. In general, young people would benefit from an increase at home of activities designed to encourage the formation of character, competence, and faith in today's youth. And it will require that you significantly change the experience base of many young people to allow them opportunities to develop the necessary perceptions and skills for successful and faithful living.

The State of Youth Ministry

The State of Youth Ministry (Barna, 2016) revealed how the social and spiritual lives of adolescents are far more complex, diverse, and challenging today due to rapid cultural changes. These cultural shifts have had a dramatic impact, markedly changing the landscape of parenting and youth ministry today. Consequently, you must partner with parents to effectively address the following challenges in order to raise today's youth to become committed disciples of Christ:

1. Rising Bible skepticism: an increasing skepticism of the Bible which many consider irrelevant.
2. Increasing loneliness: though hyper-connected via social media, youth are far more likely to say they are lonely, anxious, or depressed.
3. Pervasive pornography: many youth view pornography as a natural and normal part of human sexuality, while most churches are woefully silent on the subject with no program to help.
4. Confusion regarding human sexuality: widespread confusion on matters pertaining to human intimacy and sexuality and the need to make countercultural biblical commitments.
5. Me-first morality: emergence of a "new moral code" that places Self at the center.
6. Pressurized Christian identity: youth are afraid to speak up about their faith in the face of enormous peer pressure.
7. An era defined by achievement: teens are excessively busy and preoccupied with building an impressive resume (84–87).

These findings reiterate the words of Gary Smalley and John Trent: "We're in a raging battle for the hearts of our [children and] families that begins at the cradle and never ends this side of the grave" (18).

Connecting: Parents and YFM

> My son, keep your father's commands and do not forsake your mother's teaching. Bind them upon your heart forever; fasten them around your neck. When you walk, they will guide you; when you sleep, they will watch over you; when you awake, they will speak to you. For these commands are a lamp, this teaching is a light, and the corrections of discipline are the way of life (Prov 6:20–23).

This passage and Deuteronomy 4:9 clearly place the primary responsibility for character development and faith formation on a child's parents and the intergenerational family. Therefore, it is your role to encourage, promote, and equip parents and grandparents to assume their God-given responsibility for spiritual formation. Consequently, it is imperative for you to establish a strong connection and open lines of communication with parents, proactively building a ministry where parents are partners. Yet, it is alarming that only 23% of youth ministers indicated that getting more parents involved in spiritual formation was a goal for their ministry (Barna, 12). Similarly, a lack of parent interest and a lack of adult volunteers were two of the top challenges identified by youth and family ministers (Barna, 32). When asked why she believed it was difficult for youth ministers to capture the focus of parents and adults in their congregations, Kara Powell, author of *Sticky Faith* (2011), noted,

> Looking back, I struggled to capture the focus of parents and adults *because they were not my focus*. I gave them far too little attention and time. Our church believed the lie that they could outsource the spiritual development of our young people solely to

me as the professional youth leader—perhaps because I never told them otherwise (Barna, 2016, 34).

The weak partnership between parents and youth ministers is disconcerting, as it is imperative that parents and youth ministers recognize faith begins at home and that they foster intergenerational family and faith identities dedicated to the spiritual formation of their children. To properly address the cultural challenges facing the youth of today, families and churches need to rethink their paradigm for forming young disciples of Christ. You need to be far more intentional about equipping parents to assume the primary responsibility for the faith formation of their children in the home.

Connecting: Parents and Children

Rules plus a relationship promotes obedience, while rules without a relationship often lead to rebellion. You will never get Fido to sit or roll over on command without first establishing an amazing connection. If the relationship matters with our family dog, it is even more essential with our children. Developmental psychologist Urie Bronfenbrenner postulated that the most important factor in a child's intellectual, emotional, social, and moral development is involvement in progressively more complex reciprocal activity, on a regular basis over an extended period. This needs to occur with persons [i.e., parents] who share a strong, mutual, irrational, and emotional attachment with the child. In other words, he says, development happens in a relationship between two people who are crazy about each other (Bronfenbrenner, 1990, 27–38). Malachi describes this ideal parent-child bond as he predicts what will happen when one like Elijah comes: "He will turn the hearts of the fathers to their children, and the hearts of the children to their fathers" (Mal 4:6).

The process of creating an incredible parent-child bond involves verbal affirmations of love, meaningful touch (i.e., affection), and bonding experiences. Verbal affirmations of love demonstrate the "power of the spoken word." Parents need to express their love often. You may be surprised by the number of children who have never heard their father say, "I love you." David Mace (1983) said that affection is the single most important ingredient; it is the common bond that gives heart and strength to the shared life. Ask yourself, *What kinds of experiences have fostered a strong emotional bond with those persons to whom I feel the closest attachments?* Most likely it is people in your life with whom you share individual (i.e., one-on-one) relationship time, people you laugh (i.e., play) with, people you sweat (i.e., work) with, people you hurt (i.e., cry) with, and people you pray (i.e., worship) with. The process by which meaningful connections are established between parents, children, and youth ministers involves meaningful bonding experiences and influential relationships, as is further described below.

Connecting: Individual Relationship Time (IRT)

Most recognize the importance of family time; however, you build emotional bonds and strong families by creating strong dyadic (i.e., one-on-one) relationships. Whereas everyone has a longing for belonging, children need to feel as though they are important and they belong. When children feel important and belong, they are more constructive; when children do not belong, they are likely to misbehave. Consequently, it is important for each parent to spend individual relationship time (IRT) with each child, forming healthy attachments that prevent future problems. General guidelines for IRT suggest that it should be predictable, preferably fifteen to thirty minutes of IRT from at least one parent every day. IRT should be a time of unconditional positive regard, free of interruptions and distractions, during which it is critical to give a child undivided attention and to connect psychologically. IRT should be a time of fun and laughter, free of criticism, with appropriate physical contact (i.e., affection), and eye-to-eye contact. IRT should take place in the context of formalized "daily routines and schedules" designed to assure that certain activities are not neglected (e.g., Bible study, chore time).

Connecting: Recreational Companions

Parenting is teaching your children to find pleasure in the right things. Most people live by the pleasure principle, perhaps because it was God who created pleasure in the beginning. Consequently, people pursue pleasure in healthy or perhaps unhealthy ways. God is in favor of fun, but God is for fun in the right way.

> There is nothing better for a person than that he should eat and drink and find enjoyment in his toil. This also, I saw, is from the hand of God, for apart from him who can eat or who can have enjoyment? For to the one who pleases him God has given wisdom and knowledge and joy (Eccl 2:24–26).

Your youth activities should be intentionally designed to help parents teach their children how to find joy and pleasure in life in ways that honor God's intention for His people to find pleasure in the right things.

Connecting: Work Companions

Perhaps the greatest missing link in parenting (and youth ministry) today is work. The historical changes described above have fostered the consumer culture of childhood which has led to low expectations for children to make significant contributions to the needs of their family and community.

> In the new culture of childhood, children are viewed as *consumers* of parental services, and parents are viewed as *providers* of parental services and *brokers* of community services for children. What gets lost is the other side of the human equation: children bearing responsibilities to their families and communities. In a balanced

world, children are expected not only to receive from adults but also to actively contribute to the world around them ... to add their own marks to the quality of family life, and to contribute to the common good in their school and communities [including, the community of faith]. (Doherty, 2000, 15–16)

Unfortunately, youth ministry often becomes another context in which children are primarily consumers of goods and services. Consequently, parents are not very involved in the programs and activities of the youth ministry, and often youth leaders do not expect them to be (Barna, 2016). Being work companions not only connects youth to parents and to the community of faith, but it also provides enormous psychological benefits. When youth make vital contributions to the daily routines of family life and actively plan and participate in the "work" of the church, it cultivates an important internal sense of initiative, industry, competence, and their being *needed* by their family and the community of faith.

Connecting: Positive Role-Models and Mentors

As previously noted, today's youth are inundated with diverse value systems, worldly lifestyles, and unhealthy role models promoted by technology, including mass and social media. It is paramount for parents, youth ministers, and church leaders to effectively educate themselves on how best to protect their children from these outside influences. "Now flee youthful lusts [i.e., passions/desires] and pursue righteousness, faith, love and peace with those who call upon the Lord from a pure heart" (2 Tim 2:22). Similarly, Proverbs 18:24 declares, "Walk with the wise and become wise, for a companion of fools suffers harm." Surprisingly, only 23% of youth ministers say they offer adult-teen mentoring programs. It is imperative for youth to form influential and intergenerational mentoring relationships among the community of faith. These vital relationships teach cultural discernment and provide youth with the ability to apply faith to their everyday reality (Barna, 2016, 40).

In *How to Raise Your Children for Christ*, Andrew Murray (2016) asserts:

> Not in what we say and teach, but in what we are and do, lies the power of training. Not as we think an ideal to train our children for, but as we live, do we train them. Not our wishes or our theory, but our will and our practice, really train. It is by living a thing [the Christ-life] that we prove that we love it, that we have it, and that we influence the young mind to love it and to have it too. (261; the 1975 edition of this book includes the valuable phrase "the Christ-life")

Murray's assertion is precisely why the findings of Tim McKnight (2021) are so alarming. He observed that parents of Gen Z are not only disengaged regarding their child's use of technology, but they also fail to discuss spiritual matters with their children. In a study of students who actively attended church youth groups, only 27% of students indicated that their family regularly engaged in spiritual conversations or routinely prayed together. To paraphrase Edgar Guest's poem, *Sermons We See*,

> I would rather see a sermon than hear one any day. I would rather you walk with me than merely point the way. The eye is a more ready pupil than ever was the ear. Good advice is often confusing, but example is always clear (Guest, 1976).

It is imperative for parents to practice what they teach; as such they must be admonished, "If it is to be, it begins with me."

Connecting: Parents as Teachers

Barna (2016) noted the rising Bible skepticism of today's youth, who increasingly view biblical teachings as irrelevant. The cultural shifts that have changed the landscape of parenting and youth ministry are marketed to today's youth in 3D and living color, while most biblical teaching is done in black and white. The seminal work of David Mace (1983) provides a blueprint for character education and spiritual formation which can be employed to create activities and learning experiences that demonstrate the cultural relevance of Christ's teachings in contemporary society. The blueprint's three basic steps include (a) the presentation or *teaching* of a relational/spiritual concept, (b) the *modeling* of the concept in meaningful and effective ways, and (c) the *application* of the concept/teachings by individuals in the group. It has been said, "Tell me and I forget, show me and I may not remember, involve me and I understand." Similarly, "I have learned that people will forget what you said, people may remember what you did, but people seldom forget how you made them feel" (source unknown). For example, you probably cannot remember your preacher's sermon from four weeks ago, but you can remember your favorite scene from a movie fourteen years ago because of the way it made you feel.

Parents and youth ministers must design what I call "creative learning experiences," which *teach* biblical principles, effectively *model* biblical truths in ways that touch the hearts (and minds) of today's youth, and have youth *apply* biblical teachings by making countercultural commitments relevant to their lives. For example, Luke 10:25–37 can be used to *teach* the parable of the good Samaritan and caring for others. A powerful online video, the *Kindness Boomerang One Day* by Life Vest, can be used to *model* biblical teaching to care for others and appeal to the hearts of students. Students can *apply* these teachings by creating a "caring chain" with each link identifying an act of kindness performed by members of the youth group. When the chain reaches a prescribed length, the group will celebrate with a special activity. Parents and youth leaders need to be far more intentional about utilizing compelling or captivating videos, life stories, etc., available online and elsewhere to design "creative learning experiences" that demonstrate the relevance of biblical teachings and spiritual concepts to the everyday reality of today's youth. When you do, you will increase the probability that today's youth will embrace their identity as disciples of Christ and hold fast to countercultural commitments.

Conclusion: Identity in Christ

Unfortunately, we are losing many of our young people. John S. Dickerson asserts that nearly four out of five of today's youth will not remain faithful as disciples of Christ (Dickerson, 2013). Former Harding University professor Flavil Yeakley researched students among churches of Christ (2014). He found that approximately 58.2% of those he studied stayed faithful after leaving home and that about 12% of those who left returned to the church when they married and started having children (2014, 531). While there is variety in the percentages, the fact remains that we are losing too many young disciples (and losing one is too many).

The parable of the sower (and soils) explains how the seeds of faith planted in the hearts of children can be supplanted by the desire for other things which enters in and chokes the word until it proves unfruitful (Mark 4:18–19). One of the more surprising findings of the Barna report was that 55% of churchgoing parents consider their child's participation in extracurricular activities to be of equal importance as involvement in youth group activities (Barna, 2016, 30). This finding corresponds with the report that 74% of youth leaders say teen busyness is the main challenge to their ministry, yet 58% of parents say their child's balance of activities "is good" (Barna, 2016, 28). One plausible explanation is that these parents desire to build their child's résumé to enhance opportunities for collegiate scholarships, future employment, etc. If parents believe extracurricular activities are of equal importance as youth activities, then do not be surprised if their child decides extracurricular activities are more important. Parents can inadvertently foster their child's "desire for other things" and prioritize the pursuit of other identities which renders one's identity in Christ to be unfruitful. "Yet to all who did receive him, to those who believed in his name, he gave the right to become children of God" (John 1:12).

In conclusion, for today's youth to make countercultural commitments and remain faithful to the Lord, their greatest sense of personal identity (i.e., connection) must be in and to Christ.

Discussion Questions

1. What do you believe the author means by suggesting outcomes with children show Proverbs 22:6 to be true, yet life shows it to be a probability and not a guarantee? Do you agree? Give examples.
2. How would you answer the author's question regarding parenting being more difficult today than it was 100 years ago? Which of the historical changes in parenting do you believe have had the greatest impact? Discuss.
3. *The State of Youth Ministry* (Barna, 2016) identified a variety of cultural shifts that have changed the landscape of parenting and youth ministry. Which of these challenges have you observed, and what strategies can be employed to address them?
4. How do you explain Barna's finding that only 23% of youth ministers had a goal to get parents more involved in spiritual formation? Conversely, how do you explain the finding that a lack of parent interest and adult volunteers were major challenges?
5. What does the author mean by "families and churches need to rethink their paradigm for forming young disciples of Christ?" Discuss.
6. What kinds of experiences have fostered strong emotional bonds with those persons to whom you feel the closest attachments? How did the author answer this question?

7. The author identifies a variety of connections between parents and children (e.g., IRT, work companions, etc.). Assess the health of these connections in your child's life and identify how they can be strengthened.
8. The author uses the parable of the sower/soils (Mark 4:18–19) to suggest that parents may inadvertently foster their child's "desire for other things" and prioritize the pursuit of other identities which render their child's identity in Christ to be unfruitful. Do you believe this is a legitimate concern, and, if so, what can be done to address it?

Bibliography

Barna Group. *The State of Youth Ministry: How Churches Reach Today's Teens—And What Parents Think about It.* Dallas-Ft. Worth, TX: Barna Group, 2016.

Bronfenbrenner, Urie. "Discovering What Families Do." Pages 27–38 in D. Blankenhorn, S. Bayme, and J.B. Elshtain, eds. *Rebuilding the Nest.* Milwaukee, WI: Family Service America, 1990.

Dickerson, John S. *The Great Evangelical Recession: 6 Factors That Will Crash the American Church...and How to Prepare.* Ada, MI: Baker Books, 2013.

Doherty, William J. *Take Back Your Kids: Confident Parenting in Turbulent Times.* Notre Dame, IN: Sorin Books, 2000.

Glenn, H. Stephen, and Jane Nelsen. *Raising Self-Reliant Children in a Self-Indulgent World: Seven Building Blocks for Developing Capable Young People.* Albuquerque, NM: Harmony Publishing, 2000.

Guest, Edgar. *Collected Verse of Edgar Guest.* Cutchogue, NY: Buccaneer Books, 1976.

Howard, Ron, Director. *Parenthood* [Film]. Imagine Entertainment, 1989.

Mace, David R., ed. *Prevention in Family Services: Approaches to Family Wellness.* Thousand Oaks, CA: Sage Publications, 1983.

McKnight, Tim. *Engaging Generation Z: Raising the Bar for Youth Ministry.* Grand Rapids, MI: Kregel Ministry, 2021.

Murray, Andrew. *How to Raise Children for Christ: A Guide for Excellent Christian Parenting.* Updated edition. Abbotsford, WI: Aneko Press, 2016.

Murray, Andrew. *How to Raise Your Children for Christ.* Ada, MI: Bethany House, 1975.

Powell, Kara E., and Clark, Chap. *Sticky Faith.* Grand Rapids, MI: Zondervan, 2011.

Shaw, Hayden. *Generational Sticking Points: How to Get 5 Generations Working Together in the 12 Places They Come Apart.* Carol Stream, IL: Tyndale Momentum, 2020.

Smalley, Gary, and John Trent. *The Hidden Value of a Man.* Carol Stream, IL: Tyndale House, 2005.

Kindness Boomerang One Day. https://www.youtube.com/watch?v=SiJdoZHgri1. Life Vest Inside. DMovies Studio.

White, James Emory. *Meet Generation Z: Understanding and Reaching the New Post-Christian World.* Ada, MI: Baker, 2017.

Yeakley, Flavil, Jr. *Why They Left: Listening to Those Who Have Left Churches of Christ.* Nashville, TN: Gospel Advocate, 2014.

Chapter 11
Connecting Different Races and Ethnicities
Zack Martin

Introduction

"There is neither Jew nor Greek, there is neither slave nor free, there is no male and female, for you all are on in Christ Jesus" (Gal 3:28). I grew up with a grandmother who loved the church and God's word. At every opportunity growing up, especially in the summer, we could be found at VBS in the mornings and gospel meetings at night. It did not matter if the congregation was black or white, rich or poor, large or small, in town or out in the county; if the congregation was a part of the brotherhood, we were there.

I love the brotherhood. I guarantee that you do as well. Otherwise, you would not be reading this book. I could spend the rest of this chapter on why I love the brotherhood. When the term 'brotherhood' is used, it suggests a united fellowship of congregations (John 17:21). However, there are two brotherhoods that are separated along racial lines. Martin Luther King, Jr. stated that Americans "stand at eleven o'clock on Sunday morning to sing ... in the most segregated hour of Christian America."[1] How true this is in our brotherhood. W. E. B. Du Bois described the dividing line between white and black cultures as "the veil."[2] Within the brotherhood, the veil is intact.

The past few years in our country have shown that racial division has not disappeared. Perhaps it is the most divided it has been in my short lifetime. Racial tension is a result of every issue becoming a political issue. Leaders in the church have quickly become more despondent and burned out because the problems dividing our country and society are also dividing their congregations. So instead of showing unity to the world, we are allowing the world to destroy the church's unity. Or, as Wes Crawford calls it, "the illusion of unity" has been shattered.[3]

So then, there is no better time for the Lord's church to step up and help lead the next generation to be better and do better in connecting different races and ethnicities. I will stress this point throughout this chapter because it is important. We must be diligent in being balanced when connecting with our brothers and sisters of different races and ethnicities. On the one hand, we can stress our differences too much. On the other hand, we can ignore our differences. We are all created in the image of God, yet we are different physically and culturally. Both are to be acknowledged and celebrated. I believe that the book of Revelation illustrates this well. In heaven, John saw and heard a lot of singing. Old songs (Rev 15:3–4) and new songs (Rev 5:9) are sung in heaven by its residents and the faithful. The new song in Revelation 5 notes the differences between the faithful-they are "from every tribe and language and people and nation" (Rev 5:9). So even though we are one by the blood of Christ, we have much to offer one another with our different backgrounds and cultures. Therefore, since heaven will be a melting pot, the church on earth must follow suit.

Acknowledging the Differences

Jesus Christ is the great High Priest because He sympathizes "with our weaknesses" (Heb 4:15). Therefore, if you are going to lead the way in connecting with different races and ethnicities, you must be willing to do the hard work and go beyond "the veil" (cf. Du Bois above). Because of the color of their skin and/or their country of origin, society treats certain individuals differently. You may not understand the prejudice and discrimination that they face. Still, you need to know that it is real and negatively affects them. However, when we come together or try to connect, everyone comes with baggage or preconceived ideas about the other. So what can help us start on some equal footing?

Richard T. Hughes offers helpful advice when he discusses the vantage points of the "gospel of grace" and "the gospel of the kingdom." The vantage point of grace is what the gospel is all about and should have a direct response to how we look at our brothers and sisters. In 1 John 3:16–18, John shares that the most remarkable illustration of love is when Jesus gave His life for sinners-this is the gospel. Paul informs us that this happened "while we were enemies" (Rom 5:10). There is nothing special about us to deserve Jesus dying on our behalf. Therefore, we are all recipients of God's grace and made brothers and sisters by Jesus's blood.[4]

Therefore, as John continues to say in 1 John 3, there is no way for us to have this love and not help our brothers and sisters in need. Also, there should be no reason not to reach out to your brothers and sisters of color to see how they are feeling and allow them to debrief when another incident of injustice has occurred nationally or locally. Sometimes people of color need to know that their white brothers and sisters are there for them, whether to hear them vent, pray for them, or be a silent presence.

When Jesus inaugurated His earthly ministry, He stood in His home synagogue in Nazareth and read from the prophet Isaiah (Luke 4:18–19):

> The Spirit of the Lord is upon me, because he has anointed me to proclaim good news to the poor. He has sent me to proclaim liberty to the captives and recovering of sight to the blind, to set at liberty those who are oppressed, to proclaim the year of the Lord's favor.

This particular passage was written for Jesus to fulfill, which he did. The passage was about the kingdom of God that He came to establish. Hughes gives this as a scriptural reference for the vantage point of the "gospel of the kingdom." Remember that there is room in the kingdom for all—we now have a new identity in Christ and a new set of values to live by. However, we are still in this world where Jesus promised we would have tribulation and need each other![5]

The Key Is Contextualization

In *Loving the City*, Tim Keller encourages his readers to take a second look at American cities and form a plan to evangelize them again. There are certain negative stereotypes about those who live in cities. It seems like the media loves to share all the bad news in our cities on the six o'clock news every night. Historically, in the 1960s, when people of color could move into nicer city neighborhoods, "white flight" took place, and our modern suburbs blossomed.

As a result of "white flight," most of our cities are made up of citizens who look very different from those in the suburbs and have very different socio-economic backgrounds. Tim Keller loves the city and its citizens and provides a plan to take the gospel back to our cities. His plan is centered around contextualization. While I acknowledge that Keller comes from a different theological background than many who will read this chapter and he focuses on evangelism, I also believe that black and white congregations can use his concept to better connect to one another.

Often, it is not the gospel, nor is it the fundamental doctrines of the church, that keep white and black congregations from connecting (i.e., the role of baptism, men's and women's roles, instruments in worship, etc.). Rather, it is culture, especially our different worship cultures (i.e., some add notes and words to songs, have more leader-congregation response singing, have more amens and audience response in the sermons, etc.). It is important to note that both white and black congregations are at fault, and both need to learn how to contextualize. When it comes to helping contextualize the culture of those within the church, it may be best to talk about culture in the popular way that Keller describes. For example, Keller says that "culture is popularly conceived narrowly—as language, music and art, food and folk customs—but properly understood, it touches every aspect of how we live in the world."[6]

Each race and ethnicity must conclude that God has blessed cultures to bless others. Romans 1–3 informs us that all humans are sinners who have fallen short of God's glory (Rom 3:23). There are people from various ethnicities who may never have been exposed to Scripture, yet, as Keller points out, humanity is guilty because of God's general revelation. Man knows right from wrong through nature and our consciences, yet we choose to rebel against God anyway. However, in our rebellion against God, we still bear His image, and He still provides common grace. Keller concludes that each culture is a part of God's common grace (all are created in His image, Gen 1:26–27). Therefore, white culture has insights and creativity that can and should be enjoyed by the black culture and vice versa. How much richer and fuller our lives and congregations would be if we started to introduce other cultural "insights" and "creativity" to our people.[7]

We must be flexible regarding men's cultural issues and traditions if we are going to connect, especially through worship. Essentially, these cultural issues and traditions fall under "matters of opinion." Keller reminds us that these are areas "where the Bible has not spoken" and man has elevated "relative human cultural norms to make them absolutes."[8] Keller uses the language of Francis Schaffer in talking about "form and cultural freedom." That is, there should be freedom "in regard to church form" in areas not commanded by the New Testament when speaking to issues of a "particular time and place."[9] Therefore, humility (brought about by the gospel) and listening should be essential to move forward.

Keller shows from 1 Corinthians 9 that church members show their love towards one another when there is cultural adaption. In 1

Corinthians 9:22–23, Paul says he "became all things to all people ... for the sake of the gospel." So, it is with us. When the world sees us acting like the world indorsing "separate, but equal," why should they need the gospel? Furthermore, 1 Corinthians 10:32–11:1 is used by Keller to strengthen the argument of love and cultural adaptation. Again, I am not suggesting that one culture swallows up the other. Still, both cultures must be allowed to express themselves and have their own traditions within a mixed setting. Since the church is called to live out the gospel and to minister, "the Bible has left us free."[10] Hence, there is no excuse not to be "constantly engaged in cultural adaption."[11] Negatively speaking, this also means that there will be times when each side will need to "refrain from particular music, clothing, foods, and other nonessential practices and concepts that could distract or repulse people from clearly perceiving the gospel" (and Christian unity).[12]

Beyond Workshops and Worship Services

Since the 1960s, several racial reconciliation workshops have been held, and countless congregations have conducted annual joint worship services. However, these have not moved the needle far toward total racial reconciliation. What will help? We need to be more active and intentional in connecting races and ethnicities. Listening is essential, but before listening takes place, both sides must learn about the other side. Each side must be earnest (never stopping) in becoming "fluent in" the different cultures'

> social, linguistic, and cultural reality as possible. It involves learning to express people's hopes, objections, fears, and beliefs so well that they feel as though they could not express them better themselves.[13]

To listen, we must be in one another's lives—we must learn to trust each other and know each other, and then listening becomes much more accessible. We must start holding conversations outside of those workshops and worship services. Get together for coffee or lunch. Start inviting one another into our homes. We would do that if we were trying to convert a sinner. Why not a brother or sister of another race that attends the congregation across town? If successfully mixed congregations are going to be a reality, we must intentionally have all races involved in planning our worship services, teaching our classes, and becoming leaders. Let us celebrate each race and its cultural traditions within our congregations. Let it not be said among us that one culture is the dominant and "right" culture, and those are the rules the church will function by. After all, the gospel is at stake!

Discussion Questions

1. Is it okay to have a predominately white congregation on one side of town and a predominately black congregation on the other? If yes, then why? If no, then why not?
2. What are other ways to move beyond workshops and joint worship services to bring about racial reconciliation in our congregations?
3. How can we break down the "wall of worship style" to ensure that no dominant culture overtakes our congregations? (phrase shared with me by HCU Board member and gospel preacher, James Gray).

Notes

[1] Martin Luther King, Jr., "Paul's Letter to American Christians," in *A Knock at Midnight,* ed. Clayborne Carson and Peter Holloran (New York, NY: Warner Books, 1998), 31.

[2] W. E. B. Du Bois, *The Souls of Black Folk* (Brooklyn, NY: Restless Press, 2017), 23, Proquest Ebook Central.

[3] Wes Crawford, *Shattering the Illusion: How African American*

Churches of Christ Moved from Segregation to Independence (Abilene, TX: Abilene Christian University Press, 2013), 164–176.

[4] Richard T. Hughes, "Resisting White Supremacy," in *Slavery's Long Shadow: Race and Reconciliation in American Christianity*, ed. James L. Gorman, Jeff W. Childers, and Mark W. Hamilton (Grand Rapids, MI: Eerdmans, 2019), 226–227.

[5] Hughes, "Resisting White Supremacy," 226–227.

[6] Timothy Keller, *Loving the City* (Grand Rapids, MI: Zondervan, 2016), 7.

[7] Keller, 49–52.

[8] Keller, 53.

[9] Keller, 64.

[10] Keller, 53.

[11] Keller, 53.

[12] Keller, 52–53.

[13] Keller, 68.

Chapter 12
Connecting the Generations, Part 1
Intergenerational Ministry
W. Kirk Brothers

Introduction

"When an organ is removed from a living body, that organ dies, and often the body dies along with it" (DeVries 2004, 43). This quote, one from Mark DeVries' landmark book, *Family-Based Youth Ministry*, has been Gorilla-Glued to my heart since I first read it. Over twenty years ago, DeVries discussed the dichotomy between large numbers of young people at religious youth activities and the lack of growth in the adult population in churches. He then asserted,

> We can find the primary cause of the current crisis in youth ministry in the ways that our culture and our churches have systematically isolated young people from the very relationships that are most likely to lead them to maturity (36).

Children's ministry specialist Holly Allen highlights the generational separation in society at large and then observes,

> Among the societal changes that have contributed to pervasive age segregation are age-graded public education, the movement from extended to nuclear family, the prevalence of preschools for the young, and retirement communities and assisted care facilities for older persons (Allen 2021, 82).

Think about what we commonly see in our congregations. Many of our churches have a children's ministry, a youth ministry, a college ministry, a middle agers group, a senior saints group, and more. Now, do not misunderstand me, if you study the mountains of research on human development, you will find that there is social, educational, and developmental value to having age-specific classes and activities. Yet, I fear we may have gone too far by not giving young people enough opportunities to have meaningful interactions with multiple generations. Youth Ministry guru Chap Clark observes, "Adolescents have been cut off far too long from the adults who have the power and experience to escort them into the greater society. Adolescents have been abandoned" (Clark 2011, 210). This chapter will explore connecting generations. We will begin by looking at the evidence for making generational connections and then offer a few suggestions for making connections and working with various generations.

The Value of Intergenerational Connections

We begin our exploration of intergenerational connections by addressing the "why" question. Why should we make concerted efforts to connect the generations? What value is there in it? We will answer the question initially by looking into Scripture and then will transition to social science research.

Intergenerational Connections in Scripture

Let us begin with Scripture. A passage to which we often turn when promoting the role of family is Deuteronomy 6:6–9:

> And these words that I command you today shall be on your heart. You shall teach them diligently to your children, and shall talk of them when you sit in your house, and when you walk by the way, and when you lie down, and when you rise. You shall bind them as a sign on your hand, and they shall be as frontlets between your eyes. You shall write them on the doorposts of your house and on your gates.

While this command most definitely applies to the family, Israel would also have understood this to be a clan and a national responsibility. The use of the word "gates" in addition to "doorposts" in verse 9 may be an allusion to this. John Kohlenberger III and William Mounce observe that the term, which is found 373 times in the Old Testament, often refers "to the entrance to a city, a key point of the city's defense and a place for public hearings and decisions" (Kohlenberger and Mounce 2012, H8179). This is interesting when one considers that, at the time the Israelites heard this, they were transitioning from a nomadic society to a more stationary society (i.e., they were still living in tents). The point is that ancient Jews would have viewed the task of raising godly children as both a family and community responsibility.

In the New Testament, fellowship (*koinanía*) was the foundation of the Christian communal experience (cf. Acts 2:42). Danker's Lexicon refers to *koinanía* as "close association involving mutual interests and sharing, *association, communion, fellowship, close relationship*" (Danker 2000). It can also be translated as "partnership" (Mounce 2011). Christianity is to be a shared experience. Consider that Jesus referred to His followers as "family" (Mark 3:31–35) and the church was described as the "household of God" (Eph 2:19; 1 Tim 3:15). Would it not be logical to conclude that, as the physical family has responsibility for raising children, the spiritual family would also bear some responsibility for raising spiritual children?

Consider the quote to which we referred earlier concerning the removal of an organ from a living body. That quote makes me think of Paul's teaching in 1 Corinthians 12, where he described the church as a body in which every part matters (cf. 1 Cor 12:12–26). I know that Paul's focus was on gifts/abilities, not age/generational divisions, but I cannot imagine that he would think it spiritually healthy for children and young people to be separated from meaningful interaction with the other parts of the body of Christ. Paul further emphasized generational connections when he challenged older women to teach younger women (Titus 2:3). How can this happen if they do not spend meaningful time together?

Timothy was one of the most important leaders in the early church. He did not have a godly father (Acts 16:1), yet others stepped into the gap and helped to shape him into a servant of the Lord. Think of the individuals who influenced him: his mother and grandmother (2 Tim 1:5), the brethren in his local congregation (Acts 16:2), a group of elders (1 Tim 4:14), and the apostle Paul (2 Tim 3:10–11). This would have involved interacting with multiple generations. It seems evident to me that Scripture assumed and expected intergenerational connections.

Intergenerational Connections in Social-Science Research

My doctoral dissertation was on *Factors Motivating Church of Christ Ministry Students to Enter Ministry*. I interviewed students from twenty church of Christ affiliated schools in four countries, including eleven schools in the U.S. We identified twenty-nine factors that influenced at least some in the group. Here are some of the factors (the other factors that influenced them were not people, but internal motivations, experiences, etc.):

- #6 – Parents/Family (49.5%)
- #7 – Youth Minister (42.4%)
- #8 – Preacher (39.9%)
- #9 – Teaching in their local congregation (39.5%)
- #10 – Training outside their local congregation, i.e., camps, etc. (38.8%)
- #12 – A leader outside their local congregation (38.2%)

- #14 – An adult in their congregation (not an elder, preacher, deacon, or teacher) (34.5%)
- #15 – A college professor (31.9%) (Brothers 2010)

Take a moment to look at this list. These influences would have involved multiple generations.

The findings above are consistent with a wealth of research that has been published in the last twenty years. In their landmark research published in the book *Soul Searching*, Christian Smith and his team observed,

> Much existing research has suggested the crucial importance in adolescents' lives of meaningful relational ties to parents *and nonparent adults*—grown-up friends, teachers, mentors, coaches, and other parents—who can help watch over, care for, and provide resources to teens (Smith 2005, 226, emphasis mine).

Smith noted, "The more religiously involved teens, first, tend to be more comfortable talking with adults other than their parents" (226). Researcher Wesley Black shared his findings in an article titled, "Reversing the Dropouts," which was published in the *Christian Education Journal*. He observed, "Young adults who did not have close adult mentors during their teenager years seem to drop out more than those who did. Those with two or less older adult friends attend church less often in their adult years" (Black 2008, 42). He goes on to add, "Teenagers need to see what a walking, talking adult Christian is like. They need opportunities for interacting and dialoging with a number of adults who care for them" (44).

Research conducted by Fuller Seminary is highlighted in the book *Sticky Faith*. What Kara Powell and her team discovered is very insightful: "The closest our research came to that definitive silver bullet is this sticky finding: High school and college students who experienced more intergenerational worship tend to have higher faith maturity" (Powell 2011, 75). The team stressed that the need for adult connections continues after the teen leaves the youth group and moves off to college. "Contrary to public opinion, graduates don't want to be 'out of sight, out of mind.' Contact from at least one adult from the congregation outside the youth ministry during the first semester of college is linked with Sticky Faith" (78). Intergenerational connections are important.

Connecting the Generations

I worked on much of this chapter while in Orlando, Florida, the home of Disney World, for the Annual Meeting of the Association of Biblical Higher Education. Mark Cannister, in his book *Teenagers Matter*, notes that Disney World (while it may have height requirements for some rides) is not really segregated by age. It is designed for multiple generations to enjoy the park together (Cannister 2013, 137). While I do not agree with all that Disney does, I do find this a helpful model for us.

Multigenerational Vs. Intergenerational

Cannister makes an insightful observation when he notes that "It is essential to comprehend the differences between multigenerational and intergenerational" (137). Just because there are multiple generations in a congregation does not mean that there are meaningful intergenerational encounters happening between them. Thus, Cannister adds, "Intergenerational ministries strive to integrate multiple generations through meaningful conversations, interactions, and service on a regular basis" (137). Eric Mathis, in his book, *Worship with Teenagers*, states, "Actually, many congregations think they are intergenerational when they are actually multigenerational" (Mathis 2022, 127). He laments that these congregations have "not pursued the arduous task of moving from independent, siloed forms of ministry by age to collaborative, integrated forms of ministry organized by other frameworks" (127).

Elizabeth Nesbit Sbanotto and Craig Blomberg make some helpful observations in their book, *Effective Generational Ministry*.

Of particular assistance is their description of how generations struggle to understand each other. First of all, they observe, "Every generation takes for granted the good that went before it, reacts against the bad, and responds within its own historical context" (Blomberg and Sbanotto 2015, xix). One might add to this the tendency of older generations to be critical of younger generations and to think that society and the church are on a downhill side.

The authors also note, "A final thing to keep in mind is that *lived* experience is very different than *learned* experience" (xix, emphasis theirs). This is one of the reasons that generations struggle to understand each other. It is one thing to have read about the assassination of JFK, or the Civil Rights Movement, or September 11, 2001. It is very different to have lived through those events as a participant or first-hand witness. My father remembers being in a sociology class at the University of Tennessee—Martin when his professor announced that President Kennedy had been shot and then canceled class. I remember being in my office at the Central church of Christ in McMinnville, TN, when the youth minister, Scotty Smith, came in to tell me a plane had hit one of the World Trade Center towers.

Even for those who experienced the same events, the age at which they were experienced matters significantly in how each person and generation was impacted. The takeaway from this is that we must be very intentional in creating situations and environments in which the generations can share, grow in their understanding of each other, appreciate each other's strengths, and forgive each other's weaknesses (cf. #5 below under General Practices).

General Practices of Intergenerational Churches

Chap Clark is a champion of what has become known as "Adoptive Youth Ministry." He states, "The goal of youth ministry must shift away from segmenting young people off from everyone else to offering them a mutual, empowering, engaging and supportive new family" (Clark 2015, 85). He adds,

> To put it more clearly, the goal of youth ministry as adoption is for every child, every adolescent, and every young adult to be so embraced by the community of faith that they know they always have a home, a people, and a place where they can discover who they are and how they are able to contribute. In short, youth ministry is adopting young people into the family of God (85).

In his book *Adoptive Church*, Clark challenges churches to plan activities, programs, and gatherings that promote the adoption of young people by the whole congregation. He stresses that gathering as a church should have three primary areas of focus:

1. We gather to build trust.
2. We gather to build warmth.
3. We gather to explore Christ's Good News together (Clark 2018, 139–41).

When adults and young people gather in meaningful interactions on a regular basis, the young people learn that they are in a safe environment with people they can trust. These gatherings create genuine atmospheres of warmth and love that foster collaboration and deep sharing. Gatherings open the door for meaningful exploration of God's word that includes opportunities for young people "to share things that matter to them with the group" (141).

Mark Cannister highlights research done by Brenda Snailum and shared in an article in the *Christian Education Journal* titled, "Implementing Intergeneration Youth Ministry within Existing Evangelical Church Congregations: What Have We Learned?" (138–145). Snailum's research identified seven helpful practices in congregations seeking to become intergenerational (Snailum 2012, 165–81).

1. Establish Intergenerational Community as a Core Value. The entire congregation, not just the youth ministry, must buy in.
2. Balance Intergenerational Values with Age-Specific Ministry. Maintain age-specific ministries while pursuing intergenerational connections. Do not sacrifice one for the other.
3. Ensure that leaders are fully invested. Church leaders must champion the process and purpose.
4. Begin Where You Are. Consider what existing ministries, events, and classes can be quickly tailored to promote meaningful interactions.
5. Educate the Congregation. "Such education requires continual communication and emphasis on the philosophy, principles, and goals of becoming intergenerational" (142). Help the congregation to understand generational differences and help them to learn to love each other in spite of the differences.
6. Be Intentional and Strategic. Changes work best if accomplished incrementally, yet the movement must be consistent and intentional. Champion successes along the way, and continue to think strategically as you move forward.
7. Include All Generations and All Ministry Venues. Interconnectedness should not be reduced to adults and teens. Connect all the generations. "While incremental change is a wise approach to becoming an intergenerational community, the goal will never be fully realized until all ministry venues—including worship services, small groups, Sunday school, Bible studies, outreach events, and mission trips—become intergenerational to one degree or another" (144).

Eric Mathis adds, "To truly move toward intergenerational ministry, congregations will need to change their behavior, values, and attitudes through processes of experimentation and learning" (Mathis 2022, 127).

Intergenerational Worship

Many have lamented the generational segregation that often happens in worship (the ethnic and racial segregation in worship is also an issue to be addressed, but that is another chapter). There is a growing trend to have separate children's and teen worship on a regular basis. I see both sides of the struggle. It is difficult for young mothers to worship when fighting with small children. Human development research also reveals the value of age-targeted learning and experiences. Yet, we must not throw the baby out with the bath water. We have shown repeatedly in this chapter that intergenerational worship is important to faith development. As the research team from Fuller Seminary reported in Sticky Faith: "Involvement in all-church worship during high school is more consistently linked with mature faith both in high school and college than any other form of church participation" (Powell and Clark 2011, 75). Thus, I am not saying that it is bad to have children's Bible hour, for example. What I am saying is the evidence is overwhelming that children and teens also need large doses of intergenerational worship to mature as God intended.

In addition to worship segregation, multigenerational worship services are often unigenerational in their focus. Worship services in many congregations seem to target older Christians. I think of the older member who critiques the song leader for leading what he calls "devotional songs" by saying, "Well, are you going to lead any songs we know today?" On the other hand, some churches target teenagers as the primary audience in worship. We also have Youth Sundays in which the teenage boys speak or lead singing. Now, before moving forward, let me emphasize that there is nothing wrong with having a Youth Night in which the young men lead worship. Yet, why do they have to wait for that? Shouldn't they be regularly involved in all aspects of worship on a regular basis?

Shouldn't they be valued in choices made while planning every worship service?

One of the key expressions of generational focus is found in the song choices. Shouldn't we choose songs that speak to and from every generation? Why can't we sing "Amazing Grace" (Traditionalists), "Jesus is Lord" (Baby Boomers), "Awesome God" (Generation X), "In Christ Alone" (Millennials), "A Living Hope" (Generation Z), and "Jesus Loves Me" (Generation Alpha), in the same worship? We could sing "Just As I Am/I Come Broken" which mixes songs from the 19th century and the 21st century. Maybe the critic mentioned above needs to realize the songs he knows may not be known by others. Different songs speak to different people. Selfless, others-centered people rejoice when songs are included that bless all generations.

I am not talking about changing God-authorized forms of worship. For example, I am not calling for the addition of instruments in worship. Some say that young people will not come to worship if we do not add an instrument. Our responsibility is to please the Creator of the universe, not a particular generation. Yet, I do think we need to be more intentional in thinking about how to connect to all generations, not just the old or young when we worship. Mathis highlights the dangers of focusing on a single generation—adolescents, for example—when he says, "Yet when these young adults turn twenty, they leave church because church is no longer focused on them" (Mathis 2022, 126). Could we be more successful in keeping our young people if we had an intergenerational approach to congregational worship to begin with?

Intergenerational Bible Classes

Holly Allen specializes in children's spiritual formation and is a champion of intergenerational connections, especially for the development of children. In her book *Forming Resilient Children,* she highlights how intergenerational settings nurture children spiritually:

1. They nurture the child-God relationship.
2. They nurture the child-others relationship.
3. They nurture the child-self relationship (Allen 2021, 82–88).

An example of the impact on the child-God relationship is found in children's prayer lives. She found that the prayers of children in strong intergenerational congregations are more robust, largely because the intergenerational gatherings often begin with the generations praying for each other. The children's child-others relationships are enhanced as they have regular interaction with people of all ages struggling with some of the things they struggle with in living out their faith. Allen also stressed the value of the role of the whole family of God in helping children to develop their identity, their sense of self. I think back to participating in a class on leading in worship as a teenager with older men in the class who were new Christians. I think of one man in the class who was very shy. His courage to lead his first prayer had a profound impact on me. This would not have happened in a class with only people my age.

As a means of creating intergenerational connections, Allen is a proponent of intergenerational Bible classes. She spoke of the value of such classes during the 2022 gathering of the Association of Youth Ministry Educators (AYME). She summarized some general principles when coordinating such classes:

1. You don't want naysayers.
2. Recruit people who are enthusiastic.
3. Generally, you do not want to try it with preschoolers (ten-year-olds and up is a good starting place, or at least those old enough to read).
4. Limit the length of the class, maybe to no more than six weeks (Allen 2022).

Allen stressed that our purpose in intergenerational learning is, in part, for our children to learn something that the adults are learning while the adults are also blessed. Yet, she emphasizes that learning is more than just the gathering of information. There is what she refers to as the "relational feast" and the "emotional feast" that take place when all are learning the same thing together. It is the interactions in the class that create the magic. Multigenerational learning takes place in a typical Sunday morning worship. Yet, teaching in these gatherings is largely aimed at the adults, with some learning filtering down to those who are younger, especially by watching the adults worshiping. The difference in what Allen is suggesting is that you have multigenerational classes in which the children are the primary target. This learning then wafts blessings upward as adults are impacted relationally and emotionally, and they also have the enriching opportunity to participate in the children's learning (thus moving from merely having a multigenerational gathering to an intergenerational gathering).

Conclusion

I challenge you to explore intergenerational opportunities. I think of simple activities such as taking the teens to visit our elderly, having teens co-teach younger children with older adults, or inviting elders or their wives to share with the young people. Think of an octopus. The more tentacles that are connected to the prey, the less likely it is that the prey will get away. Generational connections are similar. Scripture emphasizes the role of the whole congregation in faith development. Research confirms that the more generations of faithful followers of God that are connected to the life of a teenager, the greater the likelihood that the teenager will not "get away" from God. Intergenerational connections matter!

Discussion Questions

1. What would you list as the top three reasons we struggle to understand those older or younger than us?
2. On an A, B, C, D, F scale, how would you grade your youth ministry's efforts to be intergenerational?
3. List some people who might serve on a focus group to brainstorm ideas for building intergenerational connections to craft a proposal that might be shared with your church leaders?
4. What are three current programs or activities in your congregation that could easily become intergenerational?

Bibliography

Allen, Holly. *Forming Resilient Children*. Lisle, IL: IVP Academic, 2021.

———. "Intergenerational Formation." Presentation at the Association of Youth Ministry Educators Annual Conference. San Diego, CA. 21 October 2022.

Black, Wesley. "Stopping the Dropouts: Guiding Adolescents Toward a Lasting Faith Following High School Graduation." *Christian Education Journal* 3.5 (2008): 28–46.

Blomberg, Craig L., and Elisabeth A. Nesbit Sbanotto. *Effective Generational Ministry*. Grand Rapids: Baker Academic, 2016.

Brothers, Kirk. "A Cross-Cultural Study of Factors Motivating Church of Christ Ministry Students to Enter Ministry." PhD diss., The Southern Baptist Theological Seminary, 2010.

Cannister, Mark. *Teenagers Matter*. Grand Rapids: Baker Academic, 2013.

Clark, Chap. *Hurt 2.0: Inside the World of Today's Teenagers*. Grand Rapids: Baker Academic, 2011.

———. "Adoptive View of Youth Ministry." Pages 73–90 in

Youth Ministry in the 21ˢᵗ Century: Five Views. Grand Rapids: Baker Academic, 2015.

_____. *Adoptive Church*. Grand Rapids: Baker Academic, 2018.

Danker, Fredrick William, ed. "*koinanía.*" *A Greek-English Lexicon of the Greek New Testament and Other Early Christian Literature*. 3ʳᵈ ed. University of Chicago Press, 2000. *Accordance Software*. Version 13.1.2. Oaktree Software, 1994–2020.

DeVries, Mark. *Family-Based Youth Ministry*. 2ⁿᵈ ed. Downers Grove, IL: InterVarsity Press, 2004.

Kohlenberger III, John, and William Mounce. "*šaʿar.*" H8179 in *Kohlenberger/Mounce Concise Hebrew-Aramaic Dictionary of the Old Testament*. 2012. *Accordance Software*. Version 13.1.2. Oaktree Software, 1994–2020.

Mathis, Eric. *Worshiping with Teenagers*. Grand Rapids: Baker Academic, 2022.

Mounce, William D. "*koinanía.*" *Mounce's Concise Greek-English Dictionary of the New Testament*. 2011. *Accordance Software*. Version 13.1.2. Oaktree Software, 1994–2020.

Powell, Kara, and Chap Clark. *Sticky Faith*. Grand Rapids: Zondervan, 2011.

Smith, Christian. *Soul Searching*. New York: Oxford University Press, 2005.

Snailum, Brenda. "Implementing Intergeneration Youth Ministry within Existing Evangelical Church Congregations: What Have We Learned?" *Christian Education Journal*. Series 3, 9:1 (2012): 165–81.

Chapter 13
Connecting the Generations, Part 2
Understanding the Generations
W. Kirk Brothers

Introduction

I did my doctoral work in Biblical Leadership at Southern Seminary in Louisville, KY. My degree involved study and research focusing on Scripture, ministry, and education (Christian higher education in specific). The educational component meant that I was exposed to various social and human development theories that one would not be exposed to in a typical theological or ministry-related degree. I learned so much that helped me in ministry at local congregations and in training teaching ministers at Christian universities. We wrestled with personality development, cognitive development, moral reasoning development, systems theory, and more. We also wrestled with generational theory. It is to this area that I wish to turn our attention. As youth ministers, we interact with elders, deacons, preachers, parents, college students, teens, children, etc. These represent multiple generations. In the previous chapter, we explored the value of intergenerational connections and some basic principles that might guide us as we form those connections. In this chapter, I wish to wrestle with the features of the generations we will likely interact with. I am grateful for the editorial input of Dr. Michael Jackson, Associate Director of the ABHE Commission on Accreditation. He is a friend and former co-worker and has done a great deal of work in the area of generational theory.

What is Generational Theory?

The term "generations" was coined by the German sociologist Karl Mannheim (*Generationslagerung*, meaning "generational setting"). Spanish philosopher Jose Ortega y Gasset also made significant contributions to generational theory. It was William Strauss and Neil Howe, especially in their 1991 seminal work, *Generations: The History of America's Future, 1584 to 2069*, that popularized this theory in the United States (Strauss & Howe 1991, 76).

Strauss and Howe summarize their perspective as follows,

> We treat generations as people moving through time, each group or generation of people possessing a distinctive sense of self. We look at history just as an individual looks at his own life. We explain how a generation is shaped by its 'age location'—that is, by its age-determined participation in epochal events that occur during its lifecycle (1991, 71–72).

They define a generation as ***"a cohort-group whose length approximates the span of a phase of life and whose boundaries are fixed by peer personality"*** (144–45). There are two key aspects of this definition: "age location/phase of life" and "peer personality." These sociologists view a phase of life (childhood and adolescence, young adult years, middle age years, etc.) as approximately 22 years (144–45). Yet, they readily admit that this is not an exact number (145). For them, "age location" refers to a group of people (a cohort) born within a 20-year span who share similar "epochal events" during their formative years (71–72). These shared experiences create what they call a "peer personality." "Peer personality" refers to a cohort-group/generation's "own unique biography" (154). More specifically, they state, "The peer personality of a generation is essentially a caricature of its prototypical member" (154).

It is important at this point in our study to stop and offer some words of caution. Generational theory is not an exact science. As you read the literature, you will see differences of opinion among the experts on details of the theory (such as the length of a cohort and the key defining events). Not all sociologists even accept the validity of the theory, or they express concern about undo emphasis on it (cf. Lavelle 2019 and Cagle 2018). We need to avoid pigeonholing people. I do believe and see evidence in my own life that shared experiences impact people in similar ways. Yet, every person is unique. There are many other factors that influence a person's actions and attitudes: individual personality, learning styles, gender, parents, upbringing, loss, suffering, etc. You also have individuals that Haydn Shaw calls "cuspers" (Shaw 2020, 9). These are people born during generational transition. For example, I was born in 1965. I am right at the beginning of Generation X, but I also have a lot of characteristics of the Boomers. My point is that while we can benefit from noting generational tendencies, we need to recognize that everyone is his/her own person and may exhibit actions and attitudes that are different from the "caricature of its prototypical member" (cf. Strauss and Howe 1991, 154). Be aware of the generational tendencies but know the person individually and personally.

Generational Boundaries

One of the key responsibilities in wrestling with generational tendencies is in deciding which years will be assigned to each generation. There are different birth date ranges in the literature related to generational theory. For example, here are some samples:

- **Julie Coates**: Veterans/GI Generation – 1920-33; Silent Generation – 1933-46; Baby Boomers – 1946-64; Generation X – 1965-1980; Millennials/Generation Y – 1980-2000; Generation Z – 2000+ (Coates 2007).

- **Mark McCrindle**: Builders – 1925-1945; Boomers – 1946-64; Generation X – 1965-1979; Generation Y (Millennials) – 1980-1994; Generation Z – 1995-2009; Generation Alpha – 2010-2024 (McCrindle 2014).
- **Elisabeth Nesbit Shanotto and Craig Blomberg:** Silent Generation – 1925-45; Baby-Boomers – 1946-1964; Generation Xers – 1965-1981; Millennials – 1982-2001, Generation Z – 2002-??? (Blomberg and Sbanotto 2016).
- **James Emery White**: Baby Boomers – 1946-63; Generation X – 1964-79; Millennials – 1980-94; Generation Z – 1995-2010 (White 2017).
- **Haydn Shaw:** Traditionalists/Builders (Combination of GI & Silent Generations) – Before 1945; Baby Boomers – 1946-64; Generation Xers – 1965-1980; Millennials – 1981-1998; Generation Z – 1999-2019 (Shaw 2020 edition, original edition published in 2013).

I looked at various articles on Generation Alpha and discovered the following dates:

- 2010 to present (ABC News, 2020; Mullen, *The New Yorker*, 2022).
- 2010-2024 (McCrindle 2014).
- 2011-2025 (*Forbes*, 2016; Pinsker, *The Atlantic*, 2020; North Carolina State University, 2021).
- 2011-2024 (Lavelle 2019).
- 2013-2025 (The Annie E. Casey Foundation 2023).

These examples both exemplify the struggles of nailing down exact dates for generations and give us some intellectual wood to whittle on as we seek to arrive at the dates we will use for this chapter. The key factors that are typically used in determining generational birth boundaries are the number of years in a typical life stage (most put it at 15–20 years), population trends (up or down), and key shared events that might shape a generation in a unique way (i.e., WW II, the assassination of JFK, or 9-11-2001). This is part art and part science.

For the purposes of this study, I am going to use the dates of Hayden Shaw. This includes combining the GI/Builder Generation and the Silent Generation under the "Traditionalist" label and using the date of "before 1945." There are two primary reasons for this. First of all, there are very few GI/Builders active in the church, and the Silent Generation took on many of the characteristics of the Builders. I also believe his dates best take into account September 11, 2001, and the pandemic in 2020.

- Traditionalists (Builders/Silents) – Before 1945
- Baby-Boomers – 1946-1964
- Generation X – 1965-1980
- Millennials/Gen Y – 1981-1998
- Generation Z – 1999-2019
- Generation Alpha – 2019-present

Characteristics of the Traditionalists, Boomers, and Xers

Next, I want to share a summary of generation information that might help you as you interact with some of the older generations (we will look at younger generations in the next chapter). Here we will highlight Traditionalists through Gen Xers. The information is largely drawn from Hayden Shaw and the research of Michael Jackson, a former Heritage Christian University employee who now works for the Association for Biblical Higher Education (as of the time of this printing). As you review the information below, I would recommend that you think of which generation the people you interact with fit into.

Traditionalists (GI Generation/Builders + Silents)— Before 1945

US Population: 22.9 Million (7%)

Teen Years: 1930–1950s

Key Events: Standard Oil broken up (1911), World War I (1914–1918), Prohibition (1920–33), first popular talking movie (1927), introduction of sliced bread (1928), the Great Depression (1929–39), the New Deal (1933–39), move from farms to suburbs (1901–70), World War II (1939–45), atomic bomb (1945).

Top TV: Networks did not broadcast to the entire US until 1951.

Top Music: "White Christmas" by Bing Crosby, "Don't Be Cruel/Hound Dog" by Elvis Presley.

What they say when asked, "What makes your generation unique?"

1. World War II or the Great Depression (tied at 14%)
2. Smarter (13%)
3. Honest (12%)
4. Work ethic (10%)
5. Values/morals (10%) (cf. Haydn Shaw, 2020, 59–68).

Baby-Boomers—1946–1964

US Population: 68.9 Million (21.1%).

Teen Years: 1960–70s

Key Events: Surge of births after World War II, economic expansion/affluence, television, the Generation Gap, Civil Rights Movement (1955–1968), *The Feminine Mystique* (1963), assassinations of John F. Kennedy, Martin Luther King, Jr., and Robert Kennedy (1963, 1968), Vietnam conflict (1954–75), Woodstock (1969), the Watergate scandal (1972–74), US and USSR limit nuclear warhead testing (1979), Love Canal evacuation (1978).

Top TV: Gunsmoke (1957–61), Bonanza (1964–66), The Andy Griffith Show (1967–68), All in the Family (1971–76).

Top Music: "Hey Jude" by the Beatles (1968), "I'm a Believer" by the Monkees (1966), "You Light Up My Life" by Debby Boone (1977).

What they say when asked, "What makes your generation unique?"

1. Work ethic (17%)
2. Respectful (14%)
3. Values/morals (8%)
4. Baby boom (6%)
5. Smarter (5%) (cf. Shaw, 2020, 69–84).

Generation X—1965–1980

US Population: 65.2 Million (20%)
Teen Years: 1980–90s
Key Events: Double-digit inflation (1979–81), Iranian hostage crisis (1979), Sony Walkman (1980), AIDS (1981), MTV (1981), household borrowing grows twice as fast as income (mid–80s), Space Shuttle Challenger (1986), Berlin Wall torn down (1989), Persian Gulf War (1991), rise of divorce, most aborted generation in history.

Top TV: Dallas (1980–84), The Cosby Show (1985–89), The Simpsons (1989–present), Friends (1994), Seinfeld (1989–1998).

Top Music: "Physical" by Olivia Newton-John (1982), "Livin' on a Prayer" by Bon Jovi (1987), "One Sweet Day" by Mariah Carey & Boyz II Men (1995).

What they say when asked, "What makes your generation unique?"

1. Technology use (12%)
2. Work ethic (11%)
3. Conservative/traditional (7%).
4. Smarter (6%)
5. Respectful (5%) (cf. Shaw, 2020, 85–102).

Ministry Considerations for Boomers and Generation X

In this section, I will lean heavily on the work of Craig Blomberg and Elisabeth Nesbit Sbanotto and in their excellent work, *Effective Generational Ministry*. We will start with Boomers and then move to Gen X. It is my prayer that this will help you as you interact with them.

Baby Boomers

Baby Boomers were in their 60s and 70s in 2023. Congregations have several elders from this group. Let us consider some priorities in ministry to Boomers (Blomberg and Sbanotto 2016, 57–79).

1. Help them to prepare for dealing with failing health. Boomers have tended to work far beyond normal retirement age and, because of medical advances, have tended to have a feeling that they will stay young forever. They are now coming face-to-face with the reality that time always wins. Consider what caregiving programs need to be in place to help aging members.
2. Teach what Scripture says about the life to come. Help them to understand what is next when they leave the borders of this life.
3. Evangelize non-Christian Boomers. Next to young people under the age of 18, this is the next ripest group for evangelism and conversion.
4. Help them to consider how best to use their remaining days. Because many work longer, they may have discretionary income that can be used for God's glory. Terry Munday states, "Boomers control 80% of personal financial assets" (Munday 2020, 87). A study by *US Trust* found that one-third of Baby Boomers in their study said they would rather leave their money to a charity rather than to their children (cited in Munday, 2020, 88).

5. Help them with their identity. Boomers tend to view their identity in terms of their careers. Teaching on identity in Christ and not career can be helpful.
6. Help them to explore meaningful ways to contribute as they age.
7. Watch for signs of depression as they retire, and have resources available to them.
8. Mentoring and grandparenting provide opportunities to have meaningful impact on the future. Provide them resources that help them to know principles of good mentoring. Create opportunities for them to mentor younger generations (Xers, Millennials, and Zers).
9. Help to offset ageism. This is a growing feature of Xers and Millennials. There is a tendency among these generations to want to move the older generations out of the way. Promote mutual respect and the value of learning from those who have gone before.
10. Emphasize intergenerational connections. "One almost always learns and grows more when one is challenged by someone who is different than when one associates solely with those who are most like oneself" (Blomberg and Sbanotto 2016, 69).

Youth ministry can play a vital role in assisting with many of the priorities mentioned above. Some key areas where you have particular influence are in mentoring, caregiving, and creating intergenerational opportunities. Your attitude and respect toward those who are older as well as what you teach in the classroom can help to offset ageism in younger generations.

Generation X

Gen Xers were in their 40s and 50s in 2023. Youth ministers interact with them as parents of the teenagers, deacons, elders, and chaperones. Let us consider some priorities in ministry to Generation X (cf. Blomberg and Sbanotto 2016, 137–65):

1. Help them to navigate their skepticism. One area where this skepticism is expressed is in relation to leadership. Gen Xers do not follow someone just because that person is in a position of leadership. They do not automatically follow someone who has a title. For them, leaders must earn respect and followership by action and authenticity. If youth ministers want to be respected by Xers, they must live authentic faith and integrity in front of them. They also do not simply obey directions because a superior told them to do so. They want to know why they are being asked to do things. Thus, when older generations tell them to do something "because I said so," they are more motivated not to obey than to obey. Thus, when interacting with Gen Xers, include the "why" when discussing things that need to be done.
2. Help them to wrestle with truth. Generation X often views truth as relative and contextual. Sbanotto and Blomberg observe, "Anything or anyone who purports to have a corner on any kind of absolute must either be a fool or a con, for almost nothing in Xers' experiences has given them reason to believe in absolutes" (138). This does not mean that we do not teach God's truth to them. It means that we do not take a top-down, authoritarian approach, but rather a friend-to-friend, mutual sharing and searching approach. It means that we seek to be patient and calm during discussions of truth. It means we understand the value of seeking to understand the context of each Gen Xer's life and circumstances. It means we do not overreact to questions. They are going to question things. That is ok. Have you ever noticed that the apostles struggled to accept the legitimacy of Jesus' resurrection at first? Yet,

when they came to believe, their belief was strong. Be patient. Be understanding. Be authentic. Be genuine.
3. Help them to feel at home: As the most aborted generation in history, they are sandwiched between two larger and louder generations. They tend to feel ignored and overlooked. Individualism and independence mark them, and they do not like large group affiliation (often including religious groups). Yet, they long for places to belong and feel safe. Help them to know that they matter. They are more likely to connect to small groups than large groups. This does not mean they will not participate in corporate worship, but it means that we provide opportunities for them to connect with safe and loving smaller groups as well.
4. Plug into their practicality: Practical theology is an area of emphasis for this generation. They want truth to be relevant. It is important that we connect Scripture to real, lived out, everyday life. They tend to be activists, not at a macro level but more at a micro level. They are less concerned about changing the world than blessing their community. Plug them into local needs such as feeding the hungry and helping the homeless. They also value creation care. Service projects that involve care for creation or that marry care for creation with meeting needs will speak to them. An example of this might be digging wells in thirsty communities in Central America or Africa.
5. Unleash their creativity and innovation: These traits are characteristic of this generation. Bring them in and give them opportunities. They are more apt to participate in and to be engaged in activities and works that they helped to create than those which someone else created. Their creativity can be a blessing, but they often do not engage because those in power are unwilling to share and unwilling to invite them in.

6. Learn from their focus on life over work: Unlike their Boomer parents, Generation X works to live instead of living to work. Many of them raised themselves because they were left at home while their parents worked. They do not want the same thing for their children. Planning too many youth and congregational activities can frustrate them because it keeps the family so busy that they do not have time to be together. They also become frustrated when they are no teen activities they can participate in or there are no activities that involve the whole family.

Teaching the Generations

Julie Coates authored the book *Generational Learning Styles* (one of my graduate school textbooks). She stressed,

> It is absolutely the case that there are wide variations within each generation, and members of generational cohorts are not social, philosophical, educational, or economic clones of each other. It is also true that generations tend to merge into each other so that the youngest Baby Boomers may have more in common with Generation Xers than with leading edge Boomers (Coates 2007, 5).

Yet, generational experiences impact learning. "Individuals screen information through a set of unique, individual filters" (9). Below are lists of features of learning and teaching for each generation.

Traditionalists

Generational Characteristics for Teachers to Consider:

- Traditional learners.
- Respect authority and seek respect in return.

- Seek a learning setting that is stable, orderly, and risk-free.
- Appreciate logic, consistency, and discipline.
- Like content connected to real-world practices or supported by precedent.

Teaching Suggestions:

- Don't make them feel "on the spot."
- Show respect for their background and experience.
- Ask permission to coach or correct.
- Make clear, logical presentations of fact.
- Provide big picture summaries (cf. Coates 2007, 58–75).

Baby Boomers

Generational Characteristics for Teachers to Consider:

- Interactive and non-authoritarian.
- Like interaction, networking, and teamwork.
- Many have authority issues.
- Winning is very important to them.
- Value learning for learning's sake.
- Icebreakers, team activities, and small groups are good, but they do not like role play.
- Tend to intellectualize rather than practice.
- Don't like to display faults in front of others.
- Like materials organized so they are easily accessible.
- Caring/fairness are important (know names).
- Like to be told they are important.
- Like to talk in class.
- Don't think that they accept your authority.

Teaching Suggestions:

- Be nice, be democratic, treat them as equals, and respect their experience/knowledge.
- Ask lots of questions and acknowledge what they know (cf. Coates 2007, 76–82).

A Boomer student at Heritage Christian University stated, "I like to know the reason for the 'rules.' If I understand the whys, then it makes sense. Please don't expect me to accept 'you must do it this way because I said so' reasoning. That's almost like an invitation to break the rules!" She went on to add, "I like having help available, but only if I can't figure it out on my own. I don't appreciate teachers who hover while I'm learning. I'm perfectly capable of asking for help and clarification if I need it." Another Boomer student highlighted these three suggestions for working with her generation:

1. Visual ... Concrete object or pictorial representation.
2. Application ... How will I use it now?
3. Scripture (of course) and research.

These students do not represent all in this generation, but their comments can provide some insights that serve as a starting place.

Generation X

Generational Characteristics for Teachers to Consider:

- Not as motivated to learn as previous generations.
- May not be as respectful of the teacher.
- Want to know what is expected of them.
- Want to know why it matters.
- Like choices and options.
- They work to live, do not live to work.

- Being best not as important (grades not as important).
- Learn best by doing.
- Want practical outcomes.
- They are visual, not big readers.

Teaching Suggestions:

- Be efficient (don't waste time).
- Be relevant.
- Work to make the classroom active with field trips, self-directed projects, discussion, etc.
- Humor can be effective.
- Be visual and use technology.
- Use color, novelty, and contrast in presentations.
- Allow frequent breaks and encourage play (cf. Coates 2020, 83–101).

One Gen Xer at HCU observed, "Learning topics must be integrated into how it is relevant to life purpose. Gen Xers are somewhat skeptical of spending time learning unless it can achieve a specific objective."

To help us to understand the differences when teaching multiple generations, consider the following. Boomers like to be in charge of their learning. Generation Xers prefer to work independently with self-directed projects. Millennials like to interact with colleagues while learning. As a youth minister, you will not only work with these generations, but you may also be in settings where you need to teach them or preach to them. Recognizing the differences in how they learn can make all the difference.

Conclusion

Perspective impacts performance! We started this chapter with a birds-eye view of generational theory and then focused in for a closer look at some of the older generations, with the younger generations covered in the next chapter. My goal in these "generational chapters" is to help you to begin to understand the perspectives of various generations. It may cause you to reflect on the worldview of your own generation. There are things we all share in common, but there are also personal, gender, and generational differences. The better we understand each other, the better we can minister to and with each other.

Discussion Questions

1. What did you find the most surprising in this chapter and why?
2. What did you find the most helpful in this chapter and why?
3. What would you say are the strengths and weaknesses of generational theory?

Bibliography

Blomberg, Craig L., and Elisabeth A. Nesbit Sbanotto. *Effective Generational Ministry*. Grand Rapids: Baker Academic, 2016.

Brown, Gennevieve Shaw. "After Gen Z, meet Gen Alpha." www.abcnews.go.com. February 17, 2020. Accessed February 17, 2023.

Cagle, Kurt. "Rethinking Millennials and Generations Beyond." www.forbes.com. August 22, 2018. accessed February 17, 2023.

Coates, Julie. *Generational Learning Styles*. LERN Books, 2007.

Dretsch, Heather. "Meet the Mini Millennials: Generation Alpha." www.ncsu.edu. October 1, 2021.

McCrindle, Mark. *The ABC of XYZ*. 3rd ed. McCrindle, 2014.

Munday, Terry. *The Great Handoff*. Dust Jacket Media Group, 2020.

Mullen, Al. "What Generation Alpha Has Already Ruined."

www.thenewyorker.com. February 23, 2022. Accessed February 17, 2023.

Pinsker, Joe. "Oh No, They've Come Up with Another Generation Label." www.theatlantic.com, February 21, 2020, accessed February 17, 2023.

Reed, Betsy. "Move over, millennials and Gen Z – here comes Generation Alpha." www.theguardian.com, January 4, 2019, accessed February 17, 2023.

Shaw, Haydn. *Sticking Points*. Carol Stream, IL: Tyndale Momentum, 2020.

Strauss, William and Neil Howe. *Generations: The History of America's Future, 1584 to 2069*. New York: William Morrow & Co., 1991.

The Annie E. Casey Foundation. "What is Generation Alpha?" www.aecf.org. Originally posted November 4, 2020. Updated February 14, 2023. Accessed February 17, 2023.

White, James Emery. *Meet Generation Z*. Grand Rapids: Baker Books, 2017.

Chapter 14
Connecting the Generations, Part 3

Generations Y & Z
W. Kirk Brothers

We now turn our attention to the two generations with whom youth workers will likely spend the bulk of their time. Discussions of these generations in religious circles will periodically refer to Old Testament passages like Judges 2:10: "All that generation also were gathered to their fathers; and there arose another generation after them who did not know the LORD, nor yet the work which He had done for Israel" (cf. McKnight 2021, 27). Information below will show that younger generations are less religious than those who went before them, yet they present wonderful opportunities and possess traits which God can use for His glory.

Ministry to Millennials (Gen Y)

We will begin our discussion with Generation Y and then transition to Generation Z. This section will be divided into three parts: Generational Characteristics, Ministry Considerations, and Teaching Considerations.

General Characteristics of Millennials/Generation Y—1981–1998

US Population: 82 million (25.2%)

Key Events: Television show rating system established (1997), Columbine High School shootings (1999), Clinton/Lewinsky scandal (1998-99), new millennium & Y2K (2000), September 11, 2001 (this has a larger impact on Gen Z), Massachusetts becomes the first state to legalize gay marriage (2004), the Great Recession (2007-09), Barack Obama becomes first Black president (2009), Occupy Wall Street (2011), heavy parental involvement, fear of low self-esteem, the Consumer Age, technology everywhere.

Top TV: American Idol (2003–), Grey's Anatomy (2005–).

Top Music: "I Gotta Feeling" by the Black Eyed Peas, "Irreplaceable" by Beyonce.

What they say when asked, "What makes your generation unique?"

1. Technology use (24%)
2. Music/pop culture (11%)
3. Liberal/tolerant (7%)
4. Smarter (6%)
5. Clothes (5%) (Shaw 2020, 104).

Ministry Considerations

The youngest Millennials would have been 25 in 2023, and the oldest would have been in their early 40s. If you work with college and young adult ministry, you are apt to work with them. Many of them are going to be volunteers for youth activities, teachers in the congregation, deacons, and parents of the smaller children. Here are some things to consider in ministry to and with this generation. Much of the following is influenced by *Effective Generational Ministry*, written by Craig Blomberg and Elisabeth Nesbit Sbanotto (cf. Blomberg and Sbanotto 2016, 167–251).

1. Listen and give feedback: For Millennials, truth is relative and personal. Being able to ask questions is also important to them. They value being heard and having feedback. They do not need

people always to agree with them, but listening and sharing feedback are important. It is critical to create an environment in which they feel safe to ask questions. They may struggle to believe in absolute truth, but the path to belief is paved with patience, openness to questions, and calm, loving responses.

2. Minister to their diversity: This generation is much more diverse that those that went before them. They are more open to different ethnicities, religions, ages, lifestyles, and relationships. They are much more comfortable with interracial marriages, and they are also more open to same-sex relationships. They are going to struggle with churches and generations that are not open to differences and that are intolerant of others.

Their diversity trait has both blessings and challenges. This is blessing in that it challenges older generations who can learn from their multicultural openness. God made a diverse world and intended His church to be for all nations. The racism and bigotry of the past are simply unacceptable among God's people. Not only have Christians acted in racist ways, but many have also been guilty of the sin of silence. We have silently stood by and said nothing while people were being mistreated around us. Millennials are watching the church and will decide whether they want to join us, in part, based on our tolerance or the lack thereof.

Yet, there can be a negative side to their tolerance. Their struggles with believing that there is absolute truth and their openness to differences can lead to an unwillingness to accept biblical teaching on such subjects as the nature of the church, appropriate ways to worship, and human sexuality. This does not mean that we do not discuss these differences between their worldview and God's worldview. It does mean that patience and humility will be important in helping them to understand and accept biblical teaching. When discussing gender identity and same-sex relationships, it will be important not only to have the courage to stand for biblical teaching but also to show love for those who live lifestyles contrary to Scripture. We must stand against sin while loving and ministering to the sinner. They will be watching for our authenticity and compassion.

3. Help them to navigate technology: Millennials are the first generation to grow up in a world in which internet access, television, and computers were available to them for much of their lives. "Millennials have a lot of information available to them but lack the skills or knowledge to adapt to it or decipher it" (Blomberg and Sbanotto 2020, 173). Thus, patiently helping them to evaluate the information they have access to will be vitally important. It is also worth noting that some Millennials have reached a technological saturation point. A 2023 article on Foxnews.com noted that many phone carriers are reissuing flip phones to meet Millennial demand for them (Knutsson 2023). A Heritage Millennial student also noted of this group, "Many still prefer paper and pen to digital formats." This resonates with me because my Millennial daughter, who graduated Summa Cum Laude, took all of her college notes by hand.

4. Help them to overcome homes that revolved around them. Like many generational traits, there are blessings and challenges related to this. Whereas Gen Xers often felt "in the way" as their parents pursued their careers, Millennials were doted on by their parents. They are the generation who all received participation trophies for every sport and whose parents put "My child is an honor student" bumper stickers on their cars. They have been told their whole lives that they can do anything. Thus, many are driven to try new things and dream big dreams. A blessing is that youth ministers and churches have opportunities to unleash this optimism and potential on doing good for God's glory.

Yet, as they move into adulthood, they learn that they cannot, in fact, do anything. Life can be brutal. Discouragement is a real possibility for some in this cohort. Churches and ministers will need to be prepared to help those who are struggling to deal with the discouragement of a real world that does not fit the fantasy world their parents created. Help them to see that in spite of the fact they have limits, God can do great things with their lives.

5. Embrace their attitude toward older adults: Millennials tend

to like their parents and trust authority more than previous generations. They do not blindly follow authority figures but do tend to be less skeptical of them. They are more apt than Boomers or Xers to respect older generations. This does not mean they do not have concerns about older generations. For example, Millennials tend to feel the Boomers and Xers struggle with tolerance and are overly rules-oriented. Yet, they are more open to the positives of older adults as well. This opens the door for intergenerational connections which can bless all involved. They do value being heard, but if things are discussed collaboratively, they are willing to accept decisions that differ from their own.

Teaching Considerations for Millennials

In her book *Generational Learning Styles,* Julie Coates summarizes generational characteristics and teaching suggestions which can be helpful to youth workers who are teaching Millennials.

Generational Characteristics for Teachers to Consider:

- They want to know what is expected up front (i.e., Is it on the test?, Why do I need it?)
- Comfortable with technology
- Traditional in many ways (research shows they connect with the WW II generation best)
- Need more structure and attention
- Motivated to learn to reduce stress and increase marketability
- Making money matters (education helps)
- Interpersonal skills and "getting along" are important
- Tend to be polite, good manners, moral code, civic action
- Like learning to be entertaining and fun
- Can quickly become bored

- Grew up with Learning Channel and Chuck E Cheese (mixes in entertainment)
- Stand-up talking is deadly (lecture)
- Like music, art, games, and creative activities

Teaching Recommendations:

- Generation of readers
- Use experiential learning
- Encourage learning communities
- Provide structure
- Provide feedback
- Use technology
- Make it fun (incorporate games)
- Be relevant
- Utilize their talents
- Allow for creativity and be creative
- Offer multiple options for performance
- Be visual
- Be organized (know where a lesson is going and why)
- Be open to their ideas
- Recognize the need for social interaction
- Give opportunities to talk
- Be fair and create respect and positive reinforcement in the learning environment
- Be positive, clear, and precise
- Break class into 20-30 minute segments with changes in activities (20 minute attention span) (cf. Coates 2007, 102–16).

Coates adds,

Unlike Gen Xers, Gen Y's will not look at you with disdain if they feel they know more than you about a specific topic. However, they will expect you to be open to hearing their ideas and to demonstrate competence as a teacher. To this generation, being 'a good teacher' is more important than knowing everything (Coates 2007, 127).

As of spring 2023, Millennials make up the largest cohort among our students at Heritage Christian University at 40.72% (Boomers—16.49%, Gen X—25.26%, Gen Z—7.53%). Nine of our Millennial students responded to an informal email survey. Their top four suggestions for teaching their cohort are listed below. I will include comments from some of them but will not use names to honor confidentiality.

1. Practical Application (82%)—One student summed up the comments as follows: "Many Millennials (in my experience) are less interested in just knowledge for knowledge's sake. We need to see what impact it actually has on living life and being 'successful' in it."
2. Visual/Variety (55%)—Although they felt it was ok to have some lecture, they learn through visuals and value teaching with variety (both in-class teaching and out-of-class assignments).
3. Discussion/Community (55%)—Create a community atmosphere in the classroom, and use discussion to unpack material and to allow for students to share their thoughts (both large group and small group discussion).
4. Evidence/Scripture (45%)—Content matters in the classroom. Base teaching on Scripture, sound evidence, and consistency with the real world. Do not abuse Scripture or make unsound arguments to advance personal points.

While willing to share their thoughts on the group, they were quick to note that they don't necessarily represent the group. One student noted, "I am a 'Millennial' though most my age (30 and up) resist the term. I'm not sure if this is representative, but I can speak for myself and some of my close friends my age." I also observed that one student referenced the fact they had shorter attention spans than past cohorts, while another said he did not buy into the myths about attention spans. This is a reminder that there are many personal differences within generations. Finally, it is worth noting that one student stressed the important of teachers living lives consistent with their teaching. He said, "It is hard to listen to someone who you do not respect." Amen!

Ministry to Generation Z

Now we turn our attention to Generation Z, the generation that today's youth ministers are spending the largest amount of time with (with the Alphas right behind them). These young people were roughly between the ages of five and twenty-five in 2023. Like the previous section, we will consider characteristics, ministry considerations, and teaching considerations.

Characteristics of Generation Z—1999–2019

US Population: 86.9 Million (26.7%)

Key Events: No personal memory of September 11, 2001, the Great Recession, student loan debt/college cost at all-time highs, internet-in-your-pocket from infancy, social media "personas," the "On-Demand Economy," anxiety epidemic, subscriber entertainment (Spotify, Netflix), increase in racial diversity, sexual fluidity.

Top TV: Big Bang Theory (2007–19), Game of Thrones (2011–19).

Top Music: "Despacito" by Luis Fonsi and Daddy Yankee featuring Justin Bieber (2017), "Uptown Funk" by Mark Ronson featuring Bruno Mars (2015).

What they say when asked, "My _____ is very important to my sense of self."

1. Professional/educational achievement (43%)

2. Hobbies/pastimes (42%)
3. Gender/sexuality (37%)
4. Group of friends (35%)
5. Family background/upbringing (34%) (cf. Shaw 2020, 123–40).

In his work *Meet Generation Z*, James Emery White points out that Generation Z is now the largest generation (White 2017, 37). He states,

> They are growing up in a post-9/11 world. They are experiencing radical changes in technology and understandings of family, sexuality, and gender. They live in multigenerational households, and the fastest-growing demographic within their age group is multiracial (39).

White highlights five defining characteristics of this important generation (see his text for the original sources he refers to).

<u>Recession-Marked</u>: Economic struggles have been a key part of their early years, and thus economic security and making a difference in the world are important to them.

As members of Generation Z develop their personalities and life skills in a socioeconomic environment "marked by chaos, uncertainty, volatility, and complexity," it is no surprise that blockbusters like The Hunger Games and Divergent, with their depictions of teens left alone to face a dystopian future, connect with them. Simply put, they are deeply worried about the present (39–40).

<u>Wi-Fi Enabled</u>: They have immediate access to information but often do not know how to process and evaluate the information they access. "The speed by which this technological revolution has taken place is stunning and makes it difficult for older generations to realize the radically different world into which Generation Z has been born" (42).

<u>Multiracial</u>: They are the most racially diverse generation in history. U.S. culture is experiencing explosive growth in Hispanic

and mixed-racial populations. "Overall, multiracial children are the fastest-growing youth group in the United States" (46).

Sexually Fluid: Gender issues and sexual identity are problems for older generations. These realities are the norm for Generation Z, and many would view Christian stances against same-sex relationships as no difference from the sin of racism. "For Generation Z, the idea of 'acceptance' is often interchangeable with the idea of 'affirmation'" (46).

Post-Christian: U.S. culture has transitioned from an Acts 2 culture, where most people had a basic belief in God, Christ, and Scripture, to an Acts 17 culture, in which the largest religious group is the group that has no religious affiliation at all (the "nones"). White notes, "As the research of the Barna Group concluded, the 'pattern is indisputable: The younger the generation, the more post-Christian it is'" (49).

Additional characteristics:

- They are eager to start working.
- They are mature and in control.
- They intend to change the world.
- They've learned that traditional choices don't guarantee success.
- Entrepreneurship is in their DNA.
- They seek education and knowledge, and they use social media as a research tool.
- They multitask across five screens, and their attention spans are getting shorter.
- They think spatially and in 4D but lack situational awareness.
- They communicate with symbols, speed, and images.
- Their social circles are global.
- They are hyperaware and concerned about humanity's impact on the planet.
- They are less active and frequently obese. They live stream and cocreate (48).

Tim McKnight references White's work and adds the following characteristics:

- ·They struggle with mental and emotional health.
- They are growing up "too slow" and "too fast."
- ·The parents of Generation Z are both over-engaged and under-engaged in their parenting (McKnight 2021, 33–38).

Haydn Shaw described Generation Z in terms of five things that haunt them:

1. Born online
2. The Great Recession
3. Diversity
4. Increased stress and openness about mental illness
5. Emerging adulthood (they emerge into adulthood later) (cf. Shaw 2020, 124–40).

One more aspect of Generation Z (and Millennials as well) that must be noted is the steady decline in religious indicators. Pew Research Center's 2014 *Religious Landscape Study* noted that 35% of those between the ages of 18 and 29 have no religious affiliation, and only 40% say religion is very important to them. A Pew research study from 2019 found that 40% of Millennials had no religious affiliation, and only 22% attended religious services weekly or more (Pew Research Center 2019).

Ministry Considerations for Generation Z

How then do we minister to this generation of young people? They are dealing with a world unlike the world in which many of us grew up. There are five areas of focus that I believe are important in helping them to mature into the likeness of Christ.

1. Help them to find peace and safety: Remember that they have experienced two economic downturns, a post-9/11 world, and a worldwide pandemic. Make sure that all settings you have control over are safe environments for them (classrooms, retreat sites, adult conversations, etc.). Also, helping them to understand peace in Christ is critical.
2. Help them to deal with stress: Depression is a growing problem for Gen Zers (cf. Shaw 2020, 137). The good news is that they are often willing to talk about their mental health and to use mental health resources (cf. Shaw 2020, 137). Youth workers need to get all the training they can get in counseling and need to know the resources available in their communities. Church leaders need to consider hiring mental health professionals to work with their congregations.
3. Help them to deal with technology: Help them to find their identity in Christ, not in social media. Also, give them tools for evaluating the strengths and weaknesses of what they access through digital sources.
4. Disciple to their diversity: Model before them a willingness to accept, minister to, and disciple people from all backgrounds. They are watching to see if Christians are legit in living out Christ's love for all people. Yet, help them to see that loving and ministering to all people does not mean that we condone or promote every life choice or belief system.
5. Mobilize them for ministry: Remember that they are entrepreneurs. The Barnes and Noble research noted, "More than one-third of Gen Z students currently own their own business or plan on having one in the future" (Barnes and Noble 2017, 6). Tim McKnight observes:

My research and experience reveal a common denominator: churches across America treat teenagers like fourth-graders rather than disciples. As youth ministers and parents, we need to set a new example and a new standard. We can grow disciples who advance the gospel and the kingdom of Christ while they are students and after they graduate. We can mobilize students who have a kingdom mindset and pursue a kingdom mission (McKnight 2021, 17).

Build on that that entrepreneurial spirit to train them to make a difference in the world. We need to believe in them and expect more. One area of opportunity is in evangelism. One of our Generation Z students at Heritage stated, "Generation Z needs to pick up and learn how to truly be evangelists."

Teaching Considerations for Generation Z

Tim McKnight listed "students" as one of his ten identifiers of Generation Z. Research conducted in 2017 by Barnes and Noble College with 13–18-year-old Gen Z students confirmed this reality. For example, they discovered that "89% rated a college education as valuable" (Barnes and Noble 2017, 4). If they are willing to learn, let us take advantage of that and teach them. There is a later chapter in this book on teaching teenagers, so we will be brief. Let us begin this section by considering some of their learning characteristics.

Learning Characteristics of Gen Z

The Barnes and Noble research cited above can give us some insight into how Generation Z learns. The researchers found, for example, that Gen Z students prefer collaborative learning (especially with friends), and they learn more by doing than by watching or listening (7–8). When the students involved in the survey were asked "what teachers could do to make learning more fun, helpful, and interactive," they identified the following as "the most helpful tools for learning":

- Class discussion – 64%
- Working through problems/concepts – 60%
- Study guides – 60%
- Textbooks – 56%
- Working in small groups – 49%
- Homework – 46%
- Notes made available online – 38% (8).

Generation Z seeks education that is engaging and interactive. When asked about the helpfulness of education technology tools, students responded as follows:

- Smartboard – 84%
- DIYL ("Do It Yourself Learning") – 81%
- Digital textbook – 81%
- Website with study materials – 81%
- Online videos (Youtube, etc) – 81%
- Social media/user-generated – 74%
- Skype – 73%
- Podcast – 72%
- DVD/movie – 61% (9).

The focus of this research was on learning in a college setting, but there is much here that youth workers can incorporate into teaching teenagers God's Word.

Mark McCrindle, in his text *The ABC of XYZ: Understanding Global Generations*, offers an interesting summary of what he calls the "post-literate" culture in which young people live:

> Today's younger generations have been born into a time that has seen the printed word morph into an electronic form. In this digital era, communication is not restricted to the spoken and written word but is multi-modal. The Internet is not a literate tool but an interactive, hyperlinked medium of discovery, sound, video and images. For today's young people, the online and web-commu-

nity created Wikipedia is more widely accessed than the printed Encyclopaedia Britannica compiled by academics. The real danger with this reliance is the collaborative nature of Wikipedia—at times sacrificing the accuracy and thoroughness of information. Ironically, today an electronic document is perceived to have more currency (and therefore accuracy) than the printed page. Books give way to YouTube videos. Written word is replaced by icons and images. A letter is replaced by a text message complete with emoticons and new forms of spelling. Education is shifting from structured classrooms to collaborative means, from textbooks to tablets and from reports to infographics and video presentations. Words in this global era are progressively replaced with symbols or universal icons (McCrindle 2014, 140).

To further emphasize McCrindle's insight, James Emery White noted that the 2015 Oxford word of the year was an emoji, 😂 (cf. White 2017, 118). Today's teachers of teenagers and twenty-somethings must take this reality into consideration.

Teaching Considerations for Generation Z

It is important to remember that students in Generation Z are visual, they are digital natives, and they have what James Emery White described as "eight-second filters." White states,

> According to the research of the National Center for Biotechnology Information, the average attention span has dropped from 12 seconds in 2000 to just 8.25 seconds in 2015. That's around a 25 percent drop in just over a decade. To put that into perspective, the average attention span of a goldfish is 9 seconds (115).

White stresses that once you have young people's attention, they can go deep and be very focused. You just need to connect to them quickly.

White gives a summary for those who teach teenagers: "Bottom line? Whatever it is we are attempting to convey, much less explain, will need to be communicated more frequently in shorter bursts of 'snackable content'" (116). With these things in mind, Julie Coates offers the following suggestions for teaching Gen Z college students in her book, *Generational Learning Styles*:

- Think digital.
- Break content into short segments.
- Make information graphical and bite-sized.
- Be relevant (respect their time).
- Provide individualized instruction.
- Use social media in learning.
- Set up students for a career.
- Provide access to resources to help eliminate student debt.
- Acknowledge that they see themselves as smart, creative, and hardworking (Coates 2007, 116).

Mark McCrindle gives what he calls "The New Four Rs" of teaching and learning for today's young people:

- Be Real—"If we are less than transparent, it will be seen. This generation can sniff a phony from a long distance" (McCrindle 2014, 160).
- Be Relevant—"Obviously what we are communicating has to fall within their area of interest. But the style as well as the content must be relevant to a generation which is visually educated and entertained" (160–61).
- Be Responsive—"Education can either be teacher-centric (obviously ineffective), curriculum targeted (it is irrelevant if a curriculum is taught but the students miss much of it) or learner focused (responsive to their learning styles)" (161).
- Be Relational—"Communicating to this generation requires more than just good content and some

interesting anecdotes—it needs openness. The more we create an environment conducive to engaging with the head (knowledge), hands (application) and heart (inspiration), the more likely the learning will be embedded" (161).

I have taught teenagers and college students for over thirty-five years. There are couple of things that seem to connect with today's young people. First of all, I have found that videos work well with both Millennials and Generation Z. Video clips can, for example, serve as great discussion starters. Start class with a video, ask a thoughtful question, and hold on because the class is about to blast off. This has also worked well when teaching the life of Christ. Movies such as *The Gospel of John* or *The Son of God* have been very helpful. Typically, we would watch a section of the movie, read the biblical text that lies behind the movie clip, and then discuss it and dive deeper. I would often begin the discussion asking questions like the following:

- "Did you feel the movie's depiction was consistent with the biblical text, and why?"
- "What was surprising to you in this scene?"
- "How did seeing the scene help you with the text?"
- "What is your #1 takeaway from this section of Scripture?"

Sometimes I would pose these questions (and others) in large group discussions, and sometimes I would assign them to small groups for discussion. After the small groups wrestled with it, they would bring their findings back to the larger group.

Second, both Millennials and Gen Zers like discussion. I would encourage you to offer variety in the discussion settings. Some students will respond well in full group discussions. It has been my experience, though, that more will open up if you break the larger class down into smaller groups and appoint a student leader to ask the questions and record the results. I also suggest that you frequently have all-girl discussion groups. They will share things with ladies that they would not share in front of guys. It is important to use small group leaders that the other students respect and give the leaders the questions ahead of time (so they have time to reflect on them). Let the leaders know specifically what is being asked of them. For example, I let them know that it is not their job to answer everyone's questions. I just want them to generate discussion and summarize the group's thoughts and concerns. Finally, I have found that there are some students who will not speak up in either of the settings mentioned above, but they will respond to digital discussions (some feel safer if they are not face-to-face with someone).

Areas of focus in teaching Generation Z

As we think about teaching Generation Z, especially in light of some of the information noted above, there are some areas where we will need to give special emphasis.

1. We must stress biblical basics and Christian evidences. Preachers and teachers can no longer say, "You know the story of David and Goliath." Many do not.
2. Another area of focus must be evangelism and teaching young people how to evangelize their friends.
3. We are going to need to help them to have a balanced biblical understanding of human sexuality that includes standing for truth while expressing love.
4. Finally, we are going to need to emphasize and explain the nature of the church and the importance of connecting to a local body of believers. The pandemic has reminded us that many do not value connection to the local church. We have been trying for too long to connect people to Christ without connecting them to His body.

Conclusion

We have highlighted the unique characteristics of today's generations over the last few chapters. Tim McKnight summarizes the features of each as follows:

> The Boomer culture was marked by borderline self-worship and could be described in the phrase 'get ahead.' The Buster culture could be described by the phrase 'get lost.' The Millennial culture could be described by the phrase 'get real.' The Generation Z culture could be described by the phrase 'get wired' (McKnight 2021, 29).

You may or may not agree with his oversimplification of the generations, but I pray that his assessment and my overview will cause you to think.

A statement made by one of our Gen Z students at Heritage might be helpful to remind us why we need to wrestle with what we have wrestled with in the last few chapters: "Although a person may have gone through similar situations as me, [as an older figure in my life] they may not fully understand the situation due to generational circumstances. I think it is important not to tell people that you understand their situation when everyone goes through things differently." This student is challenging us to take time to get to know those from other generations. Anyone who whittles knows that to carve something out of wood, you must first have a piece of wood to start whittling on. This chapter and the previous two were not designed to be comprehensive discussions of generational theory and generational connections. They were designed to whet your appetite, to give you some mental wood to whittle on, to give you a framework for further study. They were designed to give us bridges to cross as we seek to build deeper and richer intergenerational relationships.

Discussion Questions

1. What did you find most surprising in this chapter and why?
2. Based on your personal experiences, what parts of this chapter did you agree or disagree with and why?
3. Describe how this chapter might impact your ministry on a day-to-day basis.
4. Describe how this chapter might impact what you do as a Bible teacher.

Bibliography

Barnes and Noble College. "Getting to Know Gen Z - Exploring Middle and High Schoolers Expectations for Higher Education." 2017. https://www.bncollege.com/wp-content/uploads/2018/09/Gen-Z-Report.pdf.

Blomberg, Craig L., and Elisabeth A. Nesbit Sbanotto. *Effective Generational Ministry*. Grand Rapids: Baker Academic, 2016.

Coates, Julie. *Generational Learning Styles*. LERN Books, 2007.

Knutsson, Kurt. "Why Gen Zers are gobbling up flip phones and rejecting smartphones." 28 May 2023. https://www.foxnews.com/tech/gen-zers-gobbling-flip-phones-rejecting-smart-phones.

McCrindle, Mark. *The ABC of XYZ*. 3rd ed. McCrindle, 2014.

McKnight, Tim. *Engaging Generation Z*. Grand Rapids: Kregel Ministry, 2021.

Pew Research Center. "In U.S., Decline of Christianity Continues at Rapid Pace." 17 October 2019. https://www.pewresearch.org/religion/2019/10/17/in-u-s-decline-of-christianity-continues-at-rapid-pace/.

Shaw, Haydn. *Sticking Points*. Carol Stream, IL: Tyndale Momentum, 2020.

White, James Emery. *Meet Generation Z*. Grand Rapids: Baker, 2017.

Chapter 15

Connecting Congregations
Teamwork Among Youth Ministers
Will Myhan and Patrick Kershaw

One of the most important parts of youth ministry is providing students and their families the opportunity to grow in their relationship with Jesus. One of the many ways to hinder this is to segregate your students from other congregations and ministers in the area. Time spent with other youth groups can strengthen teens' relationships with Christ, and it can grow and change the mindsets of teens on what the church is and it can strengthen the church as a whole.

The Key Challenge to Cooperation

The most significant hurdle stopping youth ministers from wanting to be involved with other congregations is jealousy. You may find yourself in a community where there are several congregations where families can worship, work, and fellowship. Both of the authors of this chapter live in such a community. If you find yourself in a situation with this blessing, it may be difficult because you fear you are opening your family to seeing another ministry that they may believe is better than yours. Due to this, you could risk losing you're your people to another congregation. The challenge of jealousy is one that everyone faces because every youth minister wants students to desire to be a part of their group. Overcoming the jealousy of what other ministers and congregations have is critical to helping your students better understand the church as a whole and mature in their faith.

The Benefits of Teamwork

Planning activities with other congregations and youth workers outside of your congregation can feel like a daunting task. You are busy enough with your youth group...right? The reality is that the growth and well-being of the church as a whole should always be at the forefront of our minds, not just individual congregations. When the opportunity presents itself to be involved with coordinating area events or calendars with other youth ministers, that can be an invaluable opportunity for you to contribute to the church's growth, not just for the youth group you work with but for the churches in the area you live in as well. Let us consider and explore some benefits of working with other congregations.

It Helps Your Students Better Understand the Church

Too often, we have students graduating without connecting to the church in youth ministry. Your students are involved in everything the youth group does but have no connections to the congregation's work. We must remember that the youth ministry is not separate from the church, but the youth ministry is a work of the church. When youth groups of different congregations get together, it helps our students understand that "church" is larger than just the youth group. When you, as a youth minister, speak highly of other ministers in your area, it helps your students better understand the church's value and strength when it works together. Scripture teaches us that the church is worldwide, and it's time we start doing a better job of teaming up with each other and stop letting city limits, school rivalries, and egos prevent us from being the church!

It Helps Your Students to Be Encouraged and Influenced

You are likely a great teacher and may have prepared for this ministry for a long time, but sometimes it is terrific for your students to hear other people and how they share the gospel. As a minister to the youth in your congregation, you invest so much time into them, and sometimes your students may look at you the way they look at their parents. As with parents, things said may go in one ear and out the other, but someone else can say the same thing, and it sticks like glue (side note: parents often feel that their kids listen to the youth minister more than to them). Allowing other men and women to lead and teach your students from time to time may help them to have a deeper understanding of Scripture that deepens their faith and commitment to Jesus. In many of our middle and high schools, our students are in the minority regarding their beliefs and the convictions that guide how they live their lives. When youth groups get together, it shows our students that they are not alone. These gatherings with other like-minded teenagers allow them to find accountability partners, new friendships, and mentors to help them grow in their faith.

It Helps You Personally

Youth ministry can be tiresome and stressful, and there can be times when you are not at your best for your students. In those moments, you need teammates! You need people like Aaron and Hur from Exodus 17, who are willing to hold you up so that the fight for the souls of your students can continue. When it comes to youth ministry, you can feel like you are on an island. If you do not have people to hold you up, then your time in youth ministry can be cut short. When you are willing to work with other congregations, you will automatically build relationships with people who understand what it is like to be in the trenches of ministry. Many people in your congregations do not know what it is like to deal with the stresses of your job, but when you find those who "get it," you can open up with them about your disappointments and failures. These meaningful relationships will help you learn, grow, and become the successful youth minister that your students need you to be.

Finding Your Place

The three benefits listed above are just a small list of the benefits of working with other congregations. In the next section of this chapter, we will discuss the importance of finding your place within a group of ministers and understanding how you can use your talents to benefit the young people in your area.

Sharing the Load

Picture this, you are sitting around a table with multiple fellow youth ministers from your area, and you are about to start planning the next year of area-wide events. The men in the room represent youth groups of all sizes and makeups. These youth ministers come from various backgrounds and walks of life. Now, it is possible that you can participate in this planning session with a mindset of uncertainty and even fear. You can let concerns about how you fit in bother you or you can worry about being overburdened with maintaining your work while helping with area responsibilities. Instead, we would encourage you to choose to find confidence and support in knowing that the men assembled around that table are all there with common purposes. In some form or fashion, those purposes are to serve the Lord, provide young people opportunities, and spiritually nurture God's people into being the best they can be for His glory. When you choose the latter option, you're choosing to be a critical part of some significant work for the Lord. That mental transition from focus on individual problems to group potential can open the floodgates of possibilities.

The dynamic of working amongst a group of youth ministers can be different in different communities. You may be in an area heavily saturated with numerous congregations in neighboring cities where the youth ministers commonly get together to plan area events. You could also be part of a cluster of youth ministers that plans events for an entire region of a state that is less heavily saturated with congregations, and you may only get together once a quarter. Whatever situation you find yourself in, the comradery of working together to better the youth of your area is a task that is difficult to truly measure the value of and next to impossible to describe in words.

When you enter your planning sessions with your fellow youth ministers, you can be ready to yell "Avengers Assemble!" and get to work, or you can choose to be a back-of-the-classroom pew sitter who does not engage in the work. The hope here is that you will launch into the opportunities that God places before you and consider these thoughts as you go along.

Understanding Talents

As youth ministers, we often focus on encouraging our students to realize their talents and to remember that God made each of us differently. Yet, when a bunch of youth ministers find themselves in a room to plan events, we can suddenly forget the importance of understanding the different talents and abilities that God has blessed each of us with. Recognizing differences in our talents can greatly increase the quality of the work we do together. We need to remember that even in a room of our peers who share the same position and profession, there are many talents that each of us is blessed with. There are unique talents that you have that can bless such gatherings. Developing a group of youth ministers to plan, organize, and execute area events or multi-youth group events in many ways begins with the planners themselves understanding each other and who is best suited to plan, organize, and execute certain things. Youth ministers are not all planners or creative thinkers. That is okay. When we come together as a group, the group collectively has talents that each of us as individuals may not have. One thing that can contribute to the planning and sharing of the load amongst youth ministers is when we, as a group, have a community understanding of our individual talents. We can then harness those talents to make the overall task ahead easier. You may ask, "What talents can be useful to have amongst your group when planning events together?" Let's consider some of the talents that are needed.

Most youth ministers have at least a little creative side, but for some, they have a great deal of creative ability. If you are constantly brainstorming new ideas or projects, then you may be one of these creative types. Others have the ability to see the big picture of a project. You may lie awake at night putting together the big pieces of your next events in your mind. You may also be great at looking at the needs of the teens in your area and using their feedback to design event concepts. If these things align with how you think, then you would probably fit the bill for being a "big picture" type of youth minister. The beginnings of any event often start in the hands of these youth ministers or at least in the thoughts and concepts of youth ministers that fit in this role. If this is you, then realize that often you may be a catalyst for the start of an excellent event for your area, but you have to rely on the planners and the expeditors to help make it happen. Creative types may envision a new event or the upgrade of a current event. Big picture types get the ball rolling and help the group think about all the details of what needs to happen to make the event a reality. The planners then step in to move the project along. You also have the motivators and encouragers who keep the group going as the work piles up and the stress increases. Others are best at "day off" activities such as registration, setup, food, or cleanup. Still, others are good at follow-up and helping the group to learn and improve after the event.

If you are detail-oriented, are somewhat meticulous, or even OCD, and have a fascination with spreadsheets and other forms of organization programs. You might as well embrace the title of the planner, "The Leader," or even "Captain," as the case may be. Youth ministers who are planners may either have had influences from other secular work that contributed to having a deep-rooted desire for consistency, details being correct, and things being organized to flow properly, or they may be wired to be more of an in-control type personality. If this is you, get ready to be the note taker, more than likely at planning meetings or the one reminding people of tasks that need to be completed leading up to an event. You're valuable to planning the events, organizing the setup, and noticing the details as the events are executed.

If you love being in the thick of executing an event, are cool with life moving at 100 MPH, and always have some pep in your step that makes people want to smile or laugh, then you may be an "expeditor" type youth minister. When executing an area event for several hundred or several thousand teens, the "expeditor" youth ministers are incredibly valuable to have as part of the team. In restaurants, expeditors ensure orders are executed promptly, look great, with no mistakes, and even serve as liaisons between the cooks and servers. Suppose you are an expeditor-type youth minister at an area event. In that case, you may find yourself setting up for the worship, ensuring the meal is ready to go and everyone gets served, then wrapping back around and ensuring everything is cleaned up and back in its place after several thousand teens have come through the building. Then when it's all said and done, you can still step back through the night and learn from that night to better execute the next event. Make no mistake; the "expeditor" type youth ministers make area events work. Planners can plan, and big picture, and creative people can dream up and design, but the expeditors make it happen. If you find yourself in those shoes, then know you are invaluable to successfully making an event come together.

When it all comes down to it, you may have a little of each of these in you. Often, you'll find yourself leaning more strongly toward one of these types and that is perfectly okay. You may also find that your ministry type will change over time and that the planning team and its strengths will also change over time. There is a reason why the Avengers superheroes worked so well together. Not everyone was a Captain America and not everyone was an Ironman. They all had unique talents and capabilities that, when assembled together, could do some incredible things for good. Now let us go into our planning sessions and figure out whether we're a Captain or an Ironman. Regardless of who you are, remember the purpose of what you are doing, who you are serving, and what the ultimate goal is. Also, remember to allow others freedom and room to use their talents. If I monopolize a leadership role, I may be preventing a spiritual Ironman from using his gifts for God's glory.

Conclusion

As your fellow youth workers, we understand that students may join another youth ministry in your area at times based on your decision to interact with and have events with other congregations. While we know these times can be challenging, any decision you make that leads students to be more faithful in their relationship with Jesus, whether in your group or another group, is a significant win. When all of us are working together and have the same mind that desires teenagers to love Jesus and have a relationship with Him, then the church as a whole wins! Some of the greatest resources you have as a minister are simply across town or the next county over. We are stronger together!

Discussion Questions

1. Why do you believe that our egos can be such a driving force for not working with others?
2. How would you handle a family leaving your ministry for another one you worked with?
3. What type of youth minister do you see yourself as being? Are you a big-picture guy, a planner, or an expeditor? Evaluate your strengths and the focus for how

you work and see which of these fits closest to how you work.
4. What advantages can you think of for having a mix of the discussed youth minister types represented within a group that is charged with planning area events?

Recovery in Youth and Family Ministry

Chapter 16
Counseling Tips for Youth Ministers
Ben Hayes

It is inevitable. At some point in your youth ministry career someone will come to you for counsel, whether you are prepared for it or not. As a youth minister who was untrained and quite honestly, ill-prepared for those scenarios, I had everyone from middle schoolers to parents of the youth group come to me for help long before I had ever taken my first class in counseling.

The list of situations that I faced as a young minister included a dad leaving his wife after close to 20 years of marriage, a young man who struggled with homosexuality, and a young girl who attempted to take her own life with a shotgun to the stomach. Then there were the situations that I am sure most ministers face at any given time: a widower struggling to survive without his wife, teenagers coming to church alone and trying to figure out how to live spiritually with parents who are not, and the regular struggles of college-age students trying to find their way on their own.

It is not uncommon for youth ministers, and ministers in general, to face situations for which they are unprepared. It is also not uncommon to mishandle those situations because most are unprepared and untrained in handling such situations. After many years in ministry, and even many years in counseling, there will still be very difficult circumstances through which I am required to navigate.

If ministers are dealing with these struggles and what to do in the face of them, then you know the youth group and congregation you work with are struggling as well when they face them. Many of them long for answers just like you do. Many expect you, as the minister, to have all the answers. In 2018 a Lifeway study revealed that forty-nine percent of ministers say they never talk to their churches about mental health and that fifty-nine percent of Christians suffering from mental illness wished that their ministers would discuss it more openly. The same study revealed that sixty-five percent of their families would like for there to be more conversations about mental health in churches.

In the following chapter, you will explore the details of handling certain scenarios that you may face with the teens you work with on a daily basis. Before you get into the specifics, it is important to simply understand the mindset and general characteristics of a good counselor to young people.

The Greatest of These

What do you think is the single most important aspect of counseling? There are many different theories in counseling and seemingly thousands of techniques to choose from. Yet, the greatest predictor of the success of counseling comes down to the therapeutic relationship between the counselor and the client. The same is true when it comes to ministry. It is cliche, but it is still true: People do not care how much you know until they know how much you care.

There have been many parents through the years who have warned me before I met with their kids that they may not say anything to me. Several of the kids and teens have been upset that they are coming to counseling because they do not feel that they need it. Some parents report that their kids just do not talk with adults. Yet, in almost every single situation where I have been warned, I have not only connected to the client, but they have desired to come back. That is not said in some prideful way about my ability to counsel. It is simply proof of the power of showing love and concern for other people.

An attitude seen in Jesus and his disciples in the New Testament could be summed up like this: Love them where they are, but love them enough not to leave them there. That is a concept that should drive our work with all people. You may not solve everyone's problem but at the very least you can attempt to show compassion and help them to move forward from the difficult spot that they have found themselves in.

When you consider the work of Jesus, you see this on more than one occasion in His ministry. Yet, the starting points for each occasion are different. Consider how Zacchaeus' story was different from the man at the pool of Bethesda. One was an outcast because of his prideful power and the way he had mistreated others (Luke 19:1-10). The other was an outcast due to situations he could not prevent or change and was neglected by others (John 5:1-9). Yet, in each of the situations you see a Savior willing to get involved. He loved Zacchaeus, and He loved the man at the pool. He loved them enough not to leave them in the pitiful situation He had found them in.

We generally think of love as a feeling. Of course, emotions are certainly involved in the process of love, yet I can remember Keith Parker saying, "Love is not just a feeling that you feel like you're feeling when you feel a feeling that you've never felt before." Love doesn't always involve good feelings. Sometimes, however, love is the ability to look beyond the hurt and pain of a situation and act in the best interest of those whom we care about. Jesus did this on the cross and with the many people that he encountered daily.

There will be occasions when people arrive at your office at times that are not convenient for you. There will also be moments when you are called into action in the middle of the night. Those moments do not often feel good but remember that they still need your smile. They need your comforting words. Most of all they simply need your presence. Be aware that your posture and nonverbal actions communicate just as much as your words. Keep an open posture (arms uncrossed), smile, nod, keep appropriate eye contact, and generally help them to feel comfortable in your presence.

Tuning In

Of course, part of helping people get on the road to where they need to be is understanding fully where they are. Have you ever attempted to give someone directions to a desired location over the phone without first considering where they were when they called? Can you share with them the direction they should head in or the landmarks they should look for when you are unaware of where they are starting from? You would not do that with directions so be careful not to do that with people's lives.

Jesus was willing to listen with His ears, but He also "listened" with His eyes. Even though He had the ability to know all things, He still made sure people felt heard and seen. Consider the day that Jesus watched the people and perceived that they were "like sheep without a shepherd" (Matt 9:36 ESV). He immediately recognized Nathanael and informed him that He had already noticed him under the fig tree (John 1:48). He had noticed the man in John 5:6 and that the condition of the man revealed he had been there a long time. In the story of the rich young ruler Mark records, "And Jesus, looking at him, loved him …" (10:21 ESV).

Jesus clearly passed this trait on to the disciples who followed Him in His ministry. Luke, in the book of Acts, tells of an interaction in which Peter and John were walking into the temple when they encountered a beggar. If you have ever walked the streets of a large city or been on a mission trip to another country, you may have had similar encounters with those who are asking for help. People accustomed to such interactions will recommend not making eye contact. Yet, "Peter directed his gaze at him, as did John, and said, 'Look at us'" (Acts 3:4 ESV). Not only did they take notice of the one begging, but they also called for him to take notice of them. Later in the book of Acts, Paul took note of the people he was speaking to and preached a lesson without using a single Scripture reference. He knew where his audience was coming from, met them where they were, and loved them enough not to leave them there (Acts 17:16–34).

Attunement is a word used to describe our ability to connect inwardly with the people around us. It is paying attention to what others are saying and doing and choosing when and how to connect with those things. The more attuned—or in tune—a person is to another, the more likely that relationship will grow. The concept of attunement will also bless your ministry by helping people feel seen and heard. When kids speak to you, pay attention. When they are involved in an activity, be a part. When they come to your office to pour out their souls over whatever struggle they find themselves embroiled in, simply listen. It's a lost art but a necessary one. Most people simply want to be heard and to feel a connection. Paul stated it simply: "Rejoice with those who rejoice, weep with those who weep" (Rom. 12:15 ESV).

Have you ever experienced the frustration of being in the middle of a conversation with someone only to have them get distracted by someone else and abandon your discussion? It leaves you feeling unimportant and unheard. If you know the disappointment involved in such an interaction, then do your best to avoid it with those who may be speaking to you. If you find yourself in conversation with someone and another individual comes up with an attempt to get your attention, simply acknowledge the person but let them know you need to finish the conversation you are currently engaged in first. If they are unrelenting in their attempt to distract, take hold of the person you were first in conversation with to let them know you are not abandoning them, and then allow the distractor to finish so that you can return to the initial conversation uninterrupted. It may be difficult and take some effort, but in doing so, you have left no one feeling as if they are unimportant.

Sometimes people who are hurting will struggle to find the right words to explain how they are feeling. This is especially true with young people. They often struggle to identify emotions and connect them to the situation they are facing. Tuning in may involve "listening between the lines" and helping them connect the emotion. For example, when a teary-eyed young lady relates how she is being left out you might simply state, "I can see how much that hurts you." When a young man shares with you how he did not make the team you might respond, "I know that being on that team meant a lot to you." Open statements like this allow them to continue to explore the feelings instead of shutting the feelings down.

As ministers you want to make the hurt go away, and you might be tempted to make statements like "You do not need those friends anyway" or "Do not feel bad about that, there will be other opportunities." While those words are meant to help, they often result in bottling up the emotions, which can lead to further trouble in the long run. It is important to process the frustration, grief, anger, sadness, or whatever else they may be facing. A great resource for this kind of interaction is the book *How to Talk So Kids Will Listen and Listen So Kids Will Talk* by Adele Faber and Elaine Mazlish.

The Genuine Article

If teenagers have a superpower, it might be the uncanny ability to spot people who are not genuine. They seem to be able to quickly spot behaviors that lack sincerity. Therefore, it is important to cultivate within yourself the sincere desire to love and care for them and to do all you can to show the concern you have for them. Your work in helping them with their spiritual life is not about you. It is not for you to work your way up a ministerial ladder. The work you find yourself in should be something that you genuinely care about, and the people you work with should be people you genuinely care about.

Remember that every student is different. They are starting from a different place in life and in their spiritual walk. A key part of genuineness is helping each one to reach his or her potential and knowing what that is. Your young people will not all develop at the same speed, and they will not all reach the same places. Thus, as a leader, you need to connect to each one in love, attunement, and genuineness and adjust to their needs and stage of development. Everything Jesus did was genuine. He felt people's pain (John 11:35) and hurt for them even when they did not realize what they were doing (Matt 23:37; Luke 23:34). One of His greatest pleas was an attempt to lighten the burdens of others:

> Come to me, all who labor and are heavy laden, and I will give you rest. Take my yoke upon you, and learn from me, for I am gentle and lowly in heart, and you will find rest for your souls. For my yoke is easy, and my burden is light. (Matt 11:28–30 ESV).

There is love and concern in that statement. There is attunement to those who are hurting. There is someone gentle who is ready to help bear the burden, while at the same time being honest about expectations. Yokes are a burden. His yoke is lighter than the others you may carry in life, but it still qualifies as a burden. What Jesus realized was that people needed to be held to a standard. His genuine love not only supported people but also called people to a higher place. Taking His yoke gave them a mission and a purpose. Part of being genuine is not just comforting them in their mistakes but calling them to walk a better path. It might not always be easy, but it is much preferred over the burden of choosing the way of the world.

Youth ministry is difficult at times. It is also extremely rewarding. You have the blessing of walking kids through the time in their lives when the brain is doing some of its most substantial growth and change. So, while they may be some of the moodiest humans on the planet, they are also some of the most creative and energetic. Relationships and the way that you engage with them are some of the most important things you can do as a minister to impact them. When they feel safe and connected, they will open up. There will be things you are not trained to handle, but the relationship you have with them will allow you to safely recommend them to counselors or other helpers who can give them further guidance on those things.

Making Referrals

With that being said, how do you know when to refer your kids to a counselor and how does that process work? There are several things to think about when considering the referral of a student to a counselor. First, do I feel uncomfortable with this topic and/or giving answers regarding this situation? There are simply times that you feel "out of your league" on certain topics. If it is a spiritual question, you might first consult with the elders or another minister. However, sometimes they may speak to you about things that require further knowledge of how the brain works or how to treat mental health disorders.

There are certain concerns that prayer and reading cannot fix. You may balk at that answer at first but consider this: How many times have you told someone with a 90% blockage in their heart or with severe diabetes to simply pray and read a passage of Scripture without also having them consult a physician? My guess would be that you think that would be crazy. Mental health disorders are concerns or problems in the brain, which happens to be the most complex computer in the world. There are people who have spent their lives attempting to better understand how it works and certainly can help people find some answers for responding when that computer between the ears is not working properly.

Second, in the event that you decide a referral would be best, how do you decide whom to refer to? This can certainly be a difficult scenario. Good counselors should never push their own beliefs on their clients. Even Christian counselors are careful to allow the client's worldview to lead the discussion. However, most Christians feel more comfortable visiting with someone that they know shares their belief in Christ. In that case, it may be important to compile a list of Christian-focused counselors in your area. You may want to call other local congregations and see who the counselors are they have used. Those lists may also contain non-Christian counselors who help clients with their spirituality even though that is not their own personal worldview. Every area is different and there are some areas where seeing a counselor in person may take a significant drive. Since the beginning of the COVID-19 pandemic, telehealth has been more readily available. Most counselors do online therapy, which has helped many people in rural areas.

Conclusion

Youth ministers are on the front line of the spiritual war that young people are fighting each day. You see teens at their best and you often see teens at their worst. You understand more than anyone what the teenagers of the church and those in the community are facing. Arm yourself with love (Col 3:14), attunement (Prov 18:13), and genuineness (1 Pet 1:22). You will not only represent Jesus well, but you will also make an impact that may last for generations.

Discussion Questions

1. Have you ever encountered a situation where showing concern for someone led to an opportunity to help them in a much deeper way or even to share the gospel with them? Can you think of examples in Scripture where that happened?
2. What other Scriptures or Biblical examples can you think of that reveal the idea of attunement? Are there passages that reveal that our Father in heaven is tuned in to what we need?
3. When you think of people that you see as genuine, what qualities do you see? With that in mind, how can you cultivate those qualities of genuineness in your life?

Chapter 17
Helping Teens Deal with Addictions
Ryan N. Fraser

Introduction

Your phone rings and it is an anxious mother asking for advice pertaining to her teenage daughter who is addicted to alcohol. A father stops you in the foyer following services seeking help for his adolescent son who has been caught again watching pornography on his smartphone. The young man has confessed to his dad that he spends several hours a day looking at it and cannot seem to stop. It has become a deeply engrained habit that is accompanied by guilt and shame. A 15-year-old girl from the youth group messages you to set up an appointment to discuss her unhealthy relationship with social media along with her distorted body-image and self-esteem issues. She feels depressed and isolated from her family and peers. How may youth and family ministers respond to these very real types of situations that arise in their congregations? It is very challenging indeed!

Addiction is a painful reality in our world, especially for young people and their families. It cuts to the very core of individuals' physical, emotional, and spiritual well-being. It sabotages their inner sense of peace and stability. It wrecks hope on the jagged rocks of despair. It reduces happiness, corrodes confidence, tarnishes reputation, and diminishes joy. Christian teenagers are certainly not immune from the insidious dangers of addiction, which comes in many shapes and forms. In fact, I believe they are directly targeted by the devil who seeks to destroy their souls.

These days, teens are standing in harm's way when it comes to drug and alcohol dependence as well as various forms of behavioral addiction. Vaping, for instance, is rapidly on the rise. Technology abuse and addiction have reached epidemic proportions with online gaming, social media compulsions, and internet pornography being among the main culprits. Parents and/or legal guardians, church leaders, and youth ministers can only insulate and protect their teenagers so much from the temptations and the perverse threats to their souls that often ensnare them. Let's face it, nobody can monitor teenagers 24/7, and young people are oftentimes prone to make reckless, impulsive, and unhealthy choices that come back to haunt them and their families. It is an ongoing battle for all concerned.

This Is Serious Business

Youth and family ministers need to become better equipped to effectively address addiction from a godly and informed perspective —one that is well-rounded, biblically sound, carefully structured, and holistically formulated in approach. Counseling theory and practical theology (ministry theory and practice) both play important roles in the overarching process of pastoral diagnosis and strategic treatment. We cannot afford to bury our heads in the sand by ignoring the real issues and jeopardizing those precious young lives that hang in the balance. Far too much is at stake!

In the church, we have a hard time knowing what to do about addiction issues and how to handle them compassionately, yet proactively. In my view, addiction ought not to be seen necessarily as a sin, but rather as the consequence of sin. It is the painful and precarious condition of self-slavery and psycho-spiritual bondage that results from falling prey to Satan's destructive schemes. In John 10:10, Jesus asserts, "The thief comes only to steal and kill and destroy. I came that they may have life and have it abundantly." Addiction is spiritually deadly in nature, and it robs the abundant life right out of young people's souls.

Addiction may be defined as "the repeated involvement with a substance or activity, despite the substantial harm it now causes, because that involvement was (and may continue to be) pleasurable and/or valuable" (https://www.mentalhelp.net/addiction/). Addiction involves loss of self-control; immense spiritual, psychological (and physical), and relational damage; and a vicious cycle that results in feelings of helplessness, worthlessness, and hopelessness. The compulsive component of addiction dominates a young person's time, energy, and mental resources. Think in terms of the acronym **GAS** (keeping in mind that gasoline is an accelerant): **G**uilt, **A**nxiety, and **S**hame work together to fuel the insidious fires of addiction in young people.

The Adolescent Brain and Addiction

It is important to recognize that many changes are occurring during adolescence in the teenager's body and brain. According to researcher Lisa Chiu,

> The teen brain is like a big ball of clay, ready to change and be molded by new experiences — but it is also very messy. During this time, more synaptic pruning occurs, with stronger connections beating out weaker ones in a process called competitive elimination. At the same time, the brain is improving its connections, with neurons extending their dendritic branches and myelination of axons increasing, especially in the frontal lobes (2018, 51).

Young, adolescent brains are particularly susceptible to addictive patterns and unhealthy ways of thinking.

During adolescence, "more complex functions of the brain

develop and can be influenced by environment and experience" (2018, 51). The rapid increase in white matter volume along with myelinated fibers connecting the brain's right and left cerebral hemispheres in the region of the corpus callosum may explain why teenagers have an enhanced learning capacity. Researchers suggest, "Enhanced connections, changes in the brain's reward systems, and changes in the balance between frontal and limbic brain regions can all contribute to teenage behaviors such as increased risk taking and sensation seeking" (Chui, 2018, 51).

Chiu continues as follows:

> Unfortunately, this can be a double-edged sword, as the associated risk taking and sensation seeking also increase the risk of addiction. Some regard addiction as a type of acquired learning disorder, pointing to the overlap between brain regions involved in addiction and those supporting learning, memory, and reasoning. ... Compared to a healthy adolescent brain, adolescents who used alcohol had reduced gray matter volume and reduced white matter integrity. [B]inge drinking (alcohol) during adolescence [is] associated with lower brain activity, less sustained attention, and poorer performance on a working memory task (Chiu, 2018, 51).

The adolescent addict's neural pathways are physically altered, thereby reinforcing thought patterns and cravings for the gratification of a "fix." Thus, the brain of an addicted teenager (particularly the reward circuit of the amygdala, which regulates emotions, along with other brain structures that play roles in pleasure-seeking) is changed so that it differs physiologically from that of a non-addicted young person. This negatively impacts decision-making and often precipitates such mental processes as denial, minimization, and justification or rationalization.

A Biblical Perspective

The Bible speaks clearly about the topics of temptation, sin, and self-control, as well as the respective challenges associated with these concerns. Paul states, in 1 Corinthians 6:12, " 'All things are lawful for me,' but not all things are helpful. 'All things are lawful for me,' but I will not be dominated by anything." Later, in 1 Corinthians 10:13, the apostle asserts,

> No temptation has overtaken you that is not common to man. God is faithful, and he will not let you be tempted beyond your ability, but with the temptation he will also provide the way of escape, that you may be able to endure it.

God is constantly working in the lives of young people to provide them with a viable way to resist temptation, avoid sin, and overcome addiction.

Paul struggled at times with his own behavioral tendencies and was frustrated by his compulsions. He writes in Romans 7:15, 17–19,

> For I do not understand my own actions. For I do not do what I want, but I do the very thing I hate. ... So now it is no longer I who do it, but sin that dwells within me. For I know that nothing good dwells in me, that is, in my flesh. For I have the desire to do what is right, but not the ability to carry it out. For I do not do the good I want, but the evil I do not want is what I keep on doing.

Merely knowing what is righteous is much easier than actually doing the right thing!

Later in Romans (12:1–2), Paul states,

> I appeal to you therefore, brothers, by the mercies of God, to present your bodies as a living sacrifice, holy and acceptable to God, which is your spiritual worship. Do not be conformed to this world, but be transformed by the renewal of your mind, that by

testing you may discern what is the will of God, what is good and acceptable and perfect.

Thus, rehabilitation and transformation of mind, soul, and body are a promised prospect for those young people who struggle with addiction. There is hope for recovery and newness of life in Christ (Rom 6:4; 2 Cor 5:17).

However, adolescent addicts need to be guided in the direction of positive spiritual thinking and a godly, Christ-centered focus. Philippians 4:8 exhorts,

> Finally, brothers, whatever is true, whatever is honorable, whatever is just, whatever is pure, whatever is lovely, whatever is commendable, if there is any excellence, if there is anything worthy of praise, think about these things.

Developing the *mind of Christ* (Phil 2:1–5) requires intentionality and consistent meditation on the Word of God and His perfect will for our lives. Furthermore, it necessitates putting these God-given principles into daily practice (Phil 4:9).

The Addiction Cycle and Assessment

Regarding the teenage addict, there are common phases to the addiction cycle: (1) Initial exposure/use; (2) Continued use/abuse; (3) Tolerance; (4) Dependence/Addiction; (5) Withdrawal; and (6) Relapse.

When assessing (or evaluating) the category and severity of the addiction problem and conceptualizing a way forward, it is helpful to think in the following terms:

- Temptation (What type is it?)
- Triggers (What precipitates it?)
- Time (How much time is involved?)

- Trouble (What damage to self and others results from it?)
- Treatment Plan (What proactive strategies may be put in place?)

Limitations, Boundaries, and Referral

In working with adolescent addicts (no matter the form of addiction), it is first important to recognize your own limitations of time, availability, and behavioral health expertise. Deep-rooted compulsive struggles will likely require referral of the young person and his/her family to a licensed mental health professional and/or primary care provider for longer-term, specialized treatment. Also, it should be kept in mind that those seeking help will need to have a high level of personal motivation if they desire to pursue "sobriety" (i.e., healthy and holy living). This drive must be internally formed within the teenager much more so than by the external pressure placed on the young person by his or her parents or other outside influences.

Over the years, I have come to operate with a basic conviction that states, "People don't change unless they *have* to!" Why? It is simply far too easy to revert to one's default pattern and keep current unhealthy habits in place. Most individuals tend to take the path of least resistance. The road to sobriety requires hard work, personal sacrifice, and a huge commitment for all parties considered, but particularly the teenage addict himself or herself.

The above being said, I will now share some practical ideas of what I have found to be most effective in my pastoral counseling practice in assisting youth and their families to overcome (or manage) addiction.

Pastoral Counseling Process for Adolescent Addiction

I recommend conceptualizing your overarching addiction recovery strategy as being comprised of three 40-day segments: **(1) Cessa-**

tion; **(2) Maintenance**; and **(3) Anomaly**. (Note: In my professional experience, 28-day programs, whether residential or outpatient in design, are generally ineffective over the long haul. It is simply not long enough time to produce lasting change.)

According to my addiction recovery program, the first forty days focuses on ceasing the problematic use/behavior and replacing it with healthy cognitions (or thinking) and wholesome behaviors (or actions). The second forty days is structured to maintain the new behaviors and bolster the new positive patterns of thought and action. During the third forty-day period, it would generally be an anomaly (or unlikely) for recovering addicts to return to their former addictive/compulsive behaviors. While slip-ups and relapses do happen on occasion, they are generally not insurmountable problems.

The Significance of "40"

You may notice that the theological motif of "40 days" crops up rather frequently in Scripture. This is not a merely coincidental phenomenon! For example, it rained for 40 days and nights leading up to Noah's flood (Gen 7:4; 12). Moses ascended Mt. Sinai for 40 days and nights to receive God's Law (Exod 34:28). Moses interceded on Israel's behalf for 40 days and nights in prayer and fasting until his face shone with the glory of God (Deut 9:9, 18, 25). The twelve Israelite spies took 40 days to spy out the land of Canaan (Num 13:25). Goliath taunted Saul's army for 40 days before David arrived on the scene to slay him (1 Sam 17:16). Elijah fasted in the desert and traveled for 40 days to Mt. Horeb (1 Kings 19:8).

The number *forty* also appears in the prophecies of Ezekiel (4:6; 29:11–13) and Jonah (3:4). Jesus fasted in the wilderness before his temptation (Matt 4:1–2; Luke 4:2). After Christ's resurrection, Jesus appeared to disciples for 40 days prior to his ascension (Acts 1:3). There is something theologically significant regarding the idea of a forty-day period in Scripture.

In my view, it takes around 40 days to begin rewiring addicts' neural pathways and modifying behavioral habits/patterns (Rom 12:1–2). Spiritual renewal and brain transformation are possible due to neuroplasticity, which refers to the brain's remarkable ability to change and adapt both its structure and function through intentional and consistently engaged mental processes.

First 40-Day Segment: "Cessation"

Regular Sessions and "Detox" Period

During this first 40-day segment, it will be necessary to meet with the adolescent addict at least twice per week for consistency and built-in accountability. In the first 10-day period, there needs to be a *detox* period for purity/cleanness/sobriety. When it comes to porn addiction, for example, there needs to be no sexual activity, no pornography, and no masturbation (See Mark R. Laaser's research). Each of these elements is closely intertwined and serves to preserve the addiction problem both cognitively and behaviorally. The mind, body, and soul need sufficient time to detox and essentially reset. Alcohol and substance abuse detox should always be medically supervised due to the intense physical risks involved.

Removing Access

It only makes logical sense to eliminate (or greatly limit) access to the specific addictive vice/temptation in question. Lack of easy access removes the immediate hazard. In the case of technology, for instance, putting parental controls, appropriate usage time limitations, and access codes on the devices will be essential to keep them safe for ongoing use (if at all). If impulsive spending is the addiction, then removing credit/debit card access would make logical sense. Unfortunately, sometimes the only avenue to successfully ensure the removal of access may involve inpatient psychiatric hospitalization for a period and/or residential treatment programs.

When self-control is lacking, drastic measures often need to be taken to ensure a safe and secure environment. Do not be naïve, and thereby unintentionally enable the young addict and perpetuate the problem. Tough choices must be made if the young person is going to stand a real chance of overcoming the addiction and finding true deliverance and freedom from bondage.

"Sobriety" Calendar

Require that young recovering addicts keep track of their sobriety on a calendar that they bring to each session. It will help to have something tangible to track their progress. Relapse is generally predictable, so expect it to occur and normalize it when it happens. If they stumble, do not lecture or shame them, but show continued patience, support, and belief in them to continue fighting the good fight. Nonetheless, it is important to restart sobriety days to Day One to ensure legitimate progress and to avoid denial, minimization, or rationalization of the addictive behaviors.

Daily Positive Reinforcement

Encourage the counselee to give themselves a small, yet meaningful, daily reward for remaining clean and "sober." Doing so will facilitate positive reinforcement. Parents may also want to participate in this tangible reward system. Meet with the counselee and parents every week to facilitate an honest reporting of progress and/or any setbacks, ongoing emotional support, and personal accountability. Days 10, 20, 30, and 40 should include larger rewards for successfully achieving sobriety. These rewards may come in many forms, including special treats, gifts, fun outings, and activities, or new privileges.

Scripture Memorization

Also, I require that the young person begins memorizing the book of James, which speaks much about temptation and purity of heart, mind, and behavior. We must fight the devil's fiery schemes with God's flaming sword of the Spirit. God's Word is "living and active, sharper than any two-edged sword" (Heb 4:12), powerful, and transformative. This constitutes a measurable replacement activity to counteract and supplant the addictive cycle. Have the counselee memorize three verses per day and expect the verses to be cumulative.

Remember the story Jesus once relayed concerning the demon that was sent out of a certain man; however, that man failed to replace the demonic activity in his life with God's divine goodness (see Luke 11:24–26). Therefore, the demon later returned with seven worse evil spirits to take up permanent residency in the man's life. Jesus said that "the last state of that person is worse than the first" (verse 26b). Merely quitting unhealthy, addictive behavior without actively replacing it with something good and beneficial is a recipe for disaster.

At each session, ask that the counselee recite the verses memorized thus far. Provide praise and encouragement as well as a system of accountability. After forty days, the counselee will have completely memorized the Book of James, which will be cause for much celebration and a healthy sense of personal pride and accomplishment on their part. Next, continue the memorizing regimen with the Sermon on the Mount (Matt 5–7), Philippians, and then Colossians.

Accountability Partners and Support Groups

Discuss the establishment of accountability partners (or sponsors) with trusted, mature adults who will be prepared to check in with the young person every day (in rotation) to ask pointed questions regarding his/her sobriety progress. Accountability partners may be supplied with questions they can ask the addict regarding when he or she last failed, about triggers, and proactive strategies to fight temptation. Faith-based support groups and programs such as *Celebrate Recovery* may also serve a valuable role in supplying additional weekly structure, accountability, Christian care, psychoeducation, consistency, and spiritual growth opportunities for both the young person and his/her family throughout the addiction recovery process.

Second Forty-Day Segment: "Maintenance"

During the second forty-day segment, newly acquired skills, habits, and behaviors will be bolstered by ongoing maintenance and fine-tuning of the sobriety strategy. The young people will need to continue memorizing and reciting scripture. They will also grow in their cognizance of triggers and temptations they must fight. Ongoing rewards and daily accountability check-ins ought to be maintained. Another recovery element that may be helpful to incorporate at this juncture is that of service opportunities/projects designed to infuse an enhanced positive focus and meaningful outreach experiences into the young person's daily life.

Serving others is a proactive way to demonstrate genuine repentance while engaging in a form of restitution for previous mess-ups and mistakes. More importantly, it is a way to shift focus off oneself and onto the needs of other people. In Matthew 20:27–28, Jesus said, *"Whoever would be first among you must be your slave, even as the Son of Man came not to be served but to serve, and to give his life as a ransom for many."* Engaging in Christian service projects represents a potent antidote to addiction and a remedy to selfishness.

Third Forty-Day Segment: "Anomaly"

During the third forty-day segment, it will be unlikely that young people in addiction recovery will revert to their former vices and behaviors. By this time, their mind will have been renewed and rehabilitated as brand-new neural pathways, behavioral patterns, and mental processes have been firmly established. In Christ, a young person has real hope of being made new and whole. In 2 Corinthians 5:17, a wonderful promise is given: *"Therefore, if anyone is in Christ, he is a new creation. The old has passed away; behold, the new has come."*

Conclusion

Addiction is undeniably extremely challenging to overcome and to manage, but not impossible with God. It requires a whole lot of commitment, consistency, and compassion. Youth and family ministers are uniquely positioned to serve as helpful spiritual and practical resources to those teens and their parents who are caught in the middle of the struggle. But ultimately, it is going to be up to the young person to decide whether he or she chooses a life of sobriety or not. In the end, the battle is theirs to fight, but they need not fight it alone!

Discussion Questions

1. In what ways did the brain research noted above help you to understand teens' actions?
2. In what ways could it help you to realize that addiction involves more than just addiction to alcohol and drugs? What are some other addictions you have seen in your work with young people and their families?
3. List professional counselors/facilities in your area that can assist teens and their families.
4. How can it be helpful to understand the process that an addict goes through in recovery, even as you recognize that you will need to refer them to a professional? (unless you have the necessary training and credentials).

Bibliography

Chiu, Lisa (ed.). *Brain Facts: A Primer on the Brain and Nervous System.*

Chap. 7, Infant, Child & Adolescent Brain. Washington, DC: Society for Neuroscience, 2018.

https://www.mentalhelp.net/addiction/

Laaser, Mark R. *Healing the Wounds of Sexual Addiction*. Grand Rapids, MI: Zondervan, 1992, 1996. 2004.

Laaser, Mark R. *Taking Every Thought Captive*. Men of Valor Series. Kansas City, MO: Beacon Hill Press of Kansas City, 2011.

Chapter 18
Helping Teens Deal with Death
Bill McDonald

Introduction

Little did I know that a defining moment in my life would come on a hot Saturday morning in the summer of my sophomore year of high school. I was on top of my world; spending my time with a great youth group, getting ready to play basketball with our school team, working my way up the Explorer Scouting trail, and headed to a state office in the 4-H Club. I would not have changed a thing. All was perfect until the moment my dad walked down the hall of our home and said, "Ken is dead." Suddenly my perfect world had fallen apart.

Totally unexpected, our family was thrown into the unimaginable. The news spread like wildfire through our small hometown, and I was overwhelmed. I was upset; and more than that, I was angry. I immediately started wondering why God would allow this to happen. I quickly left the house and ran to a place where I often spent time alone. I looked at the heavens and shaking an angry fist said, "Why? why? why?" Never have I ever felt so lost and alone.

Walking with Those Who Weep

I never expected to feel this way, and I had little idea which way to go. I climbed down from where I was and headed toward the back door of our house. Waiting on the back porch were two of my best friends looking at me as if wanting to say something; but not knowing what to say. They threw their arms around me and just held on as the tears came and my emotions overflowed. I do not remember a word being said, but I do remember feeling like a great weight had been lifted from my shoulders. They did not say or do anything, but their presence assured me that I would not be alone. At that moment, that was all I needed.

Years would pass before the actual impact of that moment would be understood; but when it finally set in, it became my chosen ministry for helping the grieving. Simply put; it's not what you say, it's not what you do, it is that you "are" that is important. They helped me return to the present moment so I would not feel pressed to figure everything out in that instant. The gift of their company helped me rid myself of the feeling of being totally overwhelmed and brought some calm back into an extreme moment of confusion.

Most people find walking into someone else's heartache out of their comfort zone; but for those who are willing to walk in the valley of loss with someone, the rewards are great, and their concern is wonderfully comforting to everyone involved. This is exactly what John Durham and Bobby Morrison had done for me. They had walked into the shadow of death with me. They had not tried to give me wonderful advice, share religious platitudes, or tell me everything would be alright. They shouldered my sorrow by being with me in a very difficult moment in my life. Needless to say, I will cherish their friendship for the remainder of my days. They taught me what the "ministry of presence" means. It is the very simple sharing of life's difficulties with someone. This "ministry of presence" became a practice woven into every facet of my life's work as a youth minister, elder, funeral director, and friend. I have had the joy of sharing this idea with many people, churches, and organizations.

Lessons from My Friends

The balance of what I share in these pages will rest upon the loving example of my two friends, who cared enough to step in and walk through the valley of the shadow of death with me. The following segments of this chapter are designed to help readers deepen their understanding of what grief may look like in the lives of young people, and how we can avoid having our lack of experience keep us from loving others who need our company. The opportunity for doing good with struggling youth is everywhere; especially when we are willing to admit that loss of life is not the only cause of grief in their lives.

> Understand That You Don't Understand,
> But Do Not Allow Your Lack of Understanding
> to Prevent You from Doing What You Can.

I vividly remember how Bobby and John struggled with what to say when we saw each other a few minutes after Ken had died. As soon as they got the news, they came from their summer jobs to our home knowing they had no idea what I was feeling and having no idea what they were going to do or say. When I walked in, I could tell immediately they had no idea what to say. After a few awkward moments, we walked outside and they rebounded while I shot free throws on my basketball goal. They said very little but with loving ears, they heard me ramble about my feelings and my hurt. They listened to dozens of stories about my brother Ken. I cannot imagine how difficult that must have been for them. The sharing of grief is always something that is uncomfortable for the listener. No one I know finds it easy to participate in the pain and suffering of one they care about, but I found out through my own experience, what a valuable blessing that willingness can be to someone feeling so deeply alone.

I have always viewed this as a sacred moment when two people's hearts are joined by love and pain at the same time. Bonds are made that will forever be appreciated. In this experience, however, the comforting participant may have never tasted the bitter salt of suffering as deeply as the person they are hoping to comfort. Even if they have suffered similar losses, the differences can be obvious. Grief is like a snowflake; no two experiences of grief are the same. Helpers need to realize the task of grieving is different for each of us. We help ourselves to be more prepared when we can recognize these differences. Our journey is not like anyone else's. If we can try to keep this in mind, we will be more open-minded to the reactions we observe. We can best serve when we realize that we cannot understand what is going on in the thinking of someone else. The fear of saying or doing the wrong thing stops many people from offering the simple comfort of their presence. Try to remember, that just having someone around who cares can lighten the load and comfort the loss stricken. We do not need all the answers to help; the wisdom we gain from being present with someone in their grief helps us understand our own. Also, try to remember that it is not what you say or do, it is more about that you "are" with them and willing to be with them in their grief.

Walking With Teens Who Grieve

In walking with young people through grief, having expectations of them is a temptation that should be avoided. If I have learned anything from working with first graders through high schoolers; it is they defy expectations, especially in grief. One minute a child will be running around playing, and the next minute they are curled up with their mother, and no one else can touch them. Teen reactions can be just as varied, but sometimes their thoughts and actions become detrimental to their own health. Acting out can occur all up and down the age scale, and the ones that leave most counselors concerned are those beginning to withdraw and isolate. With their thinking and reasoning processes altered and a sense of hopelessness slipping in, their efforts to kill the pain can become desperate. One decision they make to relieve the pain can change them and their families forever. Without a caring person, who is able to walk with them, other tragedies may follow their depression.

One warning sign to be aware of and watch for is an adolescent who seems to begin avoiding many or all of the previous activities that were their favorite things to do. A drastic shift in the people they spend time with may indicate a growing change in their personalities, and in how they are spending their free time dealing with their grief. Separation from positive associates may be sparked by their changed self-esteem. You can observe these from a distance and know something is off, but showing interest in spending some time with them may give insight into how and why their habits and lifestyles have changed. Even an unwillingness to let you have a moment of their time may indicate something is off.

Grief and loss can usher young people into behavior not previously a facet of their personalities. Death of a sibling, divorce of parents, and failure to live up to their own expectations are all losses that can have negative consequences. Losing a close friend to death or to someone else can create emotional disturbances and damage healthy habits. The saddest for me are those who lose their sobriety. According to my brother's drug and alcohol counselor, the beginning of his problems began with our brother's death. He was nine years old when it happened, and his fear of losing caused him to jump from friend to friend, psychologically not wanting to get closely attached because of the possibility of losing again. He developed a cycle of not keeping a relationship long enough for it to become strong enough to develop close emotional ties, and this followed him until his death some fifty years later.

The Tasks of Grief

There are four major tasks of grieving according to J. William Worden in his book, *Grief Counseling and Grief Therapy*. Each of these tasks is a part of the grief process and needs to be addressed in every loss that occurs no matter the cause. Just as in the death of a loved one, these must be addressed by those who lose their sobriety, live with a divorce in their family, or break a leg that crushes their college football hopes. These steps help put the loss in a manageable place where life can continue in a positive way.

Task One: Accept the Reality of the Loss

Without accepting the reality of the loss, the person dealing with the loss has a hard time finding a reason to move forward. Without being able to incorporate the idea of the loss into our day-to-day thinking, one has no reason to press forward. When they continue to deny the loss, they are attempting to live in the past and find no real hope for the future. Many times, it is to avoid the pain of saying goodbye. Pain is usually the motivator that moves us toward the willingness to acknowledge our loss has occurred.

Task Two: Experience the Pain

Most young people will feel the hurt of loss in four ways: mentally, physically, emotionally, and spiritually. With mental pain, our grief is manifested in distracted thought patterns. For example, being unable to get the object of our loss out of our heads becomes all we think about. We may worry about what to do next to the point we become overwhelmed with life's smallest tasks. We cannot remember the simplest things, and struggle to do the most complicated. Concentration is a major challenge and grades may suffer. Physical pain exhibits itself in sleepless nights, headaches, and many other physical problems. Emotional pain is seen in mood swings, outbursts of anger, and social withdrawal. Spiritual pain results in anger with God, questioning His love, and showing less or no interest in the church or the youth group.

Task Three: Adjust to the New Environment

The third task is adjusting to an environment where the object of my affection is no longer present. A child may have a hard time going to sleep because the "mother" is not there to rock them to sleep. A teen whose car is no longer functioning may need to find different ways to get where they need to be. A family may need to pick up and move because they can no longer live where they are because income has been lost. For families, there are a multitude of adjustments to make, and for individuals, the challenge is often to learn to live in a world without the one they loved and depended on the most. This is especially true for those who are young and need a parent who will introduce them to life and guide them through its beginning stages. In every situation, they will need someone to walk their journey with them.

Task Four: Reinvest

One who has suffered loss must reach a point where they are able to withdraw some of the emotional energy they have invested in the object of their loss and reinvest that energy in something or someone else. Most of us have a capacity to love and a need to give our love away. When we are able to give our love away, the experience of giving helps our lives to have meaning once more. When the object of that love is taken away, reinvesting the energy of that shared love helps us heal. On many occasions, the most difficult step in mending a broken heart is finding something to do with this love energy. The best example of this may be the mother, Candace Lightner, who began the very strong organization we know as "Mothers Against Drunk Driving." While her efforts have encouraged parents across the country to rally to put an end to this highway tragedy; her efforts were possible because she was able to use the energy from the love she had for her child to do something positive with her pain. Had my younger brother not died, I am sure I would not have the drive to help others in grief that I do. Helping others allows me to reinvest my love energy for Ken in a positive way. Over the years I have been allowed to have grief classes in our high school and I assure you, they have helped me more than they have aided those in my classes. I have found it to be true that what I give away, I give to myself. Helping other people help others is and will always be a powerful way to help them help themselves.

Feelings

Feelings are neither right nor wrong; they are just feelings. What we do with those feelings, is where the right or wrong factor is found. Teens do not wake up in the morning and then decide how they feel. They wake up feeling how they feel. A person does not walk to the bathroom mirror and think, today I am going to be depressed, angry, or afraid. They simply feel what is going on inside. What is important is knowing that what I do with a feeling can certainly be right or wrong. If a youth minister can help a suffering adolescent think first and plan for a positive outcome for his or her feelings, then he can help them act first and not react. Learning to think out what we want the result of our feelings to be can help prevent outcomes no one wants. We already feel how we feel before we look in the mirror; therefore, what really becomes important is what we are going to do with the feelings we already have. For a friend or caregiver to help someone who is struggling, they need to think of positive ways to use the energy feelings can give. They can make good things happen in a powerful way. Allowing them to feel what they feel and to use that emotional power to either rebuild their self-esteem or to take positive steps forward can be a healing way to help.

Follow in the Steps of Jesus

There is truly no better place to find good working orders for helping young folks who grieve than in the way Jesus cared for the grieving in John 11. The Lord gives us a step-by-step recipe for helping the broken-hearted in his caring for Mary and Martha after the death of Lazarus.

Step 1: Be ready and willing to go, no matter the cost (John 11:1–16). Jesus did not go immediately because of the increased value of waiting a couple of days, but he went when the time was best (He had a unique plan and power that was different from ours). He went knowing there might be actions against his life and he was going whether anyone went with him or not. He was ready to go when the time was right and encouraged others to go with him.

Step 2: The Lord was willing to shed the use of euphemisms to communicate clearly what had happened (John 11:14–15). When the apostles thought that Lazarus was "sleeping," and there was therefore no real reason to go, Jesus spoke honestly in order to remove any doubt about what had happened. He simply stated, "Lazarus is dead." The use of the word sleeping to describe death to young children can be terribly damaging to their understanding of death. While they may not understand the concept of the words "dead," "dying," and "death," these words are far better for children because sleeping means their special someone will wake up. Even with teens, being honest and using the words of death will help them the most.

Step 3: He spent "one-on-one" time with Mary and Martha and answered their questions, as we must always try to do (John 11:17–37). I have found that the words "I don't know," when used honestly, are much better than any effort to explain an event we do not understand ourselves. Jesus felt the sting of the words, "If you had been here, my brother would not have died" (11:21). This is just like many counselors who hear words that cut to their hearts. Be patient and be present.

Step 4: Jesus wept with them (John 11:33–36). There are few

more moving moments in close relationships, than when tears are shared. Tears of love and concern help heal broken hearts. Never be afraid to share honest tears. "See how He loved him," the nearby said. Love that is shown is even more powerful than love that is shared.

Step 5: Finally, Jesus did all he could to alleviate their grief. He raised Lazarus from the grave. Of course, this is not something we can do, but we can walk with them, talk with them, be with them, and let them know by our love and actions that we care. Also, think of what needs they have during and after the funeral services that we, as youth workers, can help, and the church can help with.

Conclusion

You have journeyed with me through my grief and the ministry that grew out of it. I pray that the lessons I have learned in my ministry to grieving families will bless you as you minister in the name of Jesus. May God use your love for Him to bless the young people who have reason to weep.

Discussion Questions

1. How many different events or feelings can you think of that might cause a teen to experience grief besides the death of a family member?
2. Which of the major tasks of grieving do you perceive a teen might have the most difficulty completing? Why do you feel your answer is the correct one?
3. When do you think is the best time to contact a teenager following a major loss, and why do you think this timing is best?
4. Read John 11:1–44. Considering Christ's actions following the death of Lazarus and thinking about what the Holy Spirit through John decided to include in the

story, list what important lessons Christ teaches us in this passage.
5. If you have experienced the heartache of tragic loss, how can you use your grief to help young folks, when you know the grief they are experiencing is not exactly like yours?

Bibliography

Fitzgerald, Helen. *The Grieving Child: A Parent's Guide*. New York, NY: Touchstone, 1992. (Very Helpful)

Larson, Dale G. *The Helper's Journey: Empathy, Compassion, and the Challenge of Caring*. 2nd ed. s.l.: Research Pr Co, 2020. (Needed if you, like me, over-internalize the emotions of those you counsel).

Lewis, C. S. *A Grief Observed*. Annotated ed. New York, NY: Warbler Classics, 2023. (A look inside his personal pain and hurt when his wife died. This book is very helpful if the reader has not experienced a personal loss).

Schwebert, Pat and Chuck DeKylen. *Tear Soup: A Recipe for Healing after Loss*. Illustrated by Taylor Bills. 5th ed. Portland, OR: Grief Watch, 2005. (Look and find the "are" factor in this adult children's book).

Williams, Ron, and Don Williams. *Walking with Those Who Weep: A Guide to Grief Support*. s.l: CreateSpace Publishing, 2015. (Bill's mentoring led to Ron and Don's grief support ministry, visit rondonbooks.com for book and workshop information, KB)

Worden, J. William. *Grief Counselling and Grief Therapy*. 5th ed. New York, NY: Springer Publishing, 2018. (A read full of insight and information).

Chapter 19
Helping Teens Deal with Depression
Jeremy Hinote

Introduction

The teenage years can be some of the hardest years to navigate. You are at a time in your life when there are often many changes going on. You are at this place where you have one foot in the adult stage of life yet are still enjoying Disney movies, nerf gun wars, and spraying someone with silly string. Teenagers are really just little kids in grown-up bodies. At this stage in life, you are growing in your independence, wanting to do grown-up type things while also at the same time wanting nothing to do with adult responsibility.

In addition, you're going through many changes. First, your body is changing and you start to go through physical changes as you go through puberty. According to Johns Hopkins Medicine, the beginning of puberty for males can begin as early as 9 ½ years old while females can start as early as 8 years old. During this time the body goes through so many physical changes that can make it an awkward time for many. Your body is going through reproductive changes while also having other physical changes like voice changes, the shape of your body changes, body hair changes, and more.

If this wasn't difficult enough to handle at this age of life, now throw in that you're also having to deal with changes that are not just physical, but also mental and social changes. During the teen years mentally and socially things begin to adjust and change. You start thinking more abstractly. You start to think and be more concerned about life going on around you. You start to dive into the world of politics and social issues. You start to think more long-term and even start setting goals and thinking about what you want to do with your life. What job or career you will have? You start to set up your own friend/peer groups. Romantic relationships become more important to you. You start to want to have more independence from your parents. You start to drive and travel and go and do things.

Depression Is Real

These teen years can be a difficult road to travel. Between physical changes, mental and social changes, and more, it can be a hard time in life to navigate. At this age, we do not just have to deal with and go through these changes only, but often are have to fight with the other things that life throws our way. From peer pressure to school and work to dealing with pimples, navigating the social landscape, dealing with your parents divorcing, struggling with sexuality, navigating first-time romantic relationships, and more, the teen years can be so difficult to deal with that teens often become overwhelmed. They can become so overwhelmed with life, that they start to have a battle mentally and emotionally. Often the result of going through these difficulties is finding a teen who is now dealing with a mental health issue called depression.

Depression is something that is affecting more and more of our teenagers each and every year. According to the National Institute of Mental Health (NIMH), roughly 4.1 million teens in the United States struggled with at least one major depressive episode in 2020. Within that number, not all groups are affected the same. Information from NIMH shows that depression is much more prevalent in female teens (25.2%) than male teens (9.2%) and among teens who reported two or more races (29.9%). Information given to us in 2021 by a Mental Health America (MHA) report shows that severe major depression has increased in teens to 9.7%. This is an increase from 9.2% in 2020. The 2021 MHA report also shows that adolescents ages 11 to 17 were the group that was most likely to score in the moderate-to-severe depression categories when being assessed for mental health conditions.

Depression is real, and the teens in our youth groups are struggling with it. The questions are, "What do I do?" and, "How do I help these struggling teens deal with depression?" The truth is, many teens will end up coming to their youth minister for help and support before anyone else. Because of that, let us spend some time preparing you so you can learn how to support these teens in one of the most vulnerable times of their lives.

What Is Depression?

According to DSM-5 (*Diagnostic and Statistical Manual of Mental Disorders*, fifth edition), a person must have five or more of the following symptoms during the same 2-week period, and at least one of the symptoms should be either (1) depressed mood or (2) loss of interest or pleasure.

1. Depressed mood most of the day, nearly every day.
2. Markedly diminished interest or pleasure in all, or almost all, activities most of the day, nearly every day.
3. Significant weight loss when not dieting, weight gain, or decrease or increase in appetite nearly every day.
4. A slowing down of thought and a reduction of physical movement (observable by others, not merely subjective feelings of restlessness or being slowed down).
5. Fatigue or loss of energy nearly every day.
6. Feelings of worthlessness or excessive or inappropriate guilt nearly every day.

7. Diminished ability to think or concentrate, or indecisiveness, nearly every day.
8. Recurrent thoughts of death, recurrent suicidal ideation without a specific plan, or a suicide attempt or a specific plan for committing suicide.

These symptoms must cause the individual clinically significant distress or impairment in social, occupational, or other important areas of functioning.

The symptoms must also not be a result of substance abuse or another medical condition.

What Depression Is Not

- **It's not a weakness:** It doesn't mean you're flawed, weak-minded, or just sensitive. Depression is an illness. According to the Centers for Disease Control (CDC), 1 out of 5 Americans will deal with mental illness in a given year.
- **It's not a choice:** No one chooses to be depressed. It's complex and not something you just snap out of.
- **It isn't sadness:** Sadness is more or less like a head cold —with patience, it passes.—Depression is like cancer.
- **It's not bad moods and acting out:** That's what normal teenagers do.
- **Depression doesn't mean looking a certain way:** We can't just judge whether someone is depressed just by their appearance. A lot of times when someone opens up to a friend about being depressed—their reaction is, "Well, you don't look depressed."

Causes of Depression

It's not known exactly what causes depression, but a variety of issues may be involved. According to the Mayo Clinic, the following 5 items are all things that can be involved in causing depression.

1. **Brain chemistry.** Neurotransmitters are naturally occurring brain chemicals that carry signals to other parts of your brain and body. When these chemicals are abnormal or impaired, the function of nerve receptors and nerve systems changes, leading to depression.
2. **Hormones.** Changes in the body's balance of hormones may be involved in causing or triggering depression.
3. **Inherited traits.** Depression is more common in people whose blood relatives—such as a parent or grandparent—also have the condition.
4. **Early childhood trauma.** Traumatic events during childhood, such as physical or emotional abuse, sexual abuse, or loss of a parent, may cause changes in the brain that make a person more susceptible to depression.
5. **Learned patterns of negative thinking.** Teen depression may be linked to learning to feel helpless—rather than learning to feel capable of finding solutions for life's challenges.

Risk factors

According to the Mayo Clinic there are also many factors that have the potential to increase the risk of developing or triggering teen depression, they include the following:

1. Having issues that negatively impact self-esteem—such as obesity, peer problems, long-term bullying, or academic problems

2. Having been the victim or witness of violence, such as physical or sexual abuse
3. Having other mental health conditions
4. Having a learning disability or attention deficit/hyperactivity disorder (ADHD)
5. Having ongoing pain or a chronic physical illness
6. Having certain personality traits, such as low self-esteem or being overly dependent, self-critical or pessimistic
7. Abusing alcohol, nicotine, or other drugs
8. Being gay, lesbian, bisexual or transgender

Now that we have a better idea of what depression is and isn't and have a basic understanding of the potential causes and risk factors, now we move to more of the practical. Let's start by looking at the questions that most will ask when they start to possibly notice some symptoms of depression.

How can I tell if one of my teens is possibly depressed?

Well, based on the DSM-5 criteria we covered earlier, we then want to be on the lookout for some specific items along the way. According to https://suicideprevention.nv.gov/Youth/Depression/ the following are some possible signs and symptoms of teen depression.

1. **Expressed Emotions:** general sadness, hopelessness, uselessness, emotionally drained, not happy when doing pleasurable things.
2. **Physical Changes:** upset stomach, change in appetite and/or body weight, sleeplessness, headaches, joint or back pain.
3. **Behavioral Problems:** easily irritated, uncooperative, disagreeable, avoiding social interaction, avoiding or skipping school, abusing drugs and/or alcohol.

4. **Cognitive Difficulties:** focusing, finishing tasks, performing consistently in school, making decisions.

What can parents do to help? / What can I do to help?

Social: Make face-to-face time happen each day. Encourage them to go out with friends and even hang out with other families. Get them involved in an activity/sport. Get them involved with the youth group (trip, camp, youth rally, service activity, fellowship activity, etc.).

Physical: Inactivity, inadequate sleep, and poor nutrition make depression worse.

- Physical Activity: The World Health Organization (WHO) recommends 1 hr. of physical activity a day (walking the dog, taking a jog, hiking, skateboarding, shooting hoops, etc.)
- Screen Time: set screen time limits (no more than 2 hours a day—teens go to their screens to escape.)
- Nutritious Meals: healthy fats, proteins, fresh produce—get away from sugars and starches.
- Sleep: teens need 9–10 hrs. of sleep a night.

How do I communicate with a teen who is struggling with depression?

Focus on listening to understand (not lecturing). Resist the urge to criticize or pass judgment. The important thing is that the teen is communicating. The greatest good you can do is by simply letting this teen know that you're there for them, fully and unconditionally.

Be gentle but persistent. Don't give up if they don't talk and try to shut you out at first. At this age, talking about their depression can be really hard for teens. Even if they want to, they may have a hard time expressing exactly what they're feeling inside. Be respectful of their comfort level while also still trying to show your concern and willingness to want to help and listen.

Acknowledge their feelings. Don't try to talk a struggling teen out of depression (because this is often what caring adults try to do), even if their emotions/feelings/concerns seem silly to you or don't make sense to you. Often well-meaning attempts to explain why "things aren't that bad" will usually just come across as if you are not really taking their emotions/feelings very seriously. Simply being able to acknowledge the pain and sadness they seem to be going through can go a long way in causing them to feel understood and supported.

The following are appropriate things to say when a teen may be struggling with depression:

- "I am so sorry you are hurting/feeling so bad."
- "I can see you're feeling really low today. I'm so sorry."
- "It is your depression talking—it's making you see things in a negative way right now. It's not how the world really is, but it is how it feels for you."
- "I really want to help but I'm not exactly sure what to do. It's really hard for me to know what to say so please don't be upset with me if I say the wrong thing. Please tell me if I say the wrong thing or if I'm not helping."
- "Everything—including depression—goes in stages and at some point, I know you will feel better, especially if you get the right help. But it will take a little time."
- "I know this feels like it will be with you forever, but it will change. You're going to have good times here in the near future. But right now, I'm here for you as you deal with this tough time."
- "I know you may not have a lot of motivation to go to the *teen Bible study* or come to the *movies* or *play video games* right now (*fill in the blanks with any social/fun event that you want*), but you may really enjoy it, so let's do it!"

Here are some things that are usually NOT good things to say:

- "You shouldn't feel this way!"
- "Snap out of it! Get over it!"
- "It's just all in your mind"
- "You just need to pray more/go to church more/read your Bible more"
- "Yes, I understand exactly how you feel." (*Unless you've actually suffered the same problem, you don't really know how they feel. It's good to say that you can see that they're hurting, but not to seem as though you feel or have felt the same.*)

Conclusion

As we close this chapter about helping teens in dealing with depression, a major thing I want you to remember is to trust your instincts/gut. If the teen you're ministering to claims nothing is wrong but has no explanation for what is causing the depressed behavior, you should trust your instincts. If your teen won't open up to you, consider turning to a trusted third party: a school counselor, favorite teacher, or a mental health professional. The important thing is to get them talking to someone.

Discussion Questions

1. In 2020 in the US, how many teens suffered from at least one major depressive episode?
2. Who struggles with depression more—teen girls or teen boys?
3. Name the symptoms listed in the DSM 5 for depression.
4. How many of those symptoms are necessary for a depression diagnosis?
5. Name the 5 things that depression isn't.

6. What causes depression?
7. True or False? Having a parent who has had/has depression is a possible cause of depression.
8. There are a number of potential risk factors that increase the development of depression. List 5 of them here.
9. What are 10 possible signs of teen depression?
10. What are 3 things you can encourage a teen to do when dealing with depression?
11. What are the 3 major things you can do when communicating with a teen?
12. What are 3 things that you don't want to say to a teen who is dealing with depression?
13. What are 3 things that you want to say to a teen who is dealing with depression?

Bibliography

Diagnostic and Statistical Manual of Mental Disorders. 5th ed. Washington, DC: American Psychiatric Publishers, 2022.

https://mhanational.org/mhamapping/mha-data-reports (Mental Health America)

www.nami.org (National Alliance of Mental Illness)

www.nimh.nih.gov (National Institute on Mental Health)

www.psychologytoday.com (Psychology Today)

https://suicideprevention.nv.gov/Youth/Depression/ (Nevada Division of Public and Behavioral Health)

www.teenmentalhealth.org (Teen Mental Health)

www.who.int/news-room/fact-sheets/detail/physical-activity (The World Health Organization)

www.ymhproject.org/resources/ (The Youth Mental Health Project)

Chapter 20
Conflict Management
Rosemary Snodgrass

A Day in the Life of a Youth Minister

2:00 am
Justin pulls the mini-bus into the church parking lot. It is loaded with youth group kids and their luggage. They are all tired from the nine-hour drive home from CYC (Challenge Youth Conference). For the entire journey, Justin has tried to keep the emotions of the adolescents under control. Lana had broken up with Chad while they were all in Pigeon Forge. The members of the group have all taken sides in the conflict. Most of the girls seem to be on Chad's side, which baffles Justin. The boys seem to be split down the middle, some supporting Chad and some in Lana's corner. Slow service at the restaurant in Knoxville and traffic backed up from a wreck on the interstate delaying their return to their hometown, adding to the tension. Sleepy, grumpy parents are waiting in the parking lot to get their children home for a little sleep before school starts Monday morning.

2:50 am
Rodney's parents have still not come to pick him up. Rodney calls his mom's cell phone but gets no answer. Justin decides to take

Rodney home. They load Rodney's suitcase into Justin's car for the drive across town to Rodney's home. Rodney's house is in the opposite direction of Justin's apartment. Just as Justin pulls into their driveway, Rodney's cell rings. It is his mom, she is at the church building wanting to know where they are. She is angry. Rodney rings the doorbell to wake his dad to let him in the house. His dad is angry and smells of stale beer.

3:35 am

Justin arrives at his apartment. He sees that his girlfriend has left a note for him on the kitchen table, but he is too tired to read it. He goes to bed and sets the alarm on his phone for 5:00 am.

5:00 am

Justin's alarm rings, he hits snooze, then he sits upright in bed remembering that he set his alarm because he needs to get to the church building before the Senior Saints arrive to use the mini-bus for a day trip to Rainbow Omega. They are going to help clean out the greenhouses for the residents to start growing plants to sell to help support the home for adults with developmental disabilities.

5:30 am

Justin pulls into the church parking lot. "No, no, no!" he shouts in his head. Two of the elders and their wives are there in the mini-bus, cleaning it out! Justin jumps out of his car and walks over to the bus saying, "Brother Martin, I'm sorry. I'm here to clean out the mini-bus!" Brother Martin says, "We knew you would probably not get it cleaned out last night, so we just got here early to get it cleaned out before our trip today." Brother Martin and Brother Sanders have smiles on their faces, but somehow it does not feel like they are really smiling. Brother Martin's wife, Sarah, comes out of the bus holding a hand vac and says, "Justin, dear, you would never have gotten this bus cleaned out by yourself before it is time for us to leave at 7:00. This mini-bus was a mess!" She is smiling too, but not.

5:50 am

Justin gets back to his apartment planning to sleep a little while before going to Central High School for a devo with the basketball team before they leave for the state tournament. He smiles when he sees the note on the table from Mindy, his girlfriend. He decides to read it before he goes back to bed. He knows it will be something sweet she has written to welcome him home. As he reads he soon realizes the letter should have started with "Dear John ..."

Conflict—it is everywhere. It happens to us all. It cannot be completely avoided, no matter how hard you try. Bill Wilson reports that when asked, "What is the worst part of your job?" the number one response of ministers was "conflict."[1] Managing conflict effectively is a simple two-step process: 1) how we assess the conflict we are facing followed by, 2) what action (or inaction) we take to address it.[2] Your skill in executing these two steps will determine how effective you are in resolving personal conflict, as well as your ability to help others successfully navigate through conflict. In this chapter, we will examine what the Bible says about handling conflict and add some practical methods for implementing these biblical principles.

Start with Self

As you think about conflict management, one of the first things you need to do is examine your own feelings about conflict and what conflict management styles you use most often. It is very likely that you handle conflict differently in various aspects of your life. How you handle conflict in your home may be very different from the way you handle conflict in a social setting, when conducting business, or in the church. Conflict management styles are not "one size fits all," nor is there only one right way of handling every conflict. Several assessments of conflict style can be found on the internet. The following are a couple of inventories you can use at no cost: *Conflict Management Styles Assessment* found at www.blake-group.com and *Conflict Styles Assessment* can be found at www.usip.org/public-education-new/conflict-styles-assessment. A more in-depth assessment, *Style Matters* can be purchased along with training materials from www.riverhousepress.com. These assessments can provide you with useful information about your preferred way to approach conflict situations. Learning about yourself and the pros and cons of each style can be very helpful. There are also excellent resources found on the website for Mennonite Conciliation Services, www.mcs.org. Taking an assessment to find out your style can help you gain an understanding of yourself and others.

Asking yourself some hard questions can also help you gain insight into how conflict affects you. How does conflict make you feel? Angry, scared, sad, defensive, energized, and a wide range of other emotions are possibilities experienced when facing conflict. You may experience several emotions almost simultaneously. Realizing that conflict does not have to be a bad thing is also important. Conflict can be an opportunity for growth and to gain new perspectives. Do not miss the opportunity for growth because you see conflict as always negative. The emotions of others involved in the conflict will also impact how you feel. A widely accepted fallacy among Christians is that having conflict is un-Christian/sinful. Let's take a look at what Scripture actually says. Romans 14:19 (ESV) says, "So let us pursue what makes for peace and for mutual upbuilding." We can see that achieving peace may require effort. The word "pursue" also implies that this goal of peace may be elusive. The NIV uses the phrase "make every effort to do what leads to peace." Peace may be our goal, but all we can do is take action or make our best effort to do things that may lead to peace. We cannot impose peace into a situation without doing the work needed to result in peace. Earlier in Romans Paul says, "If possible, so far as it depends on you, live peaceably with all" (Rom 12:18). We cannot control the behavior of others. The only person each of us has the ability to control is ourselves and for many of us that is challenging. Ken Sande, an author, mediator, and mediation trainer, challenges each of us to ask ourselves if we are a peacefaker, a peacebreaker, or a peacemaker?[3] Many times Christians are peacefakers. They believe that avoiding conflict is the Christ-like thing to do. They try to act like they are at peace over an offense or an issue, but in reality, they are not at peace. What often happens is they allow the issue to stew within, or allow the offensive behavior to continue, until they reach a boiling point. Then they flip from peacefaker to peacebreaker. The offended and the offender could have been reasonable and rational in discussing the issues early in the conflict, but by the time it escalates to this point emotions and thoughts are difficult to control.

Becoming Peacemakers

How do we become peacemakers? Peacemaking is not the natural inclination of fallen mankind. Peacemaking requires intentional action and an examination of your heart to discover what your goal is for your action or inaction in the conflict. Failing to address the problem, peacefaking, prevents the problem from being resolved. The rationale for avoiding a confrontation is usually to keep peace while hoping the conflict will just go away. Avoiding the work to resolve the problem may seem like an easy way out, but the underlying issue remains and usually escalates. Peacebreaking is focused on winning the battle and results in broken relationships. It is putting self above others and taking action to win the contest. Peacemaking involves doing things to bring about reconciliation. Peacemaking is a way to resolve a problem and bring glory to God in the process. Jesus gave instructions on how to work toward reconciliation and peace. In the Sermon on the Mount, Jesus tells us that even if you are engaged in worship and it comes to mind that a brother has something against you, you should go right then to be reconciled with your brother. Your goal should be reconciliation, not to defend yourself or prove that you are right, or to prove your brother was wrong (Matt 5:23-24). In later instruction from Jesus in Matthew 18:15-17, we learn the process to follow if someone has sinned against you. Step one, address the issue just between the two of you. Step two, if he did not listen to you during step one, take one or two people with you to talk to the offender again. If he still refuses to listen then move on to step three, tell it to the church. Step four is found in verse 17, "If he refuses to listen even to the church, let him be to you as a Gentile and a tax collector." All of these steps are done with the goal of reconciliation.

Most people reading this book are well aware of these teachings of Jesus. Our problem is not that we do not know what Jesus taught, our problem is not knowing how to implement it or not trusting that this approach is truly the best way to handle conflict. We would rather talk *about* the brother that has wronged us than to talk *to* him. We are also hesitant to go to the brother we have wronged and admit our fault. Sometimes pride or fear may hold us back from following these instructions from Jesus. Many times, we fear the rejection or the repercussions that could come from a confrontational conversation. Unfortunately, we have very few role models to show us how to have these difficult conversations in a manner that would glorify God. TV, movies, political leaders, and very likely our friends and family demonstrate how NOT to resolve conflict in a godly manner. The greatest tragedy is the failure of church leadership to be God-glorifying examples of how to manage conflict. As youth ministers, you are in a unique position to both teach and mentor young people in how to live Godly lives in all things, including through conflict. Your interaction with them and the behavior they observe in you will provide them with a "how-to" role model. At the end of this chapter, you will find a bibliography of helpful resources. Equip yourself to handle conflict for your own benefit and for the benefit of the young people under your care. Demonstrate to them how to have those difficult conversations. Here are some general guidelines to keep in mind:

- Help them see the value of prayerful and thoughtful planning prior to starting a conflict resolving conversation. Showing them that the first thirty seconds of introducing the topic will set up the tone of the conversation.[4,5] It is so much easier to start the conversation with humility and with respect for the other person than to try to repair the damage done by starting the conversation out of anger and frustration. This could mean a delay in starting the conversation to allow yourself time to calm down and not react out of anger. It is possible that during the planning phase, you may realize that the issue is not worth fighting over. If it is something you can dismiss, then forgive them and let it go. If you cannot let it go, then proceed in working toward resolution.

- Keep the focus of the conversation on things that lead to peace and reconciliation, and avoid letting self-centeredness creep in. Identify at least for yourself, and possibly share with the other person, the goal of your conversation. Finding goals that the conflicted parties have in common is a great way to start the conversation.
- Taking responsibility for how you have contributed to the conflict and asking for forgiveness shows humility and sincerity on your part.[6] This does not mean you take full responsibility for the conflict unless that is actually the case. It may be that all you know that you have done wrong is not bringing it up earlier and you have allowed it to build up until it has become a bigger problem. Acknowledging your contribution and asking for forgiveness makes it easier for the other person to be able to do the same.
- Using "I" statements is an important way to communicate how you see the conflict. Avoid blaming and/or accusing the other person. Do not try to be a mind reader and think you know why someone did what they did or said what they said.
- Be a good listener, and try to understand the other person's perspective.

The Terrible, No Good, Very Bad Day

Let's go back to Justin and the terrible day he was having. How should he handle this situation with his elders and their wives? It would be wise to delay the conversation to a time that was not 5:30 am and they were under pressure to get the job done. Set a time that is mutually agreeable.

Justin is feeling __?__ by the elders and their wives coming to clean the bus and the attitude he *perceived* they had toward him. What was he feeling: offended? insulted? guilty? angry? Why was he feeling that way? Had he been guilty of failing to clean the bus in the past and was trying to do better? Was leaving the bus dirty something the previous youth minister had been guilty of doing? What is Justin's goal? Do he and the elders share a common goal?

Let's write a script for Justin. Justin made an appointment with the elders and their wives for Wednesday at 6:00 pm. During the time from Monday morning until Wednesday at 6:00, Justin did a lot of praying and soul searching. Justin started the meeting by saying:

> Thank you all for meeting with me. There are several things I want to say to you first and then I would like to hear your thoughts. I believe we all want to have a successful Youth Program that helps our kids grow in their faith and live lives committed to God. I think we also agree that we want to provide our Senior Saints opportunities to serve and be a light in our community. I think we see a mini-bus as a tool that can be used by both groups. When I saw you all here cleaning out the bus Monday morning I felt embarrassed and frustrated. I know that in the past I have not acted responsibly to get the bus cleaned out in a timely manner, but this time I was trying to do that. I am sorry that I have not done it in the past, and I ask for your forgiveness. I do want you to know that I was trying to do better. I had hoped that you would all be pleasantly surprised, maybe even shocked, when you arrived Monday morning and the bus was clean. I want you to know that I

plan to be more responsible about cleaning in the future. I felt that you were angry with me Monday morning, but tried to act nice to me anyway. I appreciate that. It would have made it so much worse if you had just unloaded on me. I hope that in the future we can be honest with each other about how we feel and resolve any issues we have.

I do not know how the elders would respond. I hope they would have done some soul searching too and would show love and respect to Justin. Regardless of their response, Justin has done the right thing. Sometimes we must accept that doing the right thing on our part does not guarantee that others will respond in the same way. We need to remember Paul's words, "so far as it depends on you" (Rom 12:18).

Conclusion

Conflict can be one of the most discouraging things you deal with in ministry, actually in life in general. As always, the Bible is our guide. I do not think it would be an overstatement to say that conflict is on almost every page of the Bible. Through the conflicts in Scripture, we have both happy endings and disastrous endings. We also have examples of coping with unresolved conflict. I'm sorry we are leaving Justin with so many unresolved problems, but the same biblical principles apply in every conflict. If we were in class, your assignment would be to think through Justin's other problems and write a script for how Justin should use each problem as a way of bringing glory to God in how he handles each.

Discussion Questions

1. Wrestling with some of these questions as a class: What was Justin feeling: offended? insulted? guilty? angry? Why was he feeling that way? Had he been guilty of failing to

clean the bus in the past and was trying to do better? Was leaving the bus dirty something the previous youth minister had been guilty of doing? What is Justin's goal? Do he and the elders share a common goal?

2. Work through Justin's other conflicts as a class and write scripts for how he might respond to the situations.

Bibliography

[1] Wilson, Bill, "Conflict as Blessing: Please Don't Waste This Crisis," www.healthychurch.org.

[2] Furlong, Gary, *The Conflict Resolution Toolbox: Models and Maps for Analyzing, Diagnosing, and Resolving Conflict* (1st ed. Mississauga, ON: John Wiley & Sons Canada, , 2005).

[3] Sande, Ken and Kevin Johnson, *Resolving Everyday Conflict*, (Grand Rapids, MI: Baker Books, 2011).

[4] Patterson, Kerry, Joseph Grenny, Ron McMillian, Al Switzler, *Crucial Conversations: Tools for Talking When Stakes Are High*, (2nd ed. New York, NY: McGraw Hill, 2012).

[5] Fleming, Geoff, *"What To Do in the First 30 Seconds of a Tough Conversation,"* www.crucialdimensions.com.au, 2018.

[6] Sande, Ken, *The Peacemaker: A Biblical Guide to Resolving Personal Conflict* (3rd ed. Grand Rapid, MI: Baker Books, 2004).

Additional Resources

Leas, Speed, Paul Kittlaus. *Church Fights: Managing Conflict in the Local Church.* Louisville, KY: Westminster John Knox Press, 1973

Patterson, Kerry, Joseph Grenny, Ron McMillian, Al Switzler. *Crucial Confrontations: Tools for Resolving Broken Promises, Violated Expectations, and Bad Behavior.* New York, NY: McGraw Hill, 2005.

Tripp, Paul. *War of Words: Getting to the Heart of Your Communication Struggles.* Phillipsburg, NJ: P & R Publishing, 2001.

Real-World Ministry of Youth and Families
Youth Ministry Nuts and Bolts

Chapter 21
The Youth Minister as a Leader
Jim Martin

Introduction

If you serve as a youth minister, you have a significant ministry in a congregation. You also have a significant role among the people you serve. Regardless of your age, experience, or marital status, you are a leader. You might see yourself as unworthy to be designated a leader. You might even be just a few years older than some of the very teens you are leading. Yet, serving as a leader has more to do with your intentionality than your age or experience. You *are* going to lead or influence in some way. Perhaps the more important question has to do with *where* you might be leading these students. That is, if they follow your example, your priorities, and your teaching, how will they be formed spiritually? Spiritual leadership begins with your own spiritual formation and your willingness to be led by the Lord and by those who are more spiritually mature in Christ.

Are You Willing to Be Led?

Ponder the following questions as you reflect on your willingness to be led. Be honest with yourself as you do so.

- Do you listen and seek out wise people?
- Who are you learning from right now?
- Do you accept and receive criticism?
- Do you listen—really listen—when a trusted person is trying to help you?
- Do you insist on handling your life alone or do you open yourself to the guidance of others?
- Are you willing to assume responsibility for your growth and development?
- Are you willing to manage yourself?

Your own spiritual leadership might be even clearer if you take time to reflect on how God has been working in your life before now to bring you to this place of leadership.

How has God already been at work through others to bring about this moment? Reflect on some of the important spiritual influences in your life up to this point:

1. *Who in your home significantly impacted you?* When you were growing up, were there qualities in your dad and mom that were significant as you now reflect upon your role as a spiritual leader? What in particular did you learn from your mom or dad?
2. *In what ways did a congregation impact you positively?* Was it a mission trip, a VBS, or perhaps a Bible class? Was there something that happened in the life of that church that helped prepare you to serve?
3. *Who are some of the other men and women who have significantly influenced you?* Who, in particular, impacted you for the kingdom? A family member? Ministers,

elders, deacons, youth ministers? Was there any other Christian man or woman who in some way made a difference in your life?

As you move forward in learning and maturing, remember that your service as a Christian leader begins not by reading the latest business leadership book but by first grappling with who you are as a servant (Various leadership books may be helpful, they are just not the place to begin). Jesus said that He came not to be served but to serve and to give His life as a ransom for many (Mark 10:45). The best Christian leaders are those who take their own servanthood seriously (Mark 10:43–44). Ultimately, being a leader is not something we have achieved. Rather, it is born out of our own discipleship to Jesus. In summary, consider the following:

1. A godly leader is first a servant. Servants are focused on laying down their lives for others (Mark 10:45).
2. A godly leader lives in submission to Jesus. This means that you and I take our obedience to Jesus seriously.
3. A godly leader models a willingness to be led.

As you reflect on your need to be disciplined, wrestle with this question, "Will you do what it takes to become what you need to be?" It is one thing to talk about learning to listen and serve, it is quite another thing to actually have the humility and attitude necessary to do it.

Are You Willing to Live for Others?

We have highlighted in the previous section that leaders must be servants. Spiritual leaders put others first (cf. Phil. 2:3). In 1 Thessalonians 2, Paul reflects upon his ministry as he corresponds with the Christians in Thessalonica. These reflections can give any minister an awareness of what is important. As you consider your ministry, reflect upon the following questions:

1. Are your motives for youth ministry worthy of the gospel of Jesus? Are your motives godly? (1 Thess 2:3)
2. In your ministry, how aware are you that you have been entrusted with something very valuable? (2:4) What are the implications of having something valuable like this entrusted to you?
3. What are the implications of serving to please the Father rather than ourselves? (2:4)
4. Do you refuse to seek glory from others, not letting your ego drive your ministry? (2:6)
5. Are you gentle with others, both the students and their parents, genuinely caring for them like a nursing mother might care for her own children? (2:7)
6. How might your own work ethic be worthy of respect from others? (2:9)
7. How could you be more intentional about living a "holy and righteous and blameless" life? (2:10)
8. How can you walk in a manner worthy of God and his ministry? Are you able to be transparent about your life, not hiding particular behaviors, habits, etc.?

Finally, consider these four dimensions of ministry as you consider your own leadership and ministry.

- Becoming—What are you becoming? How are you being formed? (2 Cor 3:18)
- Relating—How are you relating to other people? (John 4:19–21)
- Knowing—How would you describe your knowledge of the Lord and of Scripture? (Ps 119:66; Prov 1:7)
- Doing—How are you putting into practice what you know? (Jas 1:22)

Let us further explore each one of these dimensions of ministry.

Ministry Is Becoming

Will you lead your students toward *becoming* Christ-like people? As a youth leader, you are called to help lead your students to become more Christ-like. Think about the text you might be teaching on Sunday or Wednesday. Out of this text, what would you like to see them become in the next 24 months? Consider your own life. Your leadership is rooted in your own discipleship to Jesus. Do you wish to be a good leader as you serve as a youth minister? Do not start with techniques or tools but your own transformation. As a youth minister, your credibility deepens as you take Jesus's call on your own life seriously. To help them to become like Christ, we must become like Christ.

Ministry Is Relating

Will you lead your students in *relating* to others in a Christ-like manner? Perhaps you have known an individual who prides himself on how well he knows the Bible. Yet, what if this same individual is cantankerous, difficult to get along with, and consistently seems to damage, if not destroy relationships? Something is wrong when you and I pride ourselves on our knowledge while our relationships with others do not reflect maturity or a Christ-like spirit. My formation in Christ should not only impact my knowledge but also my relational abilities. I need to deal with my own life, given who I am in Christ. This means I no longer excuse my volatile anger, my lustful appetites, or my undisciplined speech.

One of the very best things you can do as a youth leader is to lead your students toward building relationships with others that reflect Christ's manner and life. You are helping these students not just have cognitive knowledge, but you are leading them to grapple with the relationships they have at home and at school. For example, consider the fruit of the Spirit found in Galatians (Gal 5:22–23). These are relational words that describe a particular kind of Christ-like functioning. You and I are called to model relationships that go above and beyond what others see in the world. These come as the result of the Spirit's work (Gal 5:22–23).

Perhaps one of the best ways you can lead is by helping students relate to others with empathy. Relational ministry is fundamentally about empathy. It is "feeling into" another. It is the part of us that seeks to indwell another. One of the fundamental ways we do this is by listening to the stories of one another. Empathy fuels the human spirit. As youth leaders, we are attempting to lead our students out of individualism and self-centeredness, the enemies of empathy.

We are leading them away from relating to others based on secular cultural standards, including performance, possessions, or popularity. We are leading them away from the following false identities:

- I am what I do (performance)
- I am what I have (possessions)
- I am what others think (popularity)

In contrast, we are calling students to live out of their identity in Christ. If our students were to relate to their parents or friends in a more Christ-like way, what might this look like? What is a small step that might move them to more Christ-like relationships and less self-absorbed relationships?

As a youth leader, consider your own identity in Jesus Christ. Look at your own relationships and ask if these are being transformed by Jesus. Look at your marriage, your relationship with your children, and the relationships you have within your congregation. Is the way you are relating to these people being shaped by Jesus?

Ministry Is Knowing

Will you and I lead our students in *knowing* the will of God? As youth leaders, we lead these students in knowing God, Jesus Christ, and "God-breathed" Scripture. While ultimately, Christian parents are responsible for the knowledge of their children, pertaining to

God and Scripture. Part of our stewardship in leading a youth ministry is to attend to this knowledge. Perhaps one of the best things we can do is to make sure they know the biblical drama about God's work in this world through Jesus Christ. God created the world and, after its brokenness, He set out to restore what He had made. You might walk students through a simple outline of the biblical story such as the following:

- Creation (Genesis 1 and 2)
- Crisis (Genesis 3-11)
- Covenant (Genesis 12 – Malachi)
- Christ (Matthew – John)
- Church (Acts – Jude)
- (New) Creation (Revelation)

For you to give them a road map through the Bible is an act of spiritual leadership that might be valuable to them for years.

Ministry Is Doing

Will you and I lead our students in *doing* the will of God? Our leadership often comes when we are right in the middle of "doing." Whether it is a mission trip, a service project, or a hands-on project that was relatively spontaneous, a part of leadership comes down to what we are modeling or doing. "Doing" is no option according to James 1:22. We are not just people who hear sermons, classes, etc. Rather, we are people who implement what we learn. We demonstrate leadership when those with whom we are working see that we intend to actually practice what we are learning. This is also part of our discipleship. We are not simply learning more information but are living intentional lives of obedience. When we lead with the intention to practice, we give our students a picture of what a disciple does.

Conclusion

If you are serving as a youth minister, your ministry really does matter. Your ministry begins with your own spiritual formation. Your ministry also includes your leadership before those whom you serve. You are a child of God, a part of the body of Christ, a servant, and yes, a leader. Your leadership is not the product of technique but of a very real transformation that has been and is happening in your life. Today, we serve with gratitude, understanding that our continued formation is vital to the longevity and quality of our ministry. Your leadership is a reminder that what you do in your ministry may have implications long after you leave. The question is not whether or not you are going to lead, rather it is how well and how Christ-like you will lead.

Discussion Questions

1. Consider some of the Christian men and women who have influenced you greatly. What were some of their qualities that caused you to want to become like them?
2. Youth ministers are called to take their own leadership seriously. What might the implications be for your example, your maturity, and your judgment?
3. Spiritual leadership is not based on a tool or technique but is rooted in one's own discipleship to Jesus. What implications might there be for how you are to use your judgment, express your opinion, or make decisions?
4. In terms of your own formation as a Christian leader, what would you like to see in your life as a youth minister in 24 months? What is a small step you could take in this direction this week?

Chapter 22
The Balancing Act
Managing Your Personal and Daily Calendar
Carter Hoover

Cheetahs are one of the most dangerous animals on the face of the Earth. With sharp fangs, razor-like claws, and the ability to walk stealthily upon its prey while also boasting a sprint speed of over 80mph, you would think that any animal seen as prey by this apex predator wouldn't stand a chance compared to an animal seemingly designed to excel at catching and killing its game. Did you know, however, that cheetahs only boast a 40-50% success rate on attempts to attack and kill their prey? They also frequently lose their kill to other predators (Lee 2013).

The reason for this low kill rate has nothing to do with the inability of the cheetah but rather the capability of its prey and the influence of other predators. While significantly slower and under-prepared to fight off a would-be attack, the cheetah's prey survives for two main reasons: the strong desire to live and a plan to escape when attacked. You may wonder what cheetahs and managing your personal and daily calendars have in common, but you will learn as you begin your ministry that there is a common factor between the two.

In ministry, as in life, time is precious. There is a limited number of hours in the day, and you will learn as you gain age and experience in ministry that it can be challenging to make the most of your days. There are plenty of interruptions, both necessary and unnecessary, that can distort, distract, and dispose of your time. Your job as a minister, father, husband, etc., is to learn to balance your life, as well as your calendar, as you strive daily to faithfully serve the Master.

This challenge, at times, is not easy. There are plenty of hurdles that you will encounter that will seek to draw you away from the sound advice of the Apostle Paul as he encourages the church at Ephesus to "make the best use of time, because the days are evil" (Eph 5:16). Make no doubt about it, distractions, like cheetahs, are the predator, and you are the prey. If you are to best manage your time to serve your family, your congregation, and yourself, you must be able to recognize and defend against the things that can waste your time and learn how to find ways to best utilize your time. Distractions may have the advantage of corrupting your best use of time, but your willingness to avoid them and develop a clear plan to make the best use of your time can make all the difference in the fight for your time.

Ministry is a lifestyle that is challenging to manage because it includes an unusual blend of professional and personal duty, responsibility as a Christian, responsibility as a minister, and so on. You will come to learn during your time in ministry that there are plenty of distractions that can knock you off track, but this chapter will help you to look at four behaviors that act as "time killers," four behaviors that serve as "timekeepers," and some practical ways to use this knowledge to make a plan to excel in your ministry and personal life.

Time Killers and How to Identify Them

Ignaz Semmelweis was a scientist and doctor from Hungary living in the early and mid-1800s. While you probably have never heard his name, you will most certainly have benefitted from his discovery. One day, Dr. Semmelweis was conducting a scientific study on the high mortality rate of mothers in hospitals due to infection within days of giving birth. After weeks of study, Dr. Semmelweis came to a groundbreaking conclusion: the best way to help save the lives of mothers in hospitals was for doctors and midwives to wash their hands and sanitize medical tools in between working from one patient to another.

While thinking about Semmelweis' discovery through the lens of the 21st century, it does not seem like much of a scientific breakthrough. During the 1800s, however, the concept of germs or bacteria causing infection never crossed anyone's mind. Isn't it strange to think that something so deadly was unknowingly right in front of people? Think of all the good done by Dr. Semmelweis discovering that something so small, like not sanitizing your hands and medical equipment, can be harmful. When you understand that harmful things can seem small and insignificant, you will begin to understand how small daily behaviors can cause limited production and distractions in your personal life and ministry.

During this section of the chapter, I would like for us to look at four behaviors that serve as "time killers," or attitudes that can harm your effectiveness in managing your time. I believe that the best way to avoid these challenges is to become familiar with what they are, to ask yourself how these "time killers" interrupt your life, and to make a game plan to navigate around them or stop them if you are currently practicing them.

Time Killer #1: Overextension

Overextension is the result of spreading yourself and your time too thin. There are many different areas where you can spend your time, and taking on too many responsibilities and tasks can become an unhealthy problem. While ministry can be enriching and opportunities to do good can be found all over, the pressure of saying "yes" to too many tasks can hinder your effectiveness in balancing your ministry and personal life.

My wife would tell you that this issue afflicts me often. She calls my act of overextension "picking up rocks" and often pokes fun at me for constantly looking for more "rocks" to pick up. Have you ever taken a small child to a playground and watched them begin to gather rocks? Most kids start picking up rocks one at a time that they think are interesting, but within a matter of minutes, their pockets are so full of stones that they cannot enjoy the rocks they picked up without them falling out of their pockets or hands. This same attitude can also be true in matters of life and ministry. It is easy to take on too many tasks due to the love of the church, the fear or regret of telling others "no," or countless other reasons, but we must beware not to overextend ourselves to the point that we cannot balance our personal and professional lives.

Time Killer # 2: Neglect

While it may seem harsh, many ministers fall short of their personal or professional responsibilities due to simply neglecting to do what they need to do. While there can be legitimate reasons for temporarily ignoring your responsibilities (i.e., fatigue, sickness, burnout, etc.), ministers can fall short of using their time wisely simply because they would rather spend time doing something else (or maybe even nothing) rather than focusing on what should be done. Many ministers neglect personal and professional responsibilities due to a lack of priority and intentionality. In other words, distractions like hobbies, hanging out with friends, binge-watching shows online, or simply doing anything else rather than what you should be doing, can interfere with making the best use of your time. We must combat the attitude of neglect by understanding that, as the wise teacher says in Ecclesiastes 3:1, "[T]here is a time for every matter under heaven." We must remember that while there is a time for doing what you want to do, that must come after the time of doing what you need to do.

Time Killer # 3: Perfectionism

My four-year-old son, Cade, taught me a valuable lesson on perfectionism when he and I were at odds with each other over the homework from his pre-k class. Whenever given a coloring sheet for homework, he begrudgingly grabbed a crayon and began feverishly scribbling all over the page, paying no attention to staying within the lines. When I (a self-diagnosed perfectionist) would try to teach him about coloring slowly and carefully and staying within the lines, he would look at me, shrug, and say, "Yeah, but this is faster."

While I certainly do not like to admit this, Cade does have a point about his coloring method being faster and thus returning him to playing outside or doing whatever else he would rather be doing. While striving to do a good job is not inherently a bad thing, it is crucial to understand that obsessing over perfection can hinder you from making the most of your time. While perfection is something admirable to attain, the constant pursuit of making sure everything is perfect is exhausting and ultimately leads to disappointment. You will be happier and your life more efficient when you stop chasing perfection and come to terms with being content with simply doing your best and moving on to the next task to be accomplished.

Time Killer #4: Procrastination

"Should we probably do this now? Of course. But why do today what you can do tomorrow?" I jokingly made these statements to an intern one summer while cleaning up after a week-long summer camp session. While it was a funny joke at the time because we were exhausted from a tough week of camp, there is quite a bit of sad honesty in statements like that when you begin to think about procrastination in ministry. Unfortunately, all ministers find themselves caught in the pitfall of making statements similar to mine. Comments like these reflect a problem with procrastination, and these excuses can be found everywhere. Maybe you can identify with some of the following statements have either heard or said something similar: "I do my best work when I'm under pressure." "I'll do that tomorrow when I'm well rested, have more time, or am better prepared." "I would start today, but I just do not feel motivated to get started." My warning to you about procrastination is a simple but harsh truth—if you want to be taken seriously if you want to feel or be treated like a professional, if you want to avoid wasting time, and if you want to take pride in your work and life, you have to find a way to motivate yourself to complete your work on time and in a responsible manner.

Time Keepers and How To Use Them

The legendary UCLA men's basketball coach, John Wooden, once said, "When you fail to prepare, you're preparing to fail." These words certainly echo true in ministry. As you begin your work, you will discover many different people, priorities, and activities vying for your time. Trying to juggle your daily responsibilities and priorities can sometimes feel overwhelming, which can negatively impact your mental state and your fitness to serve your family and the church. I have heard many ministers say that a great way to manage your time is by creating a daily and weekly routine to help you best manage your time. While this may work for some, I personally struggle with keeping the same routines each day or week because of the nature of youth ministry. In church work, I believe that the only routine part of ministry is constantly being out of routine. I have discovered that the best way to not become burdened by the demands of life and ministry all boils down to your preparation. Often when I feel overcome by my schedule, I can trace the source of these feelings back to a lack of preparing myself to be fit for the job ahead. Preparation for your role in ministry is key to completing the "balancing act" that this chapter is named after. I would like for you to consider four behaviors that I have deemed "time keepers," which are necessary for helping yourself stay prepared for the role of a minister ahead of you.

Time Keeper #1: Physical Fitness

This item is first on the list, not because it is the most important, but rather because it is probably the most overlooked. You don't have to look very hard online to find plenty of articles that stress the importance of a healthy physical body and the positive impact that it can have on your life. However, you don't have to look very hard to see that stressful and demanding jobs can harm your physical health. We all know that there is a certain "weight" (that's not meant to be a joke) that comes from working in ministry, and this pressure can sometimes cause a physical strain on your body. In addition, your days are usually full of helping and serving others, and often by the end of the day, most ministers do not stop to consider their own needs. I am not writing this telling you that you have to purchase a gym membership and train like a professional athlete to serve in ministry but rather to encourage you not to forget to take care of your physical body. This can prolong your ministry and help you to feel better and have more energy. Your ministry and life will flourish when your body is well-prepared and taken care of.

What does this mean for you? It's simple: find a primary care physician and go for regular checkups, try your best to eat well (I know a youth minister's diet consists of plenty of pizza and ice cream), try to get 8 hours of sleep each night, take time to decompress and find ways to help manage stress and exercise when you can (take a walk, play basketball, go to the gym, etc.). I know this sounds like the most basic advice I can give you, but as you get started working in ministry and taking care of your family, it is easy to lose sight of making sure to take care of yourself.

Time Keeper #2: Personal Faith

Nothing can dampen your faith faster than working in ministry. That sentence can seem like an oxymoron to someone unfamiliar with this line of work, but the personal faith of a minister can sometimes fall to the wayside amid your daily routine. After a full day of studying the Bible in preparation for classes, devotionals, sermons, etc., while also praying and looking out for the spiritual needs of others, it can feel exhausting to go home at the end of the day to take time to read the Bible and pray for yourself. While it may seem noble to put the needs of others over yourself, you must also remember to not let your spiritual life be moved to the back burner because of your ministry. There is a balance to be found in investing time in your faith while also upholding your responsibility of teaching others to do the same.

I would suggest a few things to help you stay prepared in your faith. First, take time in the mornings to grow in your faith, not in the afternoon or evening. Like putting on an oxygen mask on an airplane, you must help yourself before you can help others. Second, find different ways and techniques for taking in God's Word. You might listen to podcasts, read devotional books, study a passage straight from the Word, listen to sermons from other preachers and teachers, or take periodic breaks from teaching Bible classes so you can be a student yourself. Finally, remember that we must, at times, be like Jesus in Luke 5:16 and take time to withdraw from our personal and professional lives to spend time alone with our Heavenly Father.

Time Keeper #3: Sound Finances

There are numerous sources of stress that you will encounter in your life that can cause you to lose sleep at night, but nothing can be more worrisome or thought-consuming than financial distress. Financial issues can cause problems in your marriage, create a serious mental strain on you, and ultimately distract you from all other things in your life. The threat of not being able to take care of yourself or your family financially can weigh on you in a way that is different from all other worries in life. The solution to this sounds simple in theory, but, like many things, is often more difficult to carry out. First, you must manage your money. Make a budget, open a savings account, plan for emergencies, set aside money for your offering to God, and commit to saving for your future. Remember that even if you feel that the best solution to your financial woes is to make more money, no amount of money can fix financial problems if you do not manage your money properly. Second, pay your taxes. I know that you will cover this more in-depth in the tax chapter of this book, but for this chapter, keep in mind that you will meet an embarrassing and expensive demise if you forego "rendering to Caesar the things that are Caesar's" (Matt 22:21). Finally, ask for help in managing your money. I do not know of a single minister who is an expert in money management, investments, retirement, income taxes, etc. Thus, you will be blessed by finding a financial professional to assist you with your finances. Find a person you can trust to help you manage your money responsibly.

Time Keeper #4: Strong Family

While the calling to serve in a ministry is honorable and important, there is no greater call and duty that a man can have than to faithfully lead and serve his family. One of the most difficult balancing acts that you will find in your ministry will be in how you fulfill your responsibilities to your wife, your children, and your ministry. While you will feel at times that the only way to fulfill one of these responsibilities is by setting another responsibility to the wayside, as men and fathers we must prioritize family over ministry. I always try to remind myself that the work of a minister will never stop, but you cannot allow your job to overpower your family. I think that there are a few safeguards that you can put into place to help make sure your family stays strong as you balance family life and ministry.

First, set aside and guard specific times for your family. I have a rule for my family that during specific family times, there are no ministry responsibilities that can take me away from spending time with my family except for the death of a member or a life-threatening situation in someone's life. Second, highlight and help focus on the things your family finds important. My family spends a lot of time helping and being involved in my ministry, so I also want them to feel supported and helped by me in their endeavors in return. I try to do this by helping my wife with activities in her career, coaching sports, being involved in things my kids are interested in, and so on. Make sure that how you spend time with your family is balanced between asking them to give their time to you and you giving your time back to them. The dynamics of a minister's family are different from person to person, but regardless of your family situation, there is no better advice I can give you than to honor your family, spend time with them, and support them in the same way that you ask for them to support you.

Conclusion

Managing your personal and professional life is certainly a "balancing act." Unfortunately, as we think back to the illustration that we considered as we began this chapter, there are plenty of distractions roaming around like a cheetah to lure you into the destructive habits of not best utilizing your time. Hopefully, this chapter has helped you feel equipped to stay focused on what is truly important in your daily lives as you begin ministry. Just like the prey trying to escape from a cheetah, you too can learn to resist the predators of time by having a strong knowledge of the distractions that can easily lead you astray and utilizing the plan outlined in this chapter to help you stay focused on what is truly important.

Discussion Questions

1. Think about the ways that you find yourself falling prey to "Time Killers." Which ones do you think affect you the most?
2. Keeping your calendar in check often requires a great deal of introspection to see what areas of your life need help or improvement. How do you plan to track the use of your time to ensure it is best used?
3. Managing your calendar requires a great deal of preparation. What are some other behaviors besides the ones mentioned in this chapter that can help you stay prepared for your daily and personal life?

Bibliography

Lee, Jane J. "Long-Held Myth About Cheetahs Busted." nationalgeographic.com. July 23, 2013.

Wooden, John. https://quoteinvestigator.com/2018/07/08/plan/.

Chapter 23
Youth Ministry Budgets and Calendar Planning
Richard Turner and Jordan Abrams

Introduction

Welcome to a chapter that includes two of the most asked questions in youth ministry: "What does your calendar look like?" and "What is your budget?" Even though these questions are constantly being asked, the purposes behind the events on your calendar and the money that you spend are infinitely more important than the trips you go on and the amount of money that goes towards your ministry. While this chapter will seek to have practical advice regarding youth ministry calendars and budgets, we will start with the most important factor: your youth ministry purpose. For a calendar and budget to impact your ministry to the fullest potential and to help your students grow spiritually, you must know **why** you are planning events and **why** you are spending money. Your purpose should drive everything that you do as a minister.

Purpose Before Planning

An incredible passage that can help us to focus on purpose over events and money is found in Luke 10. Here, we find Jesus entering a village and being hosted in the house of a woman named Martha. While at Martha's house, Jesus begins to teach His followers. However, in the midst of Jesus's teaching, Martha finds herself distracted by the services she is providing for those who are in her house. Having noticed that her sister is sitting at Jesus's feet rather than serving, Martha angrily asks Jesus, "Lord, do you not care that my sister has left me to serve alone? Tell her then to help me" (Luke 10:40). However, rather than siding with Martha, Jesus rebukes her and lets her know that Mary has chosen the better portion (v. 41–42). Youth ministry can make the lives of leaders far too busy. There is much to do with regard to planning, organizing, and leading a variety of different events. Too many youth ministers, unfortunately, get caught up in the many activities of their lifestyles and forget about the purpose of ministry: to get our students to sit at the feet of Jesus.

To accomplish and remember this purpose within your calendar and budget planning process, we recommend examining and reexamining everything you do on a regular basis. Make sure everything you do is built around getting your students to sit at the feet of Christ. This can be accomplished in a variety of ways. For instance, our youth ministry has a motto: "Reaching In, Reaching Out, and Reaching Up." This purpose statement is meant to help our students recognize three things that all students are called to participate in within our ministry: to reach inside and grow as a Christian, to reach out to others on behalf of Christ, and to reach up to God for grace. While we utilize this purpose statement publicly in all that we do, we also make sure to utilize it in our planning. <u>Every</u> opportunity that we plan for our students to be together has at least one of these three concepts in mind. Thus, we have decided before the calendar and budget process even begins that if an event does not fit into one of these categories it is not worth putting in our plan and budget. We strongly recommend that you create a way to validate events and budgets based on your own system of teaching students to sit at the feet of Jesus. We may use the word "event" many times throughout this chapter; however, our ministries must be careful not to be event-based but to be Jesus-based. Having a strong focus on your purpose is not only helpful for students, but also allows you to demonstrate positive reasoning for your decisions when talking to parents, shepherds, and others in your church family as you all strive to make the best decisions for the youth at your congregation.

Planning a Calendar

Planning out your year can be critical to having a successful youth ministry. Planning youth events in coordination with the whole congregation helps your youth ministry not to become a separate entity of the church, but a part of the whole. Planning helps families have the opportunity to look forward and prepare for the months ahead. Planning helps coordinate opportunities for other adults to be involved in ministering to your students. Planning helps budgeting. Planning helps you, as a Christian, husband, father, and human not to be lazy, grow weary, neglect your family, or suffer in your relationship with God. With God's help, planning plays a big role in who you are and what your ministry becomes.

Our recommendation is that you plan all major events one year out. We have heard it said, "The only reason not to have a calendar planned a year in advance is laziness." We tend to agree. It is hard work and takes forethought to get a year planned in advance, but it is worth it. So how do you go about planning a yearlong calendar? We believe it is important to start by having goals. There is a variety of long-term, goal-based questions you should be asking yourself when it comes to determining your calendar:

- What are my spiritual expectations for our group this year?

- How do I plan on improving this year compared to last year?
- What are the biggest issues my students are facing?
- How can I best get families involved?

Ideally, each of these questions will allow you to plan events that are not simply "the norm" or events that call for a lot of work with little spiritual benefit. Rather, we believe that beginning by asking these questions means you will be able to create events that are purpose-driven, and this will allow you to focus on the long-term goal of getting your students closer to Christ.

While goal-based questions are important to ask in your year-long calendar planning process, it is also important for you to ask date-based questions. Some of these may include the following:

- What do the local school calendars look like?
- What are national holidays, sporting events, and days centered around families that I should stay away from?
- How spread out are my major events to allow families to enjoy time together and for families to save up funds to cover the costs of various activities?
- What are the other major church activities I should coordinate with as I plan events?
- Where am I able to find time to vacation/be with my own family in the midst of this busy schedule?

Asking all of these questions as you are planning your yearly calendar will keep you from conflict with families, will allow for the maximum number of your students to attend events, will allow families to budget for activities, and will allow for you and your families to find peace in the midst of busy schedules. As you plan your yearly calendar, make sure to ask goal-based questions and date-based questions in the midst of the process.

While long-term calendar events such as retreats, class topics, major events, and other important gathering activities are vital, make sure to plan well for short-term and routine activities as well. Creating a routine in ministry helps families and students know what to expect regularly, and they can plan to be there more often. Short-term and routine activities may include in-home Bible studies, meals, and small group events that occur within your youth ministry. While these things may not be practical to plan a year beforehand, your families and students will thank you if they are well prepared and coordinated as far in advance as you can do it. For our ministry, we tend to work in quarters. Regarding our smaller events, we try to plan them a minimum of one quarter, or three months, in advance. Remember, asking goal- and date-based questions remain important as you plan these activities. You should strive to be able to answer the following question for everything you plan: "How does this event get our students closer to Jesus?" Often, a well-planned small-scale activity will allow you to focus more on this question in the midst of your planning, and this progress will be reflected in your students' lives. It's also vital that you recognize conflicting events that may arise when it comes to short-term and routine gathering opportunities. Planning an event on the date of students taking the ACT, a major band concert, or during a much-followed sporting event often leads to conflict amongst students and their families and students and the youth ministry.

Finally, with regard to planning a calendar, it is important to address how your calendar will be communicated to families. The more you are able to communicate, the more likely your students and families will be able to participate in your youth ministry. You can do a variety of things to address the communication issue with your families. One possibility is having a Google youth calendar that you can share with all your families and post on your church's website. All major events would be available to your families through this calendar a year before and would be kept updated with smaller events three months before. Another option that we utilize is having an electronic and printed booklet called "Youth Ministry 101" that we offer to our families. This book lays out our normal events, their purposes, how to be involved, and how to receive communication about these events. We highly recommend developing a booklet like this to aid in communication with your families and with guests when they ask about the youth ministry. Next, we recommend sending weekly and monthly emails to your families regarding upcoming activities. Using apps like "Remind" to communicate quick details with families such as "Last day to sign up is today!" is another invaluable option that many ministries utilize. Finally, making positive use of social media options such as Instagram and Facebook to keep important details in front of teens and their families on a consistent basis. This level of communication can all seem like a lot of work, but we believe it is worth it. The activities we do the best job communicating to families are the events that have the greater percentage of students and their friends involved. If no one knows about what you are planning, how can it bring students and others closer to Jesus?

Planning a Budget

Planning a youth ministry budget naturally goes along with planning a calendar. As you know, most events (sadly) cost money. Planning a budget is very different for all youth ministries because they are so diverse. Budgets must be based on the events you create, the number of students in your ministry, your congregation's ability to contribute, your families' abilities to pay for events, and a variety of other situations. However, even though all budgets are vastly different, we believe there is practical advice that can be offered to all with regard to budgets.

First, we recommend that you develop a maximum cost that will come out of the youth ministry budget and out of your families' pockets for each event. For example, you would determine, "We will spend a max of [insert amount of money] from the youth budget for this event, and it will cost a max of [insert number of dollars] for each student to attend." Allowing yourself and your families to know what the cost of each event will be will allow families to be prepared financially and for you not to have to fret as your budgeted money begins to be used. Having a yearly budget for both yourself and youth families will provide much more peace and stability for your ministry.

Secondly, we recommend that you communicate with all of your families on a regular basis regarding costs. Having your families know the estimated price of big-budget items like a mission trip and camp six months to a year ahead of time allows them to be prepared financially. Coming up with a price for every event that you release to families a minimum of three months beforehand will allow for better preparation and greater appreciation from your parents.

Communicating with families on an individual basis also allows you to find out who amongst your families may struggle financially. We have developed a variety of ways to help our struggling families that we would like to recommend. An obvious option is to allow families to receive a scholarship from the youth budget by creating a budget line for this at the beginning of the year. However, we believe an option that is even better is finding affluent members of your congregation and asking them if they will add their names to a "scholarship donor list." We have a list of people from our congregation (young, old, married, widows, you name it!) written down that we ask to help pay for our struggling students when someone is having trouble paying for an event. This not only relieves pressure from the youth budget, but also allows members of our church family to participate who may not have been as active within the youth ministry.

While not all families may struggle financially, it's also important to make sure your youth ministry is not putting more of a financial burden on families than it needs to. What could you do to help a family who has multiple children within the group? One option would be charging half-price for every third child/friend from a single family. For instance, if a family has four kids, the third and fourth pay half price for a youth event. You could even add that if a family has two kids and one invites a friend, the friend will be half-price. Another important aspect of keeping youth activities from being financial burdens on your families is making sure pricey events are spread out. Especially in the summer, having back-to-back expensive events can quickly add up for your families and cause resentment towards the youth ministry. Making sure to keep expensive events at a minimum of a month apart from one another allows most families to more comfortably pay for opportunities that the youth ministry provides.

Our final piece of advice for budgeting for your families involves communication with the leadership. Youth ministers seem to constantly be struggling to get their youth budgets increased. Our greatest recommendation for this to occur is to communicate with your shepherds, financial committee, or whoever sets the budget of your youth ministry. Over the years, one of the most effective ways we have seen to do this is simply by getting a meal with those who are in charge. In this less formal environment, we are then able to lay out the purpose of events and activities that require funding. Be open to challenges and other ideas in these meetings, but also realize that building these relationships and having these conversations is vital. Too often, elders and ministers treat the budget process as a business partnership and only discuss this need in official "elders' boardroom" meetings. Having open conversations and discussions about the importance of the youth ministry with your shepherds and leaders as you all seek to help your students sit at the feet of Jesus can result in incredible blessings.

Calendar Planning and Budget Questions

- How do you balance the money you can spend on an event versus the spiritual benefit of it?
- How can you develop a calendar that is not simply event-based, but calls for your families to have consistent spiritual lives?

- What could be a unique way to find out if your families feel comfortable or uncomfortable with the cost and number of events on your calendar?
- How can you utilize others within your congregation to help plan a calendar and budget?
- How can you get help making sure all possible avenues of communication are being utilized?
- How can you emphasize the importance of your students taking part in church-wide events that are not youth based?
- How can you maximize parent involvement in each of your events?
- Can you think of other creative ways to help ease the financial burden of the families within your ministry?

Recommended Bibliography

Clark, Chap and Kara E. Powell. *Sticky Faith.* Grand Rapids, MI: Zondervan, 2011. **This book does a great job describing the importance of getting adults involved in your planning.**

    Fields, Doug. *Your First Two Years in Youth Ministry: A Personal and Practical Guide to Starting Right.* Grand Rapids, MI: Zondervan, 2002. **For those who are new youth ministers, we highly recommend this book to help you keep from making mistakes and setting yourself up for success in your first few years.**

    -----. *Purpose Driven Youth Ministry: 9 Essential Foundations for Healthy Growth.* Grand Rapids, MI: Zondervan, 1998. **This book does a great job helping you to set up events that accomplish spiritually driven goals.**

    Jenkins, Philip. *The Lunch Ladies: Cultivating an Actosphere.* Lebanon, TN: Creative Graphics, 2015. **This book does a great job describing a purpose-driven activity begun by a youth ministry.**

    Lawrence, Rick. *Jesus Centered Youth Ministry.* Loveland, CO:

Group Publishing, 2014. **This book does a great job of getting you to focus on getting students to the feet of Jesus.**

Stanley, Andy, Reggie Joiner, and Lane Jones. *7 Practices of Effective Ministry.* New York, NY: Multnomah, 2004. **This book helps teach the value of planning and taking breaks as a minister.**

Work, Mike and Ginny Olson. *Youth Ministry Management Tools 2.0: Everything You Need to Successfully Manage Your Ministry.* Grand Rapids, MI: Zondervan, 2014. **This is an incredible book to help you figure out how to plan a budget and calendar and provides many practical tools.**

Chapter 24
Youth Ministry on the Road
Michael Deese

If you are doing youth ministry, plan to do youth ministry, or if you are a youth ministry volunteer, there is a good chance that you will go on a trip with teenagers. Trips are incredible tools to use in your ministry. I have been able to plan trips to address personal issues many of our students are experiencing. I have been able to plan trips with the primary goal of bringing our group closer to each other. I have had trips that were solely for fun. Trips can also provide huge opportunities for one-on-one time with students and small group time. Each trip you make with your students is an opportunity for them to understand and see Jesus as we see Him. There is a reason we have so many who decide to become Christians while we are at Uplift, Horizons, Impact, or any other camps. The purpose of that camp is to increase the depth of each student's faith. To help them reach new places in their spiritual development. The people planning each of those events have a definite purpose and work tirelessly to make sure that purpose is fulfilled. We MUST do the same in everything we do.[1] If used effectively, we can use trips to serve our students and prepare them for a life of faith. Trust me, trips are your friend. Trips are vital for your ministry.

What Is the Why?

I always ask myself this question before I begin planning any trip: "Why are we going on this trip?" It can be for any number of reasons, but your trip and your planning need to especially focus on a spiritual connection between your students and their Savior. Make your trip about Jesus.

When planning to go to a youth rally, you should not just go because your youth minister friends invited you. Research the youth rally. Make sure the lessons are relevant. Make sure your students are interested in the youth rally. Know the schedule and the topics that will be discussed. Make sure you trust the speakers and what they might teach. Do your research before planning to go. I am always planning out my devotional and small group time based on what is being discussed at the event. I prepare and read up on some of the lessons they are talking about in the classes. I try to be as prepared as I can when taking my students on a trip.

You should never do something just for the sake of doing it. It does not matter if that is what has always been done, or if that is what is expected. Many times we get stuck in new ministry opportunities where we are *required* to do something that we find to be of no benefit to our students. It has happened to me a few times. The elders, deacons, etc., want something done, but you are frustrated because you believe there is no reason or purpose for the event or trip. If you MUST take the trip against your desires, you can always rebrand the trip. I have restructured and rebranded events that have been going on at churches for dozens of years and made them my own. I gave them a purpose in my ministry and made sure there was a reason behind the trip. There was a spring and fall retreat that was required to have at a new ministry I started. The reason for the trip was "to keep the kids busy and give them something fun to do." I completely restructured the events. I made the retreats less about having fun and made the trip about accessing a new spiritual experience. We still had games and free time, but the retreat was less about that and more about experiencing Christ. While we did have fun playing pool noodle hockey and kill ball, we also brought them a new spiritual experience and a greater understanding of their salvation. Colin Marshall and Tony Payne elaborate on this:

> We may multiply the number of programs, events, committees and other activities that our church is engaged in; we may enlarge and modernize our buildings; we may re-cast our regular meetings to be attractive and effective in communicating to our culture; we may congratulate ourselves that numbers are up. And all of these are good things! But if *people* are not growing in their knowledge of God's will so that they walk ever more worthily of the Lord, seeking to please him in all things and bearing fruit in every good work, then there is no growth to speak of happening at all.[2]

When you plan a trip, keep in mind that you are planning with a purpose and that purpose should always be grounded in pointing your students to Jesus. As far as I'm concerned, a trip to the bowling alley can point others to Jesus if structured correctly. Even a game night at your church building can still help students reach a new spiritual place. You must be intentional in everything you plan with every trip you make.

Prayer, Promotion, and Planning

Once you decide on a trip and you have your purpose behind the trip, it is important to discuss that trip with your ministry team and make sure everyone is on board with the activity. Pray with them for the event. Pray for good ideas and plans for your trip. Pray for wisdom in the planning and finalizing of your trip. After you have prayed over it and discussed it with deacons, elders, parents, volunteers, etc.; begin advertising the trip to your students. If you do not have skill in this area, pay for some professional art and advertisements to put up in your youth room and on your announcements' slides for PowerPoint presentations. Make flyers and announce your new trip or activity to everyone. There is never too much communication in ministry. Announce in class, on your bulletin, hand out flyers after services, and make a personal announcement about the trip from the pulpit. Post on social media platforms to prepare your students for the trip they get to experience.[3]

Planning: Curriculum

Another thing to consider is the curriculum used on the trip. Depending on what kind of trip you take this can be a lot of work to prepare lessons, classes, and devotional content. Sometimes, though, it is as simple as knowing what will be discussed at the event and being able to discuss it with your students. For example, if you are planning to attend CYC, always make it a point to know what will be discussed in the lessons and prepare a time for students to gather together and discuss the lesson we all heard. Another approach would be to talk about a subject that relates directly to the topic discussed. But if you are planning for a youth group retreat, the work is a little more intensive. You need to find or write your curriculum for every aspect of that event. Consider how many classes and teachers need teachers. How many devotionals will you need and who will lead the devotionals? These are all things to consider when planning a retreat. You have your purpose or theme for the event, but have you considered the level of preparation that needs to go into each of these events?

Planning: Games

It's always fun to talk about games and activities while away. Some can offer a brand-new way for your students to interact with each other. Sometimes it is just singing silly songs together but sometimes you have opportunities to play and create new games to play with each other. Each event or trip needs a way to fill in downtime. There are times when a deck of cards is more than enough to give everyone something to do, but other times students are expecting something interactive. Prepare games and bring materials to play those games. Make sure the activities that you plan and prepare are fitting for the situation you are in. Divide into teams, bring games, play sports, board games, card games, or other activities. Find ways to help your students interact with each other. There are a couple of extra things to remember. First of all, many young people are not athletic, have disabilities, or simply do not like sports. Consider this when planning and provide alternatives. What games do you have that reach the artistically inclined? Are handicapped children just forced to sit and watch? Secondly, have a backup plan in case the weather prevents the outside games you had planned from taking place.

Planning: Schedule

Make sure to have a schedule of everything you will be doing on your trip. It is important to know what time you will be eating and where. Giving an itinerary to everyone attending the event or trip you plan to take is important so they know how they can better serve while with you. Discuss with your volunteers whether there is enough rest time and activities. Remember that some of the most powerful "magic" at a retreat or camp happens during downtime or free time. Make sure your retreat is unique and stands out from others. Sometimes that takes a little extra work on the front end, but making sure things stay fresh and exciting is important for each trip you plan to make. The most important question to ask is whether or not the schedule enhances your purpose or mission or takes away from the mission of the trip. All of these things are important to consider when creating a schedule for your trip.[4]

Planning: Location and Food

Two frequently asked questions of any trip are "Where are we going?" and "What is the address?" Parents of your students want to know where their child will be while on the trip you are planning. It's important to book your housing early and have it ready to share with your ministry team, parents, and students. Give the address, show them pictures, and try your best to show your students the place or places you will be staying while on your trip.

Be sure and plan for the right amount of food. If you are even asking if there is enough food for everyone, you should just get more food. It is always better to have too much food instead of too little. When you plan your meals, snacks, and drinks, the most important thing to think about is your chef and servers. Will you be eating at restaurants, or will you need someone in your group to prepare your food? How many meals will you need while on this trip? Do they need to bring money to pay for the meals? Are there any allergies we need to be aware of? Bring snacks and drinks for the students so they can snack and enjoy a soda when there is some downtime. I will finish this by repeating what I said at first. If you think you may need more food, it is always better to have too much than too little.

Planning: Budget

Your budget is always something you must consider when planning a trip. Trips can be very cheap, but they can also make you blow your budget very quickly. I have had retreats that cost anywhere from $500 to $7,000. When you factor in all of the things we have discussed above, those things can get pretty expensive. You have speakers, song leaders, artwork and advertising, food, snacks, drinks, housing, games, curriculum, bus drivers and buses, t-shirts, and more! I have not even begun to address all the expenses that can go into making a budget, but be intentional with your time and money when you go on a trip. Be sure to plan each dollar to be used wisely and to make the trip enjoyable for your students and volunteers. Remember your purpose for spending money is to point others to Christ.[5]

Planning: Registration

Make sure your registration process is organized. You should be able to answer any and every question that is asked about a trip just from your preparedness on the front end. How many guys? How many girls? How many beds are at the venue? Do we need to bring our own sleeping bags? How much does it cost? Your registration information is important to communicate to your parents and students as early as possible. Give everyone enough time to budget and plan for every trip you plan. Make sure to communicate the dates of your trip, the age groups participating, and packing lists. How many chaperones do you plan to have on your trip? What you will be eating for each meal and when will the meals be? All of this information should be communicated as best as possible and as early as possible to reduce questions and anxieties parents may feel when being away from their child for a few days.

Chaperones and Safety

As you begin to plan your trip and activities you should always be looking for volunteers to help with your trip. As noted above, volunteers are essential to a successful trip or overnight stay. A parent met with me when I had first started my ministry and was very open and honest with me: "The way I decide if a specific trip is for my son is to look at their safety above everything else. If I believe they will be safe based on where we are staying, what activities they will be doing, and who the chaperones are; then the trip is for my son." I believe this is an important aspect of planning trips. Remember that you are traveling with precious cargo. Make sure safety is a central focus in every situation. Make sure you have enough volunteers, and make sure your volunteers are responsible and dependable.[6]

Safety Considerations

While we discuss safety and safety measures, I've always found it beneficial to have insurance forms for each student on each trip we take. Make sure that if there is an injury of some kind, you know where the closest doctor or hospital is located. Bring some First-Aid kits and bring someone trained in medical procedures to handle minor scrapes and bruises. I almost always try to take a nurse with me on every trip I take to help with minor medical procedures. Remember your responsibility is to keep the children on your trip safe. Accidents do happen; be prepared to care for them when something comes up.

You may want to look into getting background checks for your chaperones and volunteers. Many camps are now requiring it. Most parents would not require this, but it is better to give them peace of mind for the trip or event you are planning to attend. It is very important to know the people on your trip can be trusted to care for and protect the students attending. This is a recommendation but not necessarily a requirement for most churches.

Volunteers

I live by a rule in my ministry: There is no such thing as too many chaperones or volunteers. You should bring as many volunteers as you can feasibly take on a trip. We will need to deliberate on what area each chaperone can serve in, but if they are willing, I want them to be on the trip with me. I would add this caveat. Remember that those who would harm or molest children would want to volunteer for youth activities. This is one of the reasons why you should do a background check. One of our goals for each trip is to provide volunteers an opportunity to build a relationship with our students. Each student has different interests and hobbies and each volunteer has different interests and hobbies. There's a good chance a volunteer and student can connect on something, and the more relationships you have between your students and volunteers, the greater the growth in Christ for both the student and the adult.[7]

Using your volunteers effectively is very important and making sure that they all have responsibilities and purpose on the trip is just as important. I give a handout for each trip we have that has several ways they can serve. One danger of having large numbers of adult chaperones is that the event can become an adult social event. Leaders need to help adult volunteers focus on their purpose (I will say more about this below). Here are some ideas to think about when planning for chaperones to go on your next trip: First, I want them to participate in everything we are doing. Playing games? The adults should be playing with the students. Singing? Adults should sing with the students. Writing letters to each other? Adults should be writing letters to the students. There are loads of things we do on each trip and the adults are expected to participate in everything we do. This is perhaps the most important part of being a chaperone.

Another thing to remember with chaperones is that we need their support. We may be leading this event, but we cannot do it alone. It takes a team. Also, when chaperones create division, it makes it much more difficult. Chaperones need to support the group leader and should never cause any division. If they have a differing opinion, it would be more appropriate to speak privately to the group leader of the activity or event. Next, they should always look for opportunities to help. At every event, trip, or activity, there are loads of ways for our chaperones to serve. It can be to clean up, set up the table, take out the trash, etc. Finally, the most important thing to plan for chaperones is to make sure they know why they are on the trip. A chaperone's sole responsibility on the trip is to serve the students. The adults should always be willing to give up their tickets, let the kids go first, and choose the students over themselves. We are there to serve. Keep these things in mind while selecting and taking chaperones and other adults and volunteers on trips.[8]

Covering the Homefront

Something that is just as important as anything else is to make sure you have everything covered back home. I am sure you teach multiple Bible classes a week and have other responsibilities each week. You also will have young people who do not participate in the trip and they need to be ministered to as well. We youth ministers do not have the luxury of just calling up a buddy to come by and fill the pulpit. We need to make sure we are covered in all the aspects of our job. Work a week ahead, and do not allow yourself to fall behind especially when there is a trip coming up.

Youth Minister Protocol

Prepare a "Youth Minister Protocol" and share it with your elders, youth deacons, and other youth workers who can help fill in while you are away. Remember to let your elders know the bases are all covered and do not just dump everything on them. The protocols mentioned above are just basic things that most people would never think about unless they were a youth minister. This would include things such as: Who will cover your classes? Who will announce the events coming up next week? There are also personal things to consider: Do you have someone watching your dog or collecting your mail? Do any bills need to be paid while you're gone? Where will your kids stay? Remember it is your job to make sure these things are taken care of, but it can be helpful to share it with church leadership. Most of these things are not things we normally think about while we are getting ready for a trip, but they are very important to plan for because they will make the trip much easier for you on the front end.[9]

Debrief

After you finish a trip, I highly recommend sitting down with your ministry team and discussing the pros and cons of each trip. Always ask the questions: Is this trip worth going back to? Should we invest more resources into making this trip a larger part of our ministry? Make sure to discuss each trip with your students and parents as well. No matter how long you do ministry, there is always the concept of trial and error. It is always better to try new things and if they do not work for your ministry that is completely fine. Recalibrate and plan for something that does fit your ministry.[10]

Conclusion

God has given us an incredible responsibility with His children. We are given so many opportunities to plan for our students and invest in our students. Do not do anything halfway. Always give your best work and put your best foot forward. God is blessing your ministry and each trip you attend. Do not get frustrated, but instead see the opportunity for what it is or was and move on. Continue to serve God through everything you do; you will see Him work through you and your team. Remember the words of Jesus, "But whoever causes one of these little ones who believe in me to sin, it would be better for him to have a great millstone fastened around his neck and to be drowned in the depth of the sea."[11]

Discussion Questions

1. What did you find surprising in this chapter?
2. What did you find most helpful in this chapter?
3. What will you do differently in the future as a result of reading this chapter?

Notes

1 Cameron Cole, Jon Nielson, *Gospel Centered Youth Ministry* (Wheaton, IL: Crossway, 2016,) 152–155.

2 Colin Marshall and Tony Payne, *The Trellis and the Vine* (Waterloo, Australia: Matthias Media, 2009,) 82.

3 Duffy Robbins, *Youth Ministry Nuts & Bolts: Mastering The Ministry Behind the Scenes* (Grand Rapids, MI: Zondervan, 1990) 161–166.

4 Cameron Cole and Jon Nielson, *Gospel Centered Youth Ministry, 158–160.*

5 Robbins, *Youth Ministry Nuts & Bolts*, 181–185.

6 Cameron Cole, Jon Nielson, *Gospel Centered Youth Ministry*, 91–92.

7 Kara Powell and Brad M. Griffin, *Sticky Faith Launch Kit: Your Next 180 Days Toward Sticky Faith* (Pasadena, CA: Fuller Youth Institute, 2013,) 15–17.

8 Les Christie, *How To Recruit And Train Volunteer Youth Workers: Reaching More Kids With Less Stress* (Grand Rapids, MI: Zondervan, 1992) 117–122.

9 Kara Powell and Brad M Griffin, *Sticky Faith Launch Kit, 22–23.*

10 Cameron Cole, Jon Nielson, *Gospel Centered Youth Ministry*, 160–161.

11 *The Bible: New International Version* (Grand Rapids, MI: Zondervan, 1973,) Matt. 18:6.

Bibliography

The Bible: New International Version. Grand Rapids, MI: Zondervan, 1973.

Christie, Les. *How To Recruit And Train Volunteer Youth Workers: Reaching More Kids With Less Stress.* Grand Rapids, MI: Zondervan, 1992.

Cole, Cameron, and Jon Nielson. *Gospel Centered Youth Ministry.* Wheaton, IL: Crossway, 2016.

Robbins, Duffy. *Youth Ministry Nuts & Bolts: Mastering The Ministry Behind the Scenes*. Grand Rapids, MI: Zondervan, 1990.

Marshall, Colin, and Tony Payne. *The Trellis and the Vine*. Waterloo, Australia: Matthias Media, 2009.

Powell, Kara, and Brad M Griffin. *Sticky Faith Launch Kit: Your Next 180 Days Toward Sticky Faith*. Pasadena, CA: Fuller Youth Institute, 2013.

Chapter 25
Planning Camps and Retreats
Jarrod Bailey

When it comes to planning a week of camp or a weekend retreat, both take the one thing that many ministers seem to have little of ... time. Because of the general time constraints in ministry, you can lose sight of the adequate devotion to planning that is needed to have a great camp or retreat. Understand what is being said here: to have a successful, spiritual, and memorable event, it truly requires a great deal of YOUR time, so plan accordingly. You cannot begin to plan a weekend retreat or a week-long camp the month before the event. So, before reading any further, understand what is required of you in planning for a week of camp or retreat: a significant investment of your time.

Once you have committed to giving yourself plenty of time, you can start to think about the nuts and bolts of assembling a fantastic camp or retreat. Consider five questions that will help you prepare, structure, and execute your week or weekend. The answers to these five questions will help lay a strong foundation on which you can build the basic structure of your event. Without this foundation, your camp or retreat could be lacking key spiritual or physical elements that would help in the growth and development of the students, families, or individuals.

The First Question to Consider Is, "WHO?"

A foundational element of your retreat or camp is understanding the "who." Without determining who will be attending, your event can miss its focus or purpose. Begin by asking yourself, "Who is your targeted age group?" Is this camp or retreat for your kindergarten through fourth-grade students? Is this for your high school students? If so, what grade in high school? Maybe you have decided to do a camp for your families. If it is for your families, does this include all families of the church or just a specific age range? Is this for your church leadership: elders, deacons, or ministry staff? Are you planning for the couples of the congregations?

As you develop your classes, devotionals, and keynotes, make sure you have age-appropriate material for everyone. If it is a family retreat you will need class material for parents, middle school kids, and even toddlers. Think about the age groups you are dealing with and how long their attention spans are. A 45-minute keynote lesson is not designed for second and third-graders; you will lose their attention really quickly. If you are planning on an hour-long class, consider whether your teachers will have enough material for that amount of time with what you are providing them. Remember, if you are doing a middle school through high school event, that a sixth-grade student is not at the same spiritual maturity level as an eleventh-grade student. Also, consider the right speaker for your audience. If you bring a speaker to a family retreat who is not married, what does he have to offer to couples and parents? The "who" helps you tailor both the fun and spiritual activities for your event.

The Second Foundation Question Is, "WHY?"

The "why" helps you to narrow the focus of your camp or retreat. Why are you doing this event? Are you just doing it because it has always been done? The "why" can also help you focus on a theme and your purpose for the event. When you notice that there is an issue within your group or a group dynamic that is missing, maybe a weekend together or weeklong camp could help mend that issue or rebuild the missing dynamic. This also means the "why" is causing you to really analyze your group and the needs they may have. Once you fully understand why you are doing an event, you can develop a theme that is personally tailored for your group.

Your theme sets the tone for your camp or retreat. The theme should tie together with the scheduled events to make a structured, yet fantastic time together. Use your theme to design classes, devotionals, and keynotes. Make sure these aspects stay true to the theme and therefore fulfill the needs of your group. For example, if your theme deals with the idea of being together as a unified group but your keynotes, classes, or games focus on the story of creation from Genesis instead of unity from Ephesians, then you have missed the focus of your theme, and the purpose of your time together. On a side note, classes provide a great time to break down your group by age or gender for deeper discussions that apply the theme to specific groups.

The Third Question to Answer Is, "WHERE?"

Where will your event take place? As you begin looking for a place to go, there are three things to ponder here: the distance from home, the type of facility, and the cost of the facility.

Let's talk about distance. As you look at your facility, make sure you have adequate time to get there. If you plan to leave on a Friday evening around 5:30 P.M., will you make it to your facility at a reasonable time? If the facility is five hours away, your group most likely will arrive around midnight, after factoring in stops for food, fuel, and bathroom breaks. Once you arrive at the facility, it will take roughly 45 minutes to unpack everyone's belongings along with all the food. You are now at 12:45 A.M. or 1 A.M. before most can go to bed. But you have scheduled breakfast for 8 A.M., and someone will have to be up early to cook! Some things you need to factor into your potential travel time: chaperones and age groups.

Your chaperones will most likely need to wait to leave until after work, so that could possibly change the time you can leave. As you look at your age groups, how far can you travel with kindergarten through 3rd grade before needing to make a bathroom stop? Those stops take up time. My experience has taught me that if I stop for a "quick" restroom break, it will take at least 20-30 minutes. So it is important to consider the distance and time you have when picking out where to schedule your camp or retreat.

Your facilities will vary from summer camps to caves to state parks to VRBO's. As you look at the type of facility you will use, each one will provide a unique experience. When you look at a place to use, think about things that you will need: beds, showers, heat, or air-conditioning. Make sure your facility can accommodate the group you are bringing. If you book a place in the summertime and you only sleep in tents with no air conditioning, you might have some very unhappy campers. When looking at VRBO's or cabins you need to consider sleeping and shower arrangements. If you are using a summer camp, does it have heat in the cabins if you're going to use it in the fall when it's cool? Many of your facilities are popular places that other groups use, and because of this, it is possible they have a waiting list that can be up to 2 years long. Do not think you can call 3 or 4 weeks out from your event and reserve a facility. Plan way in advance!

Of course, you will need to feed all these people. Does this facility have a kitchen? What about BBQ grills or cooking equipment? Do they provide food? Some places allow you to cook, and others require you to purchase meals from their cafeteria. Some summer camps do not offer kitchens because they have their meals catered during the summer, so how are you going to feed your folks? If you are planning on grilling for a meal and your facility does not have one, what is your plan B?

The last thing to contemplate about your facility is the cost. You will see many ways facilities will charge for the rental. Many do a flat rate for the weekend. You can bring 20 people or 200 people, and the rate is still the same. Other places will do a cost per night.

This usually means a charge per person for each night of the stay. This can be costly if you do not pay attention to how much they are charging per person per night. Be cautious of added fees when renting these facilities. You might see a cleaning fee, damage fee, or even meal fee. Pay attention to the details and the fees and be willing to ask questions.

One final thought when it comes to facilities—always do a walk-through when you first arrive before letting your campers or chaperones run free through the place. Look for damages or major problems. Make notes about any noticeable damage or missing items and let those in charge of the facility know about it or come and fix it immediately. If you do not do this, you could be stuck with a damages bill. Damages or repairs can be costly!

Our Fourth Question Is, "WHEN?"

When do you plan on doing this camp or retreat? As you begin to figure this out, drag out all the calendars and lay them on your desk. Your event might have a great theme and be organized well, but if you plan it on a bad week or weekend it could be detrimental to your event. Start by looking at your personal calendar. The last thing you want to do is plan this event on your anniversary or your child's birthday. It could make for some unhappy people! The next calendar you want to look at is the church calendar. Are there any other church events planned when you want to do yours? Elders do not like it when a camp or retreat gets planned at the same time a gospel meeting is planned. After looking at the church calendar, get the school calendar out and see what is happening with the local school systems. Students might be out of school on a Friday when you want to plan your retreat. If so, it's possible several students will be gone that weekend with their families. There is a possibility that there might be a big test week coming up on the Monday right after your retreat and therefore several students cannot go. Some schools do summer school that offers different programs and opportunities for students, which could affect your numbers for summer camp. The last calendar to look at is the sports calendar, both school and city league schedules. Planning a family retreat when the city league ball is happening is not ideal because many city league games are played on Saturdays.

Looking at the time of year to plan this event, you should also consider the weather during that time of year. In the spring it is possible that there will be lots of rain or bad weather. If you look at the summer, you know it will be hot. In the fall you have football and band taking place. If you look at winter, it can be really cold, and some facilities might close for the winter.

The Final Question You Should Ask Yourself Is, "WHAT ELSE?"

What are the other things you should take some time to look at? What is your budget for this retreat? As you put a budget together you will want to consider all the costs: the facility itself, food, transportation, and maybe even printing costs for books or t-shirts.

What will you be eating for the week or weekend? What is your food budget? How many meals will you be eating over the weekend? Will you eat some of those meals away from the facility, and if so, who will pay for those meals? Are there any special needs that anyone has, like gluten allergies or nut allergies? What will you drink at your event? Will you have sodas, or will you have tea and water? Do not forget the coffee or hot chocolate! To help in this process, sit down, plan a menu, and then make a line-item list for each meal. Who will be cooking the food? Will it be you, or students, or perhaps members of the church? To help save on some cost you may want to ask the congregation to contribute to your food needs. Be cautious about what you ask for; if you are not specific enough about amounts you could end up with way too much of one item that you cannot use. Your attendees will like to snack throughout the day, so make sure you have snacks available. Finally, with food you will need utensils to eat with and plates to put the food on, so do not forget the utensils and paper goods, maybe even trash bags and toilet paper.

All events need to have chaperones. Who are you going to get to help you? Parents are always a good place to start. You can also use retired members from the congregation. At times you might allow college students to help, but make sure they are the right fit for your event. You can use non-members, but there is a risk that you run using non-members because they might not hold to the same beliefs or morals that you do.

What will you be using as far as transportation to get to your destination? Will you be using the church's vans or buses? If you are using the church's vehicles, you need to check the church calendar to make sure they are available. You will need drivers for the vehicles. Make sure you have safe drivers. Are the vehicles ready for the trip? Make sure they have the proper maintenance before you go. If you are renting vehicles, when will you pick up and drop off those vehicles? Will it cost you to add additional drivers for the rentals? Let me recommend that you always pay for the extra insurance that the rental company offers. An extra $150 of insurance that the church pays is much cheaper than an $8,000 body shop repair that the church will pay when the windows are blown out of the rented van you are driving during a summer storm. (True story!)

What are you doing for your keynote or classes when it comes to speakers? Will you be doing all the talking or will you use some of your church members? If you choose to use members from your church, give them plenty of time to prepare for their lessons. If you plan to use a guest speaker you need to plan ahead to make sure he is available. If you use a guest speaker who has to travel and be away from his family for the week or weekend, consider his travel costs, his time away from his family, and his lesson preparation time when you pay him. Where will your guest speaker stay while he is with you? Will you put him in a hotel or will he stay with you at your facility? It helps if a speaker can have some privacy to think and prepare.

What will you do for activities and games for the event? Activities are a great way to get everyone involved and help with team building. Will these activities or games take place inside or outside? Should the weather turn bad, what is your alternate plan? Make sure to remember to pack any supplies you might need for your games or activities. Keep a running list as you think about the games or the activities you will use. Look for games you can use that have a point that can help teach a spiritual application. Games that build teamwork and relationships can also be a blessing.

It is also important to consider the legal issues involved in conducting a retreat or camp. Many camps now do background checks on all chaperones. Make sure that van and bus drivers meet the requirements to be insured by the church's vehicle insurance. Some types of vehicles will require a CDL license. It is also wise to consult lawyers and medical personnel to create medical and liability releases that the parents of the teens can sign before the event. It is also important to have enough chaperone oversight to prevent couples from sneaking off together. Make sure you have clear rules for the event and enforce them fairly and graciously (this paragraph was added by KB).

Conclusion

Camps and retreats are such a great part of ministry. Special things happen when a group of people step out of their normal routines and spend some time away together. The spiritual growth that can take place over a week or weekend is immeasurable. Memories will be made that will impact people for a lifetime.

Discussion Questions

1. Discuss what times of year would be best or worst to have a retreat in your area.
2. Discuss potential problems you might have with a

church van on a trip and steps you might take to eliminate or prepare for these problems.
3. Make a list of some of the things you might try to accomplish at a retreat. (Possible purposes)
4. Discuss some of your favorite team-building games that might be used at a retreat.
5. Discuss some of your favorite themes from past camps and retreats.

Note: Jarrod was a guest speaker in my youth ministry classes for 12 years at both Freed-Hardeman University and Heritage Christian University. He always talked about how to conduct retreats and camps and the students bragged about what they learned. He had over 20 years of experience as a youth minister (McKenzie, TN) and campus minister (UT Martin). He had planned retreats for all ages. That is why I wanted him to write this chapter. He was also the heartbeat of the Board for the Ministry to Youth Conference (M2Y) which I have had the privilege of attending since its inception. Jarrod passed away a few weeks after being on the Heritage campus for an M2Y Board Meeting and shortly after turning in this chapter. Our prayers continue for Janet and their two boys in his loss. He was a spiritual giant in the world of youth and college ministry and a true friend. He is missed. I am grateful that his ministry will live on through the pages of this chapter. (KB)

Chapter 26
Planning Special Events
Larry Davenport

Introduction

Well, you are reading the chapter about planning a large event. That can mean one of two things. Either you have an event that has grown to a point that there are questions that this chapter can answer, or maybe you are just curious about what the CYC (Challange Youth Conference) guys actually do. Whatever your reason for being here, hopefully, the following sections will anticipate your questions and provide some good resources. This should be an easy chapter to write—after all, we have been doing this for twenty-five years. But, there is nothing written down. We sort of grew with CYC, and we learned as we went, which is just another way of saying that we made a lot of mistakes. In this chapter, I will share our story and identify some of the things we learned along the way.

How It All Began

So, to get started, we have to go all the way back to the 1900s: 1999, to be precise. Three youth ministers from northwest Alabama got together with the idea to have a retreat for our local congregations. Everyone reading this chapter can plan an awesome retreat, and, if we are being honest, you would have probably done a lot better job than the three of us did that first year.

We chose Pigeon Forge as the venue because it is a great location. Specifically, we chose a little Holiday Inn with a conference room that would seat about 300 people. The coordination involved four congregations, each providing $500 in seed money that was used for advertising. We invited four Christian universities to serve as sponsors, meaning they gifted CYC enough money to purchase 325 t-shirts, and each university had its logo printed on the shirt. Adults from the four sponsoring congregations worked registration tables. Board members served as master of ceremonies and song leaders, and we secured a keynote speaker, two class teachers, and entertainment from one of the Christian universities. There were about 325 in attendance (25 above capacity), and we decided to plan another CYC for the following year.

Registration

I recall that in the beginning we used the equivalent of a Google form for registration, and it changed constantly. For a large event, this is not a good way to register groups. Every day, groups would call to make changes to their registrations—and I should mention that we provided t-shirts with registration through 2004. In 2004, there were 2,600 in attendance, and I remember getting phone calls nearly every day with the changes: "I need to add two," "I need to change two extra-large shirts to two medium shirts and add two large shirts," etc. That was the last year we included t-shirts.

We needed something different, so we researched registration processes. All of the conference registration applications we found charged a per-person fee, and we simply did not want to go that route. We did not mind paying a fee, but we wanted people to be able to register by group (i.e., Main Street church of Christ could register 100 people, but it would be one single registration and one single fee). We also wanted the group leaders to be able to go in and edit their registration. We finally found such a company that would work with us: International Conference Management (ICM, www.conference.com).

From a financial standpoint, it works, but the data is available only in preset reports geared toward large corporations that book hotel rooms, meals, etc. We would love to be able to download the data into a flat file of comma-separated text that we could put into an Excel spreadsheet or Access database and manipulate the data however we wanted. We are negotiating with a software firm to develop exactly what we think would be a perfect registration tool. The data collected could be downloaded to a flat file that you could sort the way you need (by group leader name, church name, zip code, etc.), or you could even import it into your favorite software. Once it is available, we will share with you how you can access it for your events.

Every year, we get requests from individuals from other countries wanting us to sponsor his/her visas to attend CYC, and we have never attempted to enter that arena. I typically either delete or hide them from the final registration database. One year in Texas, I was in the main ballroom making final preparations for the Friday night session to begin when someone came to get me and said there were three kids from Guyana trying to check in, but they were not on the list. My initial confusion turned to instant recall—they were indeed registered, and their visit to the United States to attend multiple functions had already been sponsored via another organization. I ran to the registration table as they were leaving. I stopped them and told them we had them covered and apologized for the mix-up. They loved CYC, and we still communicate with them to this day.

Controversy

This is not something we like to talk about in the church. No one likes controversy, but I thought I would add a section about it to share an early experience and share how we handled it. Again, this is something we had to experience to learn, and there may have been better ways to handle it, but this was our solution.

The controversy emerged in our second year when we were still a young and immature retreat. The issue revolved around our keynote speaker. There was a recording of him speaking somewhere, and some disagreed with what he said. Let us pause for a second. I believe there is far more right about the church than there is wrong with it. I believe we are all trying to do what is right. Opinions abound. And when it comes to your specific event, people are going to ask questions like, "What do you allow at your conference?" "What do you not allow at your conference?" "Are you conservative?" Challenge Youth Conference is a conservative, mainstream conference. If we started listing the things that we are trying to avoid, there would still be those who think of something else they want to be added to the list. Someone once said, "If all you do is hoe your garden, then all you are left with is dirt."

Our focus in planning CYC is not on numbers, and we refuse to base success on numbers. We just want to do the right thing. So how did we handle this situation? There were congregations in our hometown that were not going to participate because of this controversy. We did not want to debate our local congregations, and we also did not believe CYC was to be a platform for this speaker. Also, the three-member board was not in perfect agreement on what to do. Ultimately, we decided to uninvite the speaker, but we also paid him. Our thinking was that he had scheduled us and perhaps turned down other speaking engagements. The question was asked, "Who can we get to replace him?" It was suggested that we invite a young, relatively unknown minister named Lonnie Jones. One board member asked if he could handle it. It was the best decision we ever made. The second year, some Tennessee youth ministers heard about us and asked if they could attend, and CYC exploded from 325 to 850. This required us to contract a convention center.

Contractual Requirements

When planning large events and entering into contracts with convention centers, there are requirements that we as event owners obligate ourselves to. The contract with the conference centers in Pigeon Forge and Gatlinburg required that we carry a one-million-dollar liability event insurance policy (if a venue asks you for a "COI," that's what they're referring to; it stands for "certificate of insurance"). Our search to secure this policy revealed that there was only one insurance company providing this service, K&K Insurance, so that simplified matters.

In the beginning, we went directly to K&K, but now we go through a local insurance agent. The price is the same either way. The difference is you can fill out the paperwork, or someone else (who knows what they are doing) can do it for you. Something that we learned after going through a private insurance agent is that exhibitors are not covered under the liability insurance policy, so now we ask exhibitors to provide their own liability insurance.

Speaking of insurance for large events, there is another policy called Directors and Officers Insurance. This protects the event organizers from many types of claims outside of the event itself.

Exhibitors

I mentioned exhibitors, so let us go ahead and say something about them. The decision was made early on that we did not want sales taking place at CYC. The only exception is when our speakers have a book or resource published. We hired a company to set up the exhibitor tables. They provide the table, skirting, pipe and drape, two chairs, and a waste basket. While it is an expense, it is a net zero expense for us because we pass the cost along to the exhibitors. And, by the way, these prices are terrific. Our price per table is $300 including electricity (yes, that is an extra charge to us). That is a bargain when you compare it to the cost of exhibitor setups at other conferences ($500-$1,000). You have to consider such things if you are going to have a large event. If your event is in the Gatlinburg/Pigeon Forge area including Knoxville, we use All Convention and Expo Services (https://acesknox.com). Using a professional trade show company is highly recommended because it makes your event look very professional.

Setting Registration Costs

CYC registration is extremely low. When we entered into the contract with the LeConte Center and told them we charged $35 per person, their jaws dropped because they had never seen a conference cost that low—most are $100 or more. We explained that this is not a corporate-sponsored event. This is an event for teenagers, and some parents are paying for multiple kids, plus hotel, plus food. Our registration costs cover the venue, lights/sound, speaker fees/lodging, insurance, legal/accounting fees, and other overhead costs. The costs for the conference center are the same whether you have 1,000 people or 12,000 people. Other items, like lights and sound, are negotiable. To host a conference in a convention center today, we would probably need at least 1,000 attendees at a registration cost of $100 per person just to break even. All of these things need to be taken into account.

Legal Issues

For many years, CYC remained under the direction of a congregational eldership, but that is not the case anymore. We still are asked from time to time, "Which congregation oversees CYC?" Here is the short answer: At the 2005 conference there were over 3,000 in attendance, and my elders asked to meet with me about CYC. In this meeting, they shared their feeling that CYC had become too large for the eldership to be accountable for. They suggested that I consult the leadership at Lads to Leaders and find out how they are organized and do the same for CYC.

That conversation resulted in us acquiring an attorney, incorporating, and then making application to become a 501c3. I asked the attorney if we could still be under an eldership, and the answer was "No," because most churches are incorporated also, and you cannot have one corporation overseeing another corporation. So, there are some legal issues that emerge with this. As a 501c3, paperwork must be filed with the IRS each year, and that involves providing a budget summary report each year. This is a good time to say that it is always okay to ask someone who has already done what you want to do. Instead of trying to figure things out on your own, ask those who have already had success in that area. We are so grateful to Gary Hogeland and Roy Johnson for sharing their experiences in planning large events.

Branding and Logos

Another thing you must consider with a large annual event is branding. So how do we come up with the cool branding and logos each year? Fortunately, we have a lot of friends and acquaintances in the church who are experts at this. Note: A big part of planning any event—large or small—is marshaling your resources. Identify your needs and surround yourself with people who have the talents to meet those needs. Here are a few of the very talented friends we have contracted with, but we would love to expand this list:

- Resources: CYC brand by Victoria Antoine, vlamarketing2209@gmail.com
- Power, In Need, Are You Listening by Brandon Edwards, brandon@fishingerchurch.org
- #forme by Jennifer Allen, jenniferallendesign@gmail.com
- Identity by Randall Turner, turner.randall.j@gmail.com

Additional Fees

We talked about the venue earlier in the chapter. As CYC grew, so did expenses. Here are some of the costs that emerged:
- Electrical

- Wi-Fi — There is free Wi-Fi at LeConte, but with the large attendance, the bandwidth drops to a level that is unusable. We have dedicated Wi-Fi at the audio/visual table to get rapid updates/changes needed for presentations.
- Insurance
- External Security — A requirement by the convention center.
- External Medical Staff — This is not required by the convention center, but it is a necessity.
- Audio/Visual — Note that, for some conference centers, you will be charged a fee if you bring in your own lights and sound instead of using their in-house services.
- Crowd Control — There are online certification courses at minimal costs. We have never experienced problems with the CYC crowd, but we have some leadership in place now who are equipped with the knowledge and training.

Lights and Sound

For the first three years, we used the in-house lighting and sound because it was available and free. In 2003, we moved to the Gatlinburg Convention Center, and there were no house lights and sound, so a youth minister who had a band volunteered to provide lights and sound for CYC. This was not our best decision, but it allowed us a chance to grow as conference planners.

Remember, we said earlier that it is always okay to ask someone for advice who has already done what you want to do. We reached out to a successful youth conference planner to ask how they handled lights and sound. Short answer, they contracted the work to professional audio/visual (A/V) companies. We were blessed to know subject matter experts in this arena. There were two deacons where I served as a youth minister who were audio/visual engineers with Sutherland Sight & Sound (https://www.sutherlandsound.com). They provided services to events like the Country Music Awards. Well, with that on their résumé, we thought we would give them a chance with CYC. I especially liked this arrangement because Greg and Charlie were in sync with how the church of Christ services are conducted, so there were no issues with our comfort zones.

Moving to the LeConte Center meant expanding our technical base to include Streamline Productions out of Knoxville (https://streamlineproductionsgroup.com), but we also retained Sutherland (Greg and Charlie) to be the quarterbacks running things. Each year, I provide a minute-by-minute schedule for the A/V guys to use. This "operations schedule" identifies every action, every video, Scripture, and song, who is coming to the stage, and what time they will be there. Everything is timed to run seamlessly from start to finish.

Let me add something here, and this is just one tiny thing that you might not notice. There are many small details that we could mention. When you plan an event, and you promote your start time, start on time. I attend many events that advertise a start time, and everyone is there and seated and ready, and it is time to begin, but someone says something like, "We are waiting on some more groups to arrive, so we will start shortly." Ok, I get it but respect those who supported your schedule. They are in their seats and ready, so start on time. The totality of attention that you pay to the smallest details, which others might consider insignificant, will culminate in their overall fond memories and the success of your event.

A lot of Jesus's kingdom parables point out the significance of the small things. Two of these are found in Matthew 13:31–33. Regarding the mustard seed, Jesus says in verse 32, "It is the smallest of all seeds, but when it has grown it is larger than all the garden plants and becomes a tree." It was the tiniest of all seeds, but it grew into a tree over ten feet tall. Small things matter. God can take these tiny things, even the seemingly insignificant planning details that no one notices, and use them as tools for planting the seed into someone's heart. One day that seed may grow into a decision by someone to submit to Jesus's authority and become a child of God. That is the way the kingdom of God works in the hearts and lives of people.

A few years back the owner of the A/V company stopped me at the end of the CYC weekend. He was shaking his head and saying, "I don't get it. I set up shows for youth events all over the country. They pay three times more than you do for lights and sound, they have bands, vendor sales through the roof, bells, and whistles, absolutely phenomenal, and you have more kids coming to CYC than they do. I don't get it. Whatever you are doing, it is working." Incidentally, he added that at the end of the weekend, they are passing the collection basket to collect enough money to pay for the conference, and sometimes they pass the basket more than once.

Teamwork and Staffing

We have an internal team of planners, plus workers who labor throughout the conference to keep it moving smoothly: registration workers, crowd control, internal security, exhibitor liaison, t-shirt staff, badge staff, etc. In addition to this team, we have our external customers/workers: participating congregations, youth ministers, parents, deacons, and shepherds. We receive daily emails, texts, and phone messages. It is our practice to respond immediately because if we do not, they will stack up quickly and we lose track. It takes a team to make things happen.

Merchandise

We receive offers from a number of organizations that want to be providers of merchandise. Many times, they will request their competitors' bids with the assurance that they can offer a better price. While that may be so, we believe it is unethical to share competitors' prices. Here are some of the great merchandise companies we are currently working with.
- Resources: Uth Stuph, https://uthstuph.com
- Gandy Promos, https://gandypromos.com
- Sunday Cool, https://www.sundaycool.com
- Sportees, http://www.sporteesonline.com

Conclusion

While CYC is a large event, we view it as a work of God, and we give Him all the glory for any success. The CYC board is grateful to serve a great God through this ministry. We also enjoy attending events that others have planned. Your events may not be exactly like CYC, but it is my prayer that this chapter has identified some resources and ideas that will assist you. Thank you for your service, and it is our prayer that this chapter will serve you well as your event grows.

Discussion Questions

1. What are some things from this chapter that you had never considered before?

2. Have you ever considered the legal issues involved in planning church-related activities, and how might this impact how you do some of the things you are doing?

3. Work together to make a list of resources in your community for the following areas:

Legal Advice
Lighting and Sound
Merchandising
Advertising/Logos

4. What would be some benefits of doing background checks with the workers for your events?

Chapter 27
Ministry to Youth Outside the US
Paul Spurlin, Jeff Johnson, W. Kirk Brothers

Introduction

God has young people all over the world. While much of this book focuses on the ministry we do in our local communities, the focus in this chapter is on possibilities for ministering to young people outside those communities. The first section of this chapter will briefly overview planning mission trips (another chapter goes into more detail). The remaining two sections of this chapter focus on two specific works that aim at ministering to young people in other countries. We pray that these examples will give you some ideas concerning what you might do.

Planning Youth Mission Trips and Planting Exposure Youth Camp

Paul B. Spurlin

Planning a mission trip and seeing this valuable work through to completion can be one of the most impactful areas of ministry. A foreign mission experience offers new perspectives through experiencing a different culture and way of life. One benefit of such experiences is that they can improve one's outlook on life and service toward others. Another blessing is the opportunity it provides for young people to use their gifts for others. Yet another blessing is the difference it makes in the lives of those who are served by such mission activities. Thus, the mission trip is a vital part of a successful youth ministry.

Preparation

There are three important considerations when coordinating any trip. First of all, there must be proper preparation and it starts with giving yourself plenty of time for planning. Personally, I suggest setting a date that is nine months to a full year away from the desired trip. Not only will this allow you to deal with all the planning components, but it will allow families with busy schedules to have the date far in advance. Allowing yourself adequate time also gives you the opportunity to find others who can help with the trip. Finding adults to assist who understand the location and have a grasp of the local culture will help with the safety and success of the trip.

Secondly, picking the right location for your group is of prime importance. Start by looking at a work that your home congregation already supports. This will improve buy-in from your eldership because it is a trusted location and work. Also, partnering with other congregations may bring more resources and help in executing a mission trip. As a suggestion, trips are easier to accomplish within English-speaking areas of the world because language can be a challenging barrier to overcome for youth group members. Thus, for first-timers, you might start in English-speaking countries and then move to other countries as the group gains experience.

Lastly, you will need to form a team of members dedicated to going on the trip and a separate team who will help you prepare for departure. Passports, documents, funds, plans for travel, food, and housing must be priorities. Fundraising is a necessity that many in your group will need help with to participate in the trip. There are different ways to work on raising the money for such a trip, so be creative. Setting a budget early will allow each team member enough time to raise the needed funds. It is also important that you take the time to train the members of your team. Everyone will need to have a better understanding of the culture, language, and safety issues before departure. Talk to local brethren in the host country about the things that need to be understood and develop a checklist of things that team members must accomplish to participate in this mission trip.

Execution

The most thrilling part of working in the mission field is that we have opportunities to continue to grow and to make disciples in all nations, just as God intended (cf. Mark 16:15; Matt 28:19). From the beginning to the end of a youth mission trip, you must maintain the focus on the purpose of the trip (VBS, Gospel meeting, evangelistic campaign, medical campaign, etc.). Share the plan from the very beginning and remind everyone consistently of the goals for the trip. In addition, create a plan to communicate with the parents of the teenagers going and the other adults that will be traveling. Send out weekly emails and strive to keep the team goals at the forefront of their prayers and minds. Most of all, shape the trip to fit the needs of the church in the location you are going to.

Develop roles for everyone on the mission team. Each team member needs a job to do and needs to feel a sense of responsibility to participate (they are not going on vacation). Part of the application for the mission trip can include having potential participants list their passions and areas of experience. Learn to delegate! Do not be a lone ranger when it comes to executing the plan for the mission trip. Working together will equal success for everyone.

Evaluation

Much can be gained by coming together after a mission trip to review the trip. Discuss what worked and what did not work. Decide together whether the goals you set before the trip were accomplished or if more work needs to be done. Ask yourselves, "Did the youth mission team make the impact that we set out to make? Did we leave the location better than we found it?"

A youth mission trip can bring people together and challenge our comfort zones at the same time. Mission trips can change people by empowering team participants to share their faith with strangers. Mission trips are important for the lives of young people, and every teenager should experience a trip. Your youth group will not only grow closer together and to Christ from spending time working together on a mission trip, but they will also learn skills that will propel them to stay engaged in the church and become leaders in the Kingdom.

Planting the Exposure Youth Camp

Exposure Youth Camp is a Youth Rally held at the Von Braun Center in Huntsville, Alabama during December 27–30 of each year and usually has around 3,000 in attendance. I am proud to be part of this good work. EYC has now been planted in London, England (2019) and Glasgow, Scotland (2023). This is a joint venture of the EYC and Ministry League leadership teams. Here are five key things we have learned while transplanting the camp:

1. Look for a location that has a need and resources to help complete the goal.
2. Set up a budget and goals for sustaining an event. Go and see the location. Start building relationships with locals. Get a lay of the land.
3. Find 3–5 local congregations who would be as passionate about this event as we are in establishing this

opportunity. For example, the Cumbernauld church of Christ plays a key role in the camp in Scotland.
4. Locate a facility in a good central location that will suit the needs of the event you're establishing.
5. Establish a curriculum for training and leadership. Find the hook for this event to draw people in to be a part of the event each year.

Dale Jenkins, who is the MC and part of the planning team for EYC, makes the following observations about what we have learned.

1. Young people are similar everywhere (no matter the country).
2. Young people, in and out of the US, love to sing.
3. Young people are deeper thinkers than adults might assume.
4. In purely secular countries, without any moral moorings, young people will push the morality envelope even further (text message, 7–25–23).

Thank you for your desire to both take teens to minister for Christ in other countries and for your willingness to minister to teens in countries outside the US.

Taking Lads to Leads Training Around the World

Jeff Johnson

Jesus said, "And he said to them, "Go into all the world and proclaim the gospel to the whole creation" (Mark 16:15). Not only must the gospel go to other countries but Christians in all countries need to be trained in both sharing the gospel and ministering in the name of Jesus (cf. Eph 4:11–16). The Lads to Leaders program focuses on training young people to minister in the name of Christ. My family has long been invested in this program. L2L has now expanded into countries outside of the United States. Three countries actively utilizing these tools with great success are India, the Philippines, and Romania. With that in mind, let me share three things that are important as you consider ministering to young people outside the US.

Intent

The book of Acts records the missionary journeys of the Apostle Paul. Paul was a missionary with a mission. He intended to take the Gospel everywhere possible. Paul did not travel simply as a sightseer. The message of his intent was clear to the Romans.

> I am under obligation both to Greeks and to barbarians, both to the wise and to the foolish. So I am eager to preach the gospel to you also who are in Rome. For I am not ashamed of the gospel, for it is the power of God for salvation to everyone who believes, to the Jew first and also to the Greek. For in it, the righteousness of God is revealed from faith for faith, as it is written, "The righteous shall live by faith" (Rom 1:14–17).

Evaluate your intent, considering Paul's efforts to continue spreading the message of salvation. Clear intent will answer the question, "Why am I doing this?" Who would dare to change the world? Jesus did, and Paul's desire was that everyone would know. Would you dare to have an intentional impact?

Imagine a world where young men and women are trained to utilize their belief in Jesus Christ to make a difference. The assault on Christianity and moral living has continued for generations. A passion for God's life-changing message drove Jack Zorn to create action statements called "Leader Pledges."

1. I am answerable to God and society (cf. Matt 22:21).
2. I will overcome pessimism and live a life of faith in God (cf. Phil 4:13).
3. I am fully responsible for my behavior (cf. Rom 14:12).
4. I am responsible for my agreements and obligations (cf. Matt 7:12).
5. I pursue honest work to meet my responsibilities (cf. 1 Tim 5:8).
6. I honor and obey my parents and respect persons in authority (cf. Eph 6:2).
7. I respect my body as the creation of God and use it for His glory (cf. 1 Cor 6:20).
8. I choose for my friends those who enjoy doing good (cf. 1 Cor 15:33).
9. I lead in building character and in demonstrating integrity (cf. Phil 2:22).
10. I lead in second-mile service to others (cf. Matt 5:41).

These leader pledges are training tools for intentional decisions to live a godly life. When these tools were penned, the expectations were high. American teachers need to improve their interpretation of the vision of changing the world. Social distractions can lower expectations.

Initiate

Selecting a place for work requires initial research. Many who have a mission in mind will want to visit other countries. For instance, Jack Zorn visited at least 15 countries while refining *Lads to Leaders*, doing mission work, and gathering information. This method can be time-consuming and expensive. Our modern world offers far more efficient alternatives. Ricky Gootam, director of the L2L Convention in India, said,

Google a country before you visit. Know your geography. Then search out someone trustworthy in the region. If you want to make a difference, you must do your homework.

Upon arrival, the first thing one must do is communicate with the local people. In Japan, for example, three languages are primarily used, and there are various dialects of these languages. India has 30 completely different languages, yet British influence has resulted in the widespread use of English. A general language used by most in a country (such as English or Spanish) may still be accompanied by different dialects. As a result, we can have a false confidence that we are communicating well, but we may not be. My father, Thomas Johnson, once commented about a mission work that he was involved in, "In Trinidad and Tobago, they speak English, but it's not the same English we speak." South America is home to a host of Hispanic dialects. People in Colombia, for example, speak a version of Spanish that is much like the Castilian Spanish spoken in the country of Spain. Much of the rest of Latin America uses a version of Spanish that is not so formal. Part of doing one's homework is learning the language or obtaining a translator proficient with the correct dialect.

It is also important to be careful to avoid using idioms. Turns of phrases and jokes often translate poorly. One Middle Eastern missionary discovered his translator had said to the audience, "He just told a joke I do not understand. Let's all politely laugh." Humor is generally good but often misunderstood. Customs and cultural differences may also lead to misunderstandings. While learning about geography and language, another homework assignment is culture. The lesson is to remove all barriers to the best of our ability.

Political limitations can be a barrier to entering a country. Awareness of those issues is important. An example of this is Ira Rice. As an American, he was not able to visit India in 1962. He decided to reach out to J.C. Bailey, a Canadian, and asked him to go to India. Bailey made the trip and converted Nehemiah Gootam.

Nehemiah then converted many of his own family as well as others. This team expanded the church in India. Nehemiah's nephew, Ricky, is a graduate of Freed-Hardeman University, serves as a gospel preacher in India, and is an influential leader in his community and the Lord's church there. He has taken civic leadership roles that have influence with some government officials. Indian officials have been impressed with the results produced from biblical training via the *Lads to Leaders* program. This all started with a conversation between Rice and Bailey.

The 2022 L2L conventions outside the US had over 4,000 participants. One outstanding student memorized 500 verses of Scripture, while many others memorized between 100 and 200. The work in India is being driven by Christians in that country, making the vetting of adult volunteers easier. Teaching others to teach at home inspires involvement and self-sufficiency. Americans are working similarly in Romania and the Philippines, but the "home court" advantage of a large group of local workers in India is having greater success.

Inspire

Support is needed to begin any mission work. Others must see the intentional vision for a work in order to respond with financial support. It is important that you have an individual or individuals who can inspire others to believe in the work. Passion and clear articulation of the mission are important. Also, if people or congregations in the United States are going to feel comfortable giving to a work in another country, they will often feel more comfortable giving to an overseeing eldership. They are at least going to want clear information concerning how the funds are going to be managed.

The Pauline letters give us a picture of a humble man who was inspired by the love of Christ. Paul was able to inspire others because he was sincere and demonstrated integrity, energy, and passion. These are the "must-have" qualities for the youth worker who goes abroad.

You can make a difference. The gospel has the power to change lives, and God left that power in the hands of human beings. What will we do with it? Being successful in the eyes of God includes having a selfless intent, being a self-starter to initiate, and possessing sacrificial inspiration to leave a lasting impression.

> Go therefore and make disciples of all nations, baptizing them in the name of the Father and of the Son and of the Holy Spirit, teaching them to observe all that I have commanded you. And behold, I am with you always, to the end of the age (Matt 28:19–20).

Future Minister Training Camps

W. Kirk Brothers

I am a product of future minister/leadership training camps in the United States and have participated in such camps since 1981. In 2010 I started serving under the eldership of the Forrest Park church of Christ in Valdosta, Georgia to plant such camps in Latin America. As of this writing, God had planted camps in 12 different Latin American countries. I will give a brief overview of what I do in case you would like to start a similar camp somewhere in the world.

The Purposes of the Camp

The goal of the camp is to train young men to be leaders and teachers in their local congregations (we have conducted one camp thus far which included young women and helped them to learn how to teach women's and children's classes). Classes in the camp include preparing and delivering sermons, personal evangelism, the eldership, biblical leadership, the minister's life and family, leading in public worship, etc.

Each evening we have a session in which campers have an opportunity to practice what they are learning in their classes during the day (speaking in front of others, reading Scripture, etc.). We divide our sermon preparation classes into two groups based on age (or three if the camp is large). All campers prepare a sermon during the week and deliver it to their classmates. We rotate doing parable sermons (textual) and sermons based on Bible characters (topical).

Another key element of the camp is that we have a torch ceremony on the last night of the camp. We will gather around a fire and sing together. We then produce a tiki torch that uses citronella oil (do *NOT* use gas or anything combustible). We talk about Jesus as the light of the world and our responsibility to be lights as well. Each camper then comes forward, takes the torch, and talks about how he will use what he has learned at the camp. We also have a graduation ceremony at the end of the week and a devotional before the graduation that is conducted by the campers.

Church camps are quite normal in Latin America. What we try to do is show the brethren how they can use such camps to pool their resources and train leaders, teachers, and preachers. We normally focus on 12–24-year-olds, but I let the local Christians make the final decision on the age range. I find that some older men want to come because they need training so they can assist in their local congregations, but they are not able to go away to a two-year preaching school.

The Philosophy of the Camp

Two key philosophies that undergird the camp are sound teaching and local ownership. I use trusted connections to identify a biblically sound and highly respected preacher to work through as the local camp director. I contact that preacher about the possibility of doing a camp. I send him a document overviewing what the camp is all about and what is required, a sample medical release, and a sample schedule or two from previous camps. I asked him to talk to the local churches and see if there is interest in doing the camp and a willingness to commit.

I bring one gringo with me from the United States (usually it is my friend Chuck Morris) and one or two men from other countries in Latin America who have experience with the camps. I often take a professor from the Bible School of the Americas in Panama. It is very common to have campers who decide to enroll in BSAM. Almost all the camp staff is made up of local Christians in that country. I raise the funds for the first two years of camps. Typically, we work with the local brethren for two years and then ask them to completely take over the camp while we move on to another country.

I share the goals of the camp and suggestions based on what has worked in the past with the camp director, but it is very important to me that the local Christians own the camp. I do not want gringos to do a camp for them. We guide, assist, and recommend, but it must become their camp. I make a point to make sure that key leadership positions are manned by local Christians, not gringos. They need to see their local church leaders in front of them, and they need to see that we respect their leaders.

The Preparations for the Camp

Once I get local church buy-in, we then need to settle on a date that works for all of us. We have done camps as short as three days or as long as seven days. We also begin discussions on possible locations. The location needs sleeping quarters, kitchen/dining facilities, at least two classrooms, one large meeting area, and, if possible, room for them to get out and exercise.

Most camps range in size from 25–35 campers. This is not your typical church camp. It is for committed young people who want to become leaders. Camp workers typically include 3–5 staff members, a counselor for every 6 campers, and a kitchen staff. We will occasionally have people who come in as guests to teach classes, but most classes are taught by the staff and counselors.

The local director works with local leaders to make these assignments.

I work with the local director on a budget. Some funds will be needed prior to our arrival in the country so we need a plan for how to transfer funds to the location in a secure fashion and for maintaining accountability for the funds. Sometimes we can do direct bank deposits and at other times we have used resources such as Western Union. In addition to the camp facilities, other expenses could include travel expenses, food, mattresses, camp supplies, and books for a camp Bible study library. Everyone at the camp is given a camp t-shirt (best advertising I know of), a Thompson Chain Reference Study Bible in Spanish, a pen/pencil, a notebook, and often one other Spanish Bible study book. It is important to remember that it is hard to prepare sermons without books to assist in the process of preparation. This is why we give everyone at the camp a study Bible (even the kitchen staff) and have a small camp library available. I also keep Spanish Bible reference books on my computer and ipad so the campers can use them if they need to.

One of the biggest challenges is securing translators. If you have gringos (folks from the United States) who are not fluent in Spanish, you will need good translators. Chuck and I use Spanish in day-to-day conversations with people but like to have a translator to assist when preaching and teaching. I frequently take a translator with me. That is one of the reasons I do not take a large number of people from the United States with me. The more non-Spanish speakers I take the more expenses and challenges I have. Yet, the other side of the coin is that taking others can also expose the young men to new people and increase belief in and support for the camp In the US. For example, it can be great to have an elder with you. Many campers will have never met one.

It is becoming more and more common for churches across Latin America to use PowerPoints and projectors in worship and can thus make it available at the camp if you let them know what you need. It can be very helpful to project the songs you will sing in Spanish. It is also helpful to have songbooks available in Spanish for use in worship and in the songleading class. If you need PowerPoints or handouts translated, you should get them to the translator many weeks before the camp, so he has plenty of time to complete the task. It is not a bad idea to sit down and talk through the presentation with your translator beforehand. Stories and United States colloquialisms can be tough to translate.

I usually submit a draft schedule to the local brethren based on what we have done in past camps. I plug the people I am bringing with me into sessions where they have strengths and ask the director to plug in all the local speakers. I let the local director know that he can feel free to move anything I suggested around, including changing speakers. Again, it is important that it become their camp and that the local leadership feel comfortable with all aspects of the schedule. There is much more we might discuss, but maybe this will give you a general idea.

Conclusion

Ministry to young people does not stop at the borders of our towns and country. It is our prayer that this chapter will inspire you to think about the possibilities of ministering to young people in other countries and locations here in the United States outside your own communities. Our desire is also that some of the tips we have shared will help you think through some of the logistics of doing so.

Discussion Questions

1. Discuss one thing in this chapter that you had never considered before.
2. Share what you see as the three most important things you learned from this chapter.

3. Name important items to research when considering outreach to another country and why you chose these.
4. Discuss some phrases, colloquialisms, and aspects of US culture that you think might be difficult to translate into other languages and cultures.
5. Discuss the difference between preaching Jesus and His church in other cultures and in transplanting US culture in other countries. Which one is biblical?

Chapter 28
Youth Ministry Internships
Bryan LeMasters and Blaine McKinney

Who we are today, our faith in God, and our understanding of what it is to be a minister were all shaped by the mentors and experiences we received in our internships. Church internship programs bless individuals and congregations by providing opportunities for the local church to invest in young leaders who have a passion for making a difference in the kingdom of God. The intern gains essential wisdom by partnering with the congregation through hands-on ministry. In this chapter, we explore the roles and responsibilities of both interns and the church leaders who partner with them.

To the Intern

Do you want to be a successful minister? Well, of course! You decided to go into ministry because you have experienced Jesus and possess a hunger for others to experience the same peace and fulfillment only found in Him. However, in any arena of life, rookies make more mistakes than those who have experience. Hopefully, you are already pondering the question, "What can I do to limit mistakes when I become a minister?" If so, this chapter is for you because we learned more about ministry in internships than in the classroom.

Why Internships Are Essential

Internships should greatly impact you spiritually. You will get to spend weeks focusing on preparing and teaching the Gospel, praying for and with individuals, and constantly being focused on the souls of others. You will witness God working in the lives of those around you and get to rejoice and weep with brothers and sisters in Christ whom you previously did not know.

A couple of proverbs highlight one of the major benefits of internships. Proverbs 12:15 states, *"The way of a fool is right in his own eyes, but a wise man listens to advice."* Proverbs 13:20 reads, *"Whoever walks with the wise becomes wise, but the companion of fools will suffer harm."* Internships are vital for your development because you receive the opportunity to be mentored and influenced by godly church leaders. Do not underestimate this blessing. For your journey, make humility your copilot. God saw fit to repeat this theme throughout Proverbs. We avoided multiple mistakes because we got to witness and talk through different scenarios with individuals who had already been down that road.

Having new experiences and meeting new people will bear fruit and open doors years into the future. Ideas and ways of organizing or structuring different elements of ministry have influenced us as ministers in our decisions. Your time in a classroom is so important, but it cannot replace the experience of partnering with other church leaders in a congregation. If at all possible, be an intern and we believe you (and the local church) will be blessed.

Primary Goals of an Internship

The spiritual example of an intern can be impactful. Good or bad, an intern can affect the culture of a youth ministry and even the soul of a child. The primary goal of your internship is to connect youth to God. Everything should go back to this. This is why you teach, share meals, organize events, and become their friend. Outside of worship and Bible class, will they witness your faith and see how important He is to you?

Teens look up to their interns. This gives you a fantastic opportunity to support and reinforce their connection to the youth ministry and the rest of the church. However, if you speak negatively about rules, events, or volunteers, then it will be difficult to connect the teens to the church. Remember most internships last a short amount of time. Although you will feel really close to many people, you will have a short amount of time with students. So, one of the best ways to make your internship have a lasting impact is to connect students to God and other Christians in their church family who can disciple and encourage them after you leave.

Finally, one of your primary goals as an intern is to mature and prepare yourself as a minister of Jesus Christ. You will develop habits and perspectives that will influence how you use your time once you graduate. Therefore, conduct yourself as if you were the minister. Be intentional about holding office hours and use the time to study, pray, and read. Do not forget to use your office hours to learn about ministry from those around you. An important question to guide you is, "If I took a full-time ministry position today, what would I lack confidence and experience with?" Here are some things to consider: interviewing for a job, recruiting volunteers, conducting weddings and funerals, premarital counseling, baptisms, handling responses during the invitation, taxes, personal Bible studies, presenting ideas to elders, training teachers, curriculum, leading the Lord's Supper, planning events, handling a disruptive student, visiting the hospital, or following up with someone who no longer attends worship. Let your answers guide your experiences and conversations.

Beyond the Job Description

Depending on the structure of your internship there may be a variance in the amount of instruction and direct management you are given. Hopefully, regardless of the exact situation, there are clear guidelines and expectations set in place. At the very least, you should do everything you can to meet those expectations. It may seem obvious, but you should do what you can to also go beyond your job description.

If you have extra time because you have completed all your responsibilities, take initiative! Go get coffee with a student who may be struggling, send cards to volunteers, call and pray with a shut-in, study more, find things to tidy up, or go ask your supervisor what more can be done. It's not about burning yourself out but maintaining the correct attitude and taking advantage of the time you have to serve the church and grow.

One additional element you should consider is your relationship with the church leadership. God's design for the church is beautiful, and one of the most special relationships is between godly shepherds and the members of the congregation. While you are an intern at a congregation, you are also a member of the congregation. Part of that includes being shepherded by the elders of the congregation. If the congregation does not have elders—find leaders who are natural pastoral figures that you can seek an intentional relationship with. Godly mentors are crucial to your development as a minister and servant. You will be blessed by the opportunity to sit at the feet of church leaders who have years of experience leading God's people. Grab lunch with them to ask questions, share ideas, and pray. Let their experiences and faith help shape you.

As a youth intern, it will be very easy to isolate yourself to the youth ministry. Remember, God's design of the church includes all ages! If you have the chance to see elements of the church's ministry outside of the youth ministry, you should take it. Go to that breakfast, nursing home service, or whatever opportunities present themselves. Use the occasion to invite a couple of youth who may not go otherwise. Building relationships in other facets of the church only helps you understand the big picture of the church better. In general, congregations consider it a huge blessing to have an intern or maybe even more than one intern. Giving chances to church members to encounter you and get to know you will also be a huge encouragement to them.

Mistakes to Avoid

Wisdom and discernment must trump good intentions. In our years of experience, we have interacted with and supervised many youth interns. We have seen many mistakes that could have been avoided with just a little bit of wisdom or discernment. Here are four mistakes you should avoid:

The first mistake you need to avoid is ministering on an island. Whether you are interning at a congregation with a youth minister or one without a youth minister, you are never alone. Seek the counsel and wisdom of leaders or other mature ministers who can mentor you. Have at least one person who has done ministry who can help you with the following: 1) make sure your event ideas are reasonable, 2) confirm lesson illustrations make sense, and 3) confirm when it is wise to have additional adult volunteers.

Second, and intricately connected to the first, is the hero complex. You are thrilled you are making connections with teens and are able to help them by sharing your experiences with them. That is really great, but make sure you are primarily connecting them *to God* as the one who supplies comfort and help and not you. Jesus is their savior. Remember the best way to help someone long-term is to connect them with God and people in their congregation who can continue to disciple them once your internship is over. In teaching and discussing the Bible, it's completely okay to say, "I do not know." Although you will naturally feel pressure to answer all questions right when they are asked, take the necessary time to study and give a good response if needed.

A third mistake to avoid is not showing love to *all* teens. Who you spend your time with will communicate who you love. We tend to naturally gravitate to people who share our interests and commonalities. Do not spend all your time with the older teens, those who are always at events, or those who do the activities you did in high school. One good practice is to use the ten minutes before Bible class to connect with those who are not as active. Spend time with those who are harder to love or overlooked. Take a genuine interest in what they care about, and you can connect with anyone.

Finally, avoid taking unnecessary risks to build connections. This is one mistake we see way too often. The combination of trying to build friendships with the small age gap between you and the teens will put pressure on you to do immature and risky things. For example, it is one thing to sneak out of your dorm with your college friends versus sneaking out with teens on a youth trip. As an intern, you are in a position of leadership and authority. Whether you like it or not, your actions define what is acceptable behavior to many teens. The music or movies you listen to or watch with them or even reference being a fan of makes a significant impact on them. Do your actions line up with what they are being taught at home and in Bible class? It is also worth noting here it is very unwise to flirt or pursue a dating relationship with anyone in the youth group while you are their intern. Mistakes are going to happen, but fewer will if you allow wisdom and discernment to guide your decisions. A simple question to ask yourself is, "If I was the youth minister, would I be okay with this?" Keep Jesus as your focus, and you will do great!

To the Church

If your congregation has the means to host an intern, we believe you should. An intern, hopefully, will bless your church, but it will also give you the opportunity to disciple a young Christian who desires to be a leader in the church. What a great opportunity and *responsibility* it is to care for someone who loves and desires to lead the church!

Questions to Ask When Interviewing

Individual congregations are autonomous, and the hiring process is certainly not uniform across churches, but at the very least, you should plan to interview your candidates. Some revealing questions to consider in the interview process include the following:

- Why do you want this internship?
- What church are you engaged with where you are in school?
- How do you serve the church now?
- Why are you a follower of Jesus?
- Why do you want to serve in ministry?
- What difference would the internship make in your development?

Compensate Them Well

Depending on your congregation's financial situation, this number will look different, but interns should be paid a competitive wage. Interns are not just cheap labor for your congregation. They are servants of God trying to help you minister to the young people in your community. Internships are crucial for the development of a growing church leader, and they should not be worried about making enough money that summer by accepting the offer to come to work for your church. You should show your interns that you value them and their time. Another way to aid in compensation for interns is to cover their ministry-related expenses (including meals).

Shepherd Your Intern

Ministry is difficult and often a thankless endeavor. Young Christians need encouragement and pastoral care, especially when they are in an official serving capacity at your church. Take every opportunity to not just pray *for* them but to pray *with* them. Check on your interns in a way that shows you care *about them* because they're a part of your flock and not just because they *serve* your flock. If/when the time comes for correction, the relationship is already primed with an aura of spiritual care and not purely a boss/employee relationship.

The Host Family Can Make the Biggest Difference

It's best to host an intern in the home of a loving family at your church. Some congregations are able to provide on-campus housing or an apartment specifically for their interns but living alone can be isolating. Their experience can also be harmful if you choose to host your intern with a family who may have the *house* to host but the wrong *heart* to host. Do not give an open invitation for hosts in your congregation, but specifically target families who have the capacity in their homes *and* their hearts to host. Find a family who will love them as one of their own, respect their privacy, and be willing to provide warm hospitality.

Prioritize Those Who Desire Full-Time Ministry

Hopefully, the goal of your internship is not just to have another worker at your congregation, but rather it is an intentional kingdom effort to help train a young church leader. We think it is important to prioritize interns interested in full-time ministry over those just looking for a summer job and *know* they have no desire to serve the church full-time. Hiring them would still be worthwhile, but choosing one who truly desires to serve a church full-time gives you the opportunity to disciple those who may really need the internship to grow as they pursue a career in ministry.

Love Your Intern

When interns first come to your church, find a way to make

them feel welcome. Maybe it's a meet-and-greet with refreshments for the whole church or something to give the whole congregation a chance to meet them when they arrive. Give them chances to be loved by the whole church throughout the summer. One example is to create a sign-up for people to take them to lunch on certain days. When they leave at the end of their service, commemorate it in your church's own way. Send them off with love and thankfulness! Hopefully, after an internship, an intern would feel comfortable suggesting your internship to other potential candidates in the future because of the way they were loved.

Conclusion

Interns, as you develop the heart of a minister, we hope you will take advantage of opportunities like internships to prepare yourself to serve the church. Congregations, we hope you see the value and responsibility you have to develop and encourage young leaders. We pray all Christians will have the chance to see the beauty, and lasting impact internships can have.

Discussion Questions

1. In what ways might an internship push you outside your comfort zone?
2. What would you include in a job description for an intern?
3. List some mistakes to avoid as an intern.
4. What are some ways a church could encourage or discourage an intern?

Chapter 29
Children's Ministry 101
Thad Looser

If you were to poll a panel of today's parents, it would likely be unanimous that parents identify their children as their most prized possession. God agrees with this notion. The Bible states, "Behold, children are a heritage from the Lord, the fruit of the womb a reward. Like arrows in the hand of a warrior are the children of one's youth. Blessed is the man who fills his quiver with them" (Ps 127:3–5a). Could it also be said that the congregation with a quiver full of them, is blessed? Most certainly.

A children's ministry, in contrast to a youth ministry, is designed to address the spiritual needs of school-aged and early adolescent children and to begin to lay a spiritual foundation for the coming years. If you are reading this book, it is because you are dedicated to God's children and their spiritual development. This chapter will identify three key components of a successful children's ministry: establishing leadership, planning activities, and mindfully ministering to the entire family. Hopefully, you will find some tips that will perpetuate your endeavors to answer your calling.

Establish Leadership

Influential leaders help to guide thriving ministries within the church. Ideally, a person leading your children's ministry should possess the following characteristics:

1. A love for young children
2. An ability to manage a room full of young children
3. A firm foundation in the Word of God
4. The time necessary to remain invested

Love as Jesus Did

The leader of a children's ministry should first love little children. There is no better example to examine for this than that of Jesus Christ. In Matthew 19:13, there is a glimpse of this example. Jesus lived during a time when many people devalued children. While His disciples rebuked those they thought were nuisances, Jesus said, "Let the little children come to me and do not hinder them." A strong children's minister should embody this same approach to children.

Each congregation has members that little children love. They are often like child magnets. Before and after worship services, these "magnetic members" radiate energy to which children gravitate. If you think about this for a moment, you can probably come up with a name of a person you know that fits this description. These members are often adults who frequently smile because communing with children is like breathing life into their bones. They sometimes give candy but always give warm hugs. Their personality screams, "I am open to blessing your life and bringing joy to your day."

On the flip side, children also know the adults from whom they stay far away. These people look down on them or raise suspicious eyebrows when children are present. These people rarely smile and usually keep to themselves. Watch the children; they will reveal those in the church family who fit the description and qualify to lead a children's ministry for the congregation. Let me share a note of caution. While young people may often know who to trust and who not to trust, in today's world, I highly recommend that you do background checks on all who work with the children in your congregation. Children can also be deceived (cf. Eph 4:14).

Chaos Manager

A children's minister must also have an uncanny ability to control a room full of children, regardless of age or circumstance. This person will be the primary voice guiding the thoughts and attitudes of your children during any given worship service. Things can become chaotic very quickly if they cannot control the room. If this occurs, learning cannot effectively take place. Often, these people already have a knack for teaching children either inside the church as experienced Bible-class teachers or outside the church in various positions or roles. It does not necessarily have to be a person who has it all figured out but must certainly be someone willing to learn, adapt, and improve their teaching style.

Rooted in the Word

Perhaps you have heard the phrase, "Children are like sponges." It is very accurate! They remember anything you teach them, including the good, the bad, and the ugly. Children can ask profound and relevant questions. Often, even the most knowledgeable among us can be stumped by a child. That is why it is essential to have someone leading them who is firmly grounded in the Word of God. They need someone who does not make answers when faced with a difficult question. Leaders should have a firm grasp of Bible basics because there are extreme consequences for those who lead young people astray (Matt 18:5–6).

Your Primary Focus

The children's minister does not necessarily have to be an employee financially supported by the congregation. Some congregations have a children's minister who is a part-time employee (partially financially supported by the church but working less than 40 hours per week). A children's ministry committee is also an adequate substitution if one person does not wish to serve independently. Having noted these options, in an ideal world, the children's minister would be a fully supported employee of the congregation who can focus his or her attention completely on the spiritual growth of the children of the congregation and their families.

Many elderships mistakenly assume a solution to the conundrum is simply asking the middle and high school youth minister to take on this role. While many may be qualified, they need more time to invest in both effectively. Children are going through entirely different circumstances in life than teenagers and flourish best with someone who is fully invested in them. Likewise, younger children deserve someone who can focus on their interests. Often, church members who work with children have a job separate from the church. That is okay as long as there is a high degree of focus and intentionality related to their role of ministering to young children.

Plan Activities

Once leadership is assigned, it's time to get busy. Speaking of busy, one of the challenges of today's families is that they are very busy, often too busy. Children are involved in school events, travel ball, video games, social media, and much more. While none of these are wrong in and of themselves, too many distractions compete to take children's attention away from the most important thing: staying connected to the Father! A well-developed children's ministry will intentionally work to provide consistent opportunities to grow closer to God while having fun. You may find the following tips helpful in your efforts to accomplish that task:

1. Be intentional about developing a consistent curriculum
2. Plan opportunities for spiritual growth and service
3. Plan fun activities
4. Do not be cheap

Note of Caution: Remember to not plan so many activities that families do not have time to just be together and be family (we can become part of the problem instead of the solution).

Curriculum Consistency

Once the right minister or ministry team is established, their first job is to develop consistency in the Bible-class curriculum across all age levels. This continuity helps the child to develop a sense of chronology within the Bible and its series of events and the themes that run throughout God's message. It is not uncommon to find a fourth-grade class deep in the story of Noah while a second-grade class is learning about the journeys of Paul. It also assures that children get the full breadth of knowledge that they need instead of just focusing on a few areas of Scripture.

Consider taking a broad look at your curriculum in its entirety. You and your team can use a few planning sessions to develop your vision of the Bible classes for all ages. Take time to identify the lessons and learning activities for each lesson and clearly understand how long it will take a child to get through the whole curriculum. One of the best things you can do for your team is to clearly define what a child should know and value when they complete the curriculum and write a map to reach those goals. Depending on the child's age and entry into the curriculum, many children will have the opportunity to complete similar lessons multiple times before graduating into the youth group. This consistency across all ages and all platforms will be beneficial in helping these lessons stick long-term.

Spiritual Growth and Service

The most important job of a children's minister is to help the children grow spiritually and develop an attitude of service like Jesus. These efforts go well beyond Bible classes and VBS. This can be accomplished in various ways, but the main thing is to continue being innovative and flexible. A few examples of learning and fun activities for your children might be weekly or monthly service projects, serving food for your widows and widowers, or hosting devotionals in which both a craft activity and a Bible story are included. In the fall season, ask children to paint or carve pumpkins that focus on a particular Bible story. You could also share an object lesson at a congregational potluck meal or plan a night where kids learn about animals and tie it to Biblical truths. The sky is truly the limit. Be creative!

Bring the Fun

Fun and engaging activities help develop an environment where children are more at ease and eventually able to absorb messages presented by the Word of God. It is no secret that children are often interested in attending events that are more entertaining. A few examples of fun activities for your children might be a movie night, outside games during the summer, a craft night, a fall festival, going to a local park, making gingerbread houses, a back-to-school gathering, eating ice cream after a Sunday night service, fishing, a celebration party for new Christians, bowling, meals after worship services, and family fun nights. Search within the culture and preferences of your congregation and find activities that will best benefit your children and families.

Do Not Be Cheap

Sufficient funding is necessary for any ministry, and a children's ministry is no exception. An investment in your children is an investment in your future. Many congregations do an excellent job financially supporting foreign missions, and they should. Jesus said, "Go into all the world." (Mark 16:15). However, doesn't "all" the world begin at home? Funds must be poured into the children of your local congregation first. In addition, when others see your congregation is serious about investing monetarily into the children, new families will join, and contributions will rise (and you can do more foreign mission work). The Lord will provide (Phil 4:19).

Minister to the Entire Family

For any Christian, support from the body of Christ equates to a more significant chance of spiritual survival. That is especially true for children. If a parent, sibling, or guardian is there to help, encourage, and nurture their spiritual growth, the devil has much more work cut out for him. The most important job for you as a children's minister is to get the family involved. While the children's minister is a small part of the "village" that helps children reach their full potential in the Lord, the responsibility ultimately falls on the parents. After all, who is asked to "train up a child in the way he should go"? (Prov 22:6) A child's home life is an outstanding predictor of future faithfulness. You can help cultivate this familial support in the following ways:

1. Communicate with parents
2. Delegate to parents
3. Plan activities that include the family
4. Connect Church and Home

I would also encourage you to brag on the parents every chance you get. It not only will encourage the parents but it will also encourage children to respect and value their parents.

Communicate with Parents

How many issues in the world today could be solved by having better communication skills? I suspect that several could. You can begin parent communication by knowing each child and connecting with each child's parent or guardian. Younger children depend on their parents or guardians to get them to church activities. For teens, it is slightly different. By that age, they all typically have phones, and many can even drive themselves to worship and events. A child's attendance and participation directly depend on the parent's decision to commit to the cause of Christ. Additionally, if the parents are not aware of an activity or event, it is unlikely that the child will either. Young children rely on their parents' commitment, and parents rely on the minister's communication.

Begin by obtaining the contact information of every parent. Add them to a messaging group and keep a line of constant communication. If they have their child at church for an event, send a message of praise, letting them know their presence was valued. If they are absent, you can text them to let them know they were missed. Using this method, the parents begin recognizing that their attendance and participation are both wanted and appreciated. They will even begin to proactively notify you if they cannot make it for an activity. Consider making newsletters for each family so they can keep up with upcoming activities. When a more significant event is planned, send an individual invitation and RSVP message to each family. Another idea is to create slides that are scrolled on a projection screen before and after worship services with announcements. It is vital to keep everyone "in the know."

Delegate to Parents

Another way to involve the family is to learn how to delegate.

Search for ways to get the parents involved. If something needs to be decorated, ask for help. If you need to organize an event, ask for assistance. Figure out what each parent's talents are and use them. Some parents would love the opportunity to plan a craft. Other parents would enjoy the opportunity to speak or teach. Even when given small jobs, parents find themselves connected to the ministry, becoming more involved in the spiritual growth of their children. The more voices involved in your children's education, the more connected the children will be to your church family.

Include the Entire Family

A children's ministry is not a babysitting service. There will undoubtedly be times when you will need the children independently, without their parents. However, including the whole family in activities benefits everyone for many reasons. When children see their parents having fun and participating in events, service projects, and devotionals, they will be more likely to engage with the lesson and learn. Parents also need to fellowship with one another in order to stay connected. Those connections are often only made if young families have opportunities to come together before their children are in their teenage years.

Connecting Church and Home

The most valuable mission trip a parent will ever take is down the hall to their children's bedroom for a Bible study and time of prayer to the Father. How can a children's minister help with this? Consider sending out a nightly devotional thought for parents to read and study with their children before bed. Ideally, these devotional themes will mimic what the children are already learning in their Bible classes at church. This process facilitates the connection between church and home. If a child is learning about Peter at church, how much more valuable will that lesson be if Peter is the focus of conversation at home too?

Conclusion

Offering an active children's ministry should be a top priority for the church because nothing is more critical than preserving God's children. The way to keep young adults and late teens from leaving the church is to provide every opportunity you can for them while they are as young as possible. A grounded child will later become a rooted adult. You can help with this effort and make a difference in the lives of the children around you. May God bless you in your calling to minister to His children.

Discussion Questions

1. What are a few of your most valuable earthly possessions? What would you do to protect them?
2. Why is it important for children to be "active" in the church before they reach middle and high school?
3. Why is it essential to involve the entire family as much as possible?
4. Name a few members in your congregation that have a unique way with children. What made you choose these people?
5. In today's society, what are common stumbling blocks for our children?
6. What are the pros and cons of providing a children's ministry to your congregation?
7. What are some "deep questions" you have heard children ask before?
8. How can you connect your parents to a children's ministry?
9. How can you turn a fun activity into a spiritual growth opportunity?
10. Name some reasons we might lose our youth to the world after high school.

Chapter 30
College and Young Professional Ministry 101
Will Sharp

Have you ever wondered how extraordinary it is when a high school student goes off to college? It is a major step in the process of "adulting." In many instances (not always the case), the 18-year-old student will leave his or her parents for the first time, live in a different city, have a roommate for the first time, live with a stranger, and must now take care of themselves with no parental supervision. The transition to college age may seem bizarre when reading it, but this is what we do as parents when it is time for our children to go off to college, or they decide to work a professional job.

Enter the Lord's church. The church must be active in the lives of college students. Why? If students are going to search for answers or lean on someone for strength, it needs to be the church of our Savior. The church and her leaders need to recognize this and take action to assist our young Christian adults. So, here are four basic principles or practices for the day-to-day work with college and young professionals that you, as a leader, can use and build upon in your local church.

Connection

Author, Chuck Bomar, observes, "They want more than a ministry to go to. They want to be connected to your Church as a whole."[1] Students want connection, and they are searching for that connection. Is the church providing that? How do we go about giving them the connection that they desire? The concept is twofold: connecting to the Word and connecting to the church. As the student goes from high school to adulthood in college (living by themselves and having more responsibilities), their faith reaches a different area, one that is no longer their family's faith but one they call their own. When a student begins to develop his or her faith, you can step in as a leader and member of your church. You have a challenging goal in front of you in which you can fulfill that need of connecting them to the Word of God.

Barna's research has found that 31% of practicing Christian students have interests in developing themselves professionally while integrating faith that they can apply to their career field.[2] Depending on whether you believe that percentage to be positive or negative, the church can meet the needs of many Christian students who want to be spiritually fed. Feeding college students and young professionals spiritually can be done by having an avenue in which ministers, members, Christian professors, and experts in their field serve both as mentors and as teachers who encourage discussion more so than just delivering lectures. The church can help students and young professionals connect to God's Word through guest speakers, personal Bible studies, small group settings, and conversations over coffee with mature adult Christian mentors.

One of the best avenues for helping young adults to connect to one another and to God is providing them with their own Bible class at least once per week. There is great value in worship and study with multiple generations, but there is also value in their being able to study with those their age. They are visual learners who frequently value discussion and deserve well-prepared and thought-out classes. Videos are valuable for unlocking discussion, but it is important that they are taught how to study and interpret Scripture and to apply it to the problems they are dealing with. It is important for teachers to take the time to get to know their students and what their questions and struggles are.

You also want them to connect to the church. Connection is made through many of the things already mentioned. Leaders need to have conversations with students; these do not always need to be theological conversations. Remember, we want to connect with them and have them connect to the church. Students connect to the Church when they are involved in the church. You give them a role, have them use their talents for the Lord, and get them to participate in an area that draws on their passions. One thing we do not want them to feel is aloneness.

> Not everyone reacts to aloneness in the same way. For example, some feel lonely, while others don't (or say they don't). Whether lonely or not, everyone is affected somehow by aloneness because we were designed to be with others.[3]

Relationships

Relationships and connectedness go hand in hand with Christian students and the church. Having a positive Christian relationship (i.e., mentor or friend) with college-aged students and young professionals takes time and effort. Take time and meditate on how much emphasis is put on others in the New Testaments, especially with the "one another" statements. The Apostle Paul wrote many of these, but two stand out; Galatians 6:2 and 1 Thessalonians 5:11. Paul writes to the church in Galatia, "Bear one another's burdens, and so fulfill the law of Christ." Writing about transgressions and temptations, Paul urges the church to help one another. Being a college student is stressful and full of anxiety; figuring out where one belongs and so much more is difficult. The church builds the relationship by helping students carry the load.

1 Thessalonians 5:11 states, "Therefore encourage one another

and build one another up, just as you are doing." Congregations are not to just encourage one individual one time and call it a day. Paul instructs them to continue to encourage and build up one another. Knowing what young adults go through, encouraging and building up goes a long way toward helping them to overcome and to keep their faith. So, in what ways can the church bear the burdens of college students and encourage them? Here are a few examples: Intentional mentorship by other members of the church, having an adopt a student program that enables members to build relationships and connect with the students, and incorporating students and young professionals into the other areas of ministry and small groups within the church.

In his book *Thriving at College*, Alex Chediak writes specifically to college-aged individuals on the importance of relationships. He states, "Relationships matter. A lot. Who you choose as your friends and mentor will permanently shape who you become. If you walk with the wise, you'll become wise."[4] If it is vital for students and young professionals to have positive relationships, then it should be our goal to be proactive in making sure this comes to fruition. One of the day-to-day aspects of the ministry to college-aged individuals is building relationships, and for this to happen, churches do not need to wait for the student or young adult to take the first step.

Leadership

Colossians 3:15–17 states,

> And let the peace of Christ rule in your hearts, to which indeed you were called in one body. And be thankful. Let the word of Christ dwell in you richly, teaching and admonishing one another in all wisdom, singing psalms and hymns and spiritual songs, with thankfulness in your hearts to God. And whatever you do, in word or deed, do everything in the name of the Lord Jesus, giving thanks to God the Father through him.

Today's society may perceive leadership as merely giving commands to others. However, that is not the case. Leadership influences the thoughts, behaviors, and development of individuals in your care. It recognizes that Jesus is the true leadership model. The type of leadership that should be applied is servant leadership and leadership begins with the heart.[5]

One of the aspects of this principle is the leadership of the students. When it comes to the practicality of college ministry and young professionals, the church needs to let young adults have ownership. When handing over some ownership to students, the church positively influences their development and behavior. A young adult given this responsibility will see that the church cares for their soul and values their input. What type of student and young professional should the church look for as a leader? The process of selecting students who are full of F-A-I-T-H can be a valuable tool.[6] These students are faithful, available, have initiative, are teachable, and have a heart for God and people.

The second aspect of this principle is the leadership of the church. Reading the New Testament, we can see how the church constantly strives to meet the needs of people (Jas 1:27; Heb 13:3; Acts 6:1–7; Acts 2:32–45). Is the church meeting the needs of college students and young professionals? This happens when the church is building connections, encouraging relationships, and has leaders in place who clearly value this age group. The church also needs to provide training in spiritual leadership and opportunities to put leadership into practice. What seems to come up when discussing college students and young professionals is their role in the church. However, the other side of the equation is the role the church should have in the lives of students. Leading this age group is about creating a sense of togetherness, empowering others by being present, being accountable for the ministry's mission, and being a mentor.[7]

Service

The last principle of the college and young professional ministry is service. The principle of service is broad. Young adults are driven to serve others. They will often readily volunteer for service projects, mission trips, and feeding the homeless. Providing them with opportunities will have a powerful impact on their spiritual development. Yet, as you think about the term "service," contemplate not only the students' service to the church and community but also how the church serves students.

> Service is one of the hallmarks of college-age ministry—but not the kind of service that might come to your mind. Instead of trying to plug college-age people into the Church by having them serve, leaders need to focus on serving college-age people.[8]

Regarding the church, to serve the college and young professionals, the church must recognize if they make this age group feel welcome or build walls. An overprotective, shallow, anti-science, repressive, and exclusive approach will encourage college and young professionals to look elsewhere for a church family.[9]

College students and young professionals are valuable members of the Lord's church. Ben Trueblood writes on the importance of the church and college-aged students:

> Being part of a church is an essential part of your college experience. There are statistics galore about the number of college students that leave the church during their college years, as well as arguments back and forth on the accuracy of the number. What we do know is that 70–80 percent of students who attended a church while in high school will not attend church for an extended period of time during their college years.[10]

College students and young professionals have talents and resources that the church may fail to recognize. Having a place for them to utilize those talents and resources will not only encourage the congregation but may decrease the percentage of students who do not attend church while in college. Serving the needs of college students and young professionals will serve the church's needs and build a community that helps young adults keep their focus on God.

Conclusion

"For even the Son of Man came not to be served but to serve, and to give his life as a ransom for many" (Mark 10:45). Jesus exemplifies servant leadership as He specifically explains His purpose and mission. When it comes to college and young professional ministry, is the church modeling after Christ, embodying the mission of serving others? College and young professional ministry is a unique area, as it involves young adults searching for answers, figuring out where they belong in the world, and what path they want to take as a career.

The practical concepts of connection, relationships, leadership, and service apply to college students and young professionals in day-to-day ministry. The four principles are, of course, not an all-inclusive list of what the ministry to young adults looks like, but these four principles can be a guide or a foundation for what you, a leader, can use to improve this type of ministry. Understand that college students and young professionals long to connect to the church. If we as leaders fail to build a community for young adults, we fail a key part of the church's mission to serve others.

Discussion Questions

1. Discuss some of the problems and issues you have faced in college or as a young adult. What role can the church have in helping students during these difficult times?

2. The Principle of Connection: Take a minute and consider relevant spiritual topics for this age group. What are they? Regarding connecting to the church, what areas of your congregation can students focus on and better the church spiritually?
3. The Principle of Relationships: What setting do you believe is the best to cultivate a positive spiritual relationship with students and church members? What obstacles might be in place when trying to pursue building these relationships?
4. The Principle of Leadership: What other tools, like the F-A-I-T-H leadership tool, could determine college and young professional ministry leaders? What characteristics of a student leader are vital for this type of ministry?
5. The Principle of Service: How can you serve the needs of college students as a church leader? How can you, as a college student, serve the church? Develop a form that lists all the areas one can serve in the church and disseminate the form to students and young professionals.

Notes

[1] Chuck Bomar, *College Ministry from Scratch: A Practical Guide to Start and Sustain a Successful College Ministry* (Grand Rapids, MI: Zondervan, 2010), 21.

[2] "Do Christian Students Want Spiritual Growth from College?" Barna Group, 4 September 2018, https://www.barna.com/research/spiritual-growth-college/.

[3] J. Budziszewski, *How to Stay Christian in College* (Colorado Springs, CO: Think, 2004), 23.

[4] Alex Chediak, *Thriving at College: Make great friends, keep your faith, and get ready for the real world* (Carol Stream, IL: Tyndale House, 2011), 85.

[5] Kenneth Blanchard, *Lead like Jesus: Lessons for Everyone from the Greatest Leadership Role Model of All Time* (Nashville, TN: Thomas Nelson, 2016), Ebook edition, ch. 1.2.

[6] Steve Shadrach, *The Fuel and the Flame: Ten Keys to Ignite Your College Campus for Jesus Christ* (Tyrone, GA: Authentic Publishing, 2003), 181–183.

[7] C. Gene Wilkes, *Jesus on Leadership: Timeless Wisdom on Servant Leadership* (Carol Stream, IL: Tyndale House, 2011), Ebook edition, ch. 8.2.

[8] Chuck Bomar, *College Ministry 101: A Guide to Working with 18–25 Year Olds* (Grand Rapids, MI: Zondervan, 2009), 175.

[9] David Kinnaman, *You Lost Me: Why Young Christians Are Leaving Church ... and Rethinking Faith* (Grand Rapids, MI: Baker Books, 2016), 92–93.

[10] Ben Trueblood, *A Different College Experience: Following Christ in College* (Nashville, TN: B&H Publishing, 2019), Ebook edition, ch. 5.1. Though his research is becoming somewhat dated, Flavil Yeakley seems to show that the adolescent departure numbers are smaller in churches of Christ (cf. *Why They Left*, 2012).

Bibliography

Barna Group. "*Do Christian Students Want Spiritual Growth from College?*" 4 September 2018, https://www.barna.com/research/spiritual-growth-college/.

Blanchard, Kenneth H., and Phil Hodges. *Lead like Jesus: Lessons for Everyone from the Greatest Leadership Role Model of All Time* Nashville, TN: Thomas Nelson, 2016. Ebook edition.

Bomar, Chuck. *College Ministry 101: A Guide to Working with 18–25 Year Olds*. Grand Rapids, MI: Zondervan, 2009.

_____. *College Ministry from Scratch: A Practical Guide to Start and Sustain a Successful College Ministry*. Grand Rapids, MI: Youth Specialties/Zondervan, 2010.

Budziszewski, J. *How to Stay Christian in College*. Colorado Springs, CO: THINK Books, 2004.

Chediak, Alex, Alex Harris, and Brett Harris. *Thriving at College: Make Great Friends, Keep Your Faith, and Get Ready for the Real World!* Carol Stream, IL: Tyndale House, 2011.

Kinnaman, David, and Aly Hawkins. *You Lost Me: Why Young Christians Are Leaving Church ... and Rethinking Faith* Grand Rapids, MI: Baker Books, 2016.

Shadrach, Steve. *The Fuel and the Flame: Ten Keys to Ignite Your College Campus for Jesus Christ*. Tyrone, GA: Authentic Publishing, 2003.

Trueblood, Ben, and Brian Mills. *A Different College Experience: Following Christ in College*. Nashville, TN: B&H Publishing Group, 2019. Ebook edition.

Wilkes, C. Gene. *Jesus on Leadership: Timeless Wisdom on Servant Leadership*. Carol Stream, IL: Tyndale House, 2011. Ebook edition.

Chapter 31
Ministry to Special Needs Children and Families
Justin and Tiffany Guin

Sterling and Emily walk into the building smiling, glossing over the chaos they endured earlier that Sunday morning. Their twelve-year-old daughter, Kate, melted down over something unknown to her parents. Kate has Autism Spectrum Disorder and is nonverbal. They frantically tried to figure out what triggered their daughter, and after an hour, Kate calmed down when given her favorite toy and some YouTube time. They finished getting ready for Bible study and worship when everything seemed okay.

The family arrived in time for Bible class. Their other children went to their classes, and they took Kate into the auditorium class with the older adults. Due to the morning's developments, they have nowhere else to take her, and they are afraid to let her go with her younger brother to class as she does on occasion. Her father locates the nearest exit, and they sit down on the last row if they need to take Kate out of the assembly. Her mother seems calm on the outside but is anxious on the inside. She does not want to be the family that disrupts Bible study and distracts others. Would there be a repeat of this morning's events? They know the church understands their situation and loves them, providing comfort and reassurance. But they are stressed nonetheless—just another typical

Sunday morning in raising a special needs child and getting their family to worship.

If you posed this scenario to families raising a special needs child in your congregation, they probably could relate to this story. It is difficult for any family to attend Bible classes, worship, and other church events. This task is especially challenging for those with special needs children. Unfortunately, many special needs parents have endured negative experiences in church settings. Amy Fenton Lee is a leading researcher and developer of special needs ministry. In her work, *Leading a Special Needs Ministry*, she interviewed dozens of parents of children with special needs. After this study concluded, she noted, "I discovered that by and large the source of the greatest relational bruising for these parents had been the church" (Lee 2016, 4). Consequently, many of these families choose to remain unaffiliated with any religious group because they feel isolated and a burden on the local church. An unkind word, mistreatment of their child, and other hurtful experiences have left this relational "bruise," and they feel unwelcome among the body of Christ.

This critique must not be true of the Lord's church. Every family must have a sense of belonging and know the congregation and its leadership value them. Such an attitude and approach follow the footsteps of our Lord. He regularly served individuals with "special needs" by today's standards. When John the Baptist's disciples asked if Jesus was the Messiah, our Lord replied, "Go and tell John what you hear and see: the blind receive their sight and the lame walk, lepers are cleansed and the deaf hear and the dead are raised up, and the poor have the good news preached to them" (Matt 11:4–5, ESV). Ministering to people with special needs was a defining characteristic of Jesus's ministry. Thus, the church must prioritize serving special needs families in their youth and family ministry.

The Impetus for Special Needs Ministry

Ask any K12 educator, and they will tell you there has been an increase in kids diagnosed with various developmental disorders. According to the latest data provided by the CDC, 1 in 6 children aged 3–17 is diagnosed with a developmental disability, which includes ADHD, ADD, Autism Spectrum Disorder, and other intellectual and physical disorders. The most significant increase in diagnoses is Autism Spectrum Disorder. In 2000, 1 in 150 children were diagnosed with ASD. In 2018, this number increased to 1 in 44, an increase of over 300%. Awareness of these developmental disorders helps the child in numerous ways, from social to educational development. Schools are more willing to test an individual if a need in the classroom arises.

Special needs issues affect congregations no matter the size of the church. This increase in diagnoses added with other disabilities, such as physical ones, creates a need in your youth ministries that must be addressed. How does the Lord's church minister to these children and their families? How does the body of Christ create an atmosphere of inclusion and belonging? What supports can the church have in their ministry plan to help strengthen their family and provide resources for their specific needs? However you answer these questions, one thing is sure, you need to have a plan in place. The church needs to develop a "we-are-in-this-with-you" type of relationship because most parents experience anxiety over whether or not the church will accept and accommodate their child with special needs (Lee 2016, 7-8).

Supporting Parents Raising a Child with Special Needs

Raising children is a stressful yet rewarding experience. The phrase, "It takes a village," is true to a certain extent. Even non-religious people understand the value of community for raising children. The phrase is better written, "It takes a church." The body of Christ seeks to strengthen each other and should be a place of edification, not anxiety. Read the end of Paul's letters and the names he mentions that helped him in his mission work (cf. Rom 16:3–16). The family of faith is one of God's most valuable resources for all people, especially for parents. As noted earlier, parents raising children with disabilities feel isolated and long for a sense of community. It is imperative for the church to fill this need. What are some practices that will help your ministries take an active role in supporting them?

Space to Vent

First, give these parents a space to grieve and vent without feeling judged. *Webster's Dictionary* defines grief as "deep and poignant distress caused by or as if by bereavement." Any sense of loss of expectation can cause grief. Whether diagnosed in utero or later in life, special-needs parents undergo grief. Their previous expectations for their child are gone, and the path is unclear. This situation creates feelings of both anxiety and grief. This author can speak from experience. When Tiffany was pregnant with Afton, we had expectations and hopes for her like any parent. When Afton was ten months old, it was apparent something was wrong as she was falling developmentally behind her peers. Later, she was diagnosed with epilepsy and Autism Spectrum Disorder. She is nonverbal and on the lower-functioning end of the spectrum. It devasted us. When Afton was about three years old, my wife stated, "You've finally stopped grieving Afton's disability." Upon reflection, Tiffany was right. I went through the grief stages, which was a difficult time. It was not until we went to an early intervention preschool that I felt I had a place to vent, allowing me to work through my grief. We also connected with other parents in similar situations. The Bell Center was an invaluable resource for both Afton and her parents. Having a place to work through the psychological effects of Afton's diagnosis put us on the path of healing and acceptance.

The church needs to be this resource for parents as they work through their grief. Romans 12:15 commands, "Rejoice with those who rejoice, weep with those who weep." Support during a time of loss is vital. During these times, resist trying to talk them through their frustrations and emotions. If a parent is hopeful, do not judge them for being in denial of their child's disability. If they are grieving, do not urge them to look on the bright side (Lee 2016, 20). Walk with them and listen. They need someone who will love them and seek to understand why they are grieving. Communicate to them, "I am with you," and you are safe to express anything to me (Williams and Williams 1996, 15). Occasionally, grief will come back, especially when their child misses milestone events their peers are celebrating. Thus, they will continually need this source of strength in their lives. Do not discount the importance of a simple text saying, "I am praying for you as you raise your son or daughter."

Not a Burden

Second, let these parents know their child is not a burden on you or your youth and family ministry. All churches must have a culture of acceptance and compassion. Do not assume parents of children with special needs know this to be true. Communicate it with them directly. Let them know the resources you have in place so they can rest assured their child is safe with you and your ministry team. Be sure to interact with their child regularly. A kind word to their child or including them in some of your activities significantly impacts these families. Understand the child may not interact with you, and he or she may avoid any physical touch. Do not let this be a deterrent. Learn their boundaries and seek to interact appropriately with them. These practices let the parents know you value and love their child.

Know Their Needs

Third, know the specific needs a child with disabilities has and let the parents know you are taking appropriate precautions in Bible classes and youth trips. Many children with special needs in the school system have an Individualized Health Plan (IHP). In this document, an authorized medical professional discloses the child's allergies, health issues, or triggers, such as seizures. Perhaps something comparable would be beneficial for your youth ministry. If a parent feels comfortable disclosing this information with you, it can be placed on file for the child's benefit. Remember that confidentiality is critical. This information must only be shared with those who *regularly* assist the child should their parents not be with you.

Ask the Parents

Fourth, ask the child's parents about any behavioral issues. If you have a child in your ministry diagnosed with Autism Spectrum Disorder (ASD), Attention-Deficit/Hyperactivity Disorder (ADHD), or Oppositional Defiance Disorder (ODD), you need to know what triggers an episode and how to address it if a parent is not with you. Also, it will help you limit exposure to situations that might set off a child. An ounce of prevention is worth more than a pound of cure. When dealing with a behavioral situation, patience and consistency are key. Knowing how to handle it beforehand will help you appropriately deal with it when it occurs. It also enables you to build trust with the parents because they know you strive to provide a safe place for their child.

Special needs parents seek belonging for their whole family. The church must not neglect them. Someone rightly noted, "When an entire segment of the population remains absent from the body of believers, that community not only remains less than it *could* be, it remains less than it was *intended* to be" (Barnes 2012, 85). Let us be diligent in reaching out and ministering to these families.

Practical Suggestions for Ministering to Children with Special Needs

As with any ministry, you need a plan to be effective; the struggle is knowing where to begin. The school system is the only point of reference most special needs parents have. The local school has some transferable ideas to help you implement a ministry plan for children with special needs.

Developing a Mission Approach and Team

What do you hope to accomplish through your ministry to special needs ministry? Crystalize the mission in a well-crafted purpose statement. As you develop a mission statement, remember your goal is not developmental progress. You are not with the child consistently enough to help developmentally, and you do not have access to an Individualized Education Plan used by the education system for this purpose (IEP). Although, there may be value in working with the parents, Bible class teachers, and members of your ministry team to develop an Individualized Biblical Education Plan for each child. Developmental progress requires hours of work with trained professionals such as special education teachers, ABA therapists, and others. You aim to provide a safe environment for the child to learn and experience God's love.

Also, develop a team approach to this ministry. There are people in your local church who are invaluable resources. You may have a combination of special education teachers, paraprofessionals, therapists, and others who work daily with children with special needs. They can provide insight and expertise that will aid you as you seek to minister to them. Perhaps God has brought them to the kingdom for such a time as this.

Facilities

In 1990, the *Americans with Disabilities Act* was passed, ensuring that all public facilities must be ADA-compliant. All facilities built after this date must meet ADA standards, including building access, restrooms, handicapped parking, etc. The church needs to make sure our facilities meet these codes and are handicap friendly for all people, no matter their age.

In addition to being ADA compliant, one thing you can add to your building is a sensory room. This room has all kinds of things children with special needs enjoy. Most items are things that are tacitly stimulating or calming. We made one of these available a few years ago at our church building, and it has become one of the most popular rooms for our students with special needs and other children in the congregation. They all use this room after services to play together. It is wonderful to watch all children play together regardless of ability.

Inclusion

One concept commonly used in the education setting is inclusion. Inclusion refers to combining typically developed children with children with special needs in a classroom setting (Barnes 2012, 83). You need some type of inclusion plan for your Bible classes. How much time will the child spend with their typically developed peers? Do you have a sensory room or another place you can take them if they only spend a portion of their time with their regular Bible class? An inclusion plan will help the teacher better prepare for everyone and provide an effective learning environment for all involved.

Conclusion: The Blessing of Ministering to Children with Special Needs

Ministering to children with special needs is no small task. It requires planning and patience. These suggestions will aid you in creating an atmosphere of inclusion and acceptance for families with children with disabilities. Walk with these parents and love their children. Be the support they need to raise their children in the discipline and instruction of the Lord (Eph 6:1), and their faith will be strengthened. Celebrate any milestone, no matter how insignificant it may seem. Create an atmosphere of acceptance. If you do these things, your ministry will reach those who are underserved and will be stronger because of their involvement. The church will be strengthened. Most importantly, God will be glorified.

Discussion Questions

1. What might life be like on a day-to-day basis for parents of children with special needs (be specific), and how can your congregation do a better job of encouraging them?
2. What are some things your congregation could do to prepare your Bible class teachers to better minister to children with special needs?
3. What changes need to be made to your congregation's facilities to accommodate those with special needs?
4. What benefit would a sensory room be in your congregation's facilities? What are some ways you can use this so that typically developed children and special needs children can interact with each other?
5. What are some special events you could plan for special needs children and adults in your congregation?
6. How could you develop an Individualized Bible Education Plan for special needs children in your congregation? What resources would be needed to develop this plan?

Bibliography

Barnes, Alyssa M. "Open Hearts, Open Minds, Open Doors:

Including Children with Special Needs in Ministry." *Christian Education Journal* 9 (2012): 81–100.

Lee, Amy Fenton. *Leading a Special Needs Ministry*. Nashville, TN: Broadman & Holman, 2016.

Merriam-Webster Dictionary. Rev. ed. Springfield, MA: Merriam-Webster Inc., 2022.

U.S. Centers for Disease Control and Prevention. cdc.gov.

Williams, Don, and Ron Williams. *Walking with Those Who Weep: A Guide to Grief Support*. Killen, AL: RonDon Books, 1996.

Chapter 32
After the Youth Group
Preparing Students for Sustained Faithfulness
Andrew Kingsley

The Case of the Missing 18–29-Year-Olds

"*Where are they?*" Mark waited by the door for the fifth Sunday in a row, hoping to finally catch them at a worship service this summer. He tried not to look anxious as he greeted the members trickling in, but he was starting to get worried about the majority of the college students. As the youth minister, Mark felt a sense of responsibility to continue encouraging the students after they had graduated from the youth group. Sure, a few of the students came back from their first year of college every summer just as faithful as ever—some even more so! But unfortunately, that was not the case for over half of them.

"*Where are they?*" The opening song was starting now and Mark was standing alone in the foyer holding the door open with hopes that they were just running late. As he stood alone, he remembered his time with these students back in their youth group days. For some of these missing students, it had only been a year since Mark had seen them full of excitement about their faith and God's mission for them. But that was when they were in the youth group.

Today, for the fifth week in a row, they were gone, and Mark was beginning to wonder if they would ever be back.

The story here is hypothetical but the reality of missing 18–29-year-olds in churches across the U.S. is quite real. The numbers are alarming, to say the least. According to recent research, 64–66% of Christian teenagers in the U.S. who are active in a church youth group leave the church for at least a year during their time in college (Kinnaman, 2019; Earls, 2019). As if this stat alone was not enough cause for alarm, the number of disappearing young adults among Christian churches has actually been trending upward in the last ten years (about a 5% increase altogether per Kinnaman, 2019). Unfortunately, this problem seems to cross most denominational (and nondenominational) lines. Thankfully, some of these disappearing students find their way back to the church before they graduate college. Others come back in their 30s when they start having children of their own. Sadly, many do not come back at all.

"Where are they?" This is a question that our church leaders (present and future) cannot afford to ignore. Whether you are reading this book as a seasoned youth minister looking for encouragement or as someone who is preparing to start serving as a youth minister soon, this chapter is intended to be an encouragement to you. My hope and prayer is that this chapter will encourage you to think deeply and prayerfully about how we may work toward producing sustained faithfulness in middle and high school followers of Christ. To that end, this chapter contains four simple suggestions:

1. build a *mindset* that *focuses on* sustained faithfulness,
2. build a *curriculum* that *teaches* sustained faithfulness,
3. build a *calendar* that *facilitates* sustained faithfulness,
4. build *relationships* that *demonstrate* sustained faithfulness.

Suggestion 1: Build a *Mindset* that *Focuses* on Sustained Faithfulness.

If we hope to keep our young people involved in the church when they leave the youth group, we (as youth ministers, parents, elders, and deacons) must start thinking about equipping students for sustained faithfulness long before they graduate. One of the very first steps in building sustained faithfulness in our youth ministries is to set our minds on sustained faithfulness as *the primary goal* of our youth ministries.

At the end of Colossians 1, Paul tells his readers why he chooses to work and suffer for the ministry given to him by God. In verses 28–29, he writes,

> Him [Christ] we proclaim, warning everyone and teaching everyone with all wisdom, that we may present everyone mature in Christ. For this I toil, struggling with all his energy that he powerfully works within me.

Paul's focus is quite clear here. Notice that Paul's ministry is focused on working *towards* the spiritual maturity of the members of the church (Olbricht, 2014). The term translated by the ESV as "mature" (τέλειος) is a significant one in the New Testament that carries the idea of "completeness" or even "perfection" (BDAG). Often, maturity in the Pauline letters refers specifically to spiritual stability and sustained faithfulness (BDAG). Paul's goal for ministry here in Colossians 1:28–29 certainly includes the sustained faithfulness of the members of the church.

This same focus is repeated in Ephesians 4:11–16. Here, Paul writes that the leaders of the church are given to "equip the saints for the work of ministry, for building up the body of Christ" (v. 12). This work of equipping and building is meant to continue "until we all attain to the unity of the faith and of the knowledge of the Son of God, to mature [τέλειος] manhood, to the measure of the stature of the fullness of Christ" (v. 13). To drive home the focus on spiritual maturity, Paul continues the long sentence with a metaphor about children and the instability associated with childhood: "so that we may no longer be children, tossed to and fro by the waves and carried about by every wind of doctrine, by human cunning, by craftiness in deceitful schemes" (v. 14).

In the passage here, the work of the leaders in the church is meant to be focused on leading church members away from the instability and inconsistency associated with childhood towards the stability and consistency of mature adulthood. Make no mistake, the immaturity presented in the passage here is a "highly dangerous condition" that "cannot be treated as a neutral state which will be outgrown in due course" (Bruce, 2008). As ministers in the Lord's church, we absolutely must prioritize cultivating spiritual maturity and sustained faithfulness in those with whom we are blessed to toil. We must have our minds focused on sustained faithfulness the moment that our students walk into our classrooms, auditoriums, and buses for the very first time. We cannot expect to be successful if we only begin to think about sustained faithfulness as the students are walking across the graduation stage or as we are holding the door open on Sundays in the summer hoping that they will come back.

Suggestion 2: Build a *Curriculum* that *Teaches* Sustained Faithfulness.

Sunday morning and Wednesday evening Bible classes are one of the best opportunities we have as ministers to encourage sustained faithfulness. These regular meetings provide us with the chance to open the Scriptures and teach them what exactly sustained faithfulness really is. It is our chance to gather with the group to focus solely on God's word and learn more about His will, His character, and His plan for each one of us! How many other opportunities do we have during the week to focus solely on the truths of Scripture with our students? What you choose to teach in the classroom and how you choose to teach are critical to building sustained faithfulness in your students.

If we are focused on building faithfulness to last after the youth group years, we must be intentional from the start about what we are putting into our teaching curriculum. As a youth minister, you are likely going to be primarily responsible for building the shape of what the teenagers in your congregation will learn in congregational Bible study for a period of 4–7 years. What an amazing opportunity to teach Christ and him crucified! What an amazing opportunity to work with students and their parents to instill a faith that lasts!

As we approach our curriculum building with thoughtfulness and prayer, we must consider how to instill lasting faithfulness in the students through what we teach. It may very well be appropriate to close out a student's time in the youth group with a sort of "capstone" class aimed specifically at helping students prepare for what lies ahead (e.g., J. Budziszewski's *How to Stay Christian in College*), but we must be intentional and prayerful about building sustained faithfulness through our classes long before the final summer. It must start from the very beginning of a student's time in the youth group. We need to work closely with the parents, elders, and other ministers of our congregations to build a teaching plan designed to instill a faith that will outlast a student's time in the youth group. For advice on building a strategic curriculum for lasting faith, see the insightful suggestions offered by Kara Powell and Chap Clark in *Sticky Faith, Youth Worker Edition* (2011), and the more recent *Sticky Faith Innovation* (Argue and Roose, 2021).

Suggestion 3: Build a *Calendar* that *Facilitates* Sustained Faithfulness.

In my own experience in youth and college ministry, many of our teens and young adults who leave the church after the youth or college group do so simply because there are no longer any church events or retreats scheduled for their particular age group. How are we preparing our students to live and serve in the life of the church without a busy summer calendar and area-wide devotionals?

When we build our calendars, we need to ask how *every single event* helps us to accomplish our overall goal of building faithful disciples of Christ. Our calendars can be powerful tools to facilitate sustained faithfulness when we are careful to ensure that we (as ministers) are holding our calendars captive to Christ, rather than allowing our calendars to hold us captive to the appetites and desires of teenagers. Youth ministry is not about building attendance at social events—it is about working with families and the local congregation to build lasting faith in our teens. If we cannot clearly demonstrate how a given event on the calendar helps us to accomplish our ministry goals, the event should either be discarded or changed in such a way that it helps to promote sustained faithfulness beyond the youth group. If we are intentional and selective with the events we put on our calendars, we will be much more likely to build faith in our students that is based on something more than a fun summer schedule.

Suggestion 4: Build *Relationships* that *Demonstrate* Sustained Faithfulness.

Beyond the classroom and the calendar, we must also work to instill lasting faithfulness in our students through the relationships that we share with them and through the relationships we help them build with other members of the congregation. In our own relationships with our students, we *must* "set the believers an example in speech, in conduct, in love, in faith, and in purity" (1 Tim 4:12). If we are not living out sustained faithfulness ourselves, we should not expect great success in instilling it in our students.

Beyond our own relationships with students, it is imperative that we help them build healthy relationships with several other adult members of our congregations. Powell and Clark, authors of *Sticky Faith*, suggest ensuring that each student builds a relationship with at least five adults in the congregation during their time in the youth group (Powell and Clark, 2011). As we help our students build healthy relationships with other adults, it becomes more and more natural for students to be present within the church in contexts other than the youth group. You may be surprised how these relationships can foster further involvement in other ministries in the church even during a student's time in the youth group.

One excellent way to promote relationships with other adults in the local congregation is through an intentional mentoring program. Whether through small groups, leadership training, guest teachers, retreat chaperones, or any other means, it is essential to connect students to the life of the church by putting them into situations where they can build trust with and receive support from older members of the church (Joiner and Shefchunas, 2012). There is no substitute for building healthy, Christ-centered relationships between our students and members of all ages in the church. Without these relationships, teens will lose most (if not all) of their Christ-centered relationships in the church when they head off to college.

What Will *You* Do?

Remember Mark? As the final chorus of the opening song came to a close, Mark shut the door to the empty foyer and went to take a seat in the auditorium. *"There's one!"* He nearly shouted the thought from his seat as he saw one of the college students he was waiting for shuffle into a back pew in the auditorium. Mark was not completely sure why the student had been missing or where he/she had been, but he was excited for the opportunity to continue his work of equipping this student for the work of ministry and the building up of the body of Christ.

We can do much better than a 34-36% retention rate in our churches and we can start improving that statistic by thinking deeply and prayerfully about our intended goals in youth ministry. We must not allow our youth groups to become spiritualized social clubs where students are constantly being entertained with just enough Jesus-themed content to keep the attendance numbers up. Instead, our youth groups must become training grounds where students are constantly being equipped for the sustained faithfulness of maturity in Christ through Scripture, prayer, and fellowship. We can do much better when we focus our minds, curriculums, calendars, and relationships on lasting faithfulness to Christ. May God be with us as we toil to preach Christ, "warning everyone and teaching everyone with all wisdom, that we may present everyone mature in Christ" (Col 1:26).

Discussion Questions

1. How do the statistics at the beginning of this chapter compare to what you have experienced with 18–29-year-olds in your congregation? (note: Flavil Yeakley gives statistics among young people in churches of Christ in his book, *Why They Left*, 2012).
2. What is the purpose of youth ministers and youth ministries?
3. How can you get started on building a complete curriculum for your congregation's youth group that encourages sustained faithfulness? What topics do you think are necessary to include in such a curriculum?
4. What sort of specific training could we give to our high school graduates to encourage them to remain faithful in their college and young adult years?
5. How can our calendars work against our main purpose in youth ministry? What dangers should we be aware of as we plan?
6. How can you work towards building positive, mentoring relationships between youth group students and at least 5 adults in your congregation (other than the students' parents)?

Bibliography

Argue, Steven, and Caleb Roose. *Sticky Faith Innovation: How Your Compassion, Creativity, and Courage Can Support Teenagers' Lasting Faith*. Pasadena, CA: Fuller Youth Institute, 2021.

Bauer, Walter, William F. Arndt, F. Wilbur Gingrich, and Frederick W. Danker. *Greek-English Lexicon of the New Testament and Other Early Christian Literature*. 2nd ed. Chicago, IL: University of Chicago Press, 1979.

Bruce, F. F. *The Epistles to the Colossians, to Philemon, and to the Ephesians*. NICNT. Grand Rapids, MI: Eerdmans, 1984.

Budziszewski, J. *How To Stay Christian in College*. Colorado Springs, CO: NavPress, 2014.

Earls, Aaron. "Most Teenagers Drop Out of Church When They Become Young Adults." *Lifeway Research*, 15 Jan 2019, https://research.lifeway.com.

Joiner, Reggie, and Tom Shefchunas. *Lead Small: Five Big Ideas Every Small Group Leader Needs to Know*. Cumming, GA: Orange, 2012.

Kinnaman, David, and Mark Matlock. *Faith for Exiles: 5 Ways for A New Generation to Follow Jesus in Digital Babylon*. Grand Rapids, MI: Baker, 2019.

Olbricht, Owen D. *Colossians and Philemon*. Truth for Today Commentary. Searcy, AR: Resource Publications, 2013.

Powell, Kara E., and Chap Clark. *Sticky Faith, Youth Worker Edition: Practical Ideas to Nurture Long-Term Faith in Teenagers*. Grand Rapids, MI: Zondervan, 2011.

Chapter 33
Youth Ministry in Minority Communities
Native American and Black
Josh Austin and DeWayne Tapscott

Jesus tasked the apostles with taking the good news "to the remotest parts of the earth" (Acts 1:8). That process started with the preaching of the Gospel in Jerusalem during Pentecost in which there were "devout men from every nation under heaven" (Acts 2:5). Before the good news went to the world, the world came to Jerusalem and heard the good news. Other cities, such as Antioch of Syria, also played a role in the expansion of the Gospel because they were cities filled with people from across the globe. The United States has long been referred to as a melting pot with people from all over the world living here. This presents unique opportunities and challenges. This chapter focuses on two representative minority communities with the goal of challenging youth ministers to seek to understand and connect as they minister to young people from diverse communities.

Ministry to Native American Young People

By Josh Austin

Every minority group in America has a unique historical background. These backstories affect people's current beliefs, cultures, and practices. Native Americans, (traditionally called Indians, but usually not a preferred term), are also referred to as American Indians, Natives, or Indigenous people. Within the general term, Native American, there are hundreds of different tribes, languages, and customs spread across the land. I am not knowledgeable about all the tribes, but I will share a few thoughts about the Navajo people, with whom my family and I have lived and worked for most of my life.

Understanding Native American Communities

Navajos primarily reside in the northeast corner of Arizona and parts of Utah and New Mexico. Many variables will influence working with the Navajo. A consideration would be if they are living in the country or an urban area. The Center for Indigenous Health notes that 7 in 10 American Indians live in metropolitan areas ("Teen pregnancy prevention program"). Other factors could be if they live on a reservation or off it and if they attend public school or a government boarding school. Alcohol, drugs, suicide, teen pregnancies, and all types of abuse are usually much higher than the national average. For example, in May 2019 the *Center for Indigenous Health* cited Native American teens as having the highest teen birth rate (4 in 10) of any U.S. group ("Teen pregnancy prevention program"). The CDC posted that in 2015 American Indian/Alaska Native suicide rates were 3.5 times higher than those among racial/ethnic groups with the lowest rates. They also state that Native youths aged 12–17 years have the highest rates of alcohol use among all racial/ethnic groups (Leavitt, 2018).

We must also remember many Native Americans were forced to attend government boarding schools and various churches from 1860–1978. Sadly, many cases of abuse happened in the name of Jesus at the schools and denominations. These tragic experiences furthered the belief that Christianity is a white man's religion and something else to be viewed in a negative light.

Broken families and homes have sadly been more of a norm

rather than an exception for generations. This is interesting because family is emphasized as a priority. For instance, I have seen examples of students ready to attend universities on scholarship, but the family needed someone to stay with an aging grandparent. The promising college student becomes pressured to stay with the grandparents instead of pursuing higher education. I am not saying this is wrong, but this demonstrates how the family is normally a priority.

Native language and religious traditions are still practiced and highly connected with personal identity. As Paul says about the Athenians, so also are the Navajos, a very religious people (cf. Acts 17). This means they see daily events as being connected to spiritual activity. For instance, a sickness might not just be a germ, but rather a message from the holy people that you are not living a life according to the traditions of old. Many people still look to the Medicine men to perform chants, spells, curses, and ceremonies for blessings. Prayers are highly valued and culturally integrated as a part of everyday life.

Tips for Ministry to Native American Communities

When working with Native youth, be patient. Love them and treat them the way you would want to be treated. Be the initiator in conversations as children raised on reservations are known to be more reserved. Have a sense of humor as laughter is comforting. Ask lots of questions and show a desire to know their family, customs, language, and beliefs. Show an appreciation for their differences, even though you might not agree with all of them. Build relationships and allow the word of God to change their hearts. Remember they have the same TV channels and social media access we do. They still struggle with lust of the eyes, lust of the flesh, and the pride of life (cf. 1 John 2:16). They still have similar things that make them happy, sad, mad, fearful, and confused. Treat everyone as an individual, and get to know them personally.

There are still some who hold a negative view towards whites and Christianity, but most people are open or at least cordial. Here are a few helpful studies for those who are skeptical of Christianity. One is to show how Jesus was not white. He was a Jew from the Middle East. We do not know His exact looks, but He was not European. Another helpful study is to show how God cared about all people, even in the Old Testament, not just the Jews. Studying about Jonah being sent to a Gentile people for example is good. A third help is to explore where the different colors, languages, and cultures of people came from by studying the Creation and the Tower of Babel.

Finally, doing some basic apologetic studies has been effective for those not knowing the God of the Bible. Ask them, "How do you know God is real?" Then explain that the Creator, God, has left evidence that points to Him. This could include, noting that if you see design in the creation, there must be a designer. The same approach can be used to show why we can know the Bible is from God, based on the evidence. Ask them, "How would the Creator communicate with people on earth?" Then explore the possibilities of visions, a loud voice, dreams, word of mouth, or written language. Emphasize that by writing the message down, it can be preserved and maintained in its accuracy.

Native youth are beloved by our God just like every other human on earth. This particular group of young people has faced some unique challenges that others have not faced in America. These challenges have often discouraged missionaries because of the "lack of fruit." I believe God has always wanted His people to especially look out for those who have been some of the most vulnerable and beaten down.

Ministry to Youth in the Local Black Churches

by DeWayne Tapscott

As you read this chapter, I want you to understand that I am speaking most directly to those in leadership in Black churches.

Many of you may serve in congregations with a different ethnic makeup. I want you to listen in on our conversation and think about what you can do in your congregations to reach Black young people and disciple them into the likeness of Christ. A significant decline has been brewing in the local Black congregation for quite some time. This decline stems, in part, from a lack of Christian training on the basics of faith and sound doctrine with the Black teenage Christians in the church. In addition, there is a lack of focus on preparing young people for leadership, including a lack of teaching on such roles as elder and deacon. Due to this lack of training, many churches are experiencing an exodus of youth. Will our Black youth be relevant or irrelevant in the twenty-first century? It depends on whether we step up and make a difference or sit back and do nothing. Let me share some additional thoughts for church leaders and youth workers to ponder.

Engage in the Community

Peter Paris notes in his book, *The Social Teaching of the Black Churches*, that traditionally, the Black Christian church has been the lifeline of the Black community (1985, 25). Without these vibrant churches in the local community, our homes and neighborhoods would be in much worse shape than they may appear to be at this moment. Many of the Black children do not come from traditional families. They are from broken homes due to divorce, from single parents born out of wedlock, or they are being raised by other family members. Due to these factors, those children look to the streets and gangs for guidance, love, and sometimes even protection.

In order to make a significant impact in society, each local congregation needs to do some "deep soul-searching." Jeremiah writes, "The harvest is past, the summer is ended, and we are not saved" (Jer 8:20). What educational information will the local congregation need to prepare the next generation to execute the struggle for greater freedom? When the leaders of the Black church fail to analyze the suffering Black community, they will hinder that community from being a beacon of light for Jesus. In *The Black Church*, William Barclay says, "Christianity was never meant to withdraw a man from life; it was meant to equip him for better life" (2010, 47). If the Church fails the community, the youth will leave because they do not see the relevance of the church in their lives.

Invest in Young People

After speaking with over one hundred ministers in the local Black churches that range across various states, the common question that needs answering is, "How do we navigate a vision of equipping our Black teenage future leaders with surviving and thriving resilience." The surveyed preachers respond, "Rarely will one find a young black Youth Minister on the payroll at a Black congregation unless in a larger city." Due to a lack of Black youth ministers, the youth department at most Black congregations suffers. If the leadership cannot relate to the youth in the Black church, they will be fighting an uphill battle. Additionally, many local Black churches lost connections with their youth during the pandemic because there was no social media ministry to minister to and support them.

In many cases, we are failing our young people. We struggle to build mature disciples with an evangelistic spirit. In *Soul Winning In Black Churches*, J. Herbert Hinkle expresses concern that many local Black congregations have lost the traditional study habits and emphasis on soul-winning which breeds an internal crisis in the Black church (Mark 16:15–16). He recommends having the following discussions with young people in a group Bible study: 1) Please explain what it means to be saved, and 2) Do you know how to teach the plan of salvation to someone who is lost? What responses do you think you would hear in your congregation? The church's main emphasis must be winning souls for Jesus Christ (1973, 45ff). In addition, we are struggling to train future leaders in the black community (elders, deacons, preachers, youth ministers, etc.).

A critical need in youth ministry is for youth leaders who are prepared and supported. Most Black youth ministry leaders experience early burnout due to a lack of support and lack of preparation. Our local congregational leaders must support, educate, and compensate our young leaders for the future. Unfortunately, Black congregations have failed to encourage their youth ministers to get a solid spiritual education. The mentoring model practiced in many Black churches is sound, but our ministers need more. They are ministering in a complex and rapidly changing world. We need to get them all the education and training we can.

The impact of positive words could change a young person, minister, community, state, and nation. But, unfortunately, as Dr. Ted W. Engstrom and Dr. Ron Jenson express in their book, *The Making Of A Mentor*, most young people have never reached half of their potential because no one has believed in them (2005, 17).

Enter Their World

There is a disconnect between the black elders (leadership) and the youth of today. Dale Andrews raised a question in his book titled, *Practical Theology for Black Churches,* as to why some Black youth feel as if they are disjoined from the church (2002, 88ff). We need to dig into this. We need to sit down and genuinely listen to young people and learn why some of them feel disconnected. To capture the youth in the local Black church, the congregation's leaders must think outside the box while bridging the gap between youth ministry and a high-tech world. We cannot survive as separate individuals. However, we can overcome our issues by working together, functioning together, and growing together as Christ would have us. Our vision must also be to find and groom young Black leaders. To maximize the potential of our youth, one must realize that there is a declining lifeline in the Black church. Church leaders must be able to reach them to teach them. For leadership to connect with today's Black youth, stop by the neighborhood basketball courts, football practice fields, baseball facilities, and high school track and field events. We need to be intentional in wrestling with what local congregations can do to connect young people to the congregation and to inspire membership to become active in recruiting young people (i.e., Feeding the youth program, youth lectures, youth vocal camp workshops, and the forgotten "Black Lads To Leaders" program).

Anne Wimberly, Sandra Barnes, and Karma Johnson give practical insight in their book, *Youth Ministry in The Black Church*. They note that the biggest problem with the local Black church is the lack of availability of mentoring and spiritual father-figure role models for our youth and their families (2013, 87). For this to happen, we must be willing to go to them and step into their world. If there is ever a time when the local Black church should be on the move for God, then the time is now so that we can prepare our future leaders for tomorrow.

Conclusion

The fact that you are reading this chapter means that you are interested in crossing cultural barriers to work with those from a different background. Thank you! This is the call of Christ, "Go into all the world and proclaim the gospel to the whole creation" (Mark 16:15). Proclaiming the gospel does not start with crossing the borders of our country and entering another nation. It starts with crossing the cultural barriers in our own communities with a message of love and hope found in our Savior. If you dare to cross cultural boundaries with courage and compassion, God will open doors of opportunity. Our divided and broken world desperately needs love, unity, and peace. Be God's instrument for healing the world, one cultural boundary at a time.

Discussion Questions

Reaching Native-American Communities

1. What did you know about Native Americans prior to reading this chapter?
2. How have the stereotypes in our old western movies harmed Native-American communities and our outreach to them?
3. What did you learn related to Native Americans that was surprising or helpful?
4. What are some things you could do to better understand Native Americans?
5. What did you learn that could help you in reaching any community different from your own?

Reaching Black Communities

1. What are some ways that you feel that we can better connect to a disconnected generation?
2. What are some ways we can enhance our Black youth and encourage them into ministry?
3. Jesus ministered to many, but He focused on a few (Matt 22:14). As a mentor for our young Black ministers, can you list five "mentees" that you know who have great potential for the Lord's church in the future?
4. What does the following statement mean to you, "Do not discourage your mentee by your silence?"
5. Name a few possible reasons why some local churches have failed to groom and train our youth for future leadership.
6. What are some steps we can take to improve our leadership training?

Bibliography

Andrews, Dale P. *Practical Theology For Black Churches*. Louisville, KY: Westminster John Knox, 2002.

Davis, Reginald F. *The Black Church*. Macon, GA: Smyth and Helwys, 2010.

Engstrom, Ted W. and Ron Jenson. *The Making Of A Mentor*. Waynesboro, GA: World Press Vision, 2005.

Hinkle, Herbert J. *Soul Winning In Black Churches*. Grand Rapids, MI: Baker Book, 1973.

Leavitt, Rachel A. "Suicides Among American Indian/Alaska Natives – National Violent Death Reporting System, 18 States, 2003–2014." Morbidity and Morality Weekly Report. *Center for Disease Control and Prevention*. 2 March 2018. www.cdc.gov/mmwr/volumes/67/wr/mm6708a1.htm

Paris, Peter J. *The Social Teaching of The Black Churches*. Philadelphia, PA: Fortress 1985.

"Teen pregnancy prevention program for Native American youth expands to Minnesota." *Johns Hopkins Center for Indigenous Health*. 2019. https://cih.jhu.edu/teen-pregnancy-prevention-program-for-native-american-youth-expands-to-minnesota/

Wimberly, Anne E Streaty, Sandra L. Barnes, and Karma D. Johnson. *Youth Ministry In The Black Church*. Valley Forge, PA: Judson, 2013.

Chapter 34
Youth Ministry in Minority Communities
Hispanic
Hector Cruz, Justo Dorantes, Jesus Gallardo, and Beto Huamani

Introduction

The Hispanic population was 63.6 million people in 2022. They accounted for 53% of the US population growth which occurred between 2010 and 2022, more than any other ethnic group (Krogstad, et al., "Key Facts About"). Opportunities to evangelize and minister to this ethnic group will only increase in the years to come. The Anglo church willing to plant and open a Hispanic ministry should see this as a special calling in obedience to the Great Commission (Matt 28:18–20). However, the Anglo church should also be mindful that reaching out to Hispanics is complex. Evangelizing Hispanic communities involves opening one's doors and welcoming newcomers who are in many respects like strangers to the Anglo community. They have a different culture, language, and a different way of thinking. Hispanics have a great heart to love and follow God. Many are also in need of salvation.

Seeking a Hispanic Minister

For Anglo churches willing to reach out to Hispanics, one of the first thoughts is to hire a Hispanic minister to be in charge of that ministry. That person needs to be very skilled and talented in dealing with all the needs of those in the Hispanic community. Some needed traits for potential Hispanic ministers are 1) Fluent in Spanish and preferably bilingual, 2) Good Bible knowledge and ability to teach God's word, and 3) Very evangelistic with a passion for outreach. A Hispanic minister must also be flexible to adapt himself and the Hispanic congregation to the supporting church's culture (so that he and the Hispanic members will not be isolated). Hispanic congregations often meet on properties owned by what are largely Anglo congregations and there is a need for the two to work in unity, relationship, and harmony. Adaptability is a key to this (on the part of both groups). The Hispanic minister also needs to know the specific Hispanic community he is working with. Just being bilingual is not enough. He needs to know the people he is reaching and be willing to reach them where they are.

Seeking to Understand

It is important to remember that Hispanic ministry requires much more than hiring a minister or simply offering a Spanish-speaking service on Sunday. With that in mind, let us explore some other considerations. It is important for the Anglo congregation to consider outreach to the Hispanic community to understand the people they are reaching. Consider both the similarities and differences between Hispanic communities and other communities. Some of these differences include culture, generations, language, and the sensitive knowledge of their legal status. The Hispanic culture is different in general from the Anglo culture. That goes without saying. Yet, there are also differences within the Hispanic culture. Guatemalans, for example, are different from Argentinians. Each country has its own unique cultural background. Also, a

Hispanic who was born in the United States is different from a Hispanic who is a new immigrant.

Language Barriers

Language is a factor as well. First of all, not all Spanish is the same. We have different dialects. Just like people from New York, Alabama, and London do not have English that sounds exactly the same, so people from Spain, Colombia, Nicaragua, and Mexico do not have Spanish that sounds exactly the same. If a person is bilingual, the transition to living in the US is much easier. For recent immigrants, often the children will learn English, but the parents will know little. This dynamic can be difficult for families.

Teens' ability to adapt to life in the US will be influenced by their knowledge of English. If they immigrated as a child or were born in the US, they will know English as a teenager. Otherwise, their struggle with language will impact all other relationships. Assistance with learning English can go a long way toward helping them build friendships in the community and the church. It is worth noting that as of 2022, "72% of Latinos ages 5 and older spoke English proficiently, up from 59% in 2000" (Krogstad, et al., "Key Facts About").

Religious Background

The dominant religion in the Hispanic world is Catholicism and this is true of Hispanics in the US as well (cf. Krogstad, et al., "Key Facts About"). While there would be theological understandings in this background that are different from what you teach and believe, it opens a door of opportunity for teaching God's word to them. Hispanics are very receptive to Bible studies. Most will believe that God made the world, that Jesus is His son, and that the Bible is His inspired word. This creates a valuable foundation for teaching them Scripture. Also, the Bible can be a valuable tool in helping them to learn English (and to learn about Jesus in the process). Many have been brought to Jesus by reading from the Gospels to learn English.

Legal Status

Legal status is an especially sensitive issue for many Hispanics. It is often difficult for Anglos to understand what drives many Latinos to come to the United States. Burkholder observes,

> Those who've arrived in the United States on a work visa are in a completely different situation from those who arrive without a visa. Speaking with Mario, he mentioned the difference in pay between Guatemala and the United States. In Guatemala he earned $6 per day; in the United States he was able to earn $100 per day. Despite the fact that he earned this money without a work visa, you can understand why people would be willing to face immense hardship to merely arrive in the United States in hope of better work.

Hispanics fall on both sides of the illegal immigration debate. As law-abiding citizens, we are not promoting illegal immigration, yet there is value in trying to understand the perspective of those who are so desperate to come. Just being aware of this situation is critical when ministering to the Hispanic community. It is worth noting that as of 2022, 81% of Hispanics in the United States were US citizens (Krogstad, et al, "Key Facts About").

Put Love into Action

Part of learning to connect with a community is learning what the needs of the community are and seeking to meet those needs. As a general rule, Hispanics, like almost every community, need love and care. They perceive our love when we visit them. They see it when we are involved in helping them in their struggles. Connect with the teenagers and learn their wants and needs but also seek to connect with their parents and learn what they are struggling with. In the process of ministry and building relationships, never let Hispanics feel like second-class citizens. Love is shown in action. We need to be involved in the lives and needs of those in the Hispanic community and seek to build personal relationships with all members of the Hispanic family, not just the teenagers. True love in action will break down barriers.

Build a Strong Relationship with the Whole Congregation

It is common for Hispanic congregations to interact closely with an Anglo congregation. Sometimes the Hispanic congregation is using facilities owned by another congregation, sometimes they are a mission work of another congregation, and sometimes they are part of a larger congregation that has separate Spanish-speaking services and English-speaking services but seeks to keep all unified under one eldership.

Working with Elderships

Hispanic ministers frequently find themselves working under the oversight of an eldership that may not be from the Hispanic community. It is important for them to be on the same page with the elders about their goals related to reaching Hispanics. Many Hispanic ministers are happy just to have 20 or 30 people in attendance every Sunday. Is that an appropriate attitude? Is that all that can be done? Is there a follow-up after a person is baptized? Are we laboring to prepare the converted to be able to reach others when they move back to their countries or other States? Hispanic ministries need to be evangelistic, but they also need to stress discipleship. They need to build faithful leaders and teachers who can minister to others. It is common for Hispanics to travel back and forth between countries and communities. If well trained, they can become informal missionaries spreading the gospel of Christ. It is important, therefore, for elders and ministers to have clear goals for ministry and for the elders to keep the Hispanic minister accountable.

Communication is key for this relationship to be strong. The Hispanic minister needs to be willing to let the elders know what is happening. For this, it can be helpful for the elders to designate an elder and a deacon to work with the Hispanic minister. The Hispanic minister can communicate with the elder and deacon and with the rest of the elders about matters concerning the Hispanic work.

Integration into the Body

Once Hispanics feel welcome among the Anglo group, they need to become part of the work of the congregation and on a path to becoming part of the leadership. They need to be integrated as part of the body of Christ (the Church). Otherwise, they may feel isolated. In some cases, Hispanics have been discriminated against in the US, even within the church because of racial profiling. Connection and incorporation are important. The Hispanic minister can facilitate the connection by seeking ways to participate in activities with the English-speaking congregation that is hosting the Hispanic congregation. Intentional planning of joint worship, service, and fellowship is important. For example, periodic bilingual worship, Christmas events, Easter egg hunts, etc., can be valuable in connecting the whole body together. We need time together to build relationships.

When having joint services and activities, we need to be aware of the fact that we may use terminology that is difficult for some cultures to understand. We may need to adjust some programs we have worked hard to create if they do not work for some communities. Let's be mindful to seek the best contextualization when doing the Lord's work and to show profound humility as we serve God.

For an Anglo church willing to host and create a Hispanic ministry, it's crucial to be mindful of the above differences when making efforts to spread the Gospel to the lost. Anglos and Latinos may be different physically, but we all know that we have the same value before God. We are creatures of God, a God that built diversity and variety into His creation. Yet, He also sought unity. We should embrace both as we minister to Hispanic communities.

Conclusion

In summary, Justin Burkholder, in an article titled, "What Churches Reaching Hispanics Need to Know," highlighted four key thoughts that can be helpful:

1. Consider the Differences—Cultural, Generational, Language, and Legal Status.
2. Think About Your Model—Be intentional and think deeply about who you are trying to reach and how best to do that.
3. Cultural Sensitivity—Get to know the Hispanic community and listen to those with knowledge and experience.
4. Call to Humility—Conduct your Hispanic ministry in such a way that Hispanics are able to have a seat at the leadership table and can have their own identity while also looking for opportunities to connect the Anglo and Hispanic communities (Burkholder, "What Churches Reaching").

Much of what he said could also apply to working with other communities, such as the Native American and Black communities which were discussed in the previous chapter. The key takeaways for this chapter should be to listen, love, and seek to understand as you minister to Hispanics and any community different from your own. Love is a language anyone can understand.

Discussion Questions

1. What are some of the unfair stereotypes that hurt relationships with Hispanic communities?
2. What opportunities are available in your community for Hispanic outreach?
3. Would it be possible to start teaching English using the Bible in your congregation, and what steps would you take to make it a reality?
4. What did you learn or find most helpful in this chapter?

Bibliography

Burkholder, Justin. "What Churches Reaching Hispanics Need to Know." 1 May 2018. https://www.thegospelcoalition.org/article/churches-reaching-hispanics-need-know/.

Heard, Samuel. "Q&A: A Hispanic Pastor's Advice for Ministry in a Multicultural Age." 13 October 2023. https://ncbaptist.org/article/qa-a-hispanic-pastors-advice-for-ministry-in-a-multicultural-age/.

Krogstad, Jen Manuel, Jeffrey S. Passel, Mohammad Moslimani, and Luis Noe-Bustamante. "Key Facts About Latinos for National Hispanic Heritage Month." Pew Research Center. 22 September 2023. https://www.pewresearch.org/short-reads/2023/09/22/key-facts-about-us-latinos-for-national-hispanic-heritage-month/#:~:text=The%20U.S.%20Hispanic%20population%20reached,increase%20in%20the%20Asian%20population.

Chapter 35
Tax and Financial Tips for Youth Ministers
Brandon Lanciloti

Introduction

Taxation for ministers is complicated and poses unique challenges for those who choose this profession. The goal of this chapter is to highlight some pitfalls to avoid and provide a few high-level suggestions for minimizing taxation, complying with the law, and maximizing after-tax wealth. The focus of this chapter will be on issues unique to ministers, so only a few general financial topics will be addressed. Undoubtedly, you will have questions after reading through this material. A few beneficial resources with many more detailed discussions related to minister taxation are found at the end of the chapter.

Qualifying as a Minister

The assumption from this point forward in this chapter is that an individual is a minister employed by a congregation to perform religious functions within the church, which can include but is not limited to administering weddings, baptisms, or funerals, conducting religious worship, teaching Bible classes, preaching, organizing or managing church religious activities, or engaging in other religious functions significant enough to make one be considered an official religious leader by a local congregation's leaders and members. Notably, the number of hours dedicated to these activities is generally irrelevant in this determination. Two people can both be ministers of a church and qualify for ministerial taxation treatment, even if one is working 50 hours each week and the other is only working a few hours each week.

When disputes about ministerial status arise with the Internal Revenue Service (IRS), the government generally ignores titles and examines the actual functions performed by the employee. One cannot simply be declared a minister and receive ministerial tax treatment if one is not actually performing the aforementioned ministerial functions within the church. Temporary interns or those still in religious training at seminary schools or other theological institutions are generally considered secular employees. Ministers who choose to go back later and receive additional religious training or continue their education do not forfeit their status as ministers by furthering their education.

Two Types of Taxes

There are two different taxes that most employees working for most organizations are liable to pay: income taxes and payroll taxes. Most secular employees who work for an employer (such as church secretaries or janitors) have their income tax liability covered by having their employer withhold a portion of their estimated annual income tax burden each pay period. The secular employee's FICA (Federal Insurance Contributions Act) payroll tax—6.2% for Social Security and 1.45% for Medicare—is deducted from each paycheck and matched by the employer, as required by law. In short, secular personnel are employees for both income and payroll tax purposes.

Ministers are unique in that they are considered dual-status employees. Ministers are considered employees for income tax purposes, which makes them eligible for the same fringe benefits (perks in addition to salary) that secular employees can receive, such as group health insurance or cafeteria plans, but also makes them eligible for the housing allowance, which is unique to ministers and is discussed later. However, ministers are considered self-employed for payroll tax purposes, which means they are not subject to FICA but instead are subject to SECA (Self-Employment Contributions Act) and must pay their own Social Security and Medicare taxes through the 15.3% self-employment tax on their IRS Form 1040 tax filing annually. Churches that withhold and match FICA taxes for a minister are actually violating the law. How ministers pay their employee-required income tax and their required self-employment tax obligations is flexible.

The easiest option for most ministers is to estimate their annual tax obligation from both income tax and SECA tax, divide this by the number of pay periods, and have the church withhold enough income tax to cover both obligations. Income tax and self-employment tax are combined on the IRS Form 1040, so over-withholding income tax enough to cover both tax obligations is a legal and convenient way to take care of these. Another option is to have the minister receive paychecks in full with no tax withheld but use the same estimation techniques and send in the estimated tax payments quarterly using either paper vouchers (Form 1040-ES) or online using IRS Direct Pay. The four annual payment due dates of April 15, June 15, September 15, and January 15 are not evenly spaced out, so plan accordingly. One minor benefit of this approach is that tax money set aside can be placed in savings and accumulate some interest between due dates. Importantly, the combined quarterly payments and income tax withholding from all other sources usually need to equal at least 100% of the previous year's tax liability and as equal in amount as possible, or the IRS may impose underpayment penalties.

Some churches recognize that secular employees only bear a 7.65% payroll tax burden while their ministers bear a 15.3% payroll tax burden. As a result, many churches want to pay half of the payroll taxes of the minister in the spirit of fairness amongst the employees. If the church elects to reimburse a portion of the minister's payroll tax burden, the reimbursement is a fully taxable bonus to the minister.

Housing Allowances

The most significant tax benefit available to ministers is the housing allowance. All secular employee pay is subject to income and payroll taxes, aside from certain deductions such as retirement withholding. Secular employees get very little, if any, income tax relief for the costs of their housing. Ministers, however, can calculate the costs of maintaining their home, establish a housing allowance agreement with the church, and then exempt that portion of their salary from income tax.

Examples of expenses that can qualify as part of housing allowance include but are not limited to, mortgage or rent payments, property taxes, down payments on the home itself or additions, homeowner or renter insurance, repairs, maintenance, landscaping, lawn care, gardening, pest control, security, furnishings, utilities, internet, trash collection, landline telephone, cable, homeowner association dues, decorations, fencing, pool installation or maintenance, computers, appliances, cookware, bedding, towels, painting, pictures, radios, televisions, cleaning supplies, carpet shampooing, floor waxing, and essential home tools. Some expenses do not qualify as part of housing allowances, such as maid services, hired labor, food, personal hygiene products, toiletries, clothing or anything else worn, hobby items, toys, games or gaming systems, and cell phones.

The IRS allows ministers to exclude from income tax the lower of the designated housing allowance amount or the actual expenses incurred. For this reason, recordkeeping is critical. Ministers should track every expense eligible for exclusion and keep receipts. Generally, credit card statements are not sufficient documentation, and physical or digital receipts are necessary. There is also no penalty for not spending all of the housing allowance. The unused portion is merely added to wages subject to income tax, which is what would have happened if a minister did not have a housing allowance in the first place. However, if a minister spends more than the allowance granted, the excess spending over the allowance is not excluded from income tax. Therefore, ministers should build in some amount for unplanned expenses to avoid accidentally forfeiting benefits that could have been legally received. For some ministers, the housing allowance is a significant portion of their compensation. For some part-time ministers with other secular jobs outside of the church, 100% housing allowances are not uncommon. The maximum upper limit on housing allowances is the fair rental value (FRV) of the furnished home plus utilities. For most locations, the estimated monthly cost of renting a fully furnished home with utilities included would far exceed anything one would spend on an owned home, so this restriction is rarely a concern. Keep this upper limit in mind before attempting to exclude earnings from income tax as part of a housing allowance when the funds are spent on significant down payments, renovations, or home additions.

Ministers living in a parsonage provided by a church can still use the housing allowance, albeit at a much smaller level. Any home costs not paid or reimbursed by the church are generally still eligible for housing allowance exclusion. However, one additional tax is added as a result of living in a church-provided home. There is no impact on income tax for ministers living in a church-provided home, but the minister must add the FRV of the parsonage to the compensation subject to self-employment tax. Nonetheless, this additional tax burden is usually far cheaper than renting or owning a comparable home at market prices. For instance, if the FRV of a home is $1,500 a month and the self-employment tax is 15.3%, the additional tax burden is less than $250 a month, which is far cheaper than paying $1,500 for rent. Ministers living in a church parsonage can also put money not being spent on rent into savings for the eventual purchase of their own home.

There are many examples of housing allowance agreements

available in the resources at the end of this chapter and online. Once a minister locates an agreement form, remember that housing allowance agreements cannot be retroactively designated. These agreements must be in place before the associated compensation begins. Generally, ministers will want the agreement to apply to future periods, so make sure that the agreement states that the amount or percentage will remain in effect unless subsequently changed. Ask the leaders of the church to have a reaffirmation of the ongoing housing agreement prior to the beginning of each year included in their leadership meeting minutes to maintain the credibility of the agreement. Copies of the signed agreement should be kept by the minister, leadership, the person in charge of church payroll, and the minister's accountant. The IRS will only ask for a copy of the agreement if a minister experiences an audit.

Tax Forms

Most ministers should receive a Form W2 from their employing churches each January. A minister's Form W2 should have wages or bonuses (excluding housing allowance) in box 1, voluntary income tax withholding in box 2, relevant fringe benefits (discussed later) in box 12, and housing allowance received in box 14. Boxes 3 through 6 should always be blank for ministers. If applicable, ministers may have boxes 15-20 filled in with state and local income tax items. Ministers receiving a W2 report their wages and bonuses (excluding housing allowance) and unspent housing allowance on the wages line of Form 1040 each year. This same number from the wages line is added to the housing allowance spent and FRV of any free parsonage provided and reported on Schedule SE of Form 1040.

Ministers should only report earnings on a Schedule C (usually used by secular self-employed people) if they have earnings from churches other than their primary employer. For instance, earnings from speaking at a revival, conference, or convention, or receiving compensation from individuals for conducting a wedding would all go on Schedule C. Traveling ministers not associated with one particular church would also use Schedule C. In times when the distinction between employee minister and self-employed minister is unclear, *IRS Publication 15-A* provides clarification on status. A more straightforward test is the directory test. A person listed on the employee or staff page of the church directory or website probably should be getting a Form W2 because the church is telling the world that they are an employee.

The only ministers who should receive Form 1099-MISC or Form 1099-NEC are itinerant ministers who have one-time or very short engagements with a congregation, as these tax forms are intended for independent contractors, not employees. Importantly, ministers who are genuine employees but get a Form 1099 anyway from their employing church (usually due to the payroll preparer's ignorance of the law) run the risk of losing their fringe benefits and housing allowance if caught, as independent contractors are not eligible for these items. A church giving a non-itinerant minister who primarily works for them a Form 1099 incorrectly tells the IRS that the person is not their employee.

Opting Out of Social Security

Ministers are subject to SECA payroll taxes unless they choose to opt out of SECA and file Form 4361 with the IRS by the due date of the tax return covering their second year of ministry earnings exceeding $400. The minister who opts out of Social Security must declare under penalty of perjury that they are conscientiously or because of religious beliefs opposed to the acceptance of public insurance such as Social Security or Medicare. In addition, the employing church of the minister must be notified of the minister's beliefs before the minister files Form 4361. The minister cannot opt out for economic, tax, investment, or financial reasons. Ministers sometimes opt out only to avoid SECA taxes, but this is an illegal and unethical act. If approved, opting out is a permanent and irrevocable decision. Many people make this irrevocable decision when they are young, broke, and have no children and later regret it once they are more financially stable and have a family. Caution is advised.

In short, ministers should not opt out unless they believe that the Social Security and Medicare systems are sinful. Opting out using Form 4361 does not mean that the minister's name is deleted by the Social Security Administration (SSA). Instead, the minister simply gets no SSA work credits from ministry earnings. A bi-vocational minister with a secular job would still be subjected to FICA taxes elsewhere and receive SSA work credits for that secular job. Ministers who do opt out should make plans to replace their benefits and survivors' benefits lost by securing independent health insurance, disability insurance, life insurance, long-term care insurance, and retirement plans. The equivalent cost of these items can easily exceed 20% of a minister's salary, so diligence and commitment are necessary to fund these things.

Ministry Expenses

The most common ministry expenses incurred by youth and family ministers are automobile mileage, books, cell phones, and miscellaneous expenses related to interactions with youth or members. If possible, it is always easier and less complex if the church pays for expenses directly and keeps the minister's personal funds from being involved. However, when the minister pays for a ministry expense with personal funds, either the church will reimburse the minister for it or not reimburse the minister and leave the minister to deduct the expense on their tax return.

If the church wants to reimburse the minister, an accountable reimbursement plan should be established. These plans allow ministers to get reimbursed for expenses that have a legitimate business purpose and are substantiated with a receipt or record within 60 days of being paid or incurred and require ministers to return any unspent funds to the church. For recordkeeping purposes, it is good practice to note the date, location, reason, description (if not evident), and beneficiaries of expenses incurred. There are many examples of accountable reimbursement plans available in the resources at the end of this chapter and online. Like housing allowance agreements, ministers and churches cannot retroactively designate accountable plans. These plans must be in place before the associated reimbursement occurs. Churches can elect to give the ministers a cash allowance for expenses up front, but this is not recommended because of the requirement that the minister return unspent funds within 60 days. If a minister misses this deadline, the IRS has the authority to reclassify all the expenses reimbursed for the entire year as taxable income to the minister.

If the church does not reimburse the minister for legitimate business expenses, then the only option left for the minister is to deduct the expenses on their annual tax return. Ministry business expenses cannot offset ministry income subject to income tax from a minister's primary employer. However, if a minister has direct expenses associated with income reported on Schedule C, those expenses can be deducted on Schedule C. For example, books purchased for general knowledge cannot be listed as an expense on Schedule C. However, if a minister drove 500 miles to conduct a wedding in another state, the mileage expenses for that trip could directly offset the earnings from conducting the wedding on Schedule C. Is there any way ministers can deduct day-to-day unreimbursed ministry expenses? These expenses can still offset income subject to SECA (self-employment) tax. For instance, if a minister had a $50,000 compensation package, with $20,000 of that designated as housing allowance, and incurred $2,000 in unreimbursed ministry expenses, that minister would have $30,000 of wages subject to income tax and $48,000 subject to SECA tax. A minister with a $50,000 compensation package, with $5,000 of that designated as housing allowance, who incurred $2,000 in unreimbursed ministry expenses, and lived in a church-provided parsonage with an annual fair market value (FMV) of $10,000 would have $45,000 of wages subject to income tax and $58,000 subject to SECA tax.

Ministers who drive their personal vehicle for ministry can be reimbursed for mileage at the IRS business mileage rate, published annually. IRS Publication 463 can provide more details about which miles are deductible, but generally, miles from the minister's home to the church building and back are nondeductible commuting miles, and most other miles driven for ministry are deductible. Recordkeeping of mileage is essential. In addition to the recordkeeping rules as mentioned earlier, ministers need to note the total miles driven on each trip and which are business versus personal miles. Many ministers forfeit deductions because they fail to keep up with daily mileage. If a minister drives to watch a youth group member play a sport and they would not customarily be there for any other reason than supporting that child as their minister, those miles are likely deductible. If the church only reimburses a minister for gas, note that the IRS mileage rate is generally much higher than the cost of gas. For instance, assume a minister drives 100 miles for church business and the church gives them $20 for gas. The IRS reimbursement rate will exceed $50 for this trip, and they were only reimbursed for $20, so they are still entitled to a $30 deduction to offset their SECA tax. Again, it is critical to keep records of the mileage and partial reimbursements one may receive.

Cell phones are a critical tool for youth and family ministers and often a costly one. Churches can reimburse ministers for cell phone costs, but the minister should provide the monthly bill to the church as part of the accountable plan arrangement. If the church gives the minister a cell phone allowance in cash upfront, there should be a reconciliation with the actual cost at least once every 60 days to ensure that the allowance does not exceed the cost incurred and that any excess is returned to the church. If the church pays the cell phone bill directly or provides the cell phone, then the recordkeeping burden essentially shifts to the church, which must merely show that the phone is not provided as a disguised form of compensation. Some other unreimbursed expenses incurred by ministers may also be deductible, such as meals purchased for youth group members or computer software used for ministry.

Many churches reimburse ministers for moving expenses, but this is not a tax-free benefit, as 2017 was the last year this was allowed. Any moving or relocation bonus or reimbursement for moving expenses are taxable bonuses to the minister. Another common misunderstanding may arise when the church pays for books or other classroom supplies for ministry usage. Those items belong to the church and cannot be taken away tax-free with the minister if they move away.

Fringe Benefits

The list of fringe benefits available for ministers is extensive and not necessarily unique to ministers, so only a few commonly used benefits will be mentioned in this chapter. *IRS Publication 15-B* has an exhaustive list of fringe benefits eligible for many employees if one wishes to research the topic further. One common restriction on many fringe benefits is the nondiscrimination rule which usually means that benefits offered cannot single out individuals to receive benefits and then exclude benefits from others. For instance, a church cannot offer to pay for the pulpit minister's education and not pay for the youth minister's education. While on that topic, churches can reimburse up to $5,250 of tuition costs or student loans per employee per year, and this is tax-free to the recipient employee, assuming the nondiscrimination rule is not violated.

Very few churches offer group health insurance plans, so most ministers are left to find their health insurance outside of the church. If a congregation offers a group health insurance plan, strongly consider taking advantage of that, especially if the church pays a significant portion of the premiums (tax-free to the minister). Group health insurance plans are the easiest way for churches to make tax-free contributions toward the minister's health insurance. However, there are a few ways that churches can reimburse a minister for health insurance acquired independently. Two popular options are Individual Coverage Health Reimbursement Arrangements (ICHRAs) and Qualified Small Employer Health Reimbursement Arrangements (QSEHRAs). The mechanics and rules of these plans are beyond the scope of this chapter, but encourage the church leaders to seek out these plans if they wish to be able to reimburse minister health insurance costs legally without creating a tax burden for the minister.

If a minister goes through the healthcare exchange created by the Affordable Care Act to shop for health insurance plans, remember to estimate income high for purposes of calculating the monthly subsidies granted. If a minister estimates low and the subsidy is determined to have been too high when they file their Form 1040 tax return, they may have to pay back a portion of the subsidy. Estimating income high when calculating the subsidies increases the chances that they will get a surprise tax credit from the subsidies they did not receive throughout the year. Note, the housing allowance you receive does not have to be included in your income calculation for health insurance subsidies through the exchange.

In general, most ministers should strongly consider having long-term disability insurance and life insurance. This is especially critical if their spouse is a homemaker. If a minister has three to six months of income in savings, then short-term disability is not essential. Most people could figure out things if they lost income for a few months, but a permanent disability or long-term recovery from an accident or surgery could wreak havoc and be impossible to sustain financially without a long-term disability plan. With life insurance, one is planning for those who will be left behind in the event of their death. Consult with an insurance specialist about the type of life insurance policy and coverage amount needed. However, a starting point for life insurance coverage is at least 10x the minister's annual income.

Very few churches offer group retirement plans such as a 401(k), so most ministers are left to work out their retirement savings outside of the church. If a congregation offers a group retirement plan, strongly consider taking advantage of that, especially if the church matches contributions (tax-free to the minister). Group retirement plans are the only way churches can make tax-free contributions toward the minister's retirement. If a minister has to go outside of the church, consider the benefits of contributing to traditional or Roth IRAs. Set aside something! A person who starts saving for retirement in their early 20s will likely have hundreds of thousands of dollars more in retirement savings at retirement than a person who waits until their 30s to begin saving because of the power of compounding interest.

If a church gives a minister extra money to put into a retirement plan outside of the church, those funds are taxable income to the minister, regardless of the type of account in which the minister subsequently places the funds. The funds are still taxable to the minister even if the church bypasses the minister and contributes the funds to the minister's individual retirement account. Ministers should seek out a financial professional specializing in investments and retirement planning to find the plan that best fits their budget and needs. If possible, ministers should work with a Certified Financial Planner because they will have a broader knowledge and long-term focus on building after-tax wealth.

Conclusion

Two excellent resources available for exploring more sophisticated tax and financial options available to ministers are the *Minister's Tax & Financial Guide* and the *Church & Nonprofit Tax & Financial Guide*, written for ministers and church leaders, respectively, which can be downloaded from the Evangelical Council for Financial Accountability (ECFA) website. The IRS also has two publications especially relevant to ministers and church leaders. *IRS Publication 517: Social Security and Other Information for Members of the Clergy and Religious Workers* and *IRS Publication 1828: Tax Guide for Churches & Religious Organizations* are both available for download from the IRS website and are full of information regarding minister taxation. For more complex research, Richard Hammar's *Church & Clergy Tax Guide*, published annually by *Church Law & Tax*, is excellent. Ministers should also consider seeking out counsel from a competent Certified Public Accountant if questions arise when exploring these tax topics. Most tax preparers have very limited experience dealing with the unique challenges of minister taxation, so ask for references from other ministers to find those preparers who are best equipped to provide assistance.

DISCLAIMER

Any tax advice in this publication reflects the author's professional judgment based on his understanding of current tax law as of July 2024. Tax law is subject to change. Subsequent changes in the information known to him, in the law, or its interpretation may affect the application of this writing. The author is not responsible for updating his advice for subsequent changes in the law or its interpretation. The information presented here is of a general nature and should not be considered as specific professional accounting advice for anyone's situation or an undertaking on the author's part to monitor a specific issue for any individual or any congregation. The author is not an attorney, financial or investment planner, securities dealer, or insurance agent, and any advice given should not be understood or treated as legal, brokerage, investment advisory, or insurance consultation. Finally, if the reader and the author do not have a mutually signed professional engagement letter in place, do not even think about saying, "He told me to do this," because the author did no such thing. While seeking professional assistance is usually beneficial, remember that ultimate responsibility for financial matters always rests with the minister.

Discussion Questions

1. How do payroll taxes differ between secular employees and minister employees?

2. What should a minister consider when establishing a housing allowance?
3. What tax form should a non-itinerate minister receive at the end of each year? Why?
4. When is it appropriate for a minister to use Schedule C on their annual tax return?
5. What should a minister consider before opting out of Social Security?
6. What recordkeeping practices should ministers follow?
7. Which fringe benefits do you believe to be the most important and how can they be set up properly?
8. Which type of financial professionals should a minister consider working with?

Real-World Ministry to Youth and Families
The Youth Minister as Teacher

Chapter 36
Essential Elements of Youth Ministry
Luke Dockery

For the last several years, I have used the following organizational structure in my youth ministry classes and when working with ministry interns to talk about the necessary elements of effective youth ministry. Although I am not absolutely claiming that this is an exhaustive list, I do think that the categories I talk about here, properly defined, basically incorporate the whole practice of what youth ministry should be. These six elements fall into three categories, with each category containing two elements: one more visible element, which is supported by a related, less-visible element. After highlighting the elements, I will then dig a little deeper into the *Learning* section by discussing curriculum planning and teaching.

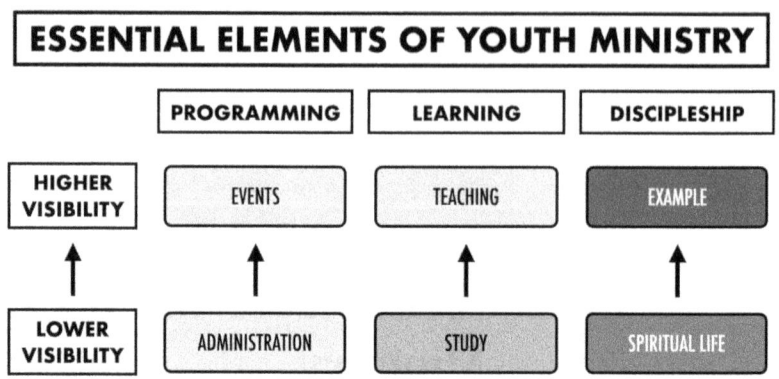

Programming

The category of *programming* refers to many of the items that most people naturally think of when they think of youth ministry—trips, special events, and regular activities that a youth group is involved in—and the behind-the-scenes planning that makes all of these possible.

Events (High-Visibility Programming)

Simply put, although youth ministry is about a lot more than *events* on a calendar, events are a fundamental and crucial part of youth ministry. Those events can be widely varied (devotionals, youth rallies, summer camps, ski trips, service projects, flag football games, eating together, game nights, etc.) and can accomplish a range of objectives (fellowship, study, service, outreach, etc.), but ultimately, if you never have events for your young people, you do not really have a youth ministry.

Events represent what is most likely the most public aspect of youth ministry, and many times, people may judge a youth ministry's effectiveness solely on the basis of the quality or perceived quality of your events. In my experience, this is also part of what draws a lot of people to work in youth ministry: the idea that you get to do fun things all the time.

Administration (Low-Visibility Programming)

It requires a great deal of planning for your events to actually *happen*, and this is where *administration* comes in. Administration is much less visible than the events themselves, but it is absolutely crucial: if you do not invest time in administrative duties, then your youth ministry simply will be unable to function.

However, youth ministry administration is about much more than putting together a calendar of events. It involves all sorts of planning and record-keeping that enable your programming to be implemented: recruiting chaperones and volunteers, organizing curriculum, keeping track of youth attendance, setting up group texts, sending out parent newsletters, and the list goes on and on.

And even more fundamentally than all of this, administration is where you make decisions about what your youth ministry is all about: why do we do the things we do? What are our goals for our students? When you think about it, it is premature to put together a list of events before you are even clear about what you are trying to accomplish.

I have found that administration can be a difficult area for many youth ministers: because most administrative tasks go on behind the scenes, no one (generally) forces you to do them, and to be honest, many administrative tasks are not very enjoyable. I do think it is possible for a youth ministry with poor administration to still have effective programming at times. But I think good administration makes consistency in quality programming much more likely, and helps to make a youth ministry much more sustainable as well.

Learning

Any effective youth ministry will make it a priority to provide an environment where *learning* can occur since we want our young people to grow up to be mature people of faith. Primarily, we want our young people to learn about God and the Bible, but it is important for them to learn other things as well. Luke 2:52 talks about how the 12-year-old Jesus grew physically, intellectually, socially, and spiritually, and in my opinion, this sort of well-rounded growth serves as a good model for what we should try to achieve in youth ministry.

Teaching (High-Visibility Learning)

Most visibly, the *learning* characteristic of youth ministry is achieved through the practice of *teaching*. Teaching occurs in formal settings like Bible classes, sermons, devotionals, worship-leading programs, and youth group retreats, and it also occurs more informally in mentoring relationships and spiritual conversations. Because a lot of people can witness you teach (including adults in some settings), this is another element where people tend to make judgments about the quality of the youth minister's work.

Study (Low-Visibility Learning)

The reality is that your teaching will not be very good for very long if you have not invested a significant amount of time in *study*. Or to put it another way, before students can learn, the youth minister must learn. Studying is not a favorite activity for many people, but it is important, and really, I believe that there is an almost endless list of sources and topics that are worth studying that help you to teach more effectively as a youth minister:

- Scripture (obviously)
- Interpretation and exegesis of Scripture

- Theology
- Ministry (general)
- Youth ministry (both theory and practice)
- Adolescent development
- Interpersonal Relationships and Conflict
- Leadership
- Church History
- Technology and Social Media
- Teaching Methods and Theory

This list barely scratches the surface of different areas of study that apply directly to youth ministry and help you to teach more effectively. We could likely brainstorm a much longer list.

Studying is another low-visibility element, and for many people, studying is not fun, and because of that, it is an element that can be crowded out of a busy schedule. Still, I do think it is true that people can tell by your teaching whether or not you have done your homework and put in the necessary amount of study ahead of time. And more importantly, if you provide a full slate of exciting and well-run events but your students never really learn anything, what have you really accomplished?

Discipleship

Intentionally, I have saved the category of *discipleship* for last, because I think it is the most important. Fundamentally, Christianity is more than the activities we do or the precepts we learn; it is a way of life as we seek to follow Jesus and increasingly be transformed into His likeness by the work of the Spirit. Effective youth ministries should help prepare young people to live according to the Way of Jesus.

Example (High-Visibility Discipleship)

Most visibly, this is accomplished through the *example* of the youth minister himself. It is hard to overstate the importance of your own personal example and the influence it has as you interact with students on a day-to-day basis and seek to build meaningful relationships with them. If you provide great events and wonderful, biblical teaching, but act in such a way that does not reflect Christ, you send a mixed message to your students and may even drive them away from the faith. Your students witness your devotion to the church, the way you interact with your spouse, the way you respond when another student misbehaves, and whether or not you cheat at dodgeball. Based on what your students see, they make judgments about the authenticity of your discipleship (and honestly, shouldn't they?). Obviously, youth ministers are never perfect, but we should live lives of devotion to Jesus and moral excellence so that we can appropriate the words of Paul to our students: "Imitate me as I imitate Christ."

Spiritual Life (Low-Visibility Discipleship)

The ability to be a good spiritual example for young people does not occur in a vacuum; it is undergirded by a robust *spiritual life* characterized by devotion to Christ and attention to spiritual disciplines. Ultimately, while good organizational skills and study habits are an important part of youth ministry, the single most important element is personal discipleship: an allegiance to Jesus Christ as the king of our lives, and a desire to help others develop a similar devotion. Personal spiritual formation is enhanced by disciplines such as prayer, Bible reading, fasting, etc., is empowered by the Holy Spirit, and is the fuel that empowers us for ministry and keeps us going when circumstances are difficult and our ministries are not achieving the results we would like.

Learning: Digging Deeper

One of the most important things you will do as a youth minister is teach young people God's word (cf. the *learning* element above). In fact, in most congregations, the young people will be taught by the youth minister more than anyone else. Thus, the quality and accuracy of your teaching are very important.

I believe that good teachers are *made,* not *born,* and that we basically develop our teaching styles and skills with experience. Furthermore, while I have taught a lot for many years, I never received formal training as a teacher, and will not pretend to give you a step-by-step guide here on how to become a great teacher. Having said that, here are some principles that can guide you both as you develop curriculum and teach teenagers.

Develop a Curriculum Plan

Although different churches vary in their youth ministry practices, generally speaking, there are two weekly blocks of time in youth ministry to teach students: Sunday morning Bible class and then some block of time in the middle of the week (often on Wednesday night). Many times, youth ministers do not have a comprehensive plan about what they want to teach and instead just come up with lesson plans week by week. This may be because the youth minister wants flexibility to address whatever seems relevant to the students at the time. Often, however, it is because the youth minister has not managed time well and invested the necessary time in long-term planning.

I once had a professor who said, "An idiot with a plan is better than a genius without one." With that in mind, I believe that rather than constantly being *reactive* to what you think students need, it is better to be *proactive* and make a plan that, over time, covers a wide variety of needs as well as the scope of the Bible. If you are convinced about the importance of having a plan and strategy about what you teach, how do you go about accomplishing that? You basically have two options: you can buy one or create one.

A lot of youth ministries buy curriculum, and there are some *advantages* to this:

- Purchased curricula are usually written by professionals, so there is likely a good deal of thought that has gone into the plan and content.
- Buying curriculum frees you up from the time involved in coming up with a plan and writing material yourself.

But there are *disadvantages* as well:

- It can be really expensive!
- Professional curricula must cast a wide net in order to be viable for purchase. Because of that, they tend to be generalized and do not always fit your particular context (whether that means doctrine, format, needs, etc.).
- Many professional curricula are more topic-focused and less focused on Scripture.
- It takes a lot of time to evaluate curricula, and very frequently you cannot even evaluate it comprehensively without purchasing it.

For all these reasons, I prefer to create my own curriculum plan to map out the content I want our students to get in Bible class.[1] My process of curriculum development has four steps.

Develop your list of topics

A good curriculum plan should have a mix of topical and textual studies, but the Bible should be central: all or most of the Bible should be covered in *some* sense. When developing a list of topics, I have found it helpful to collaborate with others, which helps check against any blind spots I may have. Furthermore, a good list of topics should emphasize the sorts of things that research indicates students need: the big story of Scripture, core Christian doctrines, the person and character of Jesus, Christian sexuality, apologetics, etc.

Determine how many teaching blocks you have

By "teaching blocks," we simply mean the number of Bible class periods or opportunities that exist for instructing students. How many years do you have your students? Most youth ministries will have students for six or seven years, depending on when students enter the youth ministry. How many times per week will your students go to class? Are there Bible class periods on Sundays and Wednesdays? Are there other opportunities for teaching students? How many weeks per year do your students go to Bible class? Are there times in your youth ministry calendar when you take a break from Bible classes (for holidays or other events)? If you multiply the number of classes per week by the number of weeks per year and the number of years you have students in your youth ministry, you will know the total number of teaching blocks you have for your students.

Fit your content to your context

After you have determined which topics you want to teach and how many teaching opportunities are available, it is time to plug your topic list into the number of teaching blocks you have. There are several issues to consider during this process:

- How many weeks will you need to allot for a given topic? It takes more time to teach Genesis well than Philippians, for example.
- Will some content be repeated? Some topics are so foundational that students need to study them more than once in six or seven years.
- Do certain teaching series fit better in certain slots? In my ministry context, we break into small groups on Wednesday nights for the majority of the time, which focus on discussion and spiritual disciplines. On those

nights, I give a much shorter lesson than I do on Sunday mornings, and certain topics fit better in this format.
- Have you left flex gaps in case adjustments need to be made? Sometimes Bible classes can be canceled because of holidays, inclement weather, or youth group travel. Make sure to leave enough flexibility in your plan to accommodate these special circumstances.

Find material to fill your plan

Now that you know *what* you want to teach, you need to write, find, or purchase the material that you *will* teach. In my own ministry, I do a combination of all of these. It is my belief that you should spend some time writing lessons; remember, *study* is one of the essential elements of youth ministry, and it is good for your own spiritual development. Additionally, a helpful practice for me has been to find other youth ministers I respect and trade material with them. While it is good to study and write your own class materials, you don't have to develop everything yourself. I enjoy sharing material I have written with other youth ministers, and some of the best series I have taught have come from friends in ministry who have shared them with me. Finally, I have purchased specific lessons or series that fit into my overall curriculum plan.[2] No one can be an expert on everything, and I believe I have added great value to our Bible classes by purchasing quality material that covered important topics about which I was not well qualified to teach.

Understand Today's Teenagers

While developing your curriculum plan and considering the objectives for your education program, it is helpful to consider some of the spiritual needs of today's emerging adults. Generally speaking, the students we are working with likely:[3]

Essential Elements of Youth Ministry

- Have a poor understanding of the historic Christian faith or what the Bible is really about.
- Struggle to put their faith into words.
- Believe that being a Christian is some form of moralism.
- Wrestle with spiritual doubts that they don't feel they can talk about with their parents or at church.
- Hold views on sexuality that are much closer to culture than Scripture, and haven't talked much about this with their parents.
- Are unconvinced of the very notion of absolute truth.
- Are at risk of developing mental health issues such as anxiety and depression.
- Are at risk of walking away from faith within the next few years.

How might this affect what and how we teach our teenagers? First, we need to be thoughtful about what we teach *explicitly*. There are certain major ideas that we need to make sure to emphasize repeatedly in our teaching such as the overall story of the Bible, core Christian doctrines, the person and character of Jesus, Christian sexuality, apologetics, and more. Second, we need to be careful about what we teach *implicitly*. We want to make sure that we are teaching historic Biblical Christianity, and not some misbegotten step-cousin.[4] Third, we need to make sure to structure our classes so that students have an abundance of opportunities to verbalize what they believe *and* what they struggle to believe. Finally, we need to figure out ways to use the time we have with students to help them develop real relationships with older, mature Christians.

Have a Clear Set of Objectives

As you are planning your curriculum and developing your classes, one of the first and most basic tasks when teaching teens (or really, anyone) is to determine what your objectives are:

- What is your purpose in teaching?
- What goals are you hoping to achieve?
- What do you want your students to know?
- How will you know *if* they know what you want them to know?
- Are you teaching primarily "mental knowledge" or do you want your students to change their behavior based on what they learn?

Unfortunately, a lot of times, I think we enter into the task of teaching without really giving much thought to objectives at all. If we are honest, sometimes our objectives might be as limited as "Cover the material I've been given" or, "Not lose my temper with the annoying kid who talks all the time in class." I have certainly been there myself!

Good objectives should be student-focused and observable. So, "I will teach my class about the apostles" is a poor objective: it is focused on the teacher rather than the student, and there is no tangible way to determine if the objective has been achieved. "The student will be able to recite the names of Jesus's twelve apostles" is a better objective, because it focuses on the student and provides criteria for determining if the objective has been met.

I do not believe it is necessary for you to write out a long list of objectives before every lesson you teach, but you should have a major goal for what you want your students to learn in each lesson or series of lessons and a plan for how you will determine if your students are meeting your objectives or not.

Use a Variety of Teaching Styles to Connect with a Variety of Students

It used to be very popular to talk about different "learning styles." My understanding is that some of those theories have been discredited, but I still believe this is generally a helpful framework to consider when reflecting on how we teach. I am not going to get overly technical here because I do not claim to be an expert on this, but I do think it is true that God made different kinds of people who are wired in different ways, and we tend to have preferences for how we like to learn.

As teachers, we need to be aware of the fact that our students like to learn in different ways, and we need to try to accommodate for that, especially over time. You might not engage every learning style in every lesson, but over time, you really do need to try to *teach* in a variety of ways in order to engage your students who *learn* in a variety of ways. Here are some different learning styles, and some examples or suggestions of how you might try to engage them:

- *Visual (spatial)* learners prefer using pictures, images, and spatial understanding. For students who enjoy visual learning, PowerPoint presentations, video clips, or having students illustrate key concepts on a dry-erase board can be helpful.
- *Aural (auditory)* learners prefer using sound to learn. This one is perhaps the easiest: some people actually prefer listening to a teacher talk! Having students listen to audio Bibles and then having them write their perceptions can be helpful with these learners.
- *Verbal (linguistic)* learners prefer using words, both in speech and writing. Students who prefer to learn in this way can benefit from having workbooks where they can take notes. It is helpful to encourage them to rewrite key concepts in their own words or to provide discussion questions for them to share their thoughts with the class. Talk about keywords and their meanings.
- *Physical (kinesthetic)* learners prefer using their bodies, hands, and sense of touch. The use of hands-on activities as object lessons to illustrate a point you are making can connect well with this type of learner, as well as having different stations or activities through which they rotate.

- *Logical (mathematical)* learners prefer using logic, reasoning, and systems. It can be helpful for these learners to point out the logical arguments that Scripture naturally gives (For example, Paul uses logic and reasoning heavily in his letters). Posing problems for your students to solve or case studies for them to work through can be effective.
- *Social (interpersonal)* learners prefer to learn in groups or with other people. For these learners, splitting into pairs or small groups to work together to answer questions or complete a task can be effective.
- *Solitary (intrapersonal)* learners prefer to work alone and use self-study. Solitary learners may benefit from quiet time to look up answers to Bible questions for themselves or spend time prayer journaling.

Related to what we said earlier in terms of long-term curriculum planning, it is important to keep different learning styles in mind and tailor different classes, quarters, and series toward different learning preferences. If you do the same thing every single week without variation, you probably have some students who are never getting to learn in their preferred style and are likely struggling as a result.

Conclusion

Clearly, youth ministry is a multi-faceted endeavor, and I do not know many people who naturally excel at all areas of it—I certainly don't! That being said, understanding the different elements of youth ministry can help us to reflect on how we are doing in the different areas and lean into our strengths while also growing in those areas that do not come as naturally to us.

Discussion Questions

1. Why is it important to pay attention to all three areas highlighted above? (Programming, Learning, and Discipleship).
2. Brainstorm additional topics, based on the list above, that might be profitable for the youth minister to study.
3. What learning styles do you best relate to? How does knowing this help you as a teacher?
4. What did you find most helpful in this chapter?

Notes

[1] I do still purchase specific lesson series from time to time; I just seek specific items that fit my plan rather than using someone else's plan wholesale.

[2] At the risk of self-promotion, I will share that I work with a group called Deeper Youth Ministry that seeks to produce reliable, well-researched, and engaging Bible class resources for youth groups. See more at www.deeperyouthministry.com.

[3] The list of spiritual needs is drawn from a variety of sources, including Kenda Creasy Dean, *Almost Christian: What the Faith of Our Teenagers Is Telling the American Church* (Oxford: Oxford University Press, 2010); Christian Smith with Melinda Lundquist Denton, *Soul Searching: The Religious and Spiritual Lives of American Teenagers* (Oxford: Oxford University Press, 2005); Kara E. Powell and Chap Clark, *Sticky Faith: Everyday Ideas to Build Lasting Faith in Your Kids* (Grand Rapids: Zondervan, 2011; Barna Group, *Gen Z: The Culture, Beliefs and Motivations Shaping the Next Generation* (Ventura, CA: Barna, 2018); Barna Group, *Gen Z Vol 2: Caring for Young Souls and Cultivating Resilience* (Ventura, CA: Barna, 2020); Jean M. Twenge, *IGen: Why Todays Super-Connected Kids Are Growing Up Less Rebellious, More Tolerant, Less Happy—and Completely Unprepared for Adulthood (and What This Means for the Rest of Us)* (New York: Atria, 2017).

[4] The description "misbegotten step cousin" comes from Christian Smith, *Soul Searching*, 171, as he describes Moralistic Therapeutic Deism's relationship to historical Christianity.

Chapter 37
Adolescent Development, Part 1
Principles of Human Development in the Context of Youth Ministry
James C. Guy

Calen is the typical goofy guy in the youth group that we define as immature. He is the class clown at school and in Bible class, often giving silly answers to even serious questions in class discussions. He stirs up others to roughhouse in the hallways, narrowly missing that feeble elderly lady on the walker. We see him as the main one who needs to be in the youth group, but we sure would like for him to grow up a bit first. Perhaps he belongs back in the junior high class. Yet, Calen has a keen ability to connect socially with his peers. In fact, much of the behavior we see reflects his seemingly innate ability to connect with people, even though we may consider it a bit immature. Contrast that with Emily, the straight-A student who can quote a lot of Scripture and answers all the questions in Bible class at a level that rivals many in the adult class. She is viewed by adults as exceptionally mature, but her peers see her as nerdy and arrogant. We would love to have that ideal teen in our youth groups who is a combination of Emily's intelligence and maturity and Calen's social ability. However, it may be more helpful for us to avoid painting a picture of the ideal teen. Doing so can seriously hinder our work as ministers, and more importantly, can hinder the growth of the people we minister to. Therefore, it is helpful to have at least a basic understanding of variations in the process of human development.

The "Normal" Individual

Perhaps the most important thing to remember about human development is to that humans are individuals. Just because something is *normal* for most teens does not mean that it is universal. Neither does the concept of *abnormal* imply inferiority. Synonyms such as *common* or *average* are appropriate, but it is imperative to remember that God created every human as an individual. Humans are all unique—even those who may be deemed abnormal on some developmental, psychological, intellectual, or even spiritual scale. This concept is reflected in Scripture, such as Paul's discussion of the body in 1 Corinthians 12, where even the "un-presentable parts" are as valuable as the most presentable parts.

A common mistake that youth ministers make is to build our ministry largely upon the students we view as the core. Instead, we should look at each individual as equally valuable and identify the strengths of each. First, this reflects the very nature of how Jesus viewed individuals (e.g. Zacchaeus—Luke 19; The woman caught in adultery—John 8; The rich man—Mark 10). Second, as ministers, we should remember that the goal of ministry is to guide and improve the spiritual lives of each individual and to help them become more like Christ. It is important to avoid a business paradigm merely focused on numerical growth and retention of numbers. This can be a challenge because the perspective of leaders can be that we are paid to grow the church numerically. God calls us to seek and save the lost, but we must remember that providing the increase (the numbers) is God's job (1 Cor 3:6). We have to ask ourselves the questions—Who do we work for? Who is our ultimate boss? What is our ultimate ministry and purpose? As we work with churches, we need to be in agreement with the leaders of the church regarding what they are really paying us to do, and we also need clarity on what God wants us to do. Our vision and the vision of the elders need to be in step with the vision of God.

However, even though we view people as unique individuals, it is helpful to understand the normal, or common, developmental processes of humans. As we do so it is imperative to keep in mind that not every individual will fit into the nice, neat categories of developmental elements associated with a particular age-associated stage.

Continuous Versus Discontinuous Perspectives

There is a theoretical perspective that human development should be viewed as *continuous* rather than having *discontinuous* stages (Berk, 2014). The terms can be confusing because stage perspectives of development follow what we might call a "continuous" pattern. However, they are referred to as discontinuous in the literature on the subject because of the distinction between the stages (i.e., they are broken into separate stages). Most well-known theorists (e.g., Piaget; Vygotsky) present their research and concepts from the discontinuous perspective, which is commonly organized by age groups.

While we will explore development primarily from this perspective, it is important to also consider the continuous perspective which essentially holds that there is little developmental difference between the child and the adult. That is, according to this perspective, differences between the child's cognitive or other functional abilities and that of the adult are simply differences between experiences and information from which to draw. In essence, this may be illustrated by thinking in terms of a child simply being a little adult, and an adult being a grown child. This concept holds that the same developmental abilities reside with the infant or young child as in the adult, but not to the same extent as with the adult who draws upon their life experiences and information. Essentially, it reflects "experience as the greatest teacher."

In contrast, the discontinuous perspective holds that while

there may be some innate abilities in the child that are also characteristic in the adult, most elements of development (e.g., cognitive, physical, emotional, social, spiritual, etc.) take place in more concrete, or neatly ordered, categories identifiable at each stage of development. Berk (2014) compares the discontinuous approach to climbing a staircase, as opposed to the continuous model which is more like climbing a gradually sloping hill. It seems clear that there is a progressive development in humans, but we also see differences based on experiences, and even youth like Emily in our example above, might be described as "advanced beyond her age." Is this because she has good genes or because her parents make her study hours every day? After all, she has no social life, or perhaps all of the above?

Nature-Nurture

One of the foundational considerations in the study of psychology and human development is the nature versus nurture controversy. For some, there is no controversy as multitudes of research studies have indicated that humans are indeed a product of both nature and nurture. On the one hand, biological developmental research has indicated genetic propensities towards certain characteristics, developmental elements, and even behaviors. Yet social psychology research clearly indicates that humans are products of their environment as well. This should never be viewed as an either/or, but as a both/and situation.

If we believe that every human who has ever lived, or ever will live, comes from "one blood" (Acts 17), and our origin is shared with the original humans created by God in His image, the genetic research which says we are products of "nature" makes perfect sense. Of course, that must be balanced with the theological importance of understanding free will, the nature of this fallen world and its impact, the uniqueness that God built into each individual (Rom 12:3–8), and the influence of others on our lives and personalities. Psychological and biological research has shown that genetics not only develop over time but can also mutate rapidly or across generations (cf. Belsky & Beaver, 2010; Runge, et al., 2014; Weder, et al., 2014). We call this "plasticity," and it is often identified in many areas of cognitive development. In other words, our experiences actually change our biological structure and to some degree circumvent our genetic predispositions. That also fits God's call for "whosoever will" to come (cf. John 3:16; Rev 22:17). To view human development solely in terms of nature stands in stark contrast to the theological perspective of free will and personal responsibility. That is if a person must act in a manner consistent with their genetic determination, that behavior is the responsibility of nature itself rather than the individual. This is not a biblical perspective. However, that does not imply that humans are not influenced by genetic propensity and other aspects of nature. Thus, there is value in thinking in terms of genetic trends for most human beings rather than genetic determination which views individuals as biological robots.

In contrast, church leaders, and others may overemphasize nurture, while at the same time condemning the concept of humanism. Humanism is an emphasis on the human ability to improve our own lives. Human nurture is the core of humanism in that it largely focuses on the environment and systemic influences on behavior. The reason the church has often condemned humanism is because some of the well-known humanists (e.g. Maslow, etc.) placed too much emphasis on human ability, potentially eliminating the need for God and redemption. But what humanism has provided is scientific evidence that humans can in fact change. It is not uncommon for grace to be given to the deacons' kids, even as they climb the roofs of the church building or get suspended from school; or the elders' grandchildren, even as they secretly have abortions, use drugs, or struggle to stay out of jail. It is easy to justify their behavior, or ability to adjust their behavior because they "come from a good Christian family." All the while, we condemn other young people with bad behavior who come from broken homes, or negative backgrounds, as being "just like their parents." This is a major flaw that we want to avoid.

Ultimately, to do a good job in youth ministry, it is important to view human development in terms of both nature and nurture. For example, a baby born with the physiological addition to drugs or alcohol will very likely experience negative consequences in their cognitive processes, behavior, emotional regulation, and other areas of development that research has clearly connected to the in-vitro exposure to the substances (cf. May, et al., 2013; Georgieff, 2018). If that child continues to grow up in the environment and atmosphere of a broken family system, is exposed to the use of substances, had negative peer influences, and other negative influences (nurture), that child has an even greater probability of problems with behavior in school, law enforcement, social issues, and socioeconomic challenges. Combining challenges in both nature and nurture, results in a child who is highly disadvantaged in terms of normal human development. Ministry to such is difficult, but again, is at the very heart of Jesus's mission and focuses on "the least of these" (Matt 25:40–45). Yet, even when that same child is placed for adoption in what would be considered a positive home environment, the natural aspects of damage to the brain, exposure to substances, and other physiological responses to the substance will continue to influence the child's ability to self-regulate and to emotionally regulate, and the child's propensity to use or abuse substances. Therefore, it is helpful to consider both nature and nurture and adapt ministry culture and efforts accordingly. One of the key Christian principles to keep in mind with any individual is grace. In some respects, a child or young adult with challenges in both nature and nurture will need an extra dose of grace. This also opens the door for opportunities to minister more broadly to families. In that way, youth ministry really is family ministry.

Developmental Theories and Theorists

While there are a number of different ways to look at human development and different perspectives on the process, it is beneficial on at least some level to view human development in a progressive manner, whether we subscribe to that as a continuous process, discontinuous stages, or a combination of the two. It is most commonly studied in terms of stages because this is an easy way to identify the progression. While all of the major theorists identified common elements across the lifespan reflective of a holistic view of humans, many are known for emphasizing a particular area of development. Let us explore some of these leading theorists.

Erik Erickson (Psychosocial)

Erik Erickson (1950) built largely upon Sigmund Freud's theories, but well combined perspectives of both nature and nurture in the understanding of human development. In his research and theories on human personality development, the individual is viewed as developing either in a positive or negative manner, depending on how they adapted to psychosocial conflicts during their lives (which he termed, "crises"). However, even though some refer to his theory as biopsychosocial (stressing biological, psychological, and social factors), his emphasis was actually more on the nurture aspect, but with the perspective of using the abilities of the mind/psyche. His theory is interesting, and helpful in youth ministry because it reflects in many ways on a "wrestling" in the mind between right and wrong. That is, we make choices based, in part, on our experiences, and those choices are processed in our minds and impact our learning and development.

Jean Piaget (Cognitive)

Jean Piaget is perhaps the most well-known human development theorist. This is in part because he is largely studied in both psychology as well as in educational contexts. Whereas Erickson focused on personality development, much of Piaget's work focused on cognitive development (i.e., thinking). His theory is largely grounded in biological development and adaptation and is presented in logical stages characteristic of a discontinuous perspective (Piaget, 1962). From birth, cognitive processes are viewed as limited to more mechanical type processes, and the ability to evaluate the world and experiences in more abstract and logical processes is developed as the child develops physically and mentally. That is, the young child does not have the biological and physiological ability to process information beyond the sensori-motor processes but develops that ability as they mature biologically.

Lev Vygotsky (Sociocultural)

Lev Vygotsky (1978) focused more specifically on the nurture aspect of human development. Similar to Erickson, his perspective emphasized the environmental influence on human development and processes, especially cognitive development. However, his nurture perspective reflected more specifically, the cultural context in which an experience takes place. Interactions with other members of the community, family, and culture, provide context for the development of thoughts and behaviors. He referred to social context, mentors, and teachers as the scaffolding that assists the young as they learn and grow (cf. McCray, 2016, 77). His theory actually built upon Piaget's cognitive perspectives to some degree, but whereas Piaget's may be viewed more from the nature perspective, Vygotsky emphasized more of a nurturing context.

Lawrence Kohlberg (Moral)

Each of the theorists includes moral development on some level in their theories. Part of moral decision-making involves cognitive ability, but there are also social and cultural influences. Indeed, one's religious culture is often intertwined with their ethnic culture, and their experiences in both arenas serve to form their personal identity. But Lawrence Kohlberg approached moral development more from the cognitive aspect, and in fact largely mirrors Piaget's cognitive development stages (Kohlberg, 1958, 1984). The application then is more to moral development than broadly to other areas. Moral development, and its companion spiritual development, warrant separate consideration of study from religious development in the context of ministry. While related, they are distinct concepts. In an effort to better understand humans as holistic beings, moral development is appropriate to study in the context of the broader aspects of human development (we will discuss moral development and decision-making further in chapter 37).

Kohlberg's pre-conventional stage of development (what is best for me) is heard in younger classes when a child says "mine" as he or she sees another child holding one of the classroom toys. At the conventional level, a person has developed a slightly more complex ability to make moral decisions, typically from the social influence perspective, with the self largely at the center of that process. This is where religious conformity is often birthed and can be argued is a stage that many never exceed. In fact, from a social perspective, it is much easier to have members of a social setting, including a religious setting, to simply follow the rules or face social consequences. Sometimes those consequences are also couched in terms of eternal consequences, but it is the social pressure that leads to the decision process.

Individuals who develop to the post-conventional stage learn to consider abstract principles of morality and focus more on what may be considered higher principles of morality apart from reward, punishment, or social pressure. It may be that these are the ones who develop more of a relationship with God, rather than obedience from fear of eternal condemnation (which should be one of our goals).

These theories and others are already impacting our congregations. The division of age groups, for example, is intentional based on views of a child's cognitive and moral development stage and ability. Let us consider other ways this research can help us in ministering to young people and their families.

Application to Ministry

Decision Making: Why, Not What

Simple observation reveals that people develop at various stages and rates and often do not reach the same maturity levels. In fact, one of the things that is emphasized in Fowler's stages of faith (Fowler, 1981) is that some never reach certain levels of moral development. At the same time, we must be careful not to place a higher value on one than the other, even though it might seem preferable for a person to be able to make a higher-level moral decision versus decision-making based on legal perspectives or social pressures. In reality, they all have their place, and all require grace. When ministering to young adults in particular, it is perhaps more important to notice *how* they make decisions than the perceived correctness of the decisions themselves. To do this, ministers must be willing to listen and be open to various perspectives, even as they may guide the young person toward the correct moral choice. Sometimes the choice or behavior itself is not the end goal, but the development of the individual as a moral agent who knows how to make good choices.

This is reflected in Scripture, even though we often miss or dismiss it. For example, Paul taught in 1 Corinthians 8:1–13, that some could eat meat sacrificed to idols without sin, and without violating their consciences. Others, however, could not eat such meat because it would be a violation of their consciences. Those who had no problem eating meat offered to idols were to be considerate of what we might call the "moral development" of the others in deciding to partake or refrain from doing so. The same principles are taught in Romans 14:1–10 regarding views of certain days, and what can be eaten. In this context, Paul goes on to warn against making judgments of others who may have different views, which especially applies to perspectives we might have of young people in the process of their moral development.

That is not to suggest that morals are relative to the individual at all. But, it is a reminder for us to view others, as well as ourselves, as individuals on a journey to perfection, but not having reached it (Phil 3:13–15; Heb 6:1–12). Our goal in youth ministry should not be mere religious conformity, but to assist young people in developing the ability to make their own decisions based on good and godly criteria that go beyond human "rules."

Age of Accountability

Human development should be considered as we view young people in the context of what we call the "age of accountability." There is no designated age of accountability in Scripture. Just because a young person was raised in a Christian home and is 12 or 13 years old, does not mean that they should be coerced into making a decision about baptism and salvation that they may not be ready for. In fact, many of the developmental theories and a plethora of subsequent research indicates that by the age of five or six, a lot of the influences characteristic of social learning theory have already been ingrained in the individual. That does not mean we designate six years old as the age of accountability, nor does it mean we designate 18-year-olds as such, though that is when society may determine a person is legally an adult. In fact, recent perspectives from youth ministers, educators, researchers, and even parents, show adolescent development is a longer process today than compared to past generations. This is reflected in the increasingly common phrase, "21 is the new 18."

Conclusion

Considering an individual's nature and nurture at the beginning of life, their social and cultural interactions throughout life, and the broad perspective of human development across the lifespan, we must learn to minister to students as individuals. If only we could get Calen to behave like Emily in class! The goofy immature in the youth group may seem less developed than the advanced student who can quote a lot of Scripture, but it may be that the latter may be less developed, able only to conform to social expectations. We may have a preference regarding who we want in our youth group, but ultimately God has called us to minister to them all individually, helping them to become who God has created them to be, not necessarily who we decide they should be.

Discussion Questions

1. Expand on the discussion of "normal" in this chapter.
2. Share your thoughts on the nature versus nurture debate.
3. How can understanding the process of human development assist us as we work with young people?
4. Share your thoughts on the discussion of the "age of accountability."

Bibliography

Belsky, Jay, and Kevin M. Beaver. "Cumulative-Genetic Plasticity, Parenting and Adolescent Self-Regulation." *Journal of Child Psychology and Psychiatry* 52.5 (2010): 619–26. https://doi.org/10.1111/j.1469-7610.2010.02327.x.

Berk, Laura E. "History, Theory, and Research Strategies." Pages 6–7 in *Development through the Lifespan*, 66th ed., 6–7. Boston, MA: Pearson, 2014.

Erikson, Erik H. *Childhood and Society*. London: Imago Publ., 1950.

Fowler, W. James. *Stages of Faith: The Psychology of Human Development and the Quest for Meaning*. 2nd ed. New York, NY: Harper Collins, 1981.

Georgieff, Michael K., Phu V. Tran, and Erik S. Carlson. "Atypical Fetal Development: Fetal Alcohol Syndrome, Nutritional Deprivation, Teratogens, and Risk for Neurodevelopmental Disorders and Psychopathology." *Development and Psychopathology* 30.3 (2018): 1063–86. https://doi.org/10.1017/s0954579418000500.

Kohlberg, Lawrence. "The Development of Modes of Thinking and Choices in Years 10 to 16," Dissertation. Chicago: The University of Chicago, 1958.

Kohlberg, Lawrence. *The Psychology of Moral Development Nature and Validity of Moral Stages*. San Francisco, CA: Harper & Row, 1984.

May, Philip A., Barbara G. Tabachnick, J. Phillip Gossage, Wendy O. Kalberg, Anna-Susan Marais, Luther K. Robinson, Melanie A. Manning, et al. "Maternal Factors Predicting Cognitive and Behavioral Characteristics of Children with Fetal Alcohol Spectrum Disorders." *Journal of Developmental & Behavioral Pediatrics* 34.5 (2013): 314–25. https://doi.org/10.1097/dbp.0b013e3182905587.

McRay, Barrett. *Teaching the Next Generations: A Comprehensive Guide for Teaching Christian Formation*. Edited by Terry Limhart. Ada, MI: Baker Academic, 2016.

Piaget, Jean. "The Stages of the Intellectual Development of the Child." *Bulletin of the Menninger Clinic* 26.3 (May 1, 1962): 120–28.

Runge, Shannon K., Brent J. Small, G. Peggy McFall, and Roger A. Dixon. "APOE Moderates the Association between Lifestyle Activities and Cognitive Performance: Evidence of Genetic Plasticity in Aging." *Journal of the International Neuropsychological Society* 20.5 (2014): 478–86. https://doi.org/10.1017/s1355617714000356.

Vygotskiĭ, L. S., Michael Cole, Sally Stein, and Allan Sekula. *Mind in Society: The Development of Higher Psychological Processes*. Cambridge, MA: Harvard University Press, 1978.

Weder, Natalie, Huiping Zhang, Kevin Jensen, Bao Zhu Yang, Arthur Simen, Andrea Jackowski, Deborah Lipschitz, et al. "Child Abuse, Depression, and Methylation in Genes Involved with Stress, Neural Plasticity, and Brain Circuitry." *Journal of the American Academy of Child & Adolescent Psychiatry* 53.4 (2014). https://doi.org/10.1016/j.jaac.2013.12.025.

Chapter 38
Adolescent Development, Part 2
Moral Development and Decision-Making Processes
James C. Guy

Introduction

In the context of understanding the moral and spiritual development of young people, it is of utmost importance to define the following terms: religion, spirituality, and morality. In many contexts, these are used interchangeably. While they certainly do intersect, they are also very distinct concepts, and worthy of consideration as such in the context of ministry. As we look at young people and find ways to help them through the process of their development, we must first understand what we are walking them through.

What Is "Religious"?

Though there is still a lot of variation, *religion* is generally defined in the research literature as related to the organized religious community, a set of teachings or beliefs, rituals and, practices, symbols, including religious leadership and organization. The term religious development is also not limited to the Christian religion. It can include any organized or identifiable religion such as Wiccan,

Buddhism, Muslim, Hinduism, Taoism, and Confucianism. But it can also include lesser organized religions such as folk religions and ancestor worship religions. Yet, it does not have to be organized around belief in a higher being. It can also be organized around certain philosophies that include transcendent concepts, without necessitating a belief in a higher being or beings. These can include concepts of the cosmos, ultimate reality, consciousness, origins of being, and beliefs about eternity in the afterlife. It has often been debated whether or not philosophies such as atheism should be included in the definition of a religion. In the broad sense, agnosticism, atheism, and even science itself may be included in the category of "religion" (and frequently is). The reason this is important is because as we examine aspects of human development in research, we are not looking at the development of a human specifically in the context of Christianity. The determination of aspects of development should also not be defined by the extent to which they adopt Christianity's shared beliefs. That is what would be referred to as religious adherence.

What Is "Spiritual"?

While there is some interaction between the spiritual and religious, *spirituality* is defined distinctly more intrinsically to include a sense of a higher being, sense of an afterlife, sense of an internal connection to a higher being, or something transcendent to the individual. It can sometimes include elements of the mind and emotions in that context as well. Some of the mental and emotional constructs might include things such as happiness, joy, compassion, and a sense of justice. It is important to distinguish between these because we often refer to religious development when we really mean spiritual development. The primary difference between them is that spirituality is more personal and intrinsic whereas religion is more extrinsic and socially constructed. Spiritual development might be illustrated by Paul's reference to the contrast in maturity between milk and meat (1 Cor 3:2). Paul was describing what we would call spiritual development rather than religious development. And while it is important to help young people grow in the "knowledge of the truth" (1 Tim 2:4), we often try to do so by emphasizing a religious development (rituals, practices), rather than a spiritual development (internal transformation and relationship with God). In 2 Peter 3:18, it refers to "the knowledge of our Lord and Savior Jesus Christ," not the knowledge of religious belief, nor even of Scripture (though other passages do). This can be an important distinction. The ability to develop religiously (growing in the knowledge of doctrine and Scripture and in spiritual habits) should be considered dependent upon the more internalized spiritual development of a relationship with Christ from the heart.

What is "Moral"?

Considering the development of young people, the religious and spiritual aspects are intrinsically connected to what we might refer to as *moral* development or moral decision-making. Morals have to do with the principles of right versus wrong that guide decisions and behavior. A related term to morals is the word *ethics*. In my *Psychology of Religion and Spirituality* course, I define "ethics" as the rules, laws, policies, or organizational social norms (including church norms) that guide us, and "morals" as the principles of right and wrong that should drive those ethics. Yet there is a reason that we often use the phrase "you cannot legislate morals." That is because morality takes place within the individual, including the need to decide whether a law or rule is in fact right or wrong. Laws are in fact the codification of mutually agreed-upon moral norms in a given society. You may not legislate morals, but legislation flows out of the internal morals of a people.

In the context of ministry, these distinctions are important when applied to our responsibilities to "train up a child" (Deut 6:7; Prov 22:6; Eph 6:4). Doing so includes some level of deciding "the way he should go." But to do that without looking at the young person as an individual essentially results in an effort to force conformity rather than to facilitate improved individual development. Not only must the young person have the capacity to understand and grasp various concepts, but also the level or characteristics of moral and spiritual development that are foundational to developing their own faith. The commonly identified levels of spiritual development also generally follow that of the broader perspective of human development levels identified in the research.

This is one of the challenges we often face in Christianity. Parents and leaders go to great lengths to be sure that young people adopt the shared beliefs regarding Christianity but may fail to see the person as an individual in the process of doing so. Additionally, forced compliance to shared beliefs and practices (religion) can actually hinder spiritual (internal) development in many ways. That in turn ultimately hinders the moral and religious development of the young person we are trying to guide. This can often give the appearance of healthy development because the person adopts the religious beliefs, but they do so out of a sense of fear, punishment, or social pressure rather than an individual and internalized adoption of the belief. They may develop religiously in the sense of practicing the expected belief system, but the practices do not emanate from an internalized spiritual sense of how the practice connects to God, others, and to self. Jesus illustrated this when he chided the Pharisees for practicing the religious rules, but "forgetting the weighty matters of the law" (Matt 23:23). In some ways, those weightier matters connected more to spiritual elements than the practice itself. We have often used this passage in the very opposite way that Jesus seems to have intended it. That is, it is often emphasized that "these you should have done" and as a side note "Oh yeah—and you should do the others also." But the emphasis here is not on the religious practice of the law, but the deeper spiritual meaning and purpose of it. Think of the term "legalism" in the context of distinguishing between the religious and the spiritual, as opposed to the interaction of the two.

Moral Development and Decision Making

Moral decision-making has been studied in many contexts, including the context of religion. It is clear from the plethora of research on parent-child relationships, that parents have a large influence on their children's decision-making processes (Hill, et al., 2018; Smith, 2009, 260), as do peers and religious leaders – including youth ministers (Smith, et al, 2005, 26, 260; Powell and Clark, 2011, 75). Much of the existing research builds upon Bandura's social learning theory, but that research has largely been conducted with children and is only one piece of the puzzle.

We do know that we all learn from our environmental and social influences. But it is also known that the parental influence on children and adolescents diminishes during college age (Hill, et al., 2018). This is likely due to a number of things including cognitive development, diminished contact with parents, and a sense of freedom without parental consequences for decisions. However, it can also stem from a more internalized spiritually-based decision-making process that builds upon prior parental and church influence. Children need to learn to obey authority because they consider that to be morally right. However, I often encourage parents to go beyond "because I said so" when instructing their children. Not only should children and young people internalize the reason to obey authority, but they need to be equipped with decision-making skills that allow them to make their own moral decisions even when there is no threat of punishment/reward from authority.

James Fowler's Research

James Fowler (1981) describes the contrast between the levels of spiritual development as the difference between being in the middle of a river and seeing only the flow of the stream around you as opposed to the more advanced ability to stand on the bank of the river and seeing the bigger picture of where the river is coming from and going. It is helpful to consider this type of development process in young people because they do need to be guided when they can only see where they stand in the middle of the river. But we also need to keep in mind that we are helping them to be able to make moral decisions standing on the bank of the river and seeing the larger picture of where decisions lead.

Lawrence Kohlberg's Research

Lawrence Kohlberg (1984) seems to emphasize the process of moral development as including moral reasoning or decision-making, as did Erik Erickson who referred to the adult midlife crisis as equivalent to the teenage identity crisis (Erikson, 1950). That makes sense as you study and work around teens and preteens. They begin to struggle with who they are, what their life is really about, whether they really matter, and their personal value in the world. While we guide them in finding healthy spiritual identity, we must also let them wrestle with that on their own internally. Otherwise, they only learn to do what we tell them which hinders the development of their moral decision-making abilities.

The Development of the Conscience

Essential to the discussion of any aspect of religious and spiritual development, and especially that of moral decision-making, must be an understanding of the development of the conscience. The conscience should be understood as an internalized construct similar to what we might consider a thermostat or compass to be. A thermostat controls or regulates the output of the HVAC unit. Similarly, the conscience regulates the decision-making processes of the person. Even Sigmund Freud, a professed atheist as an adult, identified the holistic nature of the conscience as he researched human psychology from a scientific perspective. He was studying people who are made in the image of God, even though he may not have acknowledged such. His id, ego, and superego are reflective of the decision-making process that humans go through (cf. Estep, 2010, 124). What he called the *id* equates to the "fleshly" desire to do something. The *ego* has to do with the decision-making process and involves wrestling between the "flesh and spirit" (cf. Rom 7 and 8). What he defined as the *superego* is the internalized healthy conscience that ultimately influences the decision-making process.

For us to understand the young people we work with, and to facilitate their proper development, we must consider how developed their consciences may be on an individual level, and without judgment. This is where the intersection of religion and spirituality often takes place. The conscience should be considered the spiritual element, but it is undoubtedly influenced by religious and familial experiences. For example, we may be shocked when the most well-behaved junior high girl, who is also the daughter of some of the key leaders and workers in the church, flips the bird to the boy who is irritating her in class. She then responds, "Well he was irritating me—what's the big deal?" We may believe that this young person has been taught the right ways and should understand that this thing she did was wrong. Yet, in trying to make sense of her actions, we should consider that there may be things taking place at home behind closed doors that have influenced her not only in committing the act but in the response to it. Of course, we have to be careful about assuming such and be reminded that there are many internal and external influences on behavioral decisions and the response of the conscience. Young people especially are in the process of trying to find their own way regarding the moral decision-making process.

We should be mindful of what Paul said about the conscience being seared as with a hot iron (1 Tim 4:2). However, it is easy for us to focus too specifically on the behavior, including the degree to which it fits what we define as religious development or conformity. In doing so, we miss the internalized spiritual element of what is actually driving the behavior. We must keep in mind that God created us as individuals and provided us with free will. The free will can get young people, and all of us, into trouble. But it also allows us to take risks and explore things. This exploration may or may not conform to religious expectations.

We do not acknowledge this exploration to diminish the importance of believing and practicing the truth God has set forth. It just helps us to understand that as we work with young people, they must ultimately make their own choices. Our job is simply to guide them in doing so. But as we do that, we should focus more on development of the internalized concepts of spirituality and what drives the conscience rather than only on the behavior itself. As parents and ministers, if we simply focus on trying to correct behavior, we miss important fundamental elements of spiritual development in our young people. Let them explore. Let them learn. Walk them through the process, keeping in mind that the Holy Spirit can touch intrinsic parts that we can only influence from the outside.

Application to Youth Ministry

Human development includes biological, psychological, and sociological influences on all aspects of development, including religious/spiritual/moral development. We are not machines, and the different elements of humans were created by God in His image. We are taught to love the Lord our God with all of our heart, soul, mind, and strength (Mark 12:30–31). From what we know about human development as a lifelong process, we should be careful about expecting too much too soon from our young people. Jesus himself went through the process of growing in "wisdom, stature, and favor with God and man" (Luke 2:52). What that means is we will often have to let young people experience their moral crises and arrive at decisive conclusions different than ours as they develop. Again, that does not define truth as an existential experience, but it is a reminder that we are all individuals on a journey, and we are going at different speeds. We are also in the pursuit of perfection and truth. None of us, including parents and ministers, find that perfectly. Therefore, we must be patient with our young people as they work through the challenges that come their way while walking them through the process. We provide the foundation of Scripture and a healthy concept of a God and relationship with Him but allow them to progress at their own paces. In fact, I would suggest that we need to have that same level of patience even with ourselves as leaders.

Preferences vs. Scripture

These principles should also be applied more broadly, considering youth ministry as family and church ministry. For example, at what we might consider a relatively conservative church, the young people requested to sing some of the songs often called camp or devotional songs on Sunday mornings. The adults generally did not have any concern with them singing them in their teen devotionals or at church camp, but it was not the norm in the Sunday corporate worship setting. A well-meaning deacon resisted the request because he believed that young people only wanted to sing newer songs because they were being rebellious. The deacon was drawing conclusions for which there was no evidence and was unfairly demonizing the young people.

There are other examples that might be given here. The challenge in considering requests from young people is to determine whether our responses are based on consistent and sound interpretation and application of Scripture or whether they are based on adult and generational preferences. Often, we determine right and wrong based on our preferences and what our parents taught us rather than on Scripture itself. That is an immature form of moral decision-making (cf. Kohlberg's research noted above).

If we are trying to help young people develop a sense of connection to God and His word, responding to their questions or requests with adult preferences instead of sound exegesis of Scripture, can actually cause the opposite effect. It can influence either a rebelliousness in young people against older generations seeking their conformity or they incorrectly equate the two and decide that their disagreement with humans in the church is a reflection of God himself. They then not only resist the religious connection to God's people but may often resist the connection to God as well. At a minimum, it can result in the common practice of "I'll take Jesus but not the church," or "I'm spiritual but not religious." It reminds us that the answer to our question as to why young people are leaving the church may, at least in part, be answered by looking in the mirror. Practically speaking, this means that even when young people do things differently than we think they should, and perhaps even when those things may in fact be wrong, we need to pay attention to how we walk them through that process.

Create Connections

One of the most eye-opening things in youth ministry is the spark that you see in young people when the older people involved themselves in what they are doing. At one of the congregations illustrated earlier, the college group did their thing, the young people did their thing, and the older people did their thing. They loved each other, but they did not interact well. There was a sense of tension between the different groups, largely because they had never really interacted on a more personal level. So, what we did was to invite some of the older people who were perhaps the most opposed to some of the things the younger groups did to attend some of their events. We also had the young people act as cooks and servers for some of the older group's events.

To see each group serving the other group and to see them interacting with one another, created a spark that is hard to describe. It was simply a matter of both groups understanding and accepting one another, even though they retained their distinct preferences and even beliefs in some respects. This kind of intergenerational contact facilitates the spiritual and moral development of young people and greatly improves how they respond to what we are trying to teach them. It is most effective when it includes more than just fellowship but also intentional sharing of life experiences and world views. This exchange can go a long way in helping young people to sort through their own worldviews.

Conclusion

Our emphasis should be on the spiritual development of the conscience, which then will affect the religious actions and decisions - not the other way around. That does not mean that the religious involvement does not influence the spiritual. As noted in the previous chapter's discussion of social learning, a large part of how a person develops internally is influenced by their environmental experiences. That is why it is important to be sure that how we do church includes consideration for how young people want to do church. It means we must not call something sinful just because we do not prefer it or based on misuse of Scripture. If we truly want to help young people develop into spiritual beings with internalized connections to God, and not simply "mini me's" conforming to our preferences only until they become adults, then we may have to be the ones to adapt, at least at times. If we are going to do youth ministry well, we must move beyond mere religious practice development to the holistic and internalized spiritual development of our young people that leads to godly practices.

Discussion Questions

1. What are your thoughts on the distinction between "religion" and "spirituality"?
2. Why do you think we tend to focus so much on the external actions of young people without helping them with the internal thinking that impacts their choices?
3. What are some ways we can create more intergenerational connections?
4. Discuss the challenge of separating personal preferences from biblical principles.

Bibliography

Estep, James and Jonathan Kim, eds. *Christian Formation: Integrating Theology and Human Development.* Nashville: B&H Academic, 2010.

Erikson, Erik H. *Childhood and Society.* London: Imago Publ., 1950.

Fowler, W. James. *Stages of Faith: The Psychology of Human Development and the Quest for Meaning.* 2nd ed. New York: Harper Collins, 1981.

Hood, Ralph W., Peter C. Hill, and Bernard Spilka. "Religion in Adolescence and Youth Adulthood." In *The Psychology of Religion: An Empirical Approach.* New York: Guilford Press, 2018.

Kohlberg, Lawrence. *The Psychology of Moral Development Nature and Validity of Moral Stages.* San Francisco: Harper & Row, 1984.

Powell, Kara and Chap Clark. *Sticky Faith: Everyday Ideas to Build Lasting Faith in Your Kids.* Grand Rapids: Zondervan, 2011.

Smith, Christian. *Soul Searching: The Religious and Spiritual Lives of American Teenagers.* Reprint ed. Kettering, England: Oxford University Press, 2009.

Chapter 39
Adolescent Spiritual Development
Justin Morton

For parents, youth workers, and fellow members of the Lord's church, one of our greatest concerns is the development of our young people. You want the young people you work with to be successful in whatever they choose to do. You desire for them to make positive decisions, which leads to health and happiness. However, I cannot think of anything we desire more than for our young people to grow up and be spiritually mature followers of Jesus.

Our young people are walking away from the Lord at an alarming rate. Our teenagers and young adults have stopped studying their Bibles and attending worship services. Congregations, which were once filled with vibrant, faithful young people, find themselves slowly dying. Sadly, many of those young people did not just walk away from their particular congregation, but they walked away from the Lord altogether.

What happened to all those "faithful" young people? While it may be tempting to place blame on our teenagers, maybe the problem is not with the young people but with the church's definition of what a spiritually maturing young person looks like. Many congregations view the faithfulness of young people based on external factors they can see. We deem our youth to be faithful if they attend worship services, Bible classes, and youth trips. While these contribute to the development of our young people, they do not make a spiritually mature follower of Jesus.

Faith and the Next Generation

The job of a youth worker is not to fill the pews or the bus with young people. Unfortunately, too many youth workers feel like building the numbers is their primary role. Your job is to help develop spiritually mature Christians who love Jesus with all their heart, soul, and mind (Matt 22:37–38). Youth ministers and volunteers need to focus on helping shape teens into the image of Jesus (cf. Eph 4:11–16). This is what any ministry is all about!

In 1 Peter 2, we read, "For to this you have been called, because Christ also suffered for you, leaving you an example, so that you might follow in his steps" (1 Pet 2:21). Do you remember learning how to write the letters of the alphabet? You would trace the dotted lines and curves over and over, following the pattern of the practice letters until your letters looked like the examples. This idea of following the pattern is the same way we should follow Jesus. Our lives and the lives of our teenagers should replicate our perfect example, Jesus Christ.

The eternal destination of our young people is at stake, and churches and youth workers must focus on what truly matters in youth ministry. No, it is not pizza parties, dodgeball tournaments, or lock-ins. Ultimately our ministry is not about fun and games. Youth ministry is about helping develop young people into faithful followers of Jesus. We want teens to mature in their faith and knowledge and to conform to His image. Your goal as a youth worker should be to help teens develop spiritually and to faithfully serve Jesus.

You Must Help Parents Win

One of the most vital things you can do to help with the spiritual development of your young people is to help equip and support the parents of your young people. I know many youth ministers like to think they have the greatest spiritual impact on their teens. I mean, we are the planners of some amazing events, retreats, and activities! But the truth is you are not the greatest spiritual influence in the lives of most of your youth group members. While you are "one" of the influences in your teens' lives, you are not the "biggest" influence. Mark DeVries, in his book, *Family-Based Youth Ministry*, said,

> Like a rubber band, young people may stretch away from their parents' values during their teenage years. But when they become adults, they will ordinarily return to the core values of their parents.[1]

Despite the fact that teenagers will sometimes rebel against their parents' upbringing, many times they end up finding their way back. Teenagers need to witness Christ-centered values in their homes.

Consider the young protégé of Paul. Timothy was blessed to learn from this great apostle. Certainly, Paul had a tremendous influence on Timothy. Can you imagine the wisdom Timothy gained as they traveled together or as he witnessed Paul teach and minister to individuals and churches? What a great "youth minister" Paul must have been! However, when talking to Timothy about his faith, Paul declared Timothy's sincere faith was handed down by his mother Eunice, and his grandmother Lois (2 Tim 1:5).

Paul understood something that many youth workers and volunteers need to understand. The spiritual development of adolescents starts in the home with their parents or guardians. Whether the parents take up that role or not, they are the main spiritual influences on their children. The role of primary spiritual influence should never be farmed out to a youth minister or youth volunteer. Rather, youth ministry should serve as a resource to help parents win the battle of spiritual development for their children. Jim Burns wrote, "One of the greatest common denominators in the long-term development of a loving, intimate relationship with Jesus is not the quality of our programming; it is the influence and nurture of the family."[2] Parents or guardians, who spend hours with their teenagers as they grow and mature, have a far greater influence on the spiritual development of those teens than we, as youth workers, could ever have.

As a youth minister or leader, you may create some amazing events to serve the church and the community. You may organize engaging activities and events, bringing together great crowds of young people. You may dedicate a considerable portion of your week to studying God's Word and preparing lessons to build up your teens. You may have played a significant role in the spiritual development of some of your teens. If these things are so, keep up the great work! However, please do not ever forget, that while you are an influence in the lives of your teens, you are not the main influence in their lives. That God-given role belongs to their parents. May you strive to build a ministry that helps your parents win the battle in the spiritual development of your young people.

Your Part in the Spiritual Development of Young People

While you are not the primary influence in the lives of your teens, youth ministers still have an integral role in the spiritual development of your young people. Outside of helping your parents win, what else can you do to help foster spiritual growth in the teens in your youth group? As we consider this question, let's reflect on the life of Jesus. Following the pattern of Jesus's example should be our priority as Christians, and we want to encourage our young people to strive to follow the pattern of Jesus Christ as well.

Teach Them to Love God's Word

Jesus placed a high value on the Scriptures. In Luke's account of Jesus's entrance to Nazareth, he records that Jesus entered the synagogue on the Sabbath day as He customarily did. When He read from the Scriptures, He found a passage in Isaiah that prophesied about the Messiah (Luke 4:16–20). Jesus did not simply read the Scriptures; Jesus valued the Word of God enough to know the Scriptures. When Jesus found Himself in the wilderness being tempted by Satan, He quoted Scripture (Matt 4:1–11). Jesus was able to do this because He had a deep love for the Word of God.

As youth leaders, you want your teens to make wise decisions and do what is right. Well, you cannot expect them to do what is right unless they know what is right. The Psalmist said, "I have stored up your word in my heart, that I might not sin again you" (Ps 119:11). God's Word teaches us the truth, convicts our hearts, and shows us the way to salvation. Be sure you are putting time into your own studies, so you are able to unearth some of the treasures of Scripture and teach them to your young people. Developing spiritually mature followers of Jesus, who are conformed to His image, will never happen unless young people fall in love with the Word of God.

Teach Them to Enjoy Serving Others

No matter how busy Jesus was, He always made time for others. Right after He learned of the death of John the Baptist, He got into a boat and went to a desolate place by Himself (Matt 14:12–13). Jesus probably wanted to be alone to grieve the loss of His dear friend, however, what happened next sheds light on the heart of our Lord: "When he went ashore he saw a great crowd, and he had compassion on them and healed their sick" (Matt 14:14). Throughout the Gospel accounts, we see over and over how Jesus had compassion for people (Matt 15:32–28; Lk. 7:11–17). He ministered and served like He did because of the love He had for people.

If you want to develop spiritually mature young people who are conformed to the image of Jesus, you must place great importance on serving others just as Jesus did. He came into this world, not to be served, but to serve (Matt 20:26–28). Jesus did this by ministering to others whenever He had the opportunity. As youth ministers and workers, you must help young people develop a heart to love and serve other people. We must give our teenagers opportunities to demonstrate their love for others by giving them opportunities to serve. In Matthew 22 Jesus was asked about the greatest command, but in His reply, Jesus decided to clarify that the two greatest commandments involve loving God and loving others (cf. Matt 22:37-39). What better way to demonstrate our love for both God and fellow man than through joyfully serving those around us? In order to develop spiritually mature young people who model the example of Jesus, we must help teach them to enjoy serving others.

Teach Them to Value Prayer

Jesus was a man committed to prayer. No matter how busy He was, prayer was a vital part of the life of Jesus (Matt 14:23). Jesus understood the value of a strong prayer life, giving us examples of prayers of thanksgiving (John 11:41–42) and prayers for help when making major life decisions (Luke 6:12–16). Many times we read about Jesus going away to pray to the Father (cf. Luke 5:16). He often prayed for lengthy periods of time, emphasizing the significance of those conversations with His Father.

Unfortunately, prayer is one of the most neglected spiritual disciplines for Christians today, even though the Bible has so much to say about prayer (Luke 11:9; 18:1; I Thess 5:17; Phil 4:6; Col 4:2). Those who work with young people need to be helping them to cultivate a deep prayer life. While you cannot make someone pray, you can demonstrate the value of prayer in your classes and through your personal example. When you talk about prayer, do not talk about prayer as a last resort when you are desperate. Instead, talk about prayer as your first line of defense. Let young people know that before you do anything else, you are always going to pray to your Heavenly Father. Begin and end every class session with prayer. Take time to pray individually with your teens. Demonstrate in their presence that you believe in the power of prayer in all situations, from requests to rejoicing. Remind them that the Bible teaches that the prayer of a righteous person can accomplish much good (Jas 5:16). If young people are going to be shaped into the image of Jesus, they need to learn the value of an earnest prayer life.

Never forget to discuss all the ways God has answered your prayers. Beginning your classes with prayer requests can be a great way to show value in prayer. But remember to follow up and praise God before your students when God answers those prayer requests. You can keep a list of prayer requests on a poster or bulletin board in your classroom and highlight or mark those prayer requests as God answers them. By doing this you will publicly demonstrate to them the value of prayer.

Teach Them to Seek Connections

As Christians, we all have certain connections we value. In developing spiritually mature followers of Jesus, connections with other believers play a significant role. Many of your young people may feel as though they do not have any meaningful relationships with members of the church. They may enjoy spending time with other teens in the youth group but may see the church as a place they go on Sundays, rather than a group of people who love and care for others.

When you look at the early church, one of the things you will notice is how the early church was often together and had all things in common. They were a people who had connections (Acts 2:42–

47). No wonder the early church grew like it did. People had connections with other followers of Jesus outside of their immediate family. And what about Jesus? A quick reading through the Gospel records demonstrates the importance Jesus placed on relationships. While He had many followers, Jesus chose to develop a closer relationship with twelve men. And even out of those twelve men, Jesus had a very special and unique relationship with three of them.

We all have connections with people we not only consider to be our friends but also individuals we know we can count on whenever we have a need. They are friends who feel more like family (Prov 18:24). One of the best things you can do for your young people is to intentionally surround them with a wide variety of people who are intentionally invested in their lives. Have older men and women serve in your youth ministry. Invite parents to participate in different roles for activities and events. Encourage your elders to attend youth retreats and ask them to teach one of the weekend Bible classes. Challenge your teens to "adopt" a widow or widower or a member whose family does not attend services; have them sit with these individuals during worship. Over my years in ministry, I have found that students tend to remember few of the Bible lessons I gave, but they treasure the relationships they built with adults who love the Lord and love them. Relationships with other members of God's church can have a lasting impact on the spiritual development of your young people.

Keep On Keeping On

Over the course of your time working with young people, you are going to have a lot of students come and go. Some of those students will come from a great family background with parents who follow the pattern of Jesus the best they can. Other students you serve will come from a much different background and may have little to no spiritual influence in their homes. While their parents or guardians will have the biggest influence on their spiritual lives, your influence should not be doubted. Your desire to love God and follow the pattern of Jesus can provide support and encouragement for your teens as they grow in your youth ministry.

My hope and prayer is that you will use the talents and abilities God has given you to help shape the hearts and lives of the young people you serve. You may not see the effect you have now, but someday you may find out you played an instrumental role in the spiritual development of your youth group members. And because of your time and efforts, more people will get to spend eternity with the Lord.

Discussion Questions

1. Why do many churches and youth ministries focus more on fun activities and big numbers rather than on spiritual growth?
2. How can you help equip and support the parents or guardians of your teenagers as they help them grow and mature in their faith?
3. What Scriptures teach us about the importance of spiritual growth?
4. This chapter discusses "following the pattern" of Jesus. What are some practical ways you can help mentor the teens in your ministry to follow the example Jesus set?

Notes

[1] Mark DeVries, Family-Based Youth Ministry (Downers Grove, IL: Varsity Press, 1994), 65.

[2] Jim Burns, Uncommon Youth Ministry: Your Onramp to Launching an Extraordinary Youth Ministry (Ventura, CA: Gospel Light, 2008), 66.

Bibliography

DeVries, Mark. *Family-Based Youth Ministry*. Downers Grove, IL: InterVarsity Press, 1994.

Burns, Jim. *Uncommon Youth Ministry: Your Onramp to Launching an Extraordinary Youth Ministry*. Ventura, CA: Gospel Light, 2008.

Chapter 40
Development and Discipleship
W. Kirk Brothers

An "Aha" Moment

Graduate school broadened my horizons in countless ways. One of my "aha" moments took place during my doctoral work on biblical leadership. For the seminary where I studied, discipleship was at the heart of leadership. Jesus called His followers to make disciples by going, baptizing, and teaching (cf. the three participles in Matt 28:18–20). We often act as if baptism is the finish line, but it is not. Teaching "all things I commanded you" must follow. If we can better understand the ways people develop, then we can better develop disciples who understand the will and word of Jesus. Thus, my courses, reading, and research included delving into social science research on how human beings develop their personalities, thinking, decision-making, and faith. As I wrestled with the work of researchers like Erickson, Piaget, and Kohlberg, I realized that I was learning things that every preacher, youth minister, Bible class teacher, and elder in the brotherhood should be learning. Education and psychology majors (and leadership majors) are learning these things in our Christian colleges, but not Bible majors. This chapter is my feeble attempt to begin to correct that oversight. I pray it provides you with some "aha" moments as well.

Human Development Is Biblical

Jesus, the eternal Son of God and co-creator of the world, became a human being and went through a process of human development: "And Jesus increased in wisdom and in stature and in favor with God and man" (Luke 2:52). Jesus continued to be God even in human form (cf. John 20:28), but in fully becoming human He emptied himself (cf. Phil 2:7). Thus, He needed to increase in wisdom. In one of his letters to the church at Corinth, Paul stated, "When I was a child, I spoke like a child, I thought like a child, I reasoned like a child. When I became a man, I gave up childish ways" (1 Cor 13:11). Paul understood that children and adults think differently, and they make decisions in different ways. The more we can understand about this process of human development, the better we can potentially disciple people into the likeness of Christ.

Personality Development

Theory: Erikson

There are many theorists that we might consider in this section, but I am just going to highlight the work of German-born psychologist Erik Erikson. His research with children led him to develop a psychosocial theory of human development that viewed "each stage of life as associated with a specific psychological struggle, a struggle that contributes to a major aspect of the personality" (Erikson Institute, www.erikson.edu, 2024). He referred to these struggles as "crises." As each person successfully navigated a crisis/struggle, he or she developed a characteristic of a healthy personality. Rick Yount observes, "If a child has a healthy interaction with others, and if the basic crisis of a given stage is resolved appropriately, then the child is ready for the next stage. If the crisis is not resolved, it will become increasingly difficult to resolve in the future" (Yount, 2010, 58). These "crises" to which the individual seeks healthy adaptation are trust, autonomy, initiative, competence, identity, intimacy, generativity, and ego integrity/wisdom. One might understand them as follows:

1. Trust: Realistic trust in others
2. Autonomy: Choice vs. self-restraint
3. Initiative: Self-controlled pursuit
4. Competence: Mastery, ability, areas of strength
5. Identity: True to self/others, sense of self in relation to others
6. Intimacy/Love: Committed intimacy
7. Generativity/Care: Nurture of others
8. Ego Integrity/Wisdom: Looking back with satisfied reflection on one's life (cf. Yount, 2010, 59–68).

Let me illustrate the significance of these crises. A key struggle early in life is learning whether one can trust others. My parents were foster parents. I had fourteen foster brothers and sisters in addition to my two biological sisters. Two of my foster siblings then became permanent members of our family. When my parents took my younger brother in, he was three months old and had a broken leg and a fractured arm from being thrown up against the wall. He is now in his 40s and has been loved by my family for over 40 years, yet he still struggles with trust.

In addition, every teenager is in a search for identity (cf. Erikson's fifth stage). Research conducted by Fuller Seminary resulted in the book *3 Big Questions that Change Every Teenager*. Kara Powell, Brad Griffin, and their team identified three key questions that today's teenagers are struggling with: Who am I? (identity), Where do I fit? (belonging), and What difference can I make? (purpose) (Powell and Griffin, 2021). There are those who would object to some aspects of Erikson's work, but modern research, and my life experiences, show the validity of much of what he found.

Practice

Erickson's work on personality development reminds us that we are all a work in progress. How teens adapt to the "crises" of life is largely influenced by the individuals around them. The church needs to be there for them from the moment they enter the world. Experimentation and fads are the norm for teens, as they are trying to figure out the world around them and trying to find their identity. Teens need patient and loving guides who will not freak out when they make mistakes. Here are some things we can do to help them with each stage/crisis/struggle:

1. Trust: Loving care is key.
2. Autonomy: They need advice, reassurance, and confidence.
3. Initiative: They need freedom to explore and ask questions.
4. Competence: They need learner-centered activities and help developing new competencies and a "can-do" mentality.
5. Identity: They need firm, caring, listening, and mature Christian adults mentoring them.
6. Love: They need guidance in and opportunities for positive Christian relationships.
7. Care: They need opportunities to give of themselves and their wisdom to others.
8. Wisdom: They need visits, someone to listen to them, and someone who will remember and celebrate their accomplishments (they do not need to feel pushed aside) (cf. Yount, 2010, 59–68).

James Estep and Jonathan Kim challenge us to remember that

we are all a work in progress, and we need to respect each other as we work through these crises. We need to allow kids to be kids and stumble and fall and try again as they grow. We also need to realize that each stage/crisis provides an opportunity to point young people toward God (Estep, Kim, 2010, 117–18).

Yount correctly overviews, "In general, we help individuals grow a healthy personality when we focus on success rather than failure, balance security and freedom, meet emotional needs and provide competent role models" (Yount, 2010, 82). To assist young people in becoming like Christ, we need to take the time to get to know their stories and their struggles and connect them to mature Christian adults who can model true Christlikeness.

Cognitive Development

Theory: Piaget

Next, we will consider the research of Swiss psychologist Jean Piaget in the area of cognitive development. There is so much insight we can gain from his research. I would encourage you, for example, to look at his observations relative to equilibration, assimilation, and accommodation and compare them to passages like Luke 23:35–39 (an example of assimilation) and Acts 11:1–18 (an example of accommodation, cf. Eph 4:11–16). Yet, time forces us to be brief. I want to highlight his stages of mental development. Piaget's research led him to conclude that the differences in thinking between adolescents and young children were not due simply to having more knowledge or experiences but were due to differences in how they thought and even differences in the ability to think at certain levels.

Piaget viewed human thinking as developing through four primary stages starting at birth: (1) Reflexive Thinking (think/learn using the senses), (2) Intuitive Thinking (think/learn using role play), (3) Concrete Thinking (think/learn focusing on what we can see/touch), and (4) Abstract Thinking (develop the ability to think about thoughts and abstract concepts). Terry Linhart observes that a key assumption by Piaget "was that our thinking develops from a primitive inability to perceive other perspectives than our own (egocentrism) toward a mature capacity to perceive and value the perspectives and experiences of others" (Linhart, 2016, 74).

Theory: Vygotsky

It would be inappropriate to consider Jean Piaget's theory of human cognitive development and not also consider the research of Russian psychologist Lev Vygotsky. Vygotsky emphasized the sociocultural influence on mental development. In other words, culture and social interactions impact how we think. Vygotsky stressed the value of "the more knowable other," a person who has more knowledge and experience than the learner who can guide the student in learning or in tackling a specific task. He viewed guided participation and adult-child relationships as vital. "This structured assistance in the teacher-learner relationship functions like scaffolding on a building under construction—support that can be easily removed when no longer needed" (Linhart, 77). The insights of Piaget and Vygotsky are both valuable. One reminds us that developments in thinking have internal and biological aspects, and the other reminds us that there are also external and social/cultural aspects.

Practice

Piaget's cognitive development theory helps us to consider the thinking level of our students. Small children learn through reflexes, so their classes are filled with sights, sounds, and touch. Children in the intuitive stage learn through role play, so acting out Bible stories is common. Concrete thinkers think about what they see, hear, touch, and experience (concrete or real things). Thus, art, media, and hands-on learning are valuable. They need real-life examples of the principles in Scripture (both biblical and modern examples). It is a good time to stress concrete rituals like prayer and regular Bible study. In addition, this is a great time in their development to stress memorization.

Concrete thinkers also need to be challenged to stretch their thinking so they can become abstract thinkers. The fruits of the Spirit, for example, are abstract concepts (though they are shown in concrete ways). Abstract thinkers are able to think about ideas and propositions rather than just objects or events. For abstract thinkers, we pose problems and hypothetical situations to challenge them to use their budding intellectual abilities to work through moral dilemmas and apply Scripture to life. We must challenge them to think about their thinking and whether it is molded by God's word. We ask questions to clarify their thinking, and we especially ask "why" questions.

Vygotsky's emphasis on social/cultural influences reminds us that we need to be students of cultural trends. Youth ministers should constantly be reading cultural research to understand how to adequately help teenagers to develop healthy, biblical thinking. Vygotsky also reminds us that we need to know our students' stories. Understanding the social influences in their lives helps us to guide them in thinking like Jesus. Vygotsky's emphasis on scaffolding or structured assistance should remind us that, as youth workers, we assist in providing young people the environments and mentors that help them to learn and grow. We assist them by modeling godly behavior, by thinking out loud as we reason through things, and by asking and answering questions. We also do so by creating a safe and nurturing congregational and classroom environment for learning, questions, mistakes, recovery, and spiritual growth.

Moral Development

Theory: Kohlberg

The last theorist we will consider is American psychologist Lawrence Kohlberg. I want to highlight his theory on stages of moral development. Kohlberg presented moral dilemmas to research participants and then observed how they responded. He did not focus on what the participants believed was right or wrong, but on why they thought something was right or wrong. He was interested in how human beings decide what is morally right for themselves. Here is a brief overview of the stages or types of moral decision-making that he discovered in his research.

I. Pre-Conventional Stage ("Me"-centered approach to moral decision-making)

- Punishment/Obedience (Pre-operational): Personal consequences for actions
- Instrumental Orientation (Concrete operational): What works and is best for me

II. Conventional Stage ("Authority figure/rules" approach to moral decision-making)

- Good Boy Phase: Authority/peers—Determine right or wrong based on the beliefs of peers or authority figures
- Social System/Conscience: Law/rules—Determine right or wrong based on the rules or the laws (sometimes detached from the needs of people)

III. Post-Conventional Stage ("Rights/principles" approach to moral decision making)

- Social Contract and Individual Rights: What impacts others (good is defined by society and societal needs/values)
- Universal Ethical Principles: Respect universal principles that are true and go beyond societal norms (cf. Estep and Kim, 2010, 127–28).

Terry Linhart notes, "Like Piaget, Kohlberg believed that the movement away from egocentrism was essential to mature moral decision making and that this was a significant part of the cognitive developmental work of adolescence" (Linhart, 74). People are very self-centered early in life (like the child who takes a toy from another child), but as they mature, they may base decisions on parents, teachers, or friends, or they may defer to rules and laws (possibly assuming that laws are always right). Ultimately, they move to a point where they make decisions more in line with the needs of others and/or what they consider to be universal norms of behavior or right and wrong. Our founding fathers, for example, believed that there are universal truths when they said, "We hold these truths to be self-evident ..." (Declaration of Independence, 1776).

Practice

Our ultimate goal is to assist young people in becoming mature Christian adults shaped into the image of Christ (cf. Eph 4:11–16). To do so, we need to assist them in learning to think for themselves in ways that Jesus would want them to think (cf. Phil 2:5). Kohlberg's levels of moral decision-making can assist us in this process. Remember that Kohlberg focused on why people make moral decisions. We may tend to focus merely on the moral choices of teenagers and forget to consider why they are making those decisions. Our challenge in working with teens is being able to identify what they are basing their decisions on and helping them to evaluate their thinking in healthy and biblical ways.

Ultimately, moral decisions need to be based on knowledge of and a healthy understanding of God's word. Estep and Kim observed,

> Ethics and morality imply the presence of norms. The prevalent questions become: Who establishes the norms? From where do they come? How can we facilitate the process of moral formation? For Christian educators, ethics and morality are not simply a human or societal product; rather, they are dependent on God (2010, 143).

In other words, we need to help young people base their decisions on God's will and word (cf. Col 1:9–14). Estep and Kim make the following suggestions for youth workers to help teens evaluate their decision-making:

1. Reflect critically on moral reasoning (sources of authority, line of reason).
2. Become transparent with students, sharing with them your moral processing and issues— without damaging your personal example.
3. Teach beyond the classroom but with a debriefing in the classroom, e.g., cross-cultural experiences.
4. "Scripture Saturation," i.e., early church model of teaching for reflection.
5. Cite biblical, historical, personal, and practical examples of moral solutions.
6. Distinguish facts, opinions, and judgments on moral issues.
7. Develop moral principles, reflecting Christian beliefs and commitments.
8. Character studies; but go beyond the typical "good-bad" paradigm, e.g., Abraham is portrayed as "good" while Lot is portrayed as "bad."

9. Consider the consequences and implications of moral choices.
10. Use lecture but mixed with other methods, e.g., case study (Estep, Kim, 2010, 153).

Our Mission

Let us finish this chapter focusing on developmental theory by returning to the word of God. Paul gives the marching orders for church leaders (including youth workers) in Ephesians 4:

> To equip the saints for the work of ministry, for building up the body of Christ, until we all attain to the unity of the faith and of the knowledge of the Son of God, to mature manhood, to the measure of the stature of the fullness of Christ, so that we may no longer be children, tossed to and fro by the waves and carried about by every wind of doctrine, by human cunning, by craftiness in deceitful schemes. Rather, speaking the truth in love, we are to grow up in every way into him who is the head, into Christ (Eph 4:12–15).

Understanding human development can assist us in disciplining young people toward a mature walk with God, being shaped in the image of Christ, knowing truth, and living love. We do not have to choose Paul or Piaget. Paul always takes precedence. He is an inspired apostle of our Savior. Yet, Piaget's theories can help us as we seek to obey Paul's truth.

Discussion Questions

1. What thoughts flood into your mind as you think about Jesus's development as a human being?
2. One of my doctoral professors stated, "Only about 50% of college graduates can pass formal-operational

problems proposed by Piaget" (Johnson, 2007). "Formal operational" refers to being an abstract thinker. If this is accurate, how does it impact how we teach junior high and high school students if most are concrete thinkers and not abstract thinkers?
3. How can it be helpful to know a junior high student is making moral decisions based on a parent or authority figure?
4. What is your most helpful takeaway from this chapter or something you disagree with? Explain your answer.

Bibliography

Erikson Institute, "Erik H. Erikson – Erikson Institute's Namesake." www.erikson.edu, accessed April 15, 2024.

Estep, James, and Jonathan Kim, eds. *Christian Formation: Integrating Theology and Human Development.* Nashville, TN: B&H Academic, 2010.

Johnson, Eric. "Personality and Development." Course taught at *The Southern Baptist Theological Seminary.* Louisville, KY 1–4–2007.

Linhart, Terry, ed. *Teaching the Next Generations: A Comprehensive Guide for Teaching Christian Formation.* Ada, MI: Baker Academic, 2016.

Powell, Kara, and Chap Clark. *Sticky Faith: Everyday Ideas to Build Lasting Faith in Your Kids.* Grand Rapids, MI: Zondervan, 2011.

Smith, Christian. *Soul Searching: The Religious and Spiritual Lives of American Teenagers.* Reprint ed. Kettering, England: Oxford University Press, 2009.

Yount, Rick. *Created to Learn.* 2nd ed. Nashville, TN: B&H Academic, 2010.

Chapter 41
Evangelism 101
Rob Whitacre

Christianity is a taught religion. Jesus said,

> No one can come to me unless the Father who sent me draws him. And I will raise him up on the last day. It is written in the Prophets, 'And they will all be taught by God.' Everyone who has heard and learned from the Father comes to me (John 6:44-45).

If the church is going to grow it will be because we teach the lost. We are good at training preachers. All around our nation churches of our Lord support schools of preaching by the authority Paul gave to Timothy: "And what you have heard from me in the presence of many witnesses entrust to faithful men, who will be able to teach others also" (2 Tim 2:2). Yet, this charge is not exclusively for preaching. In fact, we would all do well to acknowledge that this verse is just as much about training soul winners as preachers. Moreover, preachers and soul winners should be one and the same, but unfortunately, they are not. Far too many of us have become married to the pulpit and divorced from the people. Brethren, before we are elders, deacons, preachers, and song leaders, we should be personal workers! In fact, it should be noted that we can go to Heaven without serving in any of these capacities, but we cannot disobey the Great Commission without compromising our eternal destiny. I am not bringing into question the sincere zeal of faithful Christians to teach the lost. In addition, I do not believe the problem is in our ignorance of our Commission. The big question is, how do I do it?

This lesson is not going to be easy to digest as it will require all of us to do some introspection. Paul told the Corinthians, "Examine yourselves, to see whether you are in the faith. Test yourselves. Or do you not realize this about yourselves, that Jesus Christ is in you?—unless indeed you fail to meet the test!" (2 Cor 13:5). It will take honesty, courage, and humility if we are going to be successful.

What Do the Numbers Say?

What is the past and current standing of churches of Christ in the United States of America?

CHURCHES OF CHRIST IN THE U.S.

YEAR	POPULATION	MEMBERS	RATIO
1906	85,450,000	159,658	1 TO 535
1946	141,389,566	682,172	1 TO 207
1953	160,184,192	1,500,000	1 TO 106
1967	198,712,056	2,350,000	1 TO 84
1973	211,908,788	2,500,000	1 TO 84
1980	227,224,681	1,240,820	1 TO 183
1990	249,438,712	1,224,404	1 TO 203
2000	281,421,906	1,264,000	1 TO 222
2015	320,090,857	1,180,000	1 TO 271
2018	326,766,748	1,128,279	1 TO 289
2021	332,915,073	1,112,935	1 TO 295

Taken from the U.S. Census Bureau, "Churches of Christ in the United States" edited by Mac Lynn and Carl Royster, and The Christian Chronicle.

Can you imagine living in a time with limited resources, no internet, electronic devices, mass transportation, and media? This was the state of the church in 1906. Yet, she took the challenge of the Great Commission and began to evangelize America, cutting the ratio of Christians to non-Christians by half, in just 40 years. All of this was done during two world wars and the Great Depression! Shortly thereafter, the United States enjoyed a period of growth and increased wealth. Men came back from war and the baby boom generation was born. The population of our nation grew, but so did the Lord's church. In fact, by 1953, there was one Christian for every 106 people in this nation. During the 1960s our nation experienced a very unpopular war, social unrest, and the sexual revolution. Yet, the Lord's church continued to prosper. By 1967, there was one Christian for every 84 Americans! During the late 1970s, and throughout the 1980s, something happened that changed the impact of the Lord's church. This change caused the ratio of Christians to non-Christians to dramatically increase. Sadly, today we are now at one saint for every 289 sinners.

It is not my purpose to beat up the brethren or to create a feeling of doom, gloom, and despair, but to get our attention, and focus our energy on real answers, that can reverse the trends and spark a spiritual awakening. The solution is not hidden or costly. I would like to propose a restoration of personal evangelism, based upon the teachings of our Lord, that every Christian can do. It is not new to the Lord's church in America, and I believe it was the core reason behind the explosive growth in the early to mid-1900s.

The Principles of Soul Winning

In this chapter, we are going to do two things. First, we will examine the Biblical principles of how to be an effective soul winner. Second, we will look at its practical aspect (how it works in my world).

Defer Don't Debate

Jesus rarely answered the questions of His friends or foes. The Master's mission was to seek and save the lost (Luke 19:10), and not to play Bible trivia. His teaching method was profound and powerful. Realizing that most people do not ask the right questions, or even have the right motives, He would find a way to steer them to the heart of the matter. When the rich young ruler came to Jesus and asked, "... Good Teacher, what must I do to inherit eternal life? (Luke 18:18), He responded with a rhetorical question in order to refocus the prospect, "Why do you call me good?" (Luke 18:19). Although he was asking the right question, he was not ready for a direct answer. In the following moments, Jesus took him through a thoughtful discourse to prepare his heart for a difficult teaching. Consider the wording in Matthew's account of this conversation. "And he said to him, 'Why do you ask me about what is good? There is only one who is good. If you would enter life, keep the commandments'" (Matt 19:17). Notice the response of the ruler to Jesus, "He said to him, 'Which ones?'" (Matt 19:18). At this point in the discussion the Lord was able to reason with him using powerful penetrating precepts.

Many preachers, teachers, and elders struggle with this principle. Our first reaction is to react. Our first reply is to reply. The answer is on the tip of our tongues, and we cannot wait to give it. After all, the Bible says we should be ready to give an answer to anyone who asks (1 Pet 3:15). Until we become more interested in winning the soul than winning the argument, we will never become like our Lord. Wisdom teaches us to weigh our answers in light of the prospect's ability to digest what we are saying. As Jesus taught His disciples, He said, "I still have many things to say to you, but you cannot bear them now" (John 16:12). You cannot feed steak to a baby. We begin with the milk of the Word and allow them time to grow (1 Pet 2:2). I am not suggesting we ignore the prospect, avoid the Truth, or compromise on principle, but that we use the opportunity to answer the question with the goal of a Bible study. Playing twenty questions is not a Bible study. Think about those long Facebook posts where people "discuss" a Bible question. How many conversions result from such posts? Deferring answers is the art of steering the prospect away from fruitless and endless questions and towards an organized Bible study. Remember, he who asks the questions controls the study.

Show Don't Tell

What happens when the right questions are asked, and the prospect is ready for a Bible study? Biblical conversations and learning start happening. Deflection (deferring) is not an end, but a means to an end to get a person to a point where a study can begin. Our goal is to open the Bible and allow the Word of God to be the converting power. "The law of the LORD *is* perfect, converting the soul: the testimony of the LORD *is* sure, making wise the simple" (Ps 19:7). This was the method used by our Lord. "And behold, a lawyer stood up to put him to the test, saying, 'Teacher, what shall I do to inherit eternal life?' He said to him, 'What is written in the Law? How do you read it?'" (Luke 10:25–26). When someone wants to know what to do to be saved, do not tell them, show them in God's word! This is why Jesus said, "What is written in the law?" Moreover, have them read it. It is good to read the Word of God to them, but it is better to have them read it.

The sooner we get the Word of God into their hearts, the quicker it will dwell in their hearts.

> Let the word of Christ dwell in you richly, teaching and admonishing one another in all wisdom, singing psalms and hymns and spiritual songs, with thankfulness in your hearts to God. And whatever you do, in word or deed, do everything in the name of the Lord Jesus, giving thanks to God the Father through him (Col 3:16–17).

The goal is to maximize the Message and minimize the messenger. When we get out of the way and allow the power of God to work in the heart, even the most hardened sinners can be brought to their knees.

Bible studies need to begin and end with the Bible! We do not want the prospect to be converted to a powerful personality or creative conversationalist. "Through your precepts I get understanding, therefore I hate every false way" (Ps 119:104). Have an organized Bible study with the prospect. It does not matter what method you use as long as it is Bible based. I use "Back to the Bible" by Bobby Bates, but you might use "The Open Bible Study" by Ivan Stewart or another method. Since the power is in the Message and not the method it does not matter. The point is to get them into an organized Bible study as fast as you can.

Plant Don't Pick

Evangelistic prejudice may be the worst form of discrimination in the world. Its effects upon people have eternal consequences. I have actually heard Christians say, "He is not a good candidate for the gospel." This kind of attitude is reprehensible and completely rejected by our Lord. Even when we suspect a person is not sincere, or know they carry a lot of baggage (spiritual, physical, economic), we should not become the judge by withholding the saving message. When the lawyer came to Jesus, He looked into his heart and saw dishonesty and deception. The Scriptures say, "And, behold, a certain lawyer stood up to put him to the test, saying, 'Teacher, what shall I do to inherit eternal life?'" (Luke 10:25). The lawyer wanted to tempt the Lord and He knew it. He was not only insincere, but he was sinister. Furthermore, Luke records, "But he, desiring to justify himself, said to Jesus, 'And who is my neighbor?'" (Luke 10:29). He was also selfish and prideful. How did Jesus respond? How would you respond? Jesus not only preached the parable of The Sower and The Seed, He practiced it! Jesus planted the seed into his heart by teaching one of the most powerful parables found in the Bible, The Good Samaritan.

What about the Rich Young Ruler? Did Jesus not know he was rich? Did He not know about his covetous heart? Perhaps we know someone who is rich, greedy, and covetous and has withheld Gospel teaching. Maybe we have said, "It is just not worth my time because rich people are not receptive to the Gospel." Even though Jesus knew the rich man was a slave to money, He still loved him, and tried to teach him (Mark 10:21–22). May we do the same!

Why did Paul and Barnabas stop preaching the Gospel to the Jews? Was it the stones, stripes, and suffering they continually endured? Did Paul pick who he was going to teach? Luke records, "And Paul and Barnabas spoke out boldly, saying, 'It was necessary that the word of God be spoken first to you. Since you thrust it aside and judge yourselves unworthy of eternal life, behold, we are turning to the Gentiles" (Acts 13:46). Some people will judge themselves unworthy because they turn away from the truth. We are charged to plant the seed and not pick the soil. It is up to the prospect to determine what kind of soil he becomes.

The Practice of Soul Winning

In the fall of 2010, I received a phone call from Chris Coil, who preached for the Somerville church of Christ. He said, "Brother Rob, I need your help. I have a member who wants someone to contact her parents and teach them the Gospel." I wrote down the names, "Jackie and Sheila Birdwell" on a piece of paper and laid it on my desk. For months these names haunted me. I knew I should be visiting them, but I did not see an open door. Remembering the words of Paul, "Continue in prayer" (Col 4:2), I prayed. This opportunity came in the spring of 2011 when brother Jonathan Smith came back home from college. During a visit to my office, he mentioned a friend whose name was Evan Birdwell. Recognizing the last name I asked, "Is he related to Jackie and Sheila?" Jonathan replied, "He is their son and one of my closest friends and they are like second parents." My prayer had been answered.

I asked Jonathan if I could accompany him to their house and if he could introduce me. When we arrived, they greeted Jonathan with huge smiles and warm hugs. I stayed in the background as they invited us in to visit. I listened carefully as they told a few stories and caught up on each other's lives. Finally, Sheila looked at me and said, "Aren't you the preacher for the church of Christ?" I smiled, and said, "Yes." She then looked at Jackie, tapped him on the shoulder, and said with a bit of laughter, "I can't believe we have the preacher for the church of Christ in our living room?" My response was calculated, based upon the knowledge that their daughter had obeyed the gospel and left the Missionary Baptist church. "I bet you have a lot of questions for me." And then it began one question after another. Indeed, they were very curious about the Lord's church.

Before I arrived, I had thought about how I was going to approach this family. Learning from our master evangelist, I had decided not to give direct answers to any questions and at times to even answer a question with another question. "Do you believe only those in the churches of Christ are going to Heaven?" In the past, I was afraid of this question. I was not afraid of the truth, but I feared how the prospect would receive it. Most people are not ready for this answer because they have a misunderstanding about the church. Remembering our Master had said, "I still have many things to say to you, but you cannot bear them now" (John 16:12), I answered, "This is a great question, may I ask who told you this?" She explained that her pastor told her. Her next question came quickly. "Why don't you believe in music in church?" As a preacher, I really wanted to answer this question. First, I wanted to explain that we believe in music in worship, but not mechanical music in worship. Second, I wanted to explain Bible authority. Third, I wanted to quote Colossians 3:16–17, but I did not do any of these things. This time, I answered her question with a lead-in thought and then a question. "I can tell you have spent a lot of time thinking about spiritual matters. Why do you use mechanical instruments?" She laughed briefly and spent a few minutes explaining. These questions continued for ten to fifteen minutes. What happened next changed how I understand and conduct personal evangelism today. Sheila looked over and asked, "Jackie, why is he not answering our questions?"

Now they were ready for step two (*show don't tell*). The interest level was obvious, but I was not going to play 20 questions. I knew from experience, that this bore little to no fruit. My prepared response was, "Instead of telling you all the answers, why don't we sit around your table, open our Bibles, and see what God has said." This was not what she expected. In fact, it was a bit frightening. She looked over at Jackie with a look of concern and said, "I think he wants to have a Bible study. What would people think if they knew we were studying with the preacher for the church or Christ?" They explained how Jackie was the treasurer and Bible class teacher for the Missionary Baptists and how their friends and family would not agree with this study. Their conclusion was to do the study but to keep it private. At this point I had only one request, "May I tell my elders?" They asked, "Who are they?" I said, "Hugh Clarke, Hugh Wayne Clark, Terry Jones, Joe Lynn, and Alvin Allen." Her response is something I will never forget. "These are good men, you may tell them if you need to."

Some of you may wonder why I wanted or felt compelled to tell my elders. I was in the habit of talking to the church about our Bible studies, but this time I could not mention their names. I do this for several reasons. First, I believe in the power of prayer. I want as many prayers to be offered for the prospect as possible. Second, I want the church to look for the prospects and go out of their way to build relationships. Third, it is an opportunity to motivate and teach the church about personal evangelism. This time, I spoke generally. I told the church God had opened a huge door in this community to teach a family the Gospel. I knew if this family obeyed the Gospel, it could have far-reaching effects.

Jonathan and I came to their home for the first study. We sat around their kitchen table, passed out the little "Back to the Bible" booklets, opened our Bibles, and began. Prior to the study, I had spoken to Jonathan about the role of the "silent partner." The key word is silent. You do not want to gang up on the prospects. Their role is to help them find books of the Bible, clarify words when you misspeak, or help answer a question if needed. It did not take long for Sheila to have a question. "Brother Rob, what do you believe about the end times?" This really had nothing to do with John 8:32, and the question asked in the booklet. It is very important not to chase rabbits, so I said, "Sheila, this is a great question that deserves an answer. I have found that most questions are answered in the study. Would you permit me to finish the study and then, if you have any additional questions, I will answer them?" I encouraged her to write it down for a later time. This happened several times during the first two studies.

At times, these studies can become very emotional. At one point, Shelia wanted to tell us about her conversion or religious experience. To her, it was very real and heartfelt. It involved an accident, a dream, and the voice of God. These situations must be handled very carefully. We should never challenge the sincerity of the prospect. We should not deny their deeply held beliefs. We are not the Judge. It is important to allow the Word of God to work in their hearts and uncover the Truth. Once again, I did not respond, but thanked her for sharing, and complimented her on being such a religious person. At the end of each study, I could tell they were learning and seeing the Truth for the first time. They saw inconsistencies between the Baptist doctrine and the Bible. They freely admitted that they were not rightly dividing the Word of God regarding the Old and New Testament. They understood how God wanted them to observe the Lord's Supper each Sunday. They accepted the truth about vocal music versus mechanical music. The truth is very liberating. It helps people see through the darkness and fog, or Satan's deceits. The studies were going great, and we could not wait until lesson 3.

Before the third study, several things took place. First, I wanted to know as much as possible about the Missionary Baptists. This sect is much different from other Baptists. Therefore, I called their daughter Scarlett, who had been converted and was living in Summerville, Tennessee. I asked her about her parent's faith and her conversion. She told me about how she had been "excommunicated" after becoming a Christian. Her excommunication took place at her home and was witnessed by Jackie and Sheila. Scarlett said she was ready with her Bible in hand. To her surprise, they never quoted a Scripture or even tried to restore her. It was more procedural and ceremonial. I later learned how this had really bothered Jackie and Sheila, creating a seed of doubt in their minds. The other event was even more powerful. Scarlett said that several of her friends tried to get her to come back to the Missionary Baptists. On one occasion someone asked, "Why did you do it? Why did you leave us for them?" Her answer is one of the most powerful and impactful statements I have ever heard, and one I will never forget. She said, "Do you really want to know, because if you know what I know, you will do what I did." She could not ignore the truth and did not want to live with doubt. The word of God is greater than any word man can speak. As she saw it, "My only choice was to obey."

Knowing this would be a very difficult study, I had asked not only the congregation but many other brethren to pray for them to have a receptive heart and for Jonathan and me to be wise, bold, and loving. Just before our arrival, Jackie sat down with his wife and had a private conversation about where this was heading. He acknowledged how they had learned a lot about the church of Christ, and how he could see some of the things they believed were wrong, but that he had no intention of converting. He said, "Brother Rob is expecting us to be baptized and join the church, and I am not going to do it." Sheila replied, "Then neither am I." As before, we sat around the table and began with a prayer. This time, I had them fill out a little survey to help them navigate through the confusion of their denominational conversion. They had no problems answering the few questions. The most important question was, "If you have been baptized, were you saved before or after baptism?" As with almost every person we study, their answer was before. Our last study begins with an overview of sin and then moves to salvation. When we came to baptism, I stopped and opened my notebook to pull out a chart. I do not always use these charts, but this time I knew we needed to spend some extra time on baptism. The chart is titled, "In Christ," and it is an expanded version of a diagram that is in the "Back to the Bible" lesson three study booklet. First, we looked at Scripture after Scripture that showed all the things that were in Christ. Second, we looked at how faith, repentance, and confession move us "towards" Christ, but not "into" Christ. Finally, we looked at two clear and powerful Bible passages about baptism (Gal 3:27, Rom 6:3–4). The conclusion was inescapable. I could see their countenance change as they came face to face with the truth about their spiritual condition. I decided to close the study early as the time was right. "Jackie, what are you going to do with what you have learned?" He looked at me and said, "Rob, I know exactly what I need to do." Suddenly Sheila looked over with a stunned face, nudged Jackie in the side, and replied, "You said we weren't going to do that!" Jackie explained how he had no choice but to obey. Sheila also expressed a desire to be baptized into Christ.

Thinking they were ready, we proceeded to invite them to the baptistery, but there was a problem. Jackie said, "Rob, we can't do it tonight." I was stunned! What could be stopping them? I began to take them to Scriptures that help people see the urgency of Gospel obedience, but none seemed to change his mind. You see, Jackie and Sheila were long-standing members of a local Missionary Baptist congregation, and he was their Bible class teacher and treasurer. He finally said to me, "Rob, you don't understand. I hold the bag [money bag], and I need to resign and give them the money." I could understand his reasoning, but I knew their souls were too important to delay. After additional study, we finally left trembling for their souls.

Over the next few days, I asked the congregation to pray fervently for this family, explaining they were near the kingdom. I told the elders what had transpired and they began praying. Each day I took my family by to visit during the evening hours. We picked strawberries out of their garden, and talked about life, as I waited for their resignation. During one visit, Sheila told me she wanted to be baptized in running water. Although I knew the Scriptures did not require it, I was quick to accommodate. The next morning one of our elders took his machines down to a local creek to dig it out. I was not about to let something so little, disrupt their gospel obedience. One lesson I learned years ago is to know when to fight and when to fold. It is okay to lose small battles in matters of judgment and opinion, as long as we win the war for the soul!

It was a Wednesday evening and still no word from either Jackie or Sheila. I must admit that I was very anxious and had not enjoyed a good night's sleep since the last study. As I was visiting with church members in the auditorium, in walked Jackie and Sheila. I was surprised and relieved in the same breath. I gave them a big hug and welcomed them to our services. Members of the congregation began to ask if this was the family for whom they had been praying. I did not believe they would respond that evening to the invitation. I did not know if he had resigned, and I knew she wanted to be baptized in the creek. As the invitation song began, they walked out into the aisle and walked down towards the front pew. Tears filled my eyes as I walked up to meet them. I was overwhelmed with joy. It was one of the most impactful events in the history of the congregation. The power of the cross was on full display. This couple wanted to become Christians! No mention was made of the creek, so we took their confession and baptized them into Christ.

Conclusion

Our situation is not hopeless. There are thousands of couples just like Jackie and Sheila waiting for someone to teach them the gospel. We have churches full of potential teachers and a world full of students. We have evangelized America before, and we can do it again. From 1946 to 1953, (seven years), the Lord's church cut the ratio of Christian to non-Christian in half. At one point, 1 out of every 84 people you meet in this nation was a Christian. We have the power to do the same in our generation if we focus on training every Christian to be a soul winner.

*For more information please contact me: Rob@housetohouse.com or go to our website: evangelism.housetohouse.com

Discussion Questions

1. Why is it so important for youth workers to be evangelistic?
2. What are some reasons that some youth workers and congregations are not evangelistic?
3. Discuss some things your congregation and youth group could do to become more evangelistic in the next year.
4. Make a list of five people you know who are not Christians and then decide which one you are going to approach in the next week seeking a Bible study.

Bibliography

Bates, Bobby. *Back to the Bible*. Lessons 1–3. Glad Tidings Publishing. n.d.

Lynn, Mac, and Carl Royster, eds. *Churches of Christ in the United States*. 2018. Nashville, TN: 21st Century Christian.

Royster, Carl, ed. *Churches of Christ in the United States*. 2024. Nashville, TN: 21st Century Christian.

The Christian Chronicle, christianchronicle.org, February 2009. Article is no longer available but is referenced in a January 1, 2010 article titled, "2009 in Review: Membership Decline Top Story," which is available in digital form.

U.S. Census Bureau, census.gov. 2018.

Chapter 42
Teen Evangelism
Philip Jenkins

$8 Hunger Strike

There we were, waiting in car-buying purgatory. The salesman and I were sort of at a stalemate. He said a price. I said a price. He wasn't budging. Neither was I. I had asked my dad to come along for the experience, because, well, he's sort of a master negotiator, and I wanted to make sure I got the absolute best deal possible. And so my Dad, in an effort to illustrate to the salesman just how cheap I could be, told a story from my teenage years that I had *completely* forgotten.

> When my sons were in high school, they were eating us out of the house and home. We just couldn't have enough food in the house. So I sat them down and said, "Ok, boys. I know you have to eat, and I know how much you like to go out to eat. But from now on, when you go eat somewhere, you get $8 each. Now, you can go over that amount—if you want to order a steak, that's fine—but just know that if you go over the $8, you've got to pay the difference."
>
> Philip sat there for a minute, thought about it, and said, "What if we don't spend it all? Can we keep what we don't spend?"

Without thinking too much about it, I said, "Sure." Next thing I knew, Philip had stopped eating, just so he could keep the money!

Laura Numeroff famously wrote, "If you give a mouse a cookie, he's going to ask for a glass of milk" (2015, 4). If you give a teenager money, he is going to do something with it. He may not handle it the way you would (which could be a good thing or a bad thing!). A teenager may approach money differently, but one thing is for sure: They are going to do something with it! What I have seen to be beautifully true is this: *If you give a teenager the Gospel, they are going to do something with it.*

The Snacks at the Gas Station Took All My Money

In youth ministry, you get to watch teens learn about … well … a lot of things, but I'll say, "money" this time. There are hard lessons learned, usually in the form of a Six Flags trip.

> Honey, here's $75 for you to spend today on lunch and supper.
>
> Ok. Thanks, Mom.
>
> Now, that has to last you all day, so don't spend it all at—
>
> Ok, thanks Mom! Bye!

Kid gets on church bus.

After only one gas station bathroom break, he arrives at the park with $1.63 left.

Part of growing up is learning how to handle money. Failure to talk to our children about money would be irresponsible. It would stunt their growth and development. If they have not been trained, if we do not share with them our own lessons, shortcomings, and victories with money, we are robbing them of a valuable teacher:

experience. If we want them to be blessed by it, we need to show them how to be blessed by it.

Wait a minute, what are we talking about again? Oh yeah, evangelism. Part of growing up is learning how to handle *the gospel*. Failure to talk to our children about *the gospel* would be irresponsible. It would stunt their growth and development. If they have not been trained, if we do not share with them our own lessons, shortcomings, and victories with *the gospel*, we are robbing them of a valuable teacher: experience. If we want them to be blessed by *the gospel*, we need to show them how to be blessed by *the gospel*.

Equipping Teens to Evangelize

Make no mistake: the gospel and money are *completely* different, but the point is valid. The gospel is the most valuable form of currency we have been given, but if we do not show the next generation how to handle the currency of the gospel, <u>we are blowing it</u>! So how can we equip teens to share the gospel currency, the free gift that cost Jesus everything?

Entrust Students with the Gospel

> These twelve Jesus sent out, instructing them, "Go nowhere among the Gentiles and enter no town of the Samaritans, but go rather to the lost sheep of the house of Israel. And proclaim as you go, saying, 'The kingdom of heaven is at hand'" (Matt 10:5–7).

It's sort of crazy to think about Jesus sending the "Matthew 10" version of the apostles into the nearby villages to preach the gospel of the coming kingdom! At this point in their spiritual maturity/development, perhaps it was more like sending "teen apostles!" Jesus had heard their theology, witnessed their immaturity, and knew their flaws. Yet He still sent them. He still let them play an important role in the kingdom work.

We may ask, "But Jesus! Wasn't it early in their training? Didn't they still have so much to learn? Wouldn't they say the wrong thing or mess up?" Though He might well have answered, "Yes," He still entrusted the message to them. He also entrusts the message to us in our immaturity, in our weaknesses, and in our flaws. Do not excuse teens from being commissioned (Matt 28:19–20). Instead, entrust them with the mission. As disciples of Christ, it is theirs just as much as it is yours. Equip them and challenge them to take the gospel wherever they go.

Teach Students How to Speak the Truth in Love

"Rather, speaking the truth in love, we are to grow up in every way into him who is the head, into Christ ..." (Eph 4:15). Are there two words that are more abused in the world right now than "truth" and "love"?

"Just find your truth."

"I'm just tryin' to live my truth, ya know?"

"Love is love."

We live in a world filled with people content to define things however they choose. To put it one way, if you do not like the way Webster defines a word, just go to Wikipedia, and make your own edits. Define it for yourself. Our students find themselves in a culture where my definition is as good as anybody else's, where truth is a moving target, and where the most unloving thing you can do is tell someone that they are wrong.

Students (disciples!) must learn to ask, "What does God say about (fill in the blank)? What does God think about (fill in the blank)? How does God define (fill in the blank)?" Christians understand (or at least they should!) that every aspect of life—our identities, our thoughts, our actions, our desires—must be laid alongside God's will. His truth is truth, regardless of how it makes me feel. What He calls good we must call good. What He calls evil we must call evil. What He calls love is love. We do not get to define those things, for we are not God. God does because He is.

Perhaps now more than ever, what our world needs is Christians who will *show* what truth and love actually mean. I recently used the following illustration with our students. Imagine having a friend that comes to you and says, "Hey, I'm thinking about dating this person. What do you think?" You *know* that if your friend dates this person it is going to be a train wreck. You *know* that this guy or this girl is bad news. You *know* the kind of reputation they have. You *know* the way people are going to look at your friend. And you *know* that your friend does not need that kind of mess in his or her life.

You have a decision to make: will you speak the truth in love? You could decide to speak the truth without love. What would that look like? It might sound like this:

"Um, are you serious?!? How dumb *are* you? You really don't know the first thing about a good relationship, do you? I mean, of all the idiotic things you have asked me over the years, this one takes the cake! You have zero sense. Remind me to never come to you for relationship advice. You have no self-respect and none from me either."

Did you speak the truth? "Yep, I sure did!" one might answer, "And if you don't like it, that's your problem!" No. If you were a jerk, that is a "you" problem. You did not follow God's Word. God says to speak the truth in love.

Alright, same scenario: a friend comes to you and says, "Hey, I'm thinking about dating this person" (and you know it's going to be a bad, bad situation) and asks, "What do you think?"

What would it look like to speak lovingly but without truth?

"Well, I think you should be able to date whomever you want to date, and if people have got a problem with it, that is their problem. Just live your truth, you know? I mean, sure, he cheated on the last four girls he dated, but deep down he's a good person. I think you should give him a fair shot. I know he has a bad reputation, but who are we to judge? Plus, you're a good person! You could change him! I mean, sure, he stole his mom's car and punched a cop, but it was only because he was drunk. He would have *never* done it if he was sober...I mean, I have never personally seen him sober, but he's a great guy."

Did you speak lovingly? Yes. But did you speak truthfully? No. It's sort of like smiling and waving while your friend drives her car off a cliff.

Final scenario: "Hey, I'm thinking about dating this person. What do you think?" What if you spoke the truth in love?

"Well, I guess a few things come to mind ... the first is that I care about you. I love you and the last thing I want is for you to get hurt. I know the reputation that this person has, and I do not want to see you hurt emotionally, and I do not want to see you hurt spiritually. Have you thought about how this relationship could impact your relationship with God? What would you tell me if our roles were reversed, and I was coming to you for this very same advice?"

Truth minus love does not equal God's will. It's hateful. Love minus truth does not equal God's will. It's dishonest. Truth plus love equals God's will (Eph 4:15). It's truly loving.

Create Opportunities for Students to Pass Out Invitations

Jesus tells a powerful story about invitations in Matthew 22:

> The kingdom of heaven may be compared to a king who gave a wedding feast for his son, and sent his servants to call those who were invited to the wedding feast, but they would not come (Matt 22:2–3).

God could have shrugged, said, "Well, I tried," and have given up. Actually, that is the opposite of what happens.

> [Then he] said to his servants, "The wedding feast is ready, but those invited were not worthy. Go therefore to the main roads and invite to the wedding feast as many as you find." And those servants went out into the roads and gathered all whom they

found, both bad and good. So the wedding hall was filled with guests (Matt 22:8–10).

In essence, God says, "New plan: go invite people until you get a yes. Go everywhere. Good people, bad people, as many as you can find. Bring them. I want them to meet my Son." God has done the hard work. He has set the table and prepared the feast. He has signed, sealed, and addressed all the invitations, and He's put them in our hands. All we have to do is pass them out.

If you want students to become evangelistic, we need to remind them of just how important invitations are. That youth retreat, that summer camp, that night out with the youth group, just might be the place where their friend gets introduced to Jesus for the first time. I cannot help but think of a former 9th-grade student of mine named Spencer who happened to invite a friend to come on a retreat with us. The friend came, had a blast, and came back home telling his mom and dad about the new church home he had found for them. The next Sunday, Christian brought his entire family with him.

A few weeks later, Christian's younger brother was baptized. A few short weeks later, his older brother was baptized. A few weeks after that Christian was baptized. Christian kept coming to church. His senior year rolls around. At the eleventh hour, he decides to attend a Christian university. He decides he wants to be a Bible major. He does a youth internship one summer.

One Wednesday evening during the school year Christian shows up at church. He went to school two and a half hours away. "What are you doing here?" I asked. "Um, I'm actually here tonight to baptize my dad." And he did.

Fast forward the clock, Christian marries a Christian. He graduates with a Bible degree. He decides he wants to be a youth minister. He decides to come to work alongside me as our two-year youth ministry resident intern. After two years, he leaves Mt. Juliet to serve another congregation as their youth minister. And the story only gets sweeter with time and faithfulness: recently his younger brother Patrick married a wonderful Christian girl. The two of them are also serving the youth at another congregation.

Just think about how powerful this is! That entire story probably never have happened if not for a piece of paper with information and a ninth-grade student who said, "Hey, I've got a friend who might come on our spring retreat." Invitations are powerful things!

Include Students in Your Bible Studies

Some of the coolest moments in youth ministry happen when the friend that one of your students invited expresses an interest in being baptized. Those super cool moments get cooler when we invite "the bringer" into that study. It allows the bringer to see what a one-on-one Bible study looks like, it makes it less awkward having another person in the room, and perhaps most importantly of all, it encourages the bringer to keep bringing, reminding them that they played an important role in their friend's story.

A Team Sport

I'm not the biggest fan of old "preacher stories," but I absolutely love this one. Late one night, a man went overboard on a massive cruise ship. Thankfully, a witness happened to see him hit the water. "Man overboard!" she cried out. One of the crew members on board shined a massive spotlight into the ocean. "There he is! I see him!" The crew alerted the captain who then turned the boat around. Another crew of men and women quickly lowered lifeboats into the water. Divers entered the water and pulled him back into their boat. By this time, he had taken in a great deal of water, so when they hoisted him back aboard the ship, a team of paramedics on board administered CPR. After a few minutes, they were able to get him breathing again, and the man rested all night in a room where he was monitored closely by a nurse. The next day, the man woke up thankful to be alive. Relieved and overjoyed, he began to plead with the nurse, "Please, tell me who it was that saved my life!"

The nurse was not sure what to tell him. Was it the woman who cried out for help when she saw him fall into the water? Was it the person who shined the spotlight into the water to locate the man? Was it the captain who turned the boat around? Was it the crew in the lifeboats? Was it the divers? Was it the ones who administered CPR? Or was it the nurse who stayed up with him all night long to closely monitor his vitals?

When someone is saved, it is never just one person who is responsible. It is not just the person who baptizes them. It is the person who invited them to church for the first time. It is also the person who said, "Hey come sit with us," on the first visit. It is the person who invited them to go out to eat after church. It is the person who gave them a ride home. It is that Bible class teacher who learned their name and looked for them the next week. It is that guy who called them up to play a game of pickup basketball with some other guys from church one night.

And on and on and on ….

Let's remember that evangelism, saving souls, is a team sport, and let us all do our part.

Discussion Questions

1. Why do you think our culture struggles with the concepts of truth and love?
2. Take a moment and share your conversion stories with each other (if in a classroom session) or write your conversion story down if you are reading this chapter alone.
3. How can helping teens articulate and share their conversion stories be helpful in evangelizing other teens?

4. What are some things your congregation and youth group could do to do to better welcome visitors?

Bibliography

Numeroff, Laura. *If You Give a Mouse a Cookie*. Illustrated ed. New York: HarperCollins, 2015.

Chapter 43
Evangelizing College-Age Young Adults
Colt Mahana and Jody Apple

The gospel message of Jesus begins with His humility as God taking the form of man. This same attitude of humility afforded Jesus, as God in the flesh, the opportunity to connect with mankind in an intensely personal way, sharing in our experiences. God was willing to go to the greatest lengths to redeem humanity.[1] This model of humility is the starting place of all evangelism, including college-age young adults.[2]

A Humble Approach

This humility demonstrated by Jesus is also the same humility God requires from us. It directly impacts the effectiveness of our evangelistic efforts. The pride and arrogance that led to Adam and Eve's fall in the garden also contribute to our fall. Others are watching to see if the way we live our lives matches the principles we teach. The need to guard our hearts from being prideful is all the more urgent.[3] If we approach this subject with utter humility (following the example of Christ), acknowledge that we each deeply need God to redeem us, and allow our hearts to be shaped and molded by God, then evangelism is allowed to function the way God intended.

Humility is central to the foundation of our faith and essential to successful evangelism. Humility allows one thing to become clear: we all need a savior.

Human experience is diverse. We have unique life experiences and diverse ways of thinking. We may come from different cultures or subcultures. Even when we experience the same situation with other people, we perceive that experience in various ways. We are individually unique. That is beautiful! You have things you can teach me if I am humble enough to accept that I do not know everything you know. There are things you can learn from me if you are humble enough to accept that you do not know everything I know. If we can learn to listen open-mindedly with humility, we become more approachable to others.[4] In His divine knowledge, God designed the Gospel to be universal—so that all of mankind, throughout time, can understand His will.[5]

If we hope to disciple others as Jesus has discipled us, we must be aware of our pridefulness and provide a loving example of humility. I pray often that the gospel's message be unhindered by my flaws.[6] Our winning of souls will find success only if the gospel of Christ has first convicted us and brought us to change.

Mentoring Through Your Example

Young adulthood is a time when young people may tend to be self-focused. They are exploring their options in courses of study, careers, relationships, religions, spiritual experiences, and more. They may be in college, preparing themselves for their future. Some may be diving straight into the workforce. Many of these young adults are experiencing new forms of independence.

Young adults are also seeking mentorship in various areas of life. Just as Jesus mentored His disciples through His example, so must we mentor our young adults. No mentorship is as important as spiritual mentorship. Being surrounded by good mentors who encourage and support them spiritually and emotionally during this time in life is critical to helping them establish real faith. A heart that is ever humbled before God by understanding our own need for redemption, enables the ability to influence others to approach God the same way. Too many talk about faith without a walk that matches. Students need mentors who model how to admit their weaknesses and shortcomings. These young adults crave relationships and are looking for guides they can relate to, especially with someone who can show them how to posture their heart before God. Only when we have the proper heart posture are we ready to turn our attention to the methods used to evangelize. Once our hearts walk humbly before God, our attitudes, mindsets, and actions, overflow from the abundance of gratitude we have for God's grace. Mentors who live out their faith in all parts of life can have a long-lasting impact on these young people.[7]

Evangelistic Foundations: The Greatest Commands

The best model for sharing the good news of Christ is Jesus Himself. Through His heart of humility, He imparted truth to His disciples. They in turn shared the same truth with others. His compassion for others did not detract from His focus on accomplishing the will of God. From the time Jesus left His Father, continuing throughout His life and ministry on earth, humility defined Him. If we are to change hearts, we must be humble enough to change ourselves first, with God's help.

Jesus was repeatedly questioned, and in some cases challenged. One of those questions came from a scribe among the Pharisees who asked about the most important of all the commandments. While the request came as part of a series of questions from Sadducees and Pharisees designed to challenge Jesus, Mark's account seems to imply that the question from the scribe was sincere (cf. Mark 12:28–34). We read that the scribe was pleased with the answer Jesus gave and the Savior told him, "You are not far from the kingdom of God" (Mark 12:34). There were, by some counts, more than six hundred distinct commands that made up the Law of Moses (cf. Baker and Kohlenberger, Mark 12:28).

What sums up the entirety of the Old Testament text relative to our love of and service before God? Depending on where you stood theologically, your group might focus on *one* commandment or group of commandments while someone else, claiming to be equally devoted to the Mosaic Law, might focus on *another*. We usually sum up Jesus's response to the question in two principles: the first, love God—the second, love your neighbor. That is the usual way, with a bit more explanation in respective contexts, that Jesus responded to the challenge. In Mark 12, however, Jesus adds an important context for the commands to love God and neighbor, "Hear, O Israel, The Lord our God, the Lord is one." Jesus first emphasized the singular existence of a holy God. Flowing from that singular existence of a holy God were the coordinated great commandments. Love *that God first*, because there exists *only one holy God*. Love your neighbor second, because that is the *most natural* and *practical* way in this life that our love for God is to be manifested. It is that second great commandment that serves as the impetus for evangelism.

Evangelism Part 1: God Exists

Because God exists and because God exists singularly as the Creator and Sustainer of all that exists, He must be worshiped, exclusively. Because God exists and must be exclusively worshiped, we, by divine design and divine directive, are to share that message of His existence and holiness with others, with *all* others. When we share the good news with others, they can not only recognize the existence of that singular holy God but they can also choose to worship Him as He desired. Loving our neighbor naturally leads us to share the evidence, i.e., proof, of God's singular existence with others. That is the first part of evangelism.

Evangelism Part 2: God Is Worthy of Worship

Sharing that this singularly existing God has been and always is holy, and thus worthy of worship, is the second part of evangelism. God's holiness leads us to worship Him in holiness. It prompts us to teach others not only that God exists, but that His character inherently requires us to (voluntarily) worship Him in the way He desires. Getting us to the point that we can be in the presence of a holy God ...that is where changing ideas about God's existence and God's nature becomes grounded. It requires us to change not just our thinking, but to live consistent with that thinking. It involves the process by which we are changed in thought and every other aspect of life. We teach others how to humble themselves before the Holy God. We teach by demonstrating how to die to every practice that worships and glorifies self and by living wholeheartedly before that God.

Evangelism Part 3: Total Submission to the Holy God

Young people are converted by the singular truth of God's existence as the sole deity, and they are converted by the singular truth that this God alone has been and will always be worthy of worship. They are also converted by their willingness to give up everything they have and everything they are, to become a servant of this holy God. When souls learn these key truths and then yield to these key truths, they will, in faith, repent of their sins and surrender to death by laying down their lives through immersion into Christ (Rom 6:3–7) —with their gain being remission of their sins and being made holy before God (cf. 1 Pet 1:13–16). Because of that initial decision, they will hopefully, remain true to that commitment—staying dead to sin and self (Gal 2:20). This process of recognizing and respecting a singular existing and holy God, worshiping that singular holy God, and submitting to His will in faith, repentance, and baptism applies with equal force to every soul that becomes a child of God, including young adults.

Teaching that Focuses on the Three Key Principles

As we mentioned above, college-age young adults are at a unique juncture in life. They are being introduced to new ideas, new philosophies, and new world views. The evangelistic outreach of the local body of Christ must touch them where they are—with an awareness of their unique position in life: out of their parents' homes becoming adults, in route to establishing their own homes, perhaps within a few short years. The basic three principled approach—a singular holy God exists, He alone is worthy of worship, and submitting entirely to that singular—holy God means, we love God, so we love people. This must inform how we reach college-age young people.

Principle #1: A Singular Holy God Exists

To help them understand that God exists, we must present Christian apologetics, first ancient, then modern. However, we may need to rethink *how* this is taught. While these things need to be taught in Bible classes, seminars, lectureships, workshops, and special events —this is best accomplished in a more relaxed one-on-one setting. These conversations can happen naturally in the organic structure of your everyday life as you bring them along to walk with you. If they hear you teach these concepts in a Bible class or seminar, but never hear you talk about these things in everyday life, they may not be as easily sold on a life in Jesus.

Principle #2: He Alone Is Worthy of Worship

Our singular holy God must be worshiped as He desires. This includes learning everything that God wants us to know about His character and how to approach Him, in worship, in prayer, in every aspect of life. He is a holy God and desires people to be holy in approaching Him. We must make sure that ministry with young adults includes teaching and example that helps them to grow in understanding and practice of what God wants in worship. Also, worship is intended to be done by people who have been unified in Christ and have the mind of Christ. This permeates every aspect of congregational life, worship, Christian living, community, and serving others in Christ. Young people are not wanting to feel like a part of just a college group; they want to be a functioning part of the church. The best way for young adults to learn biblical worship is through complete incorporation into a local body of believers.

Principle #3: Submit to His Will

The holy God exists, and He desires to be worshiped according to His will, by each person. Necessarily, this means His will must also be shared with the world. Those who receive His will in obedience, demonstrate their sacrificial love for God. Loving God, according to His will, by default extends to your neighbor. That is, every person. Many of them will not be where you are spiritually. This means that converting young adults should include training them to share the message of Christ with others motivated by their love for God.

Evangelism, then, will always be the end result of the first two principles—and in order to be effective, evangelism must be tightly tied to the first two principles. Everything we do to reach young adults must focus on the practical aspects of submission to Christ initially—via faith, repentance, baptism (alluded to above), and submission to Christ continually. While a changed life has a beginning, a converted life has no end.

Practical Application

We want to give you some ideas that are practical and immediately usable if you have a group of college-age young adults. Mentor students by inviting them into your home and model how a healthy, godly, family functions. If you have not experienced this, or do not know what this looks like, seek it out! The power of seeing a godly family, lived out healthily is convicting, emotional, and inspiring. We often have students come to our home for a good home-cooked meal. While they are here, the television remains off and our phones are placed in another room. We make every effort to give them as much of our undivided attention (challenging to do with four children) as we can muster. Our children are involved because we want evangelism to be a family ordeal. This conveys to our guests the subtle message that they are important and worth our time and attention. As fast-paced as Jesus's ministry was, He was never too busy to see the person before Him in each moment. We want people to experience this Jesus characteristic through us as well. We want them to know who we are because He lives through our lives. We show them who we are, primarily by how we act toward them, making them feel seen, safe, and interested.

We encourage you to listen and learn how open and comfortable they are or are not. Sometimes young people put up dense walls while others are open books. If the person is fairly closed-off, this could be the result of past trauma, emotional hurt, physical abuse, church hurt, etc. We sometimes soften our approach by playing a game that gets them comfortable talking.[8] We also find that doing something they are interested in helps to lower walls as well. If they are more of an open book, sometimes we ask them to share their story. It is important that when this conversation starts, we intentionally set aside "fixing them" and just listen. We are not there to correct, rebuke, or instruct in any way, during this moment, unless, of course, they *ask* for guidance with something specific. We are there to listen, make them feel heard and seen, and ultimately, understand them as a person. We mostly ask questions that demonstrate a genuine interest in them and will inform us about who they are. This can prove to be incredibly helpful later as other interactions take place. Many times it paints an informative picture of where someone is spiritually, emotionally, relationally, and mentally. Our guests participate in vulnerability when they share their stories with us. They invite us into their lives, trusting we will continue to show the same Jesus they have seen in us from the beginning. We must become sensitive to these stories and the needs of these individuals. Every person will be different, so what follows from this initial step will need to be tailored to each person accordingly.

Conclusion

We pray for your success in reaching the college-aged in your area, knowing they can bring so much life to a congregation. Throughout this process, remember this is not about you. It is about allowing God to use you in softening hearts and exemplifying Christ.

Discussion Questions

1. Why is humility foundational to evangelism?
2. What are the dangers of neglecting to ground young adults in belief in the existence of a holy God worthy of worship?
3. How should the fact that more and more young adults in our country have no religious affiliation at all change how we do evangelism?
4. What was the most helpful takeaway from this chapter?

Notes

[1.] A helpful resource for exploring this further is Frank Chesser's *Portrait of God*, (Huntsville, AL: Publishing Designs, 2004).

[2.] A word of caution is needed here. When we subcategorize groups in the church, we often alienate these groups from the rest of the body. The model most clearly seen in Scripture is a multi-generational, intergenerational church functioning as a complete body. Though the college age group is a specific target group within the greater context of the whole church, we present our model of evangelizing these young adults as usable for all ages.

3. We are human. Pride is an issue we all struggle with at times. Becoming aware of this and actively pursuing humility when we are made aware of our pride, whether through self-realization or listening to others who recognize prideful notions within us, affords us the opportunity to teach by example. This can have a far greater impact on those we are trying to teach than presenting a lesson on humility while demonstrating pride.

4. Listening open-mindedly means we are looking for the nuggets of truth that can help us grow while we are striving to share nuggets of truth to help them grow. This give/take approach allows others to feel like they have something to offer to the conversation.

5. We are sensitive to those with mental or physical conditions that might prevent one from comprehending the gravity of sin. God is sovereign, merciful, and just. We choose to leave room for Him to handle those situations as He deems.

6. Most people tend to think they are right most of the time. Our willingness to admit where we are wrong and to change breeds humility in the minds and hearts of others. To disciple others, we must first be willing to be discipled ourselves. Gregory, Keukol, *Tactics*, (Grand Rapids: Zondervan, 2019) is a valuable resource for considering different ways to engage people. Also, you may want to check out the classic by Dale Carnegie, *How to Win Friends and Influence People,* Internet Archive, 1981. <https://archive.org/details/HowToWinFriendsAndInfluencePeopleBy/mode/2up>.

7. We have implemented men's and women's groups to provide mentoring for our young people. This has proven to be one of the most successful and needed parts of our ministry. We have used, with good success, the *Men of Valor* series by Mark R. Laaser, *Seven Principles of Highly Accountable Men* (Kansas City, MO: Beacon Hill Press of Kansas City, 2011); *Taking Every Thought Captive* (Kansas City, MO: Beacon Hill Press of Kansas City, 2011); *Becoming A Man of Valor* (Kansas City, MO: Beacon Hill Press of Kansas City, 2011). This provides a platform for us to begin challenging boys to become men through pursuing God. Accountability is already built into this approach. We have seen women's groups function similarly

when tailored to the needs of young women being worked with. We have compiled a list of suggested resources that we have used and continue to see being helpful in working with young people.

We also have found dating to be a topic needing much discussion. Gary Thomas's, *The Sacred Search* (Colorado Springs, CO: David C. Cook, 2013) is a valuable resource for practical guidance in shaping the hearts of young people to look for godly spouses. Another major struggle many young people of this age is the world of sexual impurity. Online and off, returning to sexual purity will probably be a part of ministering to this age group. They will need help healing (over time, some require professional help) so we have provided several resources in the bibliography that come highly recommended by professionals who work in the field of counseling. This is critical to helping them purify their hearts before God. It's also important to help them understand the beauty and goodness of the sexuality that God created them with. Because this has been so taboo to talk about, it is causing major problems in the way our young people think about the good sexuality God created them to enjoy. When a student (or young adult) has gone far enough into this journey of sexual healing, we give them the book *A Celebration of Sex*, usually as a wedding gift, encouraging them to read it with their spouse.

These recommendations come with a word of caution: if you struggle in this area, go on the journey of healing for yourself first, before you start trying to help others. There will be things you will not understand if you have not gone on this journey of healing yourself, including understanding how addiction rewires the brain, and what accepting God's forgiveness means.

8. There are several card games available that serve the purpose of simply starting conversations for building deeper relationships. Some decks contain questions that range from religious to family topics to simple "would you rather" scenarios. These are great tools to have on hand for easing into some of these conversations especially if this is not an area that comes naturally for you. We find that most students enjoy games like this because they crave connec-

tion. Whatever resource you choose to use, make sure it is something that can spark conversations or allow you to get to know the young person(s) you are interacting with.

Bibliography

Baker, Kenneth L. and John R. Kohlenberger III, eds. *The Expositor's Bible Commentary*. Abridged ed. Accordance Software. Grand Rapids: Zondervan, 1994.

Bonhoeffer, Dietrich. *The Cost of Discipleship*. New York: Touchstone, 1995.

Carnegie, Dale. *How to Win Friends and Influence People*. Public Archive, 1981; https://archive.org/details/HowToWinFriendsAndInfluencePeopleBy/mode/2up.

Carns, Patrick. *Facing the Shadow: Starting Sexual and Relationship Recovery*. 3rd ed. United States: Gentle Path Press, 2015.

———. *Out of the Shadows*. 3rd ed. Center City, MN: Hazelden Publishing, 2001.

Chesser, Frank. *Portrait of God*. Huntsville, AL: Publishing Designs, Inc., 2004.

Duvall, Scott J., and J. Daniel Hays. *Grasping God's Word*. 4th ed. Grand Rapids: Zondervan, 2019.

Foubert, John D. *How Pornography Harms: What Today's Teens, Young Adults, Parents, and Pastors Need to Know*. Bloomington, IN: LifeRich Publishing, 2017.

Habermas, Gary and Michael R. Licona. *The Case for the Resurrection of Jesus*. Grand Rapids, MI: Kregel Publications, 2004.

Koukl, Gregory. *Tactics: A Game Plan for Discussing Your Christian Convictions*. Grand Rapids, MI: Zondervan, 2019.

Laaser, Mark R. *Healing the Wounds of Sexual Addiction*. Grand Rapids, MI: Zondervan, 2004.

———. *The Seven Principles of Highly Accountable Men*. Kansas City, MO: Beacon Hill Press of Kansas City, 2011.

———. *Taking Every Thought Captive*. Kansas City, MO: Beacon Hill Press of Kansas City, 2011.

———. *Becoming A Man of Valor*. Kansas City, MO: Beacon Hill Press of Kansas City, 2011.

McDowell, Josh. *The Beauty of Intolerance*. Uhrichsville, OH: Shiloh Run Press, 2016.

McDowell, Josh and Sean. *Evidence that Demands a Verdict*. Nashville, TN: Nelson, 2017.

McDowell, Sean. *A Rebel's Manifesto*. Carol Stream, IL: Tyndale Elevate, 2022.

McDowell, Sean, and J. Warner Wallace. *So the Next Generation Will Know*. Colorado Springs, CO: David C. Cook, 2019.

McDowell, Sean, and John Marriott. *Set Adrift*. Grand Rapids, MI: Zondervan, 2023.

Rosenau, Douglas E. *A Celebration of Sex: A Guide to Enjoying God's Gift of Sexual Intimacy*. Nashville, TN: Thomas Nelson, 2002.

Thomas, Gary. *The Sacred Search*. Colorado Springs, CO: David C. Cook, 2021.

Chapter 44
Basic Bible Study Tips
Properly Handling God's Word
Ryan Gallagher

Why It Matters

Never has the importance of proper Bible study and exegesis been made clearer to me than during a monthly Bible bowl gathering we attended several years ago. During the written portion of our Bible bowl challenge the students were to answer a series of questions and the results would be tallied for a group score. One of the young ladies, who we will call Anna, was taking the test and asked me for help. I explained that I would not help her cheat on a Bible bowl test, of all things, but that if she wanted to "think out loud" I would listen. The question that was puzzling to her was, "Who was the chief of sinners?" She said, "I'm just so confused. I know we are studying 1 Timothy and that Paul wrote the letter to Timothy, so it seems like Paul would be the one making that statement." I was proud of her logical (and correct) conclusion, but then she said, "But it can't be Paul!" I responded, "Then who do you think it is?" She confidently stuttered, "Well, Jesus of course!" I simply stared at her in utter disbelief, knowing we had not only lost the Bible bowl that night but had some serious work to do in our approach to Bible study.

The Bible bowl fiasco stands out as one of the funnier moments I can recall in doing youth ministry, but it has simultaneously fascinated me. This young lady had done a good job of recognizing authorship and the intended audience of the letter, but she had, at the same time, allowed her gut instincts and preconceptions to take over in searching for the truth. She later explained her thought process, saying, "When the verse said, 'chief of sinners' I was thinking about how Jesus was master over sin and death when He defeated Satan at the cross." Again, her theology was intact, but the way she got there, and her handling of the text was lacking. So, the question left for me to answer was, "How do I make responsible Bible students of those with whom I work?"

Handling the Word

The quick and easy answer is that I must become a responsible Bible student first and foremost and then my goal should be to pass on these traditions to others. Paul specifically addresses this matter in his second letter to Timothy. "Do your best to present yourself to God as one approved, a worker who has no need to be ashamed, rightly handling the word of truth" (2 Tim 2:15). I have seen hundreds of youth and family ministry job descriptions and postings describing the desired qualities of the man a local church hopes will inspire and lead their students. Each of these queries has varying lists of qualities that have value and purpose, but if the emphasis of the youth and family program is not hinging on the ability to "rightly handle the word of truth," at best, we will only be producing good citizens, not exceptional Christians.

The word translated as "rightly handling," ὀρθοτομέω (*orthotomeō*), is only used here in the New Testament. It can be defined as guiding "the word of truth along a straight path" (BDAG 722). In the Septuagint, the Greek translation of the Old Testament, it is also used in Proverbs 3:6, a passage that teaches that the one who trusts in the Lord will have his paths "made straight" by God. It appears that Paul's standard of a good minister of the word is one who will properly discern the truth without wavering off the straight path. This is no easy feat. There are seemingly as many interpretations of certain passages as there are interpreters. However, with the right discipline and dedication to staying on the straight course, we can rest assured that we can "know the truth and the truth will set [us] free" (John 8:32, my edit).

Steps for Properly Handling God's Word

There are literally hundreds of good resources dedicated to hermeneutics (the interpretation of the Bible) and how to properly study the Bible. One of the best approaches I have seen is set forth by George Guthrie and Scott Duvall in their *Biblical Greek Exegesis: A Graded Approach to Learning Intermediate and Advanced Greek*. I would like to offer a simplified adaptation of that material, specifically omitting the steps in which knowledge of original languages is necessary (99–165). This method is intended to help in personal Bible study and the study and preparation for classes, sermons, or any other type of material or presentations intended for teaching or ministering.

Personal Preparation

The first step in properly handling God's word is, undoubtedly, the most neglected: personal spiritual preparation. Too often, the text is approached hurriedly and in an information-gathering frenzy without preparing ourselves to receive it. Think of the words of James, "If any of you lacks wisdom, let him ask God, who gives generously to all without reproach, and it will be given him" (Jas 1:5). Before we begin to study any passage from Scripture we must begin in prayer. A simple prayer for clarity of understanding, an openness to the truth, humility to change what needs to be altered in our actions and thinking, and the discernment to be able to communicate the inspired words to receptive hearts are critical as we study. Countless times I have skipped this step in favor of speedily getting my work done. When I do this, I always come up lacking in depth of understanding and fail to do justice to the Scriptures. It does not matter if this is a devotional reading for personal reflection or a specific study for a specific presentation. The results will be the same if we are personally prepared; that we will come to the full "knowledge of the Son of God" (Eph 4:13).

Crucial Questions

Once we have prepared ourselves mentally and spiritually, we need to zoom out and think about things generally. Ask yourself several questions: Who is the author of this book? When was it written? To whom was it written and for what purpose? Does this book fit a particular genre? You may need to consult the introduction in a commentary or a good Old or New Testament introduction book. These questions may seem boring or nitpicky, but they are invaluable in grasping the full picture of what we are trying to discern. So many exegetical fallacies could be avoided by merely thinking through who wrote a particular passage or identifying its genre (i.e., is it poetry or a narrative record?).

Working with Words

After this, it is helpful to begin zooming back in and identifying difficult words or concepts conveyed by the verse(s). If you are proficient in the original languages, you may take time to look them up in a lexicon or do another grammatical study, but often that is not the case for many youth ministers. I suggest reading your passage in at least five different translations, being certain to use a mixture of word-for-word, dynamic equivalent, and paraphrases. A great example of this would be in reading 1 John 2:2 in the English Standard Version where we are told that Jesus is the "propitiation for our sins." The New International Version calls Him the "atoning sacrifice for our sins," while the Contemporary English Version says that "Christ is the sacrifice that takes away our sins." Without opening a commentary or Bible dictionary we have a good understanding of John's original intent. However, I would encourage you to further your depth of study by consulting concordances, lexicons, theological dictionaries, and Bible dictionaries after checking other translations. I would also encourage you to get all the training you can in biblical languages (Hebrew & Greek).

The Biblical Context

Next, we need to, once again, use the wide-angle lens and zoom out to consider how this passage fits into the broader biblical context. For example, Matthew 27:46 records Jesus crying out, "My God, my God, why have you forsaken me?" A quick read of that passage tears at our heartstrings for Jesus's despair, but when we realize that this is a quote from Psalm 22:1, there is more than meets the eye. The original context of Psalm 22 shows David's desperation quickly turning to praise due to God's steadfast love and ability to deliver in the face of any persecution. Jesus knew how to "rightly handle the word of truth." So, at the very lowest point of the physical life of Christ is also a signal of coming victory seen only when we consider the broader scope of His statement as it was used in the Psalter.

Consider Commentaries

Once these other steps have been followed it may be helpful to check a commentary or other special study (article, sermon, etc.) on your text. Often the commentary is the quick draw for students of God's Word. The problem with introducing the commentary too early in the process is the unintended consequence of only being able to think in relation to the purposes and thinking of that particular author. Do you remember step one? Prepare your soul and mind to be open to the truth. The commentary can quickly narrow our approach and hinder legitimate interpretation. With that being said, even though the best approach is to let the Bible speak for itself and interpret itself, sometimes there are verses that are just plain "hard to understand" and a good commentary can ease that trouble (1 Pet 3:16). I recommend comparing at least three different commentaries to get a different perspective.

Apply the Text

The final step that we hope to achieve is an application of the text. Leon Morris begins his commentary on John by calling that gospel "a pool in which a child may wade and an elephant can swim," drawing on the assumption that it is both "simple and profound" (Morris, 3). This metaphor holds, not only for John's gospel but for the entirety of Scripture. Our students are going to be coming to us from a variety of backgrounds and will not have standardized Biblical knowledge from which to draw. So, while we may enjoy swimming deep in the text and catching nuances and undercurrents of the Biblical narrative, we cannot risk our students drowning in that same pool. Just like you teach children to swim gradually by introducing them to water and slowly helping them to gain their confidence until they can swim on their own, we must ease our students into the meat of the Word.

Our Responsibility

As ministers tasked with "making straight the paths" of truth, there is a heavy burden on our shoulders to help our students realize that God's Word really is "living and active, sharper than any two-edged sword, piercing to the division of soul and of spirit, of joints and of marrow, and discerning the thoughts and intentions of the heart" (Heb 4:12). Answering the question, "What does this mean for me?" is the most basic way of handling application. If you cannot say with confidence how a particular passage applies to your own life, you may need to study further or wait to teach that text. If we cannot communicate what the text means to us, then we cannot expect our students to find meaning from the same text. Andrew

Root says that "youth ministry is, after all, *ministry*, and the practicing Christian community is its 'curriculum' — a curriculum that is meaningless unless participation accompanies cognition" (32). So, the question must not only be, "What does this mean for me?" but "What does this require of me?" Application must not cease with understanding the blessings of God, but it must move us to live differently.

Perhaps it is this final question that fuels the apprehension that so many have towards truly delving into the word of God the way we should, and even more so, in our willingness to teach it to others (Jas 3:1). Far too many youth ministries have spent hours developing logos, t-shirt designs, and retreat themes without having first considered the broader implications of how the Scriptures should inform those tools of ministry. Our prayer ought to be that we let the word be a "lamp to my feet and a light to my path" (Ps 119:105).

Conclusion

When Paul told Timothy to "rightly divide the word of truth," he offered one other caveat: that he be "a worker who has no need to be ashamed." (2 Tim 2:15). I believe Timothy's right to be proud of his work came in part from his work ethic but had more to do with how he taught others the word of God. He had a directive to seek the truth, stick to the truth, and share that truth as a worker of the gospel. That's something to never be ashamed of.

You may never have a student who claims that Jesus is the chief of sinners and I hope you never do. Center your ministry on Christ. Make the bedrock of your work the study and application of His Word, and allow God to give the increase (1 Cor 3:7).

Discussion Questions

1. Do you believe a youth and family ministry program should make Bible study the core of all it does? Explain.

2. What are some personal dangers of failing to "rightly divide" the word of God?
3. What are some church-wide dangers of failing to "rightly divide" the word of God?
4. Name some common errors you have seen in Biblical interpretation.
5. What are some steps that could have prevented those errors?
6. Which of the steps listed above is the most important to you? Why?
7. Which of the steps listed above is the most challenging to you? Why?
8. Discuss the relationship between our personal Bible study and the studies we conduct with students and parents.

Bibliography

Danker, Frederick W., Walter Bauer, and William Arndt. *A Greek-English Lexicon of the New Testament and Other Early Christian Literature*. Chicago: University of Chicago Press, 2000.

Guthrie, George H. and J. Scott Duvall. *Biblical Greek Exegesis. A Graded Approach to Learning Intermediate and Advanced Greek*. Grand Rapids: Zondervan, 1998.

Morris, Leon. *The Gospel According to John. The New International Commentary on the New Testament*. Grand Rapids: Eerdmans, 1995.

Root, Andrew. *The Theological Turn in Youth Ministry*. Westmont, IL: InterVarsity Press, 2011.

Chapter 45
The Youth Minister as Theologian and Scholar
Nathan Daily and Ed Gallagher

We are not youth ministers and have never been youth ministers and would never want to be youth ministers. Once upon a time, we were both youth ministry interns, so there's that. But that was long ago, and there is little either one of us would like less than to play with teenagers. When we escaped high school, life improved dramatically; we do not want to go back. Have we made it clear enough? We are not one of you. We are not approaching this topic from the standpoint of a youth minister but from the standpoint of theologians and scholars. Take our advice with however much salt you need.

We assume you guys want to connect kids to God, that that is the primary reason you do this job. We recognize that there are multiple ways to connect kids to God, and that maybe the most important one is not actually through Bible study. Perhaps more important is community, friendships, getting kids involved with the church, the body of Christ. Perhaps worship is also one of the top ways to connect kids to God, especially worship songs, and reflecting together on the life and death of Jesus by means of the Lord's Supper. Sometimes drama builds these connections; we well remember our teenage selves committing to follow Bonnie Tyler's advice to "turn around" and not give ourselves to drugs and sex. With all the different, legitimate, and effective ways to do your primary job—connecting kids to God—we acknowledge that being a theologian and scholar is not on the top of your to-do list.

Theology and Scholarship

But everything is theological (everything contributes to how we "think about God")—the only question is whether something promotes good theology or bad theology. A pizza party promotes a theology. Capture-the-flag promotes a theology. So does a lock-in. Does the design and implementation of each activity promote a theology of thanksgiving or gluttony, teamwork or competition, community or cliques? Certainly, worship promotes a theology, and skits do. There is much to say about the theology of a pizza party based on what the apostle Paul writes in 1 Corinthians 11:17–34. And if we order pizza not primarily to fill people's bellies but to connect them to God, then we cannot escape theology. You do know what the first half of the word "theology" refers to, right? (hint, "God")

Being a scholar is not for everyone, but good theology is for everyone, and scholarship is a route to get there. There are different routes to theology—natural theology, for instance (see, e.g., Wright 2019)—but any Christian theology must be grounded in Scripture (certainly Jesus's theology was, e.g., Matt 5), and that is doubly true for a restoration movement that has called people back to the Bible. Reading the Bible is not always an easy enterprise, and different interpretations abound. One way of cutting through the noise of conflicting and often weird interpretations of Scripture is through scholarship. Scholarship not only offers interpretation but discusses and evaluates the positives and negatives of various interpretations.

(At this point, we would like to talk more about the problems of our current moment, including the internet, and the ready availability of information and the simultaneous erosion of people's ability to sort through and evaluate that abundant information, the proliferation of conspiracy theories, etc.—and therefore our need to be critical and thoughtful in assessing the sources of information we trust and being reflective about why we trust these particular sources of information. But we're running out of space. See, Postman 1985, Carr 2020, Hiestand and Wilson 2015).

That does not mean you need to be a scholar to work with young people, but it will help you—help you to both ground kids in good theology and to persuade them of your viewpoint—if you are able to recognize good scholarly resources and incorporate them into your ministry. This essay attempts to give you some pointers toward that end, a kind of how-to guide.

Tips for Growing Theologically

You have several goals as a youth minister, among which are surely the following: (1) present an example of a caring adult with vibrant faith so that the kids in your youth group will see a living servant of God and want to become the same; (2) teach your kids how to navigate life; (3) help them not to get suckered into the latest theological fad; (4) create joyful Christians who understand the basis of their faith and know how to think through issues. Basically, you have the same goal as the apostle Paul who speaks of "warning everyone and teaching everyone with all wisdom, that we may present everyone mature in Christ" (Col 1:28). To get the kids in your youth group to be mature in Christ, you need to present a mature faith yourself, one that wrestles with Scripture and is open to asking tough questions. Here are some tips for coming to a more mature faith through study of Scripture.

Tip #1: Talk to Older Ministers and Elders.

Ask them questions about Scripture, about church work, and about God. Pitch your ideas, your interpretations of Scripture or your thoughts on application of Scripture and solicit their feedback. Learn to hear viewpoints other than your own. This is accomplished through practice, the practice of speaking with people of different ages and with diverse backgrounds and experiences. As a community of believers, the church brings together people who would not otherwise exist together. To grow theologically, you will need access to others who have been there and who have seen it, to those who are not just like you, to those who have experienced growth themselves and are willing to mentor.

Tip #2: Read Books

How do you know which books to read? Well, start with this book, the one you are holding. And you know what? You're already doing it! Excellent job! Do we need to tell you that you will not agree with everything you read or that you need to eat the fish and spit out the bones as you read? Surely, you have heard those exhortations enough that we can skip them. And surely you know that there are a lot of bones in "brotherhood" books, interpretations that you will—and should!—disagree with even if the author were your own preacher. You do disagree sometimes with the way your preacher interprets Scripture, right? Since all books, no matter who wrote them, have elements, interpretations, statements, that you will reject, there is no need to limit your reading to a particular set of authors or a particular theological position. If you already know or agree with everything you read, what is the purpose of reading? Of course, you will want to be critical in your reading of any book. ("Critical" means reading closely and carefully, keeping your thinking cap on.)

Scholars often disagree with one another; literally, that's what their job is, to find where people have been thinking incorrectly about something and to propose a better way. You are not really looking for what all scholars believe—there's no such thing. But there are positions that are more well-accepted than other positions. Look for those positions and learn why they are so well accepted. Of course, a consensus can be wrong. You always need to be critical of the books you read—not skeptical, but not trusting either. Always ask, "How do you know?" If you're going to read scholarly works, you need to recognize what those works can give you. They are not going to give you the final answer to things but a new way of seeing, and they can give you data, more information than you previously had.

You need to be humble about your own knowledge. By the way, "humility" itself is a good theological principle that you will encounter repeatedly in Scripture (Green 2012, Smith 2016, 1 Pet 5:5). As Augustine wrote many centuries ago, "There is hardly a page in the Bible which does not proclaim the message: 'God resists the proud, but gives grace to the humble' [James 4:6]" (*On Christian Teaching* 3.75; trans. Green 1997: 85). You will want to inculcate humility in your youth group through teaching and modeling. You can model humility by being open to changing your opinions and being excited, joyful, to learn new things.

We will recommend some specific books in a moment, but a good rule of thumb is to choose books by recognized authors and published by recognized publishing companies. Here's a suggestion: every year the magazine *Christianity Today* gives awards to a bunch of books touching on different aspects of theology and ministry. Seek out this annual list of award-winning books.

Tip #3: Have a Big-Picture View of Scripture

Come to appreciate and teach the storyline of the entire Bible, from creation to new creation, with the crucifixion as the pivot (see Neh 9; Acts 7). Read Scripture not just to determine what you should do right now but also to learn how to think about God and the human condition. Who is God? What has God done? What will God do? Ground your youth group in the doctrines of the church and worship that churches of Christ have long emphasized, and help them see a bigger story of God's workings in the world and how our actions cohere with his purposes, and how all of Scripture (even the boring or seemingly irrelevant parts) reveal God's truth.

There are a lot of books that might help you along these lines. Some of our favorites include C. J. H. Wright (1992, 2010, 2023), Levenson (1993), Bauckham (1993), Ferguson (1996), Hays (1996), N. T. Wright (1992, 1996, 2016), Hurtado (2010), Moberly (2013), DeSilva (2018), Provan (2017), Smith (2009), and Barclay (2020). You could also check out the other books (besides the one you are holding) that HCU Press has produced. And there are also podcasts, for example, the Bible Project (and videos at YouTube) and On Script.

Most of these specific suggestions that we gave have to do with Scripture, but there are plenty of books on other aspects of youth ministry—for instance, covering research on adolescent faith development, or faith retention among young adults, or teenage religious practices. Keep up to speed with this data. The *Christianity Today* lists will help you. Also, find your nearest theological library to access databases (esp., ATLA and JSTOR) that contain the most recent research.

Tip #4: Become Familiar with the Biblical Languages

Learning Greek and Hebrew is not for everyone, but it's awfully helpful for those involved in connecting others to God. For whatever reason, God chose to communicate his message in these particular languages. Having a basic knowledge of Greek and Hebrew—even just an understanding of the alphabet, how to pronounce words, and how to use Bible software to search for words and look them up in a dictionary—can be immensely helpful in Bible study. Moreover, having a basic grasp of how our Bible came to us (Meade and Gurry 2022) can be helpful in your personal study and in answering perennial questions. You should not imagine, however, that reading the New Testament in Greek or the Old Testament in Hebrew is the gateway to completely new insights in Christianity, or that Greek and Hebrew words are richer than English words. For the most part, the major English translations of Scripture are just fine. They do a good job. But we should not treat them as if they are the original text. Doing a word study of "peace" might be helpful, but running a search on *eirēnē* (Greek for "peace") makes more sense if the goal is to understand what the New Testament says about peace. (But do not do any word studies before reading Silva 1990.)

Different Strokes

Academic study is not for everyone, and even a youth minister—an employee of the church appointed by the elders to guide other people in the things of God (i.e., someone who might be expected to be unusually devoted to Scripture)—does not necessarily need to be a reader. Youth ministers can be valuable to kids in different ways. And good youth ministers are busy youth ministers, so they know that there is always more to do than they have time for, always something that needs to receive less attention at times. That may include time in study, if that's what you enjoy less than counseling people, or evangelizing, or designing and implementing meaningful activities that connect kids and families to God. We do not mean that it is okay to let personal Bible study go by the wayside. That is not okay, certainly not for a youth minister responsible for the souls of other people. If you do not want to be involved in daily Bible study and prayer, you are going stink at youth ministry; even if you can attract a crowd, you are not going to be connecting them to God. Go find something else to do and stop mooching off the church.

What we do mean is that some people enjoy and excel in studying beyond personal Bible reading, and some people enjoy and excel at other things. You should, of course, attempt to excel at everything (Matt 5:48!), but some aspects of ministry will get more of your attention than others. If reading the types of books we have recommended here does not excite you, well, you still need to read them. Set a goal to read maybe a book a month. Look, even if you are not a reader, some of the kids in your youth group will be. Some of those kids are going to be quietly desperate for deep conversations about God and Scripture, and they are going to want a knowledgeable and trusted adult to help them think through some stuff. Are you going to be able to think through this stuff with them? You need to read.

Discussion Questions

1. What does Paul mean in Colossians 1:28 when he talks about people being mature in Christ? What does such maturity look like? How does one get there?
2. Do you agree that everything is theological? Can you see how a pizza party or a lock-in would promote a theology? Can you think of examples of things that are not theological?
3. To what extent should all Christians be devoted to Bible study? Is it okay for some Christians to be more devoted to Bible study than others? Should all Christian leaders be particularly devoted to Bible study?
4. Have you known people who were unwilling to consider positions contrary to their own? Is that a characteristic of faithfulness, or stubbornness? How should we incorporate the virtue of humility into our theology?

Bibliography

Barclay, John M. G. *Paul and the Power of Grace*. Grand Rapids: Eerdmans, 2020.

Bauckham, Richard. *The Theology of the Book of Revelation*. Cambridge: Cambridge University Press. 1993.

Carr, Nicholas. *The Shallows: What the Internet is Doing to Our Brains*. New York: Norton, 2020.

DeSilva, David. *An Introduction to the New Testament: Contexts,*

Methods, and Ministry Formation. Downers Grove, IL: IVP Academic, 2018.

Ferguson, Everett. *The Church of Christ: A Biblical Ecclesiology for Today*. Grand Rapids: Eerdmans, 1996.

Green, Joel B. *Practicing Theological Interpretation: Engaging Biblical Texts for Faith and Formation*. Theological Explorations for the Church Catholic. Grand Rapids: Baker, 2012.

Green, R. P. H., trans. *Saint Augustine: On Christian Teaching*. Oxford World's Classics. Oxford: Oxford University Press, 1997.

Hays, Richard B. *The Moral Vision of the New Testament: A Contemporary Introduction to New Testament Ethics*. San Francisco: HarperSanFrancisco, 1996.

Hiestand, Gerald, and Todd A. Wilson. *The Pastor Theologian: Resurrecting and Ancient Vision*. Grand Rapids: Zondervan, 2015.

Hurtado, Larry W. *God in New Testament Theology*. Nashville: Abingdon, 2010.

Levenson, Jon D. *The Death and Resurrection of the Beloved Son: The Transformation of Child Sacrifice in Judaism and Christianity*. New Haven, CT: Yale University Press, 1993.

Meade, John D., and Peter J. Gurry. *Scribes and Scripture: The Amazing Story of How We Got the Bible*. Wheaton, IL: Crossway, 2022.

Moberly, R. W. L. *Old Testament Theology: Reading the Hebrew Bible as Christian Scripture*. Grand Rapids: Baker, 2013.

Postman, Neil. *Amusing Ourselves to Death: Public Discourse in the Age of Show Business*. New York: Penguin, 1985.

Provan, Iain. *The Reformation and the Right Reading of Scripture*. Waco, TX: Baylor University Press, 2017.

Silva, Moisés. *God, Language, and Scripture: Reading the Bible in the Light of General Linguistics*. Grand Rapids: Zondervan, 1990.

Smith, James K. A. *Desiring the Kingdom: Worship, Worldview, and Cultural Formation*. Grand Rapids: Baker Academic, 2009.

Smith, James K. A. *You are What You Love: The Spiritual Power of Habit*. Grand Rapids: Brazos, 2016.

Wright, Christopher J. H. *Knowing Jesus through the Old Testament*. Downers Grove, IL: IVP, 1992.

Wright, Christopher J. H. *The Mission of God's People: A Biblical Theology of the Church's Mission*. Biblical Theology for Life. Grand Rapids. Zondervan, 2010.

Wright, Christopher J. H. *The Great Story and the Great Commission: Participating in the Biblical Drama of Mission*. Acadia Studies in Bible and Theology. Grand Rapids: Baker, 2023.

Wright, N. T. *The New Testament and the People of God*. Christian Origins and the Question of God. Minneapolis: Fortress, 1992.

Wright, N. T. *Jesus and the Victory of God*. Christian Origins and the Question of God. Minneapolis: Fortress, 1996.

Wright, N. T. *The Day the Revolution Began: Reconsidering the Meaning of Jesus's Crucifixion*. San Francisco: HarperOne, 2016.

Wright, N. T. *History and Eschatology: Jesus and the Promise of Natural Theology*. Waco, TX: Baylor University Press, 2019.

Chapter 46
Tips for Teaching Teenagers
Jeremy Gargis and Joey Barrier

Of all the things that we can choose to do in life, few carry more importance than teaching young people about the love, character, grace, and expectations of God. Teaching people of any age is great work, of course, but when you consider the impressionable minds of young people and the onslaught of worldly thinking that is thrust upon them, the need for effectively teaching teenagers cannot be taken lightly.

Any time we teach we must consider the seriousness of what we are doing. The words of James 3:1 should be a motivator for us; "Not many of you should become teachers, my brothers, for you know that we who teach will be judged with greater strictness." When we open the holy Word of God to expound upon it, it cannot be something that we are disingenuous about. It is paramount that we put time, effort, and serious consideration into what we are doing. All of that brings us to tip number one.

Tip #1: Actually Teach the Bible

If we are really in the business of helping people arrive at a better understanding of God's expectations and the riches found in

Christ, then we must always start squarely in the Word! Sure, there will be a need at times to motivate our teens. There will be times when we need to make an emotional appeal to some. But this should only come through the Bible and the motivation and emotion that it applies.

For instance, all of our young people are going to struggle with some specific issues that need to be addressed. Let's say, for instance, that the issue is addiction. While some research data related to addictions can be helpful to them, teaching them that our bodies belong to the Lord (1 Cor 6:19–20) is the place to start. What if the issue is anxiety? Again, helping them realize that they are not alone, and providing them with some tangible resources will be a difference maker, but providing them with Biblical examples of people facing the same problems and God providing for them needs to be step one.

There are plenty of good resources to be had out there, but if we choose to place more merit in any resource other than Scripture, we fail our students. Teach the whole counsel of God! Start with Scripture and draw topics from it rather than trying to make the Scriptures fit into your topic. Teach the Bible!

Tip #2: Do Not Make Assumptions as to Your Students's Knowledge

For far too long we have made a mistake when we assume that all of our students know familiar passages or biblical accounts and narratives. We may say something as seemingly safe as, "You all know the story of Noah and the flood," but what about those students that were not raised coming to church and have no idea what you're talking about? What about the visitor that was unsure about coming with a friend in the first place and has never cracked a Bible open? There is a very real possibility that any time we make a claim such as the one above there will be someone present that proves it false.

A better way to frame such a statement would be, "Some of you may remember what the Bible tells us about Noah." You could also simply tell the story without any reference to who may or may not already be familiar with it. It is important when teaching a class full of students from different homes and backgrounds that we do not make anyone feel as though they don't belong because they do not know some things that the majority of the students do. Perhaps the most effective way to keep teenagers from coming to Bible classes and worship is to make them feel like they are not good enough or are not wanted. This could very well end up being how we make them feel if we make statements that indicate that they should have knowledge of something when they do not. Do not make assumptions as to your students' knowledge!

Tip #3: Be Comfortable with Who You Are

It can be tempting at times to try to present ourselves as something that we are not when we spend time around teenagers. Whether you are from an entirely different generation than them or simply do not seem to have very much in common with them, we at times give in to presenting ourselves in something other than a genuine way.

I can tell you from experience that teenagers are some of the most effective folks in the world at seeing through a disingenuous presentation. Whether you are pretending to be someone that you are not, or that you know more or less about a particular subject than you actually do, or any other thing, teenagers can spot a fake.

On the other side of this, I can also tell you from experience that regardless of differences in personalities, hobbies, interests, etc., teenagers are appreciative of people that simply present themselves as who they are. We have no need to make any excuses for being in a different stage of life than our students, or to apologize for having different interests. We are there to teach them the Word of God, and we will find more success by being real with them than we will ever have if we try to present ourselves as something that we are not.

Additionally, while being personal with our students, it can be extremely helpful to share personal life experiences with them. Allowing teenagers to learn from our various successes and failures can help them to see more clearly how to handle various things that they are facing. The more we can be honest with our students, the more we increase our likelihood of having a positive impact on them and becoming someone that they can trust to share their burdens with. Be comfortable with who you are. A word of caution here. It is great to be real but be careful not to glorify yourself when telling stories. It can quickly turn teens off. Also, remember that overemphasizing your mistakes can cause them to doubt whether you should be teaching them.

Tip #4: Make Sure Your Students Know that They Are Loved

It has always been easier for mankind to hear something they would rather not hear when it comes from someone who loves them. This is certainly the case when it comes to teaching teenagers. Because of human nature, there will be times when all of us will want to do things that are contrary to God's desires. This is only exacerbated by the physical, mental, and hormonal changes that teenagers are going through. Because of this, there will be many times that we will have to address issues that our students are having. We will inevitably find more success and willingness to listen when we have cultivated those relationships with love and consistency.

How do we make sure that they know they are loved, though? It is not as difficult as it may seem. The answer is: Just be there. Are your students performing in a concert or recital of some kind? Be there. Are they playing in a sporting event? Go watch them and tell them how much you enjoyed watching them compete. Have they lost a grandparent to death? Show up at their house or at the funeral home to help with some of the funeral arrangements. Did they have a rough breakup with a boyfriend or girlfriend? Tell them you love them the next time you see them and maybe even give them their favorite candy.

Sometimes, in order to be able to most effectively show love to our students, we will have to do a little bit of reconnaissance work behind the scenes. You might need to ask their parents or close friends what their favorite treats are. You might need to find out what other people they look up to so that you can send those role models to them. The number of things that may be necessary for us to do in order to make sure that our students know that they are loved may seem burdensome, but none of that work is fruitless. If we are going to make a lasting impact on their lives, it is of utmost importance that our students know that they are loved.

Tip #5: Do Not Lump All Students into One Category

We all have different backgrounds, interests, and knowledge. Some of us are more capable in certain aspects of life while being surpassed by the capabilities of others in other aspects. This is certainly true of the students you will be teaching and we need to keep that in mind as we prepare and deliver classes.

One of the areas where this frequently plagues us as teachers in teenage classes is that we use the same examples consistently without providing examples that would make all of our students feel more included. Perhaps the most frequently used example in these classes is sports. We may talk about how conditioning and practice for a sport are not fun, but they prepare us for success when it matters the most, or we may talk about how when we are tired we need to pay extra attention to doing things the right way to be successful. Using sports as an illustration can be a very good thing so feel free to do so. Yet please do not just use sports as an illustration. If your group of students is like most groups, less than half of them will be playing sports. Sure, they will be able to understand the main point of the example even if it is not as impactful to them as it is to those who do play sports, but if that is the only way we illustrate our lessons, we could potentially make those non-sports-playing students feel less important. Remember also that you may have students with physical disabilities. For many of them, playing in athletic activities is not even a possibility (and may be difficult to talk about).

When drawing application from the things that our students take part in, we need to include more things. We could use band or chorus to illustrate the way that Christ functions as one body, though made up of many members. When a band plays or a chorus sings, if all perform perfectly in tune, but one is off, things will sound bad. Or, we could include those who take part in dramatic productions in school or the community by using the illustration of learning lines rather than using a sports team's practice from time to time. You can also pull great illustrations from the world of art.

The point is that we need to celebrate the diversity of our students instead of running the risk of making some of our children feel cut off from the group because they do not take part in any particular activity. Our students will have many similarities, but also many differences. Take care not to lump them all into one category.

Tip #6: Address the "Hard Things."

There will be all sorts of difficult things to deal with in youth ministry, or any kind of ministry for that matter. When you are dealing with teenagers, you will have the highest of highs when they make choices that make you proud, but also the lowest of lows when they make less-than-desirable decisions. There will be periods of time that make things seem easier than they really are, but also hard times that seem like there is no good way to handle them. Students will ask questions with easy answers, but also questions that will make your head hurt.

These "hard things" could include any number of issues, but perhaps the first one to address is difficult Biblical passages and teachings. Jesus said some things that are hard for us to wrap our minds around. Trying to put some of those into perspective for a teenager who is pulled in multiple directions because of the world that we live in is no small task. But, those sayings of Jesus and other Biblical authors are there, and we cannot ignore them! Go on the offensive and choose to address them. If questions arise that have no simple answer, spend the necessary time in class and, perhaps in private with a smaller group, to provide understanding. While we will never know God's will perfectly, we are in the business of helping teenagers come to a better knowledge of it, and we must take that seriously.

Another "hard thing" could be dealing with the fallout of a teenager's bad decisions, or circumstances in their lives that are beyond their control. Times like these remind us of why tip number four (make sure your students know that they are loved) is so important. You want to be a person they can go to when things are bad. When these times come, and they will, you must address them. A teen struggling with addiction who had the faith in you to share that information with you does not need you to help them hide it, they need you to help them overcome it! A teen that has been being abused in any fashion does not just need you to talk to, they need you to help get them out of a bad situation, and help them rebuild trust in people. An unmarried teenager who is pregnant, or got a girl pregnant, needs to understand that being pregnant is not a sin. Sure, sin took place to get to where they are, but that, just like any other sin, can be forgiven, and they need your support.

Conclusion

One of the most important things we do in ministry is respond to difficult questions, situations, and decisions. Not only will how we choose to handle these "hard things" affect our ability as ministers, but it will also affect how those looking to us for help will move on with their lives. Make sure that you address these hard things and do so using Scripture. Do not assume they understand; make sure that they do. Do this as who you are, a mentor, not trying to only be a friend to them. Reassure them that you love them and are there for them, and remind them that their individual situation matters. In my opinion, ministry, especially youth ministry, is not easy. However, it is certainly worthy and rewarding work and, when performed effectively, will impact the Kingdom of God in a very positive way. Do the hard work!

Discussion Questions

1. Which of these tips stands out to you as being of utmost importance?
2. What additional tips do you think others would find helpful in a classroom setting?
3. Why is having an intimate knowledge of your students so important when preparing Bible classes?
4. What are some ways that we can make all of our students feel involved and valuable?
5. How can we employ discipleship through the Bible class?

Chapter 47
Preaching and Songleading Tips for Youth Ministers
Andrew Philips

Effective youth ministry not only provides spiritual growth opportunities for students, but it also plugs them into the life of the larger church family. Helping teenagers do that will require a youth minister to be involved with adults in the larger congregation, which can be termed an "authoritative community" (Dean 2010, 72). Leading in worship provides a chance for the youth minister to connect with the entire church. Here are a few ways to make the most of those preaching and song-leading opportunities.

Preaching Tips

Effective Preaching Is the Product of Careful Preparation

If you do not preach often, it can be an anxiety-inducing proposition. One of the most effective ways to deal with nerves before speaking is to prepare thoroughly (Lucas 2019, 10). If you are preparing to preach to a group of 100 people for 30 minutes, then you will, in a sense, be asking people to invest 50 hours of human time. That responsibility demands dedicated study. Since ministry schedules are rarely predictable, carving out the time to prepare will require discipline and effort. For this reason, it is challenging to assign a certain number of hours to spend on each sermon. There will be some occasions where you simply do not have as much time available as others, yet our goal should always be to spend the time necessary to go through the preparation process.

While there are various ways to map out the sermon preparation process in the homiletic literature, here is a practical, non-academic guide to building a sermon, at least as I have experienced it:

Phase 1 — Initial Excitement

"You know what I should preach about ... ."

You either have an idea for a specific text/topic or you see what is coming up on the preaching calendar and you are eager to start.

Phase 2 — Intense Study

"This is fascinating ... ."

You are reading and reflecting on the text, consulting other sources, and you realize this is a deep, rich study.

Phase 3 — Total Loss

"I have no idea where to go next."

You look at a blank page and try to imagine how to craft a sermon that conveys the richness of what you have studied. This is my least favorite phase. Some weeks I have an idea quickly and it does not last very long, but there are other weeks where I spend more time here than I would like.

Phase 4 — Uncertainty

"I have an idea, but I am not sure about it ... ."

You start working on the idea you have finally selected for the sermon, but you keep erasing, rewriting, and starting over. This phase is tough but important.

Phase 5 — The Beginning of Clarity

"This is starting to come together, but parts of it still feel weak and incomplete."

You start to sense some progress. There is still a long way to go, but you can feel some momentum start to build.

Phase 6 — *Now We Are Getting Somewhere*
"I think the overall structure of the sermon is good, but I need to make sure I am illustrating and explaining it effectively."

Now you know what the overall message will look like, and you can start working on the details. You are not quite done, but the end is in sight. A great deal of sermon improvement can occur in this phase.

Phase 7 — *Final Touches*
"Let me look over this and see if anything needs to be changed."

You inspect the sermon carefully to make any final changes. It might be tempting to skip this phase, but it is important.

Phase 8 — *Excited to Preach!*
"This could be good ... ."

You are eager to preach your sermon. Your enthusiasm has moved up from Phase 3 back to the levels of excitement in Phases 1 and 2.

Phase 9 — *While Preaching*
"That didn't come out the way I planned it ... ."

This is the preaching phase. You make slight adjustments while delivering the sermon, based on the feedback you are receiving from your listeners. While it is hard to avoid self-critique during a sermon, it is important to stay in the moment and focus on what you are saying.

Phase 10 — *The Ride Home*
"What I should have said was ... ."

This is the phase right after the sermon, where you reflect on what you should have done differently. This phase cannot be avoided, but it should not last indefinitely. Allow yourself to think about what you could have done differently, and you may even write down some notes to think about for next time, but then allow yourself to think about something else.

Effective Preaching Considers the Listeners

One of the first steps in preparing to speak publicly is to

consider your audience. Of course, God is the primary audience when we come together to worship, but the words of a sermon are directed to those who are sitting and listening to you. When you speak regularly to teenagers, it can be easy to forget that adults do not always understand the pop culture references, terms, or music that everyone in the youth group knows. Be sure to use illustrations that everyone can understand. Be yourself; there is no need to act like someone who is decades older than you are. Just be sure to keep your audience in mind.

When you preach to a congregation, you are often speaking to people who have been Christians for decades, as well as those who have only begun their journey of faith. You will be addressing people who are married, others who are single, and still others who have lost a spouse. Some will have schedules packed with work duties and family obligations, while others may feel isolated and are looking for ways to connect with others. As you develop your sermon and are finding ways to apply your message, imagine a cross-section of your church members sitting around the table with you. How will your message address their daily concerns? What concrete examples might be the most helpful for each situation?

Preaching a sermon also provides the congregation with an opportunity to get to know you better. They already appreciate the hard work you put in every day to help teenagers grow spiritually, and preaching opportunities give you a chance to help every other member of the church grow. Taking the time before and after the sermon to greet people and talk to them can also help you build those relationships.

Effective Preaching Grows Out of Your Study

Serious study is a good safeguard against plagiarism. Nearly everyone who prepares a sermon uses resources like Bible reference books, commentaries, or podcasts. Yet there is a difference between employing those tools wisely during sermon preparation and using them to shortcut the study process. The first approach will result in personal spiritual growth as well as carefully crafted messages. The second approach might work occasionally, but it will not sustain your ministry over the long haul. As scholar Jack Lewis once wrote, "We will not win the war for the minds of men with borrowed sermon outlines" (Lewis 1985, 105).

All of us will draw on resources when preparing a sermon. There are seldom any sermon ideas or illustrations that never occurred to anyone else before we thought of them. Yet we must use resources responsibly by citing them and giving credit where it is due. We do not have to provide a complete bibliography of each source, but when we clearly refer to them during a sermon, we build credibility among our listeners (Carter 2002, 9). Remember, the sermon preparation process is not just about the kind of sermon you will preach in a few days, it is also about the kind of minister you will be in the next few weeks, months, and years. When you study, you are not only preparing a sermon; you are also preparing yourself. There may be something you learn while studying that does not fit in that message but helps you answer a question in a Bible class a few weeks later. If you have not spent time studying, you are robbing yourself of the opportunity to use what you have learned later.

Song Leading Tips

Youth ministers are typically called on to lead worship in a variety of settings. Some will be small group devotionals or Bible classes; others might be in larger assemblies. Of course, you will want to adjust your style to the number of people you are leading. For instance, when you are leading a devotional in someone's living room, it might not be necessary to stand up, use hand motions in a 4/4 beat pattern, and project the words on the wall. When you are leading the whole congregation on a Sunday morning, however, all those elements can be helpful. Here are principles to remember when planning to lead the congregation in worship on Sunday.

Effective Worship Leading Begins with Thoughtful, Prayerful Preparation

If you are in ministry long, there will likely be a time when you are asked to lead singing on short notice and pick out songs only minutes before worship begins. This should be the exception, though, and not the rule. Just like a preacher will spend hours preparing a message, the worship leader should spend time reflecting on what songs will help Christians focus as they praise. Of course, meaningful worship does not have to be completely scripted, but it should be carefully anticipated and planned.

Spend time discussing the sermon with the preacher. What message does he want people to be thinking about when they walk out of the church building? Once you know the answer to that question, it becomes the controlling influence on what songs you select. Read the text of Scripture for that morning. How will the words you sing help people focus on the text being preached? What verses will drive home the point of the message? Some topics make that job easier than others. It does not take nearly as long to think of songs about heaven as it does to locate songs for a sermon on materialism. But if you spend enough time considering that week's topic, you will almost always be able to find a few songs that would be more appropriate than others.

Thoughtful preparation will also help the flow of the worship assembly. You can set a tone by beginning with an upbeat, familiar song. Since we sing better when we stand, it is a good idea to stand for the first song(s), as well as the song(s) right before the sermon. This allows people a chance to stand up and stretch, and it generates energy and enthusiasm. If you plan to lead a new or unfamiliar song, make sure to do it between familiar songs. It is a good rule of thumb not to begin or end a worship service with an unfamiliar song.

Effective Worship Leading Involves Truly Leading

Starting a song is one thing, and leading a song is another. In small group settings, someone can start a familiar song and be confident that everyone will stay together. With a larger crowd, though, the leader needs to be assertive. To do that in a large environment, use a microphone (when provided) and hand motions to keep time. Few of us like the sound of our own voice, and for that reason, you may shy away from a microphone. But no matter how it might sound to you when your voice is hard to hear, the song is hard for everyone to follow. When your voice is loud enough, the congregation will sing louder and more confidently. Even if you think your voice is so loud that you do not need a microphone, it is still best to use one. Remember that there are often people in the auditorium using hearing aids, and they rely on the microphone. It will also keep you from over-singing and wearing your voice out quickly.

As far as hand motions are concerned, the basic beat patterns are relatively easy to learn. You do not have to know how to read music to direct with hand motions. If you know the 4/4, 3/4, or 6/8 beat patterns, you can lead almost any song in worship. These numbers are called *time signatures;* the top number tells you how many beats are in a measure, and the bottom number tells you which note gets one beat (in the case of those three, either the fourth note or the eighth note). Using these beat patterns is not as common as it used to be, so if you would rather not learn those, you can always keep time with a simple up-and-down arm motion. No matter how loud your voice is, this direction will help larger groups stay together. This is a fine line; you want to be noticeable enough to keep everyone together without being distracting.

Effective Worship Leading Relies on a Variety of Songs

We all have our favorite songs, and it can be tempting to keep coming back to songs we enjoy leading or that we feel like the congregation sings especially well. But just like a balanced diet needs more than one food group, a congregation's worship diet needs more than one type of song and more than one set of familiar favorites. Keep a record of the songs you lead each week, either digital or analog so that you can spot which ones are led most often. Also, remember that your favorite song is likely someone else's least favorite, and vice versa (so be careful about announcing publicly which songs you do not like). Leading worship regularly will require leading some songs you might not enjoy as much as others.

It will also require considering when songs were written. Each generation grew up with songs that "speak their language," and since worship involves multiple generations, the song selection will need to span multiple generations as well. If you work in youth ministry, you will be familiar with new songs that not everyone in the congregation will know. Leading singing provides an opportunity to teach those songs, and it also gives you a chance to lead older, more familiar songs as well. Both are important. Singing older hymns sends a comforting message that you have not forgotten about the songs that have sustained Christians for generations, and including newer songs lets the younger generation know that worship is for them as well.

Conclusion

Both preaching and leading singing will give you the chance to use your gifts and abilities to the glory of God, and they will also provide important moments to connect with the entire church family. May God bless you as you take full advantage of these opportunities.

Discussion Questions

1. What goes through your mind as another person is speaking? How can this help you to think about what is going through the minds of those in your audience?

2. What causes you to pay attention to a message? How does this knowledge help you to think about how to reach others?
3. Think deeply about this question: *Are you preaching sermons that flow out of deep personal Bible study and reflection or sermons produced by AI or created by another preacher?* Which approach honors God the most? Which approach will better prepare you to minister to others in the future?
4. What are some things you might do to better understand the members of your congregation so you can better apply your sermons?
5. What is the ratio of old songs to new songs in your congregation? Is there a balance? If there is no balance, what can you do to improve the situation?

Bibliography

Dean, Kenda Creasy. *Almost Christian*. New York, NY: Oxford University Press, 2010.

Lewis, Jack. *Leadership Questions Confronting the Church*. Nashville, TN: Gospel Advocate, 1985.

Lucas, Stephen E. *The Art of Public Speaking*. New York, NY: McGraw-Hill, 2019.

Shelley, Carter. "Preaching and Plagiarism: A Guide for Introduction to Preaching Students." *Homiletic* 27.2 (2002):1–13.

Chapter 48
Writing and Publishing for Children/Teens
Jeremy Pate

In one form or another, most youth ministers will incorporate writing as a part of their ministry to young people. Some are ministering to a wider range of young people (often including elementary students), while others are focusing primarily on preteens and teenagers. Whether you are writing bulletin articles, blogs, Bible class material, family Bible study curriculum, or books, this chapter will offer some practical advice on how to write more effectively in your ministry.

Technology has provided a wealth of options when it comes to preaching and teaching God's Word. Videos, podcasts, PowerPoint, social media platforms, and other forms of modern communication have opened up possibilities that were unheard of in previous generations. Some may even be convinced that these modern advances have completely replaced the written word in terms of how we can best communicate truth to young people. However, since God—in His eternal wisdom—chose to give us His revelation by means of the written word, there is a sense in which the medium of writing will always be relevant.

Youth ministry is currently serving and mentoring an entire generation of students (known as Generation Z) who have never

not had access to the Internet and portable digital technology. In fact, many of our youth ministers ***themselves*** are still in this same age group. This generation (born roughly between 1997 and 2012), has been dubbed "digital natives," and is currently spending approximately 5–9 hours every day looking at a screen for entertainment purposes. According to one recent study, less than 30 minutes of this time is spent ***reading***, creating digital art or music, or writing.[1] This creates unique challenges in many areas, including the realm of writing.

Although I am certainly no expert in this area, I have learned much, especially through my role as Youth Publications Coordinator at Apologetics Press, that may be helpful. I believe there are some sound and helpful principles that can be applied in this particular area of ministry. For your consideration, I humbly submit three characteristics that should describe the writing that we do in our ministry to children and teens (later in this chapter, we will briefly discuss the publishing aspect of writing):

- Our writing should be **SCRIPTURAL.**
- Our writing should be **SUITABLE.**
- Our writing should be **SUPPLEMENTED.**

Our Writing Should Be Scriptural

As we think about the first important characteristic of what we write for children and teens, we should always start with the Scripture. God's Word is the ultimate source of truth, life, and instruction, and anything/everything that we write should be saturated with and centered on what the Bible has to say. This means that we need to do the following.

Study the Word

We need to read/study God's word for ourselves on a regular basis. We cannot teach others something that we do not already know and believe ourselves (Deut 6:6ff.), which would certainly include the things that we write. As youth ministers (and as Christians in general), it is vital that we cultivate healthy, consistent, and informed Bible study habits (2 Tim 2:15). Surround yourself with good resources and Bible study tools, and make sure that you are growing in your knowledge of God's Word (2 Pet 3:18). These study habits will provide the appropriate "fuel" for your writing.

Be Proactive and Balanced

Writing benefits from structure and balance. In Youth Ministry, there always seems to be a "fire" that needs to be put out, which means that we can sometimes allow our ministry to be driven or directed ***reactively*** instead of ***proactively***. If we only write in response to the latest challenge, problem, or crisis, we will almost certainly be unbalanced in our approach to Scripture within our writing. However, if our writing is coming from a personal, consistent (and perhaps even a systematic) study of God's Word, we are more likely to achieve a balanced approach and less likely to seem reactionary in our writing.

Avoid Three Key Mistakes

Wrong Sequencing: Reverse Engineering/Proof Texting

In our efforts to proclaim the "whole counsel of God" (Acts 20:27), we need to resist the urge to use God's Word as a way to prove what we have already decided to say/write. There are certainly appropriate ways to allow the Scriptures to answer any given problem or situation that we might be facing, but we need to make sure that we are not twisting God's Word to say what we want it to say instead of what it actually says (2 Pet 3:16).

Wrong Sources: Secular/Denominational Source Material

There is nothing inherently wrong with consulting secular or denominational sources as part of our balanced and comprehensive study on any given topic/issue; however, we must be careful not to allow these sources to become our ***primary*** sources, with the Bible simply being used to "back them up." If we find ourselves quoting the Pew Research Center or C.S. Lewis more than we quote God's Word, we might want to adjust our approach.

Wrong Stimulus: "Feeding the Machine" (writing because we have to)

With the advent of social media, daily posts, Twitter, etc., many youth ministers may feel the pressure to write/say something every single day. This is not a good reason to write, and is yet another reason why our Bible study habits are so important. If we allow the demands of producing content to be the engine behind our writing choices, we will inevitably make mistakes in the areas of being scripturally sound and centered.

Our Writing Should Be Suitable

When writing for children and teens, it is important to write suitably. This means that we need to adapt what we have gleaned from our study of God's Word to suit the age/maturity level of our intended audience. Keep in mind, that we are not ***modifying*** God's Word; we are simply ***adapting*** it. Let's consider the two categories of "children" and "teens":

Suitable for Children

When writing for children (ages 5–12), here are a few suggestions:

Writing and Publishing for Children/Teens

Assistance

Seek outside advice/assistance from someone who has a background in elementary education. Odds are, we will not automatically have the kind of experience needed to know precisely how to write in age-appropriate ways for younger age groups. Do not be afraid to reach out to others in your family or congregation who have experience in these areas. Maybe there is a 1st or 2nd-grade teacher in your congregation, or maybe a family member has a degree in early childhood development. Use these resources to help guide your writing choices when dealing with younger age groups.

Association

Use lots of illustrations, examples, and stories from the world that children live in. If you are having trouble with this, just ask someone who is raising children, or take a trip to your local bookstore to look through a few of the books that are being marketed to the kids in your area of ministry. Notice the vocabulary that is used, the structure, and the simplicity of communication style; try to emulate these things in your own writing. Consider taking a quarter to teach the 1st or 2nd-grade Sunday morning Bible class, so that you can get a better grasp on how to approach that particular age group in your writing.

Abbreviation

One of the common pitfalls when writing for children is writing too much. Do not try to communicate too much information at once. Most writing for kids is short, simple, and concise. If you are writing a Bible lesson, a book, or a story for a young child, try to keep your word count within an appropriate range.

Suitable for Teens

When writing for teens (ages 13–18), here are a few suggestions:

The Angle

Whether you are writing a short devotional, a longer Bible class lesson, or an online post for social media, try to give your teens an immediate reason to keep reading. This might be a story, a question, or a proposed scenario. Think of some books or movies that have immediately "grabbed" you and try to adopt some of those same methods in your writing. This is one place where you **can** use "reverse engineering." In other words, start with the lesson that you want to teach and work backward in your thinking. Try to think of a creative/interesting way to introduce your lesson. It might help to pick up a few books that are geared toward teens and read the first paragraphs of those books. Which ones make you want to read more? Which ones do not? Why? Because of the nature of the "angle" that is needed to draw the reader into the topic, write the opening of the lesson *after* you have already written your lesson.

The Approach

Give them the "milk" and "meat" of God's Word but develop your own approach towards doing this. Your approach will incorporate a unique personality and writing style and will essentially become your "voice." The authors in Scripture can serve as examples of this. They all communicated Divine truth, but their unique "voices" were utilized by God to carry this out. They did not all write with the same style or vocabulary. Again, it might be helpful to take a look at some of your favorite books, articles, etc. and notice the approach that those writers take. How do they keep your attention? In what way do they structure their writing that makes it easier (or harder) to read? Learn from others and write with proper grammar and spelling but also make sure the words sound like you and not someone else.

The Application

Give teens real-world applications that can improve, challenge, and transform their lives. A lesson without an application is less likely to engage a teenager in the first place, much less help them develop their faith.

Our Writing Should Be Supplemented

In addition to scripturally based and suitable writing, we need to use all of the appropriate resources available to us and supplement our writing with images, videos, and interactive and engaging materials.

Images/Pictures

Although there is much debate in the educational community about the validity of the learning styles model (i.e. visual learner, auditory learner, reading/writing learner, kinesthetic learner), there is no question that we live in a visual society, and that appropriately chosen images can help us learn. When it comes to choosing images to go along with your writing, here are some things to keep in mind:

Use Images Carefully

Not every picture is worth 1,000 words, so choose carefully. If you need help, ask an "artistic" friend for some advice. There are almost always parts of your writing that "call out" for images (as well as those that do not), so try to figure out what those parts are and find the right kind of image to use.

Use Images Legally

Do not steal images. When searching online for images, use the "Usage Rights" tool (on Google) to make sure that you do not violate any copyright laws. You can also ask your elders if they would be willing to buy you a subscription to an online service (if you use a lot of images on a regular basis, this is going to be your best option). Some good options are *Shutterstock*, *Dreamstime*, *Lightstock*, and *123RF*. There are also free images available on sites like *Unsplash* and *Canva* (both have free and purchasable images).

Use Images Artistically

THE LAW OF CAUSE AND EFFECT

THE DIVINE EXCEPTION:

So, how did the Universe get here? The Bible tells us, "In the beginning ____ created the heavens and the Earth" (Genesis 1:1). But if we already said that every material effect must have an adequate cause, then who or what ____ God?

Doesn't the Law of Cause and Effect apply to God, too?

TRUTH:

Since God is supernatural and *not* material (John 4:24), He is the Divine exception to this law, and the one and *only* reasonable explanation for the existence of the Universe. The Law of Cause and Effect, in fact, *demands* it.

7

> SCAN THIS QR CODE TO WATCH THE VIDEO:
> **"WHERE DID GOD COME FROM?"**
> ERIC LYONS/RUNNING TIME-4:12
>
> **ANSWER THESE QUESTIONS AS YOU WATCH THE VIDEO:**
>
> 1. By definition, an _____ spirit ("the everlasting God") cannot _____ have a cause.
>
> 2. Matter is no more an eternal essence _____ a cause than God is a physical being _____ a cause.
>
> 3. Asking "Where did God come from?" is like asking "When did eternity _____?"
>
> 4. The fact is, a logical _____ explanation for the origin of the "original" ball of matter that supposedly led to the Universe does not exist.
>
> 5. The Universe is either _____, or something or someone _____ of the Universe must have created it.
>
> 6. The Scientific Laws don't apply to God, because God is not _____.
>
> 7. If matter is not eternal, and cannot create itself, then the only logical conclusion is that something or someone outside of nature who is _____ caused the Universe and everything in it.
>
> 8

Using images artistically is also important. Try to place your images/pictures in such a way that they enhance your text/writing instead of competing with it. If you need inspiration or ideas, pick up a book or a Bible class curriculum that uses images in an artistically pleasing way and try to emulate some of what you see. Take advantage of software programs that can help you use your images in the most appealing way. As an artist/designer, I use Adobe products (Photoshop, InDesign, Illustrator, etc.), but there are lots of other good options out there that can help you in this way

(*Canva*, for example). If you are less artistically inclined, many of these programs have pre-loaded templates that can help you get started.

Videos (with QR codes)

It might be the case that in your writing, you want to direct your students to a video that either goes into more detail regarding your subject or gives a helpful illustration. You can generate a QR code in most software programs and give your students immediate access to videos via their smartphones or tablets. Again, make sure that you are linking/sharing a video legally. **NOTE:** Apologetics Press and World Video Bible School have hundreds of free videos on their websites that you can link/share with your students.

Interactive/Engaging Materials (books, workbooks, etc.)

Whether you are writing an online blog post, a classroom handout, or a bulletin article, it can be helpful to give your students an interactive supplement. This may be a booklet with fill-in-the-blank questions for your Bible class, a shareable PDF document that they can send to their friends, or a downloadable quiz that you make available at the end of each quarter. The more interactive and engaging you can make your writing, the more people you will reach!

Publishing Considerations

There are a number of options available when seeking to publish material. Here are a few possibilities to consider:

Self-publishing

If you want to do your own publishing, here are a few suggestions that you may find helpful:

- *Write something good/helpful* — Do not publish your writing simply because you want to be a "published author." Make sure that you have something helpful to offer, and that your motives are to advance the Kingdom and win souls for Christ.
- *Have others proof/edit your work* — Here at Apologetics Press, everyone who writes must go through a rigorous proofing process. This process can be frustrating, but it always produces a better product. Find some people you trust who can help you proof and edit your writing.
- *Have a professional do your cover/layout/design* — Unless you are an artistic person, you might want to ask someone else to do your artwork/design. This is especially important if you are publishing a book.
- *Choose a publishing platform* — There are many platforms online that can help you self-publish your writing. A simple Google search will reveal dozens of options.

Brotherhood-associated Publishers

There are a number of publishers associated with churches of Christ. Some examples are Kaio Publications, Apologetics Press, 21st Century Christian, Gospel Advocate, and Heritage Christian University Press (the publisher of this book). You can check with any of these companies and see if they would be interested in publishing your work.

Creating Online Resources

Create/build your own website and offer free resources. If you are simply seeking to put your writing out into the world to help and encourage others (and not to make money), you can make it available online for free.

Conclusion

Culture has changed down through the centuries and will continue to do so. Yet, with each of these changes, the written word has survived. It may be read digitally instead of from a scroll, but it continues to have an impact none-the-less. Our writing will live on long after we draw our last breaths. Let us not only invest time in writing but let us make sure that our words are scriptural, suitable, and supplemented. Let us write in a way that helps young people to learn and glorifies the God whom we serve!

Discussion Questions

1. Why is it so important to make sure that your writing is based on Scripture?
2. What are some good reasons to write? What are some "not-so-good" reasons to write?
3. Why is it so important to incorporate images, videos, and interactive elements into your writing?
4. What are some important things to remember when writing for children?

Notes

[1] https://technosapiens.substack.com/p/commonsensemedia

Chapter 49
Teaching Christian Evidences to Teenagers
Kyle Butt

It Is a Different World

If you had asked my youth group in high school 30 years ago if we knew a person who claimed to be an atheist, you would have gotten blank stares. Out of 40 of us, some might have known how to define the word atheism. But I am confident that less than two of us would have known a person who was an atheist. In fact, I would guess that the first time I met someone who I knew claimed to be an atheist was when I was in my 20s working in the field of Christian evidences. Atheism was virtually unknown where (and when) I grew up. Sure, there were kids who did drugs, had sex, stole, and a host of other sinful behaviors. But there were hardly any kids who claimed not to believe in God.

That was 30 years ago. Fast-forward to the year 2024, and the situation in the United States is very different. For several years I taught Bible classes for the 15–18 year-olds at summer camp. I started asking my class each year this question: "How many of you know someone who is an atheist?" The first year I asked it, 32 of the 42 kids in the class said they knew an atheist. The second year I asked it, 30 out of 40 knew an atheist and some mentioned that they had friends who were atheists. The third time I conducted the survey, 40 out of 52 knew an unbeliever. After one class, a young man explained to me that he was not sure he believed in God and thought he was an atheist. The last time I remember asking a group of teenagers this question, 80 out of 86 of the teens personally knew an atheist.

As you can see, things have changed dramatically in one generation. Due to the fact that the current generation of teenagers has never lived in a time without the Internet, they have been flooded with ideas, both good and bad. Thirty years ago, hearing anything about atheism was rare because there were so few atheists, and they had no real way to spread their message. The number of atheists in the United States has increased significantly, though they are still a very small minority in this country. But their numbers are on the rise because they have used media outlets to spread their teaching. They do not plan to stop, either. One leading atheist named Dan Barker described himself as an atheist "evangelist." He said, "I can now literally say that I have taken atheism to the ends of the Earth." He added, "If we can divert just one young mind from going into ministry or from wasting time and money on religion, we have made the world a better place."[1] Of course, nothing could be further from the truth. Barker's statement is mentioned here only to show that atheistic evangelism shows no signs of slacking. That is why it is absolutely imperative that we teach Christian evidences to our teenagers. The apostle Peter explained that Christians should always be "prepared to make a defense to anyone who asks you for a reason for the hope that is in you; yet do it with gentleness and respect" (1 Pet 3:15). Our teens are living in a new age when they will be called upon to be ready to defend themselves against the false, destructive teachings of atheism. It is our job to arm them with the truth.[2]

Gentleness and Respect

First, it is paramount that we recognize unbelief for what it is—a sin. There is no virtue in doubting God's existence or the inspiration of the Bible. Jesus plainly stated that "unless you believe that I am he, you will die in your sins" (John 8:24). Doubting the three pillars of the Christian faith—God's existence, the inspiration of the Bible, and the deity of Christ—is a sinful condition that will cause a person to be lost eternally. God has provided more than enough evidence to prove beyond any reasonable doubt that Christianity is true. Those who reject this evidence will have to answer to God.

We as Christians, however, must bear in mind that those who struggle with unbelief are still people. They were made in the image and likeness of God. Yes, it is true that they are enemies of the cross of Christ, and many of them are attempting to teach error that is very harmful. We need to remember, however, that Jesus instructed us to love our enemies (Matt 5:44). We must teach our teens to firmly and boldly disagree with those who present the false teachings of unbelief, but to do so in a kind way that shows them we care about their souls. It is often the case that those who oppose Christianity are just as interested (or more) in how we present the truth as they are in what we are actually saying.

Who Wants That Kind of Faith?

It is unfortunate that multitudes of Christians completely misunderstand the basic concept of faith. For many people, faith is a warm feeling in their hearts when they have failed to find evidence to justify their beliefs. Modern dictionaries have done much to engrain this false definition of faith into Christianity. For instance, *Webster's Ninth New Collegiate Dictionary* states that faith is "a firm belief in something for which **there is no proof**" (emphasis mine). *The American Heritage Dictionary* published in 2000 gives a primary definition of faith: "belief that does not rest on logical or material evidence." I have been employed as a Christian apologist for almost 25 years, and I believe this incorrect view of faith has been a primary reason that young people abandon Christianity.

The idea that faith is an "experienced feeling" that does not require reason and evidence does not coincide with what the Bible teaches about faith. The Christian philosopher Dick Sztanyo correctly noted:

> There is not a single item in Christianity, upon which our souls' salvation depends, that is only 'probably' true. In each case, the evidence supplied is sufficient to establish conclusive proof regarding the truth of the Christian faith.[3]

The false view that faith is "a leap in the dark" without adequate evidence gives atheists plenty of ammunition to use against "Christianity." If believing in God is not established by rational, logical evidence, then that idea should not be accepted. A famous atheist named Sam Harris wrote: "In fact, every religion preaches the truth of propositions for which no evidence is even *conceivable*."[4] He is wrong. But since many Christians teach that faith is not based on evidence, he thinks he is right. Another famous atheist named Richard Dawkins said: "Christianity, just as much as Islam, teaches children that unquestioned faith is a virtue. You don't have to make the case for what you believe."[5]

Both of these unbelievers showed their lack of knowledge of what biblical faith is. Biblical faith is based on truth and reason, as the apostle Paul succinctly stated in Acts 26:25 when he said, "I am speaking true and rational words." The prophet Isaiah emphasized this truth about biblical faith when He recorded God's invitation to the Israelites: "'Come now, and let us reason together,' says the Lord" (1:18). Luke, in his introduction to the book of Acts, pressed the point that Jesus's resurrection was attested by "many infallible proofs." For one to believe in the resurrection requires faith, based on infallible proofs.

Sadly, too many Christians open the door for the skeptical

community to bash Christian "faith," when, in reality, the "faith" that is being destroyed was never biblical in the first place. Teenagers simply must be taught that Christianity is provable, validated by reason, and based on real evidence.

Far too often, misguided Christians make the mistake of saying things like the following, "It takes more faith to be an atheist than it does to be a Christian. I just don't have enough faith to be an atheist." The false view that faith is "a leap in the dark" is the concept that Christians have in mind when they say this. According to a proper definition of biblical faith, however, it is only because of the massive amount of strong evidence that true Christians hold to their beliefs. What it takes to be an atheist is not faith. To be an atheist, a person must choose to completely deny the concept of biblical faith and hold to irrational ideas that have been repeatedly disproven. Biblical faith is a firm belief in that which can be shown to be true. Biblical faith says that we can know God exists,[6] we can know Jesus is His Son, we can know the Bible is His Word, and we can know that we are saved. Faith is not a leap into the unknown but an honest-hearted, firm commitment based on what is known.

Be Comfortable with Questions

Never discourage questions, and remember that it is okay to say that you do not know every answer. Teenagers know when you do not know what you are talking about. Yet, many times, we have tried to present the idea that we have all the answers, and they should just take our word for things and not investigate for themselves. Sometimes our approach seems to be, "Please don't bother us with pesky questions that we have not formed a cookie-cutter answer to." For instance, preachers and parents told many young people in the previous generation that dinosaurs never existed, and they were imaginary creatures concocted by evolutionists to spread the false theory. Consider the damage done when those young people realized that their faithful, godly parents were terribly misinformed about dinosaurs. What else had their parents told them that was wrong? Did their parents know anything about science?

How will you respond when a teenager asks a question such as: "How can starlight be visible on Earth, when the star is millions of light years away, if the creation is only a few thousand years old?" In such a case, it is often a great strategy to say, "I don't know, let's study it together." Or, "Here are some possible answers, but we just are not sure." Open and honest discussions concerning things about which we are unsure can be one of the best ways to help teens think for themselves. Show them that Bible-believing Christians have nothing to fear from such honest inquiry. In fact, we are instructed by God to "test everything, hold fast to what is good" (1 Thess 5:21).

Cowardice Can Be a Leading Cause of Unbelief

A minister who has worked with a Christian Student Center on the campus of a state university for many years told this story. He said that throughout the years he has seen many university students be challenged about their Christian faith by various professors. Often such professors will ask all those who believe in God to stand or raise their hands. The professor then proceeds to ridicule the idea of God and explains to the class how foolish he or she thinks such an idea is. Many students who are Christians are so intimidated and afraid of being ridiculed that they refuse to stand up for their belief in God. They do not raise their hand, stand, or in any way acknowledge that they believe in God or are Christians.

The minister talked about one student who did stand up for her beliefs. She explained to the professor that belief in God made perfect sense, and she was not going to be bullied into cowardice. When she came back to the student center to talk to the minister, what do you think upset her the most? It was not the professor's actions, but the fact that many of her fellow students, whom she knew believed in God, refused to stand. She was heartsick that so many of her peers did not have the courage to boldly defend their beliefs. The minister stated that he often talked with students who were too scared to stand up for their belief in God. He related how they felt shame and guilt and wished that they had seized the moment to stand for the Truth.

Such confrontations can be defining moments in the lives of these young people. If they stand, they are emboldened to defend their belief. They think back to that moment when they defied the professor and the cowardice of the class, and it is something that they cherish their entire lives. If they do not defend their belief, they often attempt to validate their cowardice. Instead of later admitting that they were too scared to stand for God, they look for reasons to justify their actions. Their cowardice frequently leads them to cast a jaded eye on the evidence for God and the Bible and to begin to "doubt" the validity of such evidence. Due to the human desire to view ourselves in the best possible light, these students rationalize that they remained seated, not out of cowardice, but because the belief in God has some problems and cannot stand up to the scrutiny of such learned men and women as university professors. Those who refuse to stand often see such confrontations as defining moments as well. Yet, sadly for them, their decision pushes them toward a life of intellectually dishonest skepticism.

How can young people ready themselves to use such confrontations to their advantage? The simple solution is that we must teach them to decide before they ever face the situation exactly what they will do. In Daniel 1:8 the Bible explains that Daniel "resolved that he would not defile himself." That means that he decided beforehand what he would or would not do before he ever encountered the temptation. He made up his mind not to disobey God, and when it came time to put that determination to the test, his mind was already made up. Just like Daniel, we must encourage our young people to decide before they ever go to college or a university that they will stand up for their belief in God, the Bible, and Jesus Christ.

With the majority of university professors claiming to be atheists and the number of unbelievers increasing daily, make no mistake, our young people will be challenged. If they determine beforehand that they will stand for their belief, when the time comes, they will be ready. If they do not purpose in their hearts ahead of time, there is a much greater chance that they will cower to the pressure of intimidation. Let's prepare our young people to stand in the face of opposition and equip them to use such confrontations as moments that shape them into warriors for the Truth. All the Christian evidences in the world will not help teenagers if they do not have the courage to stand up for the Truth.

A Practical Resource

While the bulk of the chapter has covered some very broad and "philosophical" aspects of teaching Christian evidences to teens, a practical discussion about how to teach the basic information to teens is in order. There may be better ways to do this, but in the quarter of a century that I have been employed at *Apologetics Press*, what will be presented here is the most effective way I know.

Apologetics Press has specifically and strategically designed a teen curriculum that can be taught once a quarter for four years. It is composed of four books in the *Defenders* series. The books are titled *Defending God*, *Defending the Bible*, *Defending Jesus*, and *Defending Your Faith*. Included in the written texts are 25-40 videos (per book) that correspond to the material. They range from 2-9 minutes in length and are designed to be used as introductions to the class, or as supplements to the discussion. It is my firm conviction that if a teen goes through this series, that young person will be thoroughly equipped to defend the three pillars of Christianity and will know where to go and how to find answers to other faith challenges. At the end of such a program, most likely graduation from the youth group, I would suggest that the teacher or church gift the teen an *Apologetics Press Defending the Faith* study Bible. This resource is a 2500-page, full-color study Bible that provides the most thorough Christian evidence instruction available. It is the compilation of more than 40 years of writings by members of the church on the various subjects it addresses.[7] Were this approach to be accepted by large numbers of congregations in our brotherhood, we would have some of the most well-prepared young people of any religious group in the world.

Discussion Questions

1. In your opinion, why does the church need to be teaching Christian evidences? Were you taught such material in your teen years? If so, what impact did it have on your faith?
2. Why do you think the commandment to defend our faith in the Bible comes with the caveat of doing so with gentleness and respect? What happens when these elements are missing? Give examples of biblical characters exhibiting these characteristics in their defense of Christianity.
3. Contrast the generally accepted view of faith with biblical faith. What damage can be done by accepting an incorrect view of faith?
4. What can happen if a person confidently teaches something he or she does not really know? What are the benefits of saying, "I don't know, let's study it together"? What type of attitude does each of these responses exhibit?
5. Jesus explained that Christians would need the courage to "enter by the narrow gate" (Matt 7:13). What does that have to do with a discussion of Christian evidences? Why is the ability to be different so important to the Christian life?

Notes

1. Dan Barker, *Godless* (Berkely, CA: Ulysses, 2008), 320, 324.

2. Some material for this chapter has been modified from material written by the author for prior publication through Apologetics Press and used with permission.

3. Dick Sztanyo, *Faith and Reason* (Montgomery, AL: Apologetics Press, 2021), 7. Also available in electronic format at: https://apologeticspress.org/wp-content/uploads/2021/08/far.pdf.

4. Sam Harris, *The End of Faith* (New York: W.W. Norton, 2004), 23.

5. Richard Dawkins, *The God Delusion* (New York: Houghton Mifflin, 2006), 306.

6. For class resources for teens on these subjects see Kyle Butt and Eric Lyons's *Defenders* series: https://store.apologeticspress.org/collections/new-and-featured-products/products/defenders-god-his-existence?_pos=3&_sid=bb40d928c&_ss=r.

7. I believe the benefit of these materials outweighs the inevitable risk of this seeming like self-promotion and the pushing of materials by Apologetics Press.

Chapter 50
Teaching Teenage Women
Lori Boyd

What a privilege it is to be a teacher—a privilege that should be handled with great care and humility. I think of the words spoken by Peter Parker's Uncle Ben in Sam Raimi's 2002 *Spider-Man* movie, "With great power comes great responsibility." This sounds something like these words written in the Gospel of Luke nearly two thousand years ago, "Everyone to whom much was given, of him much will be required, and from him to whom they entrusted much, they will demand the more" (Luke 12:48). If you are a teacher, particularly a teacher of young people, you have been entrusted with much, and you hold the awesome power of influence. Do not take lightly what that requires of you and the responsibility it implies! You have been entrusted with precious souls, and your influence reaches past the bounds of this life, eternally into the next. However, while the work of a teacher is both serious and significant, it is also a blessing that comes with immeasurable rewards. Is there anything greater than planting and watering seeds of faith? Is it possible to define the joy that comes with watching those seeds grow?

In Proverbs 20:15 we read, "There is gold and abundance of costly stones, but the lips of knowledge are a precious jewel." As a teacher, yours are the lips of knowledge, and the Holy Spirit wants you to know that they are like a precious jewel. There is value in passing along knowledge, and even more, the knowledge of God and His Word. With that in mind, as we consider how we should approach teaching teenage girls, I'm going to use the word "JEWELS" as an acronym for tips that I hope will help you in this beautiful, worthy, ever-unique endeavor.

"J" — Judge Not

When it comes to teaching teenage girls, it's important to remember that the classroom should be a "judgment-free" zone. I'm not talking about the condemning judgment that Jesus warns about in Matthew 7:1-5, or even the righteous judgment that is referred to in John 7:24. By "judge-not" I simply mean that you should not have pre-set opinions about the students in your class. You should avoid drawing conclusions about the girls you are going to be teaching without knowing more about them. This is not only true with young people, but any time you serve as a teacher in any setting, be mindful of what you may *not* know about your audience. You may not know everyone's personal history, religious background, or the challenges they have faced. You may not know the ways they have been hurt, the sins or temptations they struggle with, or what it is that each person is seeking. Take care in what you say and how you say it, being sensitive to what you *do not* know about your students. Teach the truth but do it in love and with kindness (Eph 4:15, Prov 3:3). What you do not want to do is create an environment where someone does not feel welcome or feels like they are not "good enough" to be there, or where they feel unfairly judged.

Another part of "judging not" that I think is especially important with young people, is understanding that your difference in age lends itself to differences in many other areas: differences in perspective, communication, priorities, relationships, and maturity. Teenage girls are at a different place in life and subsequently, a different level of growth than you are, in every aspect—physically, emotionally, mentally, socially, and spiritually. Keep that in mind as you are teaching. The things that are important to them, may not be important to you, or it has been a long time since they were. Try considering the world again through the eyes of a teenager. Approach the students in your class with an open mind, a willingness to listen, an appreciation for who they are and where they are in life, and love them unconditionally.

"E" — Engage

When it comes to teaching teenage girls, you need to engage them. Make your class interesting! I do not mean that you have to tell lots of jokes and funny stories; in fact, too much of that can be distracting. I do think that using stories, personal experiences, and anecdotes can be helpful in communicating the ideas that you are trying to teach. People of all ages connect to stories, and they can be effective in holding the attention of the students in your class as you relate spiritual truths to them. You might also think about incorporating "hands-on" activities for the girls to work on during or after your lesson. Sometimes, I like to use worksheets or outlines that can be filled out as I talk through the lesson, or I encourage the girls to take notes. Other times, I might bring an actual craft or service project that can be completed before the end of our class time that reinforces the main point of the lesson.

Another way to engage teenage girls is to incorporate technology into your teaching and also use it as a means of communication. Young people today do not know life before the digital age. They do not remember a time before computers and cell phones—technology has always been a part of their world. We should meet them there! Create slides or videos to go along with your lessons. Use social media platforms to reach out to them during the week, to invite them to class, to share Scriptures and encouraging words, or to send reminders about something you have discussed in class. Provide them with online resources that you know to be reliable when it comes to Bible teaching and encourage them to explore those websites when they are studying or searching for answers to faith-related questions.

You can also engage the girls you are teaching by allowing them to suggest ideas on what they would like to study. It might be helpful to take a survey and ask for responses to specific questions like: What topics of study do you think would benefit you the most? In what areas of your spiritual life do you feel you need the most growth? Which men and women of the Bible, or which book of the Bible, would you like to know more about? Reflection on the answers that they give to these questions will help you choose lessons that are relevant to the girls and ones in which they will be personally invested.

Finally, do not forget to engage parents and guardians. Keep them informed on what you are teaching and ways that they might reinforce the lessons you are sharing in class or in devotionals. Ask them for input on subjects they would like for you to address, particularly ones they feel are especially needed or would connect well with their children. The importance of communication cannot be overemphasized—not only with the teenage girls you are teaching but also with their families. Be open and available for discussion and always willing to listen.

"W" — Weigh

As we work through these tips for teaching teenage girls, keep in mind that they are not in any specific order, although there are a couple of tips that I think are especially important—this "W" being at the top of the list: Weigh the importance of your role. Teaching is vital for the growth and preservation of the church and is not something that should be taken lightly. In James 3:1, the Bible says, "Not many of you should become teachers, my brothers, for you know that we who teach will be judged with greater strictness." Those words were not written to discourage people who are able to teach from becoming teachers, but to communicate the importance of teaching and the preparation that it requires, especially when it comes to the teaching of God's Word. We have to be careful not only about what we teach and how we teach but also the motivation from which we teach. Our aim should be to instruct and edify according to the truth and with a spirit of humility. Teaching should never be a selfish pursuit, for attention or personal gain. Rather, it should be an act of service that willingly flows from the heart of one who loves God, loves His Word, and loves helping others come to know His will. You play a part in molding the faith of those you teach, whether through building or reinforcing foundational concepts, or in helping them establish, restore, or strengthen their relationship with God.

Understanding the weight of your role as a teacher of young women should motivate you to make prayer and Bible study priorities in your life. Teaching is an extraordinary and noble task, leaving life-long impressions, and must be well covered under an umbrella of prayer. Make prayer an integral part of your teaching—in the class setting and in your personal life. Pray for wisdom. Pray for understanding. Pray for God's help and His guidance. Pray for the ones you are teaching. Also, as a teacher, you need to be a good student of the Bible, too. Study and learn so that you can help others study and learn. There is nothing more important than teaching the truth, but you have to *know* it in order to *teach* it.

"E" — Encourage

Teachers should be encouragers! The Greek word for "encourage" is *parakaleó*, literally "to call for" or "to call to one's side" (cf. 2000 BDAG 764). It carries with it the idea of comfort and exhortation. The image is of one who brings another close to her side in order to strongly advise, but also to provide support and care. Teaching teenage girls provides you with a unique opportunity to fill the hearts of your students with encouragement. Life can be difficult, and this world is not an easy place in which to live, especially for young people. Satan works hard for their souls, and they are the targets of his fiery darts day in and day out. They are bombarded with evil—it is quite literally all around them—temptations, lies, complacency, the pressure to conform. It can be exhausting and disheartening. They need to be loved. They need to be edified. They need to be encouraged.

Encouragement comes in many forms. It can be offered through words—written or spoken. It can be shared through your presence—simply being there when someone needs you, maybe with no words spoken at all or maybe with hours of conversation. It can be passed along through a smile, through laughter, or through tears. It can look like a drawing, it can taste like a favorite kind of candy, it can sound like a song. It can be anything that comforts a heart. Encouragement drives away fear, uncertainty, and doubt; and instills confidence, peace, courage, direction, and hope.

One final suggestion about encouragement for you to consider. If you are in a regular teaching position and you have many of the same girls in a classroom or devotional setting week-to-week, help them get to know each other. Foster relationships within your group and coach them in becoming encouragers for one another. As Barnabas of the Bible was referred to as the "son of encouragement" in Acts 4:36, teach your girls to be "daughters of encouragement!" It's also important to make guests feel welcome and to not let them leave without feeling encouraged. Then, be sure to invite them back. God knows the importance of encouragement. We read about it throughout Scripture (cf. Eph 6:22; 1 Thess 4:18; 5:11). It is something we all need and something we can all give. As a teacher, choose also to be an encourager.

"L" — Lead

This tip is another that I would have put at the top list if I were working through them in order of importance. As a teacher, you are a leader, and your students look to you as an example. They listen to what you say, and they share what you say with others. They watch you, not just in the classroom, but even outside of the classroom, when you may not be aware that they are watching. Lead them well. Paul said, "Be imitators of me, as I am of Christ" (1 Cor 11:1). The word "imitators" is from the Greek word *mimētēs*, which is the root of the English word "mimic." It expresses the idea of copying, emulating, or following someone or something (cf. 2006 Mounce 352-53). Paul was telling the Christians in Corinth to pattern themselves after him, as he patterned himself after Christ. Ask yourself the question, "If the girls I'm teaching follow my example, will it cause them to look more, or less, like Christ?" Remember though, teachers are not perfect. We are each on our own journey to becoming more and more like Christ. We should not try to make our students think that we have it all together and never miss the mark. Young people see right through that! They need to know that the church is made up of broken people who know they are broken and sincerely want to be whole.

Part of leading by example also means that you are more than ready when you stand in front of your students to teach. Teenagers can tell in a second when you are trying to stumble through a lesson for which you have not adequately prepared. Study well so that when you present your lesson you can explain it well. Study ahead of time so that you can thoughtfully create teaching points that are practical and relatable. Study regularly so that you can share your study habits and strategies with your students. Show them how you are taking steps to grow your own faith. When I worked as an assistant manager of the Cardiac Care Unit at Vanderbilt, I had a manager who used to say, "It's my job to teach you how to do my job." She believed that it was her responsibility to prepare me to become a manager one day. As teachers of young women, it would serve the kingdom well if we would adopt that same mindset: It's our job to teach them how to do our job. Be a teacher who prepares the hearts and minds of future teachers.

"S" — Sharpen

The final letter stands for the word "sharpen," inspired by these wise words found in the book of Proverbs, "Iron sharpens iron, and one man sharpens another" (Prov 27:17). We can understand how iron is used to sharpen other forms of iron, but how do people sharpen other people? The Cambridge Dictionary defines sharpen as "to make something stronger, or to improve something" (dictionary.cambridge.org). As the teacher of teenage girls, it is your task and your privilege to sharpen the students in your class; and you can be sure that your students will sharpen you as well.

There are many ways you can sharpen the girls you are teaching. First, challenge them! Challenge them by presenting them with the truth found in Scripture and then challenge them to be changed by it. Challenge them to continually seek the truth, and challenge them to share it with others. Sharpen your students by asking them questions, and be ready to answer the questions that they ask you. Young people today are smart and curious. They want to know the "why" behind the things they are told. We should use reason and evidence as we talk about the Bible and matters of faith. If you do not know the answers to their questions…find the answers and follow up! Sharpen your students by taking them deeper into the Word. Move past surface-level meanings of biblical accounts and help them begin analyzing at a deeper level, making thematic connections and practical applications. Whet their appetite for the meat of the Word, and when they are ready, begin the transition from milk to solid food (1 Cor 3:1–3; Heb 5:12).

Keep Shining!

Teacher, your lips of knowledge are like a jewel—precious and valuable. Do not underestimate how you shine in the lives of the girls you teach. Shine with intention and with an awareness of your purpose. Shine by creating a judgment-free space. Shine by presenting engaging and meaningful lessons. Shine by continually weighing the importance of your role. Shine by offering much-needed encouragement to the ones you are teaching. Shine by serving as a leader worthy of imitation (because of who you imitate). Shine by sharpening your students—making them stronger in faith today than they were yesterday. Keep shining, teacher. May God bless you in your service, and may He be glorified through it all!

Discussion Questions

1. As a teacher, what is the danger in making assumptions, or forming preconceived opinions, about the girls in your class?
2. What are some strategies that you can use in order to engage students in the lessons you are presenting?
3. What does it mean to "weigh the importance of your role" as a teacher?
4. In what ways can you provide encouragement to the teenage girls you are teaching?
5. Why is it important to lead by example? What are some practices you can incorporate in your own life that will help you become a better imitator of Christ?
6. What are some examples of how you can "sharpen" your students?

Bibliography

Cambridge Online Dictionary. www.dictionary.cambridge.org. Cambridge University Press and Assessment, 2024.

Danker, William Frederick, ed. *A Greek-English Lexicon of the New Testament and Other Early Christian Literature*, 3rd ed. Chicago: The University of Chicago Press, 2000.

Mounce, William D., ed. *Mounce's Complete Expository Dictionary of Old and New Testament Words.* Grand Rapids: Zondervan, 2006.

Chapter 51
Teaching in the Children's Classroom and VBS Planning
Lauren Moss

Children's Classes Matter

"Why is the sky blue?" "How does a penguin stay warm in the cold?" "Why do kids have to go to bed earlier than adults?" Kids are always so full of questions. Yet, it seems this has been the case for centuries upon centuries; even Joshua suspected the children of the Israelites might ask for an explanation.

> When your children ask in time to come, 'What do those stones mean to you?' then you shall tell them that the waters of the Jordan were cut off before the ark of the covenant of the Lord. When it passed over the Jordan, the waters of the Jordan were cut off. So these stones shall be to the people of Israel a memorial forever (Josh 4:6b–7).

Although the idea of sharing the works and wonders of the Lord with children was no new concept to the Israelites (Deut 6:4–7; 11:19), Psalm 78 shares perhaps the most beautiful reason to tell the coming generations of God's wondrous deeds.

> He established a testimony in Jacob and appointed a law in Israel, which he commanded our fathers to teach their children, that the next generation might know them, the children yet unborn, and arise and tell them to their children, so that they should set their hope in God and not forget the works of God, but keep his commandments (Ps 78:5–7).

Why should you teach children about God? To have the right answers to the questions they ask? To merely pass along a shared family tradition? To solely have a place for them to go while their parents attend a class? Rather, the psalmist says it best, you teach children "so that they should set their hope in God."

In most congregations, Bible classes serve as either the main core of the children's ministry or sometimes the children's ministry in its entirety. Children's classes accomplish so much of what we seek in children's ministry at large; children are learning to know God better while also being connected to godly mentors and peers. Ideally, Bible classes help our children to both know and feel God's love. You may already see the purpose of teaching children but need help with the logistics of it. Here are a few categories to dwell on as you consider teaching in the children's classroom.

Curriculum

The first question may aptly be *what* to teach. Children's classes typically run from birth to the last grade before middle school, typically 5th or 6th grade. Of course, an older student will be able to understand a more complex spiritual truth than a younger student. While a two-year-old may be able to say and believe "God loves me," that truth can be expounded upon to "God loves all people very much; He sent His Son for us" in Kindergarten, and then beyond to "God proved His unconditional love for all people through the sacrifice of His Son Jesus Christ" in the upper elementary years. "Scope and sequence" are terms used in the education realm to describe what is going to be taught and the order in which the topics/texts are going to be addressed in a curriculum plan (cf. 1991 Ford 67). The simplest way to build a scope and sequence for these grades and ages is generally by following the structure and order of the Bible. As you strive to develop a scope and sequence for your children's Bible classes, consider beginning with the upper grades and working your way down. What do you want kids to know before they enter youth ministry? Are there certain portions of Scripture you want to focus on more than others? Start by building the scope of your last few years of children's Bible classes around that, then simplify the list of lessons covered in lower elementary grades. Simplify even further when considering what to teach preschool students and infants and toddlers, respectively. This may look like covering *most to all* narratives regarding Abraham when teaching upper elementary grades, but only focusing in on God calling Abraham, God's promise to Abraham, and Isaac's birth and sacrifice in younger grades.

Focus the most heavily on narrative portions of Scripture; the narrative portions are more concrete for children to understand and by doing so you will also accomplish the goal of giving a better understanding to the redemptive Biblical narrative at large. Old Testament wisdom literature and poetry, parts of the major and minor prophets, and most of the New Testament letters lend themselves better to short series or supplements than they do to large portions of your essential curriculum rotation. For instance, children would struggle to understand an entire study of all 150 psalms but would greatly benefit in elementary grades by learning a few psalms to understand the context of the book and how it fits into the Bible. In this case, involving a few psalms written by David when studying his kingship would be helpful.

You may choose to purchase curriculum or write your own. If purchasing, focus on content and teaching strategies, as additional or alternative visuals, ideas for learning activities, games, crafts, etc. can easily be found from other resources and added to a baseline curriculum. Online sources like BibleFunforKids.com, FreeBibleImages.org, Pinterest, and more can all be helpful in this regard. If writing your own curriculum, include ideas on how to introduce the lesson, how to teach or tell the text, simple ways to apply what is learned, and activities like crafts or games to help the content stick.

Instruction

Generally speaking, the more interactive you can make a children's Bible lesson, the better. Ask yourself not merely "How can I tell them this story?" but "How can I help them *experience* this story?" Howard Gardner's Theory of Multiple Intelligences and various other theories on learning styles illustrate this well (cf. 2011 Howard, *Frames of Mind*, 2016 Jones 86–98). Some students will learn well by hearing something told verbally, but far more will gain the knowledge by experiencing it visually, musically, interpersonally, etc. Include visuals whenever possible, whether they be printed pictures of the narrative or objects related to the lesson. You do not need a large budget or the best materials to succeed in this regard; use what you have around you. For instance, show a picture of yourself as a baby when teaching on Hannah praying for a child. Walk outside and look at the stars as you discuss God's promise to Abraham or at the trees as you teach about Zacchaeus. Have students share what their favorite animal is as you teach on Noah and the ark.

There are many other simple ways to help students experience God's Word in a memorable way. Various people in the Bible likely did not have the same exact voice, nor should you when you are portraying them. Changing your voice slightly helps children differentiate who is speaking in a longer narrative. Get the children's minds to think more deeply about the content by having them place themselves in the story. Intertwine questions like, "How would you feel if you were an Israelite who saw the Egyptians chasing after you out of Egypt?" into your storytelling. Involve students while telling the story by having them act it out or draw sketches on a whiteboard of each scene as you read. Involve kinesthetic movement by labeling one side of the room "yes" and the other "no" and having them walk to either side of the room to show their answer to your question.

Classroom Management

Because of children's need for structure and direction, when teaching them, you are not only *instructing* but quite literally *managing* them. Classroom management is the term that encompasses everything other than your actual instruction: your pacing, your preparation, your anticipation of potential disruptions, etc. A good rule of thumb to keep in mind while planning is that children's attention span is generally around one minute per year of age. So, for instance, when teaching five-year-olds, you will want to change the activity or location in the classroom or introduce a new task every five minutes or so. Realistically, this could look like having them sit at tables working with play dough as students enter class, then standing up for an introduction to the story, sitting on a rug for the instruction itself, doing a craft while sitting at the table, then playing a game while standing up again, etc. Managing the classroom involves anticipating distractions, like having an activity ready on the table before students arrive or singing a song as children transition from one activity to the other.

Another part of managing a classroom well is discerning safety and security needs. Have each child's parent or caregiver fill out an information sheet. You should have emergency contact info and the answers to other pertinent questions that will help you serve children and their families best. Does the child have any food allergies or medical needs to be aware of? Are than any other special needs you should be aware of to provide the appropriate support to the child? Consider using a background check system for volunteers and always seek to have at least two volunteers in each room. The latter is an easy step to take toward safety in the case that a volunteer or child have an emergency and also helps provide legal safeguards for children, teachers, and the congregation.

VBS Planning

Vacation Bible School is potentially the most open door to outreach most congregations have already built into their calendars. When planning VBS, all the previously mentioned considerations still apply, but there are some added questions to consider as well. When choosing content to cover, be sure to consider whether the specific sections of the narrative are more easily understandable to unchurched children and families. Stories steeped in nuances that would take multiple other lessons to explain, such as some narratives from the prophets, would probably be best to avoid with families who are possibly being introduced to God for the first time. Start with the question, "What do we want children who attend VBS to walk away knowing?" and build your theme and lessons from there. With this in mind, lessons for VBS need to be cohesive, whether in narrative or in application. You will want one common thread running through each lesson. When applying an overarching theme and title to your VBS, consider how that theme lends itself to VBS decorations and crafts, games, activities, etc. There are many VBS themes and curriculum available for purchase from various curriculum companies if time or resources do not permit creating your own.

    Logistically speaking, VBS is an event that demands organization. Start with having a registration avenue for parents to provide pertinent information for children; name, grade/age, emergency contact information, allergies, and medical notes are good places to start. Take it a step further by having an address field and then mail notes from VBS leaders to children afterward or use the list constructed to invite families to other events. You will often see a rotational model at VBS. This allows VBS leaders to prep only one aspect as groups of children rotate into their space. For instance, if you chose to have a lesson, game, craft, and snack rotation for each day of VBS, a game leader could only prepare one game related to the lesson but execute the same game as each of the four different groups of students rotate through their room or station each day. This takes far less preparation than having one leader be responsible for teaching and additionally choosing appropriate crafts and games on their own. You can then assign one to two group leaders to each group of students to lead the children around to their different stations. This group leader would also be responsible for the arrival and dismissal of students, being aware of allergies or medical notes, etc.

Communication is a huge part of keeping VBS organized. Do the leaders for each aspect of VBS know their room assignments, time restrictions, and materials available to them or that they are responsible for creating? A meeting for major leaders one to two months before VBS and a meeting for all leaders and volunteers one to two weeks before VBS will be helpful in giving appropriate materials and instructions, schedules, t-shirts, and more. Consider also communication with those families attending VBS. Do they know where to drop off and pick up their children? If they have never been to the building before, how easy is it to find that location and what additional signage and communication will you provide to make those transitions smoother?

Conclusion

Take a moment to reflect on your favorite childhood teacher. What made that person a good teacher? He or she was probably well-prepared, creative in instruction, and made learning fun. Yet, without actually knowing the person in question, it can certainly be said that part of the primary reason that person was your favorite teacher was her or his character. Good teachers instruct well, but great teachers are also kind and patient with their students, show they truly care, and give support beyond the confines of the classroom walls. Truly, the lives of the best teachers are reinforcements to the Bible lessons they teach. They are living, breathing examples of Christ's love in action. When contemplating where to start as a teacher, your lesson content is certainly important, but do not forget what you are teaching your students unintentionally by your example.

In the long run, what do we want our kids to learn? Faithfulness despite trials? Servanthood in a selfish culture? Godliness in an ungodly world? What do we *truly* want to teach our children? Let us start by living it ourselves.

Discussion Questions

Read the account of Jesus calming a storm in Mark 4:35–41 to answer the following questions.

1. If you were teaching this to children, what would you want them to walk away knowing about God?
2. What are some ways to be sure you are appealing to different learning styles (visual, auditory, kinesthetic, etc.) while teaching this passage?
3. Name three crafts, games, or activities to involve in your lesson that would relate back to either concrete objects, scenes, or people or an abstract spiritual application from this text.
4. How might your classroom management look different while teaching this passage to a fourth grader versus a four-year-old?
5. What are three other Bible stories that would work cohesively with this one in narrative or application for a VBS theme or short unit? What common thread runs through those three accounts and the original passage in Mark 4?

Bibliography

Ford, Leroy. *A Curriculum Design Manual for Theological Education.* Eugene, OR: Broadman Press, 1991.

Gardner, Howard. *Frames of Mind.* 3rd ed. New York: Basic Books, 2022.

Jones, Karen. "Multiple Intelligences and Learning Styles" in *Teaching the Next Generations*, Terry Linhart, ed, Grand Rapids: Baker Academic, 2016.

Chapter 52
Curriculum Development for Teaching Teens
Billy Bearden

Sunday School Matters

The Bible class hour, more popularly known as "Sunday School," is a vital component of the church's past and deserves our attention, especially as Youth Ministers who have the privilege of influencing teens for a living. Sunday School has a long and fascinating history that can be traced back almost to our nation's founding. This designated time, which started for children, has become a staple across all ages in the church today. However, Sunday School is not just the church's past but the future. When you break it down, the Sunday School is where teaching, discipleship, ministry, fellowship, and evangelism can take place.[1] Ira North, in his book *Balance*, gives special attention to the significance of the Bible School, saying, "As the Bible school goes, so goes the congregation."[2] I would agree with North and continue that thought by saying that as the Bible class goes, so goes the youth group. It would be difficult to argue that Sunday School does not work, but it only works when we work the Sunday School. Without an intentional, well-thought-out curriculum developed with our teens in mind, we cannot effectively use the Bible School to the fullest extent.

The Big Picture

Teaching teenagers and being part of their spiritual growth from sixth to twelfth grade is my favorite part of youth ministry. There is something special about introducing teenagers to biblical truth and encouraging them to take ownership of their faith through these developmental years. The Latin word "curricula" actually means a "Rracecourse" or a "racetrack," which is appropriate in the church setting.[3] Remember that this process is not a sprint but a marathon. This spiritual race (Heb 12:1) that these students are running is a long, strenuous adventure, so what we teach them is important. Do not get me wrong, getting to relive my glory days playing some kickball or eating pizza for the fifth straight week has its perks, but nothing compares to the time inside the classroom, seeing students question, strengthen, and work out their faith in ways that are relevant to them. However, from many conversations I have had over the years, the curriculum development side of teaching youth can be one of the biggest challenges regarding some of the behind-the-scenes aspects of the job. With events scheduled, games and recitals to attend, the time needed for prepping the following Sunday or Wednesday class, etc., the actual development of curriculum can become a last-minute effort that ends up having to get done before the new quarter of classes start. This cycle can be overwhelming and burdensome if not dealt with seriously. One of the best things a youth minister can do is reserve time to go ahead and map through the year looking at what is needed and planning it out. Building a solid curriculum is usually not one of the top items on our to-do list as youth ministers. Building a strong curriculum is probably not something your youth group students will get super excited about and brag to their friends at school about to try and convince them to come to Bible class. However, if there is anything worthy of our time, it is spending time in meditation, reflecting on where our youth are and what they need while figuring out how to frame that in view of God's Word that has been provided to us.

What We Aim to Accomplish in Building a Curriculum

Our kindergarten through fifth grade Bible classes often focus on Bible facts and trivia. Most educators will tell you that students learn best in these early developmental years by memorizing facts through repetition. This usually takes place with the help of hands-on learning opportunities like coloring sheets, crossword puzzles, Bible Bowl tests, etc. This teaching style is appropriate for first or second-grade students because it is on their learning level. However, when a student moves into the youth group, our methodology for teaching should look different. Sure, there are still many elements of memorization and being able to relay facts that are integrated into the classroom, but teenagers now need to be making practical applications of those facts.[4]

Is it wrong to spend an entire quarter studying the book of Romans? Absolutely not! Is it wrong to study the book of Romans in preparation for a Bible Bowl-type event where the goal is to be able to relay facts from the book of Romans? Again, I would say no. Where the problem lies for me is the intention behind teaching the book of Romans. The question to ask would be, why is the book of Romans being taught to the high school and middle school classes on Sundays? Is it because the quarter is starting soon, and that would be an easy topic to cover, or am I helping our teens discover truths within this book and walking them through practical applications in their lives? At the youth group level, our aim should not be to fill class spots with any and every topic we can think of or learned in college, but rather to fill our class time with the things God's Word provides that will help our teens live out their Christianity in a hostile world.

Where do we even start? Let me share one way to help focus your aim before developing a curriculum plan. Something that helps me put this in perspective is breaking down the time we spend with teens in the classroom. If my math is correct, there are 8,760 hours a year, and out of those 8,760 hours, if we have a 45-minute Bible class time on Sunday morning and Wednesday night, we get a total of 78 hours in a formal teaching setting with our teens (retreats, camps, and youth rallies can add to this time). Keep in mind that this is only true if the student comes to every class and there are no special events during class time. However, that is the reality of it. So, what will we do with the 78 hours we have been given? As we begin to dive into some key steps for building a curriculum, let's keep a few important things in mind about the goal/aim of our curriculum:

1. We aim to help direct students to the church and obey the Gospel.
2. We aim to help encourage faithfulness and discipleship to Christ.
3. We aim to encourage proper decision-making as young Christians.
4. We aim to help students understand the problem and the solutions.
5. We aim to help grow and widen students' knowledge of the Bible.
6. We aim to prepare students for what is next.

Planning Out the Curriculum

There are many paths you can take when it comes to developing a good curriculum for your youth group. Because of the different methods and styles, there may not be a "one size fits all" approach, but the most successful plan is goal-oriented, personal, and organized. A quarter-to-quarter decision, although others may never notice it, does not fit that description. You must find a method that works for you as the youth minister but also one that works for your specific group. Whether you work out of a committee or have a deacon in charge of the curriculum, the youth minister needs to be hands-on in this process. No matter the type of curriculum adopted, one thing to remember is that 90% of the curriculum is the teacher.[5] As the youth minister, you will be the primary teacher for these teens; even if you are not teaching a given quarter, you will often be present in the room and leading by example, so you need to be involved in developing the curriculum.

Start laying the curriculum out with the end in mind. When most of the work is done on the front end, it is easier to adjust as time goes by. I suggest starting at the 30,000-foot view and planning for the big picture. For me, this begins by looking seven years down the road because, in most youth groups, students spend seven years in your youth program. The aim is to ensure that within those seven years, you have done your job as the youth minister to provide what your teens need. The good news is after you have worked through this plan, you can rework some of those classes and teach them to an entirely new group of students. Taking on a seven-year plan does not take place overnight, so where do we begin? Let me walk you through my process:

Step 1: Survey

I like to first start by surveying where our current curriculum is by asking myself questions like the following:

- Does this current curriculum reflect where our students are spiritually and culturally?
- Does what we are teaching speak to essential matters that teens deal with daily?
- Is our current Bible class material evangelistic in nature?
- Is the current material on an appropriate level for both middle school and high school students?

I also like to "survey" where I am and where I recently was. Not that long ago I was in a youth group and was going through similar things teens today go through. Spend time reflecting on what you needed as a teen:

- What did I wish my youth minister had talked about during my time in the youth group?
- What type of studies would have helped me when I graduated high school?
- What were some of the most memorable classes from my time in the youth group?
- In addition to doing some personal/internal surveying, I then like to survey the parents of our teens. Asking questions like:

- What are the top 10 things you want your middle school/high school student to study/learn about in Bible class?
- What are some of the questions your teens are asking you at home?
- Is there any topic that you would like advanced notice of before we discuss it in class?

After surveying parents, it is also good to get feedback from the current students. A simple student survey can take place at the beginning or end of a class period on Sunday or Wednesday. It can be relatively short, just getting an idea of where the students currently are and where they want to go. Ask questions like:

- What topics are you interested in/would be helpful for us to study as a group?
- What questions do you have about the church?
- What topics do you have difficulty finding answers for when peers ask?
- Can you explain your faith to someone else who may not have faith?

If you have elders in your congregation, you will also find it a blessing to sit down with them and get their input on what the young people need to be learning in their Bible classes. You will not only gain valuable insight but will get better buy-in from them on the plan.

Step 2: Laying It Out

Once you spend considerable time surveying the current curriculum, parents of your teens, and the students themselves, it is time to start working through all the feedback. When it comes to breaking it down, there are two primary ways to develop a curriculum:

1. Topical/Theme-Based
2. Textual/Content-Based

You can place many subcategories under these, but this is the primary way the curriculum is broken down. Doug Fields and Duffy Robbins dedicate a lot of time to this breakdown in their book, *Speaking to Teenagers*.[6] The goal is to have a good balance based on the feedback you receive. After you have created your balance, you can then be more creative and dress the classes up with clever titles and subtitles. When beginning the process of putting ideas to paper, there are some key attributes to remember about the curriculum you are developing. It would be best to keep the main goal in mind when reading through the feedback. For example, several students may say they want to study the book of Revelation. Opening a book of the Bible and studying it chapter by chapter does not seem like a bad idea on the surface. Many would applaud your effort to stick to a verse-by-verse approach to Bible class. However, by keeping the main goal in mind, you can quickly determine if studying the Book of Revelation verse by verse is a wise use of time for your group. Remember, as youth ministers, you have minimal time each week. Does a 45-minute Bible class on Revelation for 13 weeks fit with the goal of your youth group curriculum you are trying to build, or is it just a "fun" book students are interested in studying? I am not saying that you should not study Revelation but that you need to consider carefully how you will study it and at what age the students will be exposed to it. There has to be a balance when choosing. When sorting through feedback, always keep in mind that the final product needs to be Bible-centered, Christ-focused, practical, and flexible.

The way the curriculum is laid out needs to be balanced, but the teaching approach should also be balanced. Teaching a combined group of middle and high school students has its benefits, but middle and high school students do not always need the same thing at the same time. Do not hesitate to break down your students in creative ways at various times, such as;

- Middle school and high school split classes.
- Guys and girls split class.
- High school guys and girls split class, and middle school guys and girls split class.
- Small groups during class.
- Lecture-based or heavy discussion-based.

For example, here is a one-year curriculum plan I developed based on the needs of the youth group I work with:

One Year Curriculum

Winter Quarter Sunday Class
Middle & High School: Life Lessons from Genesis (Combined)
Winter Quarter Wednesday Class
Middle & High School: Spiritual Disciplines (Combined with Small Groups)
Spring Quarter Sunday Class
Middle School: Parables of Jesus (Split Class)
High School: Parables of Jesus (Split Class)
Spring Quarter Wednesday Class
Middle & High School: Why Believe the Bible? (Combined)

Summer Quarter Sunday Class
Middle School: The Power of Prayer (Combined and Split Class Mix)
High School: The Power of Prayer (Combined and Split Class Mix)
Summer Quarter Wednesday Class
Guys Class: The One Another Statements (Split Class)
Girls Class: The One Another Statements (Split Class)
Fall Quarter Sunday Class
Middle School: Churches in the Shape of Scripture (Split Class)
High School: Survey of the Book of Acts (Split Class)
Fall Quarter Wednesday Class
Middle & High School: Weird, Gross & Awkward Stories in Scripture (Combined with Small Groups)

Step 3: Implementation

After putting in all the work to gather feedback and decide what is needed, it is time to finalize and implement the curriculum plan. This phase might seem like a no-brainer, but some details still need to be ironed out to ensure all the hard work up to this point comes together the way it was intended. A few items to complete during this phase would include:

- **Present to Youth team/Eldership:** It is a great idea to share your vision and what you plan to teach for the year with this group of men responsible for shepherding the flock. Gain their support and keep updating them regularly on how classes are going. Do not be afraid to ask for their advice or let them know of any concerns. Have your youth deacons know this information as well.
- **Class Titles:** This is where creativity comes into play, creating catchy titles and graphics to draw/keep students' attention.

- **Selecting Teachers**: Who will be teaching what specific classes? The youth minister could teach them all, but are there some topics or quarters it would be better to have an elder, deacon, or parent involved in the teaching rotation? Because this outside teacher probably does not do ministry full time, they need plenty of advanced notice to prepare for the class you have asked them to teach.
- **Class Material**: Where are you getting your class materials? Are you writing the individual classes or using a book or outside resource?
- **Visuals/handouts**: It can be time-consuming, but wise to appeal to all aspects of learning. Knowing this in advance gives you time to create a PowerPoint presentation, find helpful videos or apps, and provide handouts for the class.

Aim for the Inside

At the end of the day, it ultimately comes down to a student's internal faith, not their involvement in activities, that matters most. Of course, we would love to have every student at every event we plan, but more importantly, we want students to grow in their faith and love for God and His church. So, what are we doing as youth ministers to promote that goal? Take your curriculum seriously and challenge yourself to regularly evaluate how and why you are teaching what you are.

Discussion Questions

1. What are the top 5 things I feel I need to teach in my youth program, and what are the top 5 things I want to teach in my youth program? What are some differences between these "wants" and "needs"?

2. What is the danger of waiting until the last minute each quarter to decide what to teach? Conversely, what are the benefits of planning a long-term curriculum to work from?
3. We often look at curriculum development as a burdensome/time-consuming task. However, what other practical elements of building a strong curriculum should we keep in mind that may not have been discussed in this chapter?

Notes

1. Thom S. Rainer, *High Expectations: The Remarkable Secret for Helping People in Your Church* (Nashville: Broadman & Holman, 1999), 47.

2. Ira North, *Balance: A Tried and Tested Formula for Church Growth* (Nashville: Gospel Advocate, 1983), 64.

3. David Powell, *Organization & Administration of the Bible School* (Henderson, TN: Freed Hardeman University), 22.

4. If you would like to dig deeper into applying research to appropriate teaching methods for various ages, see chapter 4, "How We Develop as Thinkers," in *Created to Learn* by William R. Yount.

5. H.W. Byrne, *Christian Education for the Local Church* (Grand Rapids: Zondervan, 1963).

6. Doug Fields and Duffy Robbins, *Speaking to Teenagers: How to Think About, Create, & Deliver Effective Messages* (Grand Rapids: Zondervan, 2007), 112–113.

Chapter 53
At-Risk Spirituality
Lonnie Jones

"You can sacrifice one man for the mission; But you cannot sacrifice the mission for one man."
   Sgt. Joe Carter (SWAT officer)

"Then I spent a long time thinking 'bout the ones the wolves pulled down."
   Stephanie Davis (*Wolves*, sung by Garth Brooks)

It should be known that my waking nightmare is one of the downsides of youth ministry: I tend to dwell on the kids I don't reach. The statistics vary, but it is clear that we are losing far too many of our young people (one is too many). Motivating them by fear does not work. Yet, Satan is claiming our kids at an alarming rate, and we cannot stand by and watch. We must do something (2 Cor 5:11, 19–21).

"A sower went out to sow ..." (Matt 13:3).

"What man of you having a hundred sheep, if he loses one of them ..." (Matt 18:12).

These two parables seem to say two different things. How do we integrate the shepherd with the sower? How can one know when a wayward teen is a case of stony or thorny ground or whether the teen is a sheep who wandered off? Have you felt the frustration? I do not know the number of times this has echoed in my mind.

I have watched seeds (teens) being spiritually eaten, strangled, and trampled. I've seen sheep (teens) wander off and wander back. I have seen sheep wander off never to be seen or heard from again. What I want to know is which ones will make it and which ones will not. Who needs the extra effort? Which ones should I spend the time with?

God is the knower of hearts. God has told us to be sowers and shepherds. Not every seed produces. Not every lamb survives. It is not for us to ask God about the hearts of others and how sincere or faithful they are or will be. It is for us to ask about our own hearts and whether we are being faithful in our jobs as sowers and shepherds. That may be the answer. Some things are out of our hands, and some things are not—at least not yet. Losing people is a tough subject. I am torn as I write this chapter. I will let you listen as I think out loud and wage the war in my mind and soul.

On the Outside Looking In

Ever stood in the outside of a circle and listened to people sing a beautiful song, wishing someone would share the words with you? Ever been chosen last on a team? Ever been invited to a party and knew that if you didn't show up, no one would notice? Ever been in a large gathering, surrounded by people, and still been alone? I have.

Those who have never been an outsider will not be able to relate to some of this but really need to read this and take it to heart. When young people, or any people for that matter, come and visit our assemblies, classes, or events, they will return or not return based on whether or not they feel like outsiders. New members will remain active or become inactive based on how involved and a part of things they feel.

Making someone feel *a part* as opposed to making someone feel *apart* requires a significant amount of genuine effort and concern. People feel *apart* if their only contact with "church folks" is at church activities. People feel *a part* if they talk on the phone, receive cards, and are invited to hang out with others. People feel *a part* when they are invited to work and share in the things that need to be done. The only difference between the words *a part* and *apart* is a matter of a little space between the words. Likewise, *apart* or *a part* is determined by whether or not people can climb over our walls and close the space between us and them. And sometimes it is because they cannot or will not climb over their own walls to close the gap.

Defining "At-Risk"

The phrase "at-risk" refers to young people who, because of environment, attitude, aptitude, or other variables, are at risk of dropping out, participating in inappropriate risk-taking, using drugs, joining gangs, getting killed, or generally failing to thrive. The spiritually at-risk may be harder to identify. When a child is exhibiting a poor attitude, lack of interest, or just has those signs that make you fear for their spiritual well-being, it can be hard to confirm that something serious is going on. You may not have a lot of success confronting parents on hunches and gut feelings.

For instance, here is the profile of a young man. He was raised "in the church," is sexually pure, and is not acting out violently. He is honest, controls his temper, and has a good relationship with his mother and father. Is he at risk? Why, we need fifty more just like him! It is pretty easy to assume that, but this young man is wrapped up in externals. He is all show and no go. His heart is not right. How do I know? When asked to give something up, he refused. The thing he was asked to give up was not wrong. It was just more important to him than God. Jesus asked the rich young ruler to place his treasure in heaven, take up the cross, and follow. The young man's religious "All these I have observed from my youth" did not seem to matter. He went away sad. He was "at-risk" not because of his actions, but because of his attitudes (see Mark 10:17-22).

Many take the first step to being spiritually at-risk when they have a shift in perceptions. As they make choices which are different from their peers, they make distinctions between their value systems and the value systems of others. When two people disagree and one claims to have the right to hold an opposite opinion yet seeks validation for their position, then feelings of isolation and separation will often begin to be present themselves.

"I guess I was wrong. I just don't belong. But hey, I've been there before ..." are the words from a song (written by Dewayne Blackwell and Earl Bud Lee). There is a phenomenon in working with teenagers in which they "feel" as if they do not belong. At some point in our lives all of us want to "belong." Being liked, treated nicely, included, and talked to are generally things that we say go along with "belonging." There are places and groups where anyone new or different does not have a place or welcome. Youth ministry should make a careful attempt so that others feel cared for and accepted. In most places, we do not do all that we could or should.

This, like a lot of swords, is double-edged. What do we do when we feel assured that everyone is treated with warmth and openness, yet someone still says, "I don't feel like I fit in." Maybe the words "Things are just different" are a complaint you might hear. Others say, "I think the whole youth group has changed." The real question of belonging is really quite personal. If someone does not belong, then what is wrong? Let's look at some scenarios.

The group is supposed to be a Christian group, yet one student may feel that he/she is the only one attempting to be Christlike. In this situation, saying, "I don't fit," is pretty valid. Of course, more often than not, the opposite is true. The problem may be the one, not the whole group. We may have a Christian group with one individual who does not share the same ideals with the others. There really is a difference of those who talk the talk and those who walk the walk (see Eph 4:1–3). It is much easier to place blame on others than it is to evaluate ourselves on that level (see also 1 Cor 5:9–13).

Of course, young people who hang with the party crowd, or are too worried about popularity and are engrossed in counterculture, are at-risk spiritually. Here are a few other signs. It is my experience that teens are at-risk if they come to worship or Bible classes only as spectators. They lack the desire to make a contribution. Posture and attentiveness may serve as signs that the body is present but the heart is elsewhere.

A teen is spiritually at-risk if his or her primary peer group is not made up of Christians. This can include dating non-Christians. The one caveat I will add to this is that I would rather see our girls date Cornelius than the rich young ruler. I've seen the aftermath when a young lady falls for the superficial, slick, "spiritual used car salesman" who blossoms in the culture of a Christian college but cannot maintain it or really does not have it to start with.

Christians should participate in the world as lights. Being at-risk spiritually could involve a young person who is a leader at school but does not seem to exert any leadership among Christian peers. It is not a sin to miss devotionals, camps, retreats, mission trips, and such like. Yet, a successful student is seen as one who participates in a variety of activities and not just the classes and assemblies. This sort of "at-risk" is a little more difficult to define, and it is almost impossible to confront.

People talk about not fitting in. I have even heard folks talk about God not liking them. People want to blame their failures and disappointments on a God whom they do not honor. They often do the same with the youth group or church as a whole.

Is it legitimate when people claim that others have kept them from being involved in the works and programs of a congregation? When the desire for service and spiritual participation is there, how can others keep us from it? Devotion and desire seem to be able to outweigh circumstances and excuses. Why are you here? Did you come to serve or to be served?

Turning Over the Water Dish

I used to have this dog named McKenzie. He had a water dish. The "wonder dog" drank water twice a day. Now, before you call the animal cruelty people, let me explain. He could have water all day. He seemed to prefer playing with the dish. I would give him fresh water, he would drink a little, and then he would pour it out. I tried several approaches to keep him from wasting his water, but none of them worked.

Just once I would have liked to ask him, "McKenzie, why don't you have any water?" Just once I would have liked to hear, "I poured it all out and went thirsty all day so I could chew on the pan." Involvement really is a tricky business. People decide to be uninvolved and use some reasoning which sounds good, but it is not good. There are opportunities to drink deeply from the things that are going on, yet they choose to turn over the bucket.

One year between April and July, McKenzie learned not to pour his water out because there was a drought. Thirsty dogs do not pour their water out. People who want to be involved will be involved (spiritually or emotionally thirsty people). People who do not want to be involved will not be involved. The question in youth ministry should never be "Why isn't there any water?" but rather, "What happened to this bucket? Was someone drinking from it or playing with it?"

Another reason people do not feel they belong could be one of growth. An individual can experience growth that his or her immediate peer group has not yet accomplished. It is very easy to perceive an "at odds" feeling if your perspective has changed due to maturity. It is tough to lead peers. In some cases, people develop and fail to assume the lead, and another comes to maturity and takes the lead. Then it is very easy to feel left out or passed by. Just watch the transition at middle school. By eighth grade, you have athletes, academics, band kids, and cheerleaders. Peer groups change; lines are drawn. We do not allow kids to quit high school because the group around them changed (Eph 4:7, 11–15; 1 Cor 12:20–31). Let us help them to not quit the church.

The Climbing Club

The climbing club works like this. Someone hears about rock climbing, and they get curious. If there is enough real interest, then eventually we find a day, when someone gets to go on his or her first climbing trip. Most people start out with a few small rappel drops. Once in a while, someone wants to start out climbing. I usually drive and bring my personal gear. I carry the monster backpack, two rope bags, the rope pads, and the helmets. The guest usually carries their lunch. I explain, demonstrate, calm, tie, and retie everything. I do all the belaying and none of the climbing. When we finish, I untie, coil, pack, and carry everything back to the truck.

Some people have their curiosity sated and enjoy the experience. Some people do not have a good time and do not want to come back. Other people join "the climbing club." Sometime during this period, I quit calling them and they started calling me. "Hey, I'm out of school (or off work) Thursday. Let's go fight some gravity!" During this period, they usually buy their own harness, belay device, some shoes, and once in a while someone even buys a new rope. On these later trips, I don't carry all the gear. I don't do all the rigging and setup. The person has to belay while I climb. I've even had other people take their own vehicles.

Not once in all my years and all the climbers I have known has anyone ever said, "You know, when I first started taking these trips, you used to carry everything and buy everything, but now you don't. I can't believe you don't treat me like a guest anymore. I feel like such an outsider. I think I'll quit." Most people like the fact that they can share the load. They are members, not visitors.

We expect some things from members that we do not expect

from guests. Sure, members still ask for help. They are also expected to offer help. "I want to be a part" means I want to work; I want to share; I want to grow; I want to treat visitors to the kinds of things I enjoyed when I first started (cf. Eph 4:14–16).

There was this one time when a regular climber and newer climber made the same trip with me. The new guy offered gas money. He asked questions about wear and tear on the gear and replacement costs. He even said, "If you carry that bag in, I'll carry it out." The more experienced guy was suddenly embarrassed. He had been on a bunch of trips. He had never offered any of this. He felt really uncomfortable. He did not need to quit. He just needed to change some things so that as people outgrew him, he did not have any reason to feel bad. Everyone grows at a different pace. Just because someone does not grow at the same rate does not mean they do not belong.

Poor self-esteem is a legitimate problem among young people. It is a poor excuse for not being real and hiding behind that barrier and letting it prevent involvement. Remember attention, belonging, and support? If folks are real, then they can be loved. It is when one projects an image and I minister to the image and not the real person that we both mess up.

We do injustice to Paul's instructions to the Galatians when we are not real enough to let people know we are afraid so that they can help us bear and share burdens (Gal 6:1–2). First Corinthians 12 says that we are a body. We are connected. "If one member suffers, all suffer together; if one member is honored, all rejoice together" 1 Cor 12:26). People who are afraid will not talk about the things that really need addressing. They act as if they are fine or point to things that are symptoms but not the real problem. Then one day we walk in, and they are gone.

The Goat

The morning had started with Sissy (one of the many dogs we have known over the years) throwing a proverbial fit in the backyard. I had walked out to check on her and heard the sounds of an animal in great distress. Not very far into the woods behind our house I discovered two small goats and two large dogs. One goat was tangled in the branches of a fallen tree. The other goat was lying beside him. They were both wet and stained with blood. The larger of the two dogs was attacking the goat still standing. I used conflict resolution tactic number .357 (magnum). The dogs left. As I attempted to free the goat, I could see that he was afraid. He was hurt. I knew that if I left him there, he would just get tangled up again. I began to work my way to the house. My progress stopped at the end of the chain. The goat would not move. I tugged on the chain, and he got up. We took about three steps. The goat sat down. "Look, goat, you know you should not even be here. You have run away from your master, and you do not have the good sense God gave a ... . Anyway, you don't have the sense to get away from trouble." The goat lay down.

Dragging a goat through the woods is not a pretty sight. But hey, I'm not a morning person. About halfway to the house, I thought about those paintings where someone has shown Jesus carrying that little lamb. I just could not picture Jesus dragging that little lamb. I could not see the great shepherd or any shepherd dragging a wounded, frightened animal through the woods.

I am not a shepherd. Yet I have responsibilities with a flock. If they do not want to come back, do we just let them stay out there in their ignorance and wait on the dogs to come back? Galatians 6:1–2, 2 Timothy 2:24–26, and Luke 15 all offer perspectives on this topic of dealing with the weak, lost, and rebellious. Does it make a difference when dealing with goats instead of sheep?

Everyone in a congregation gets a turn in the youth group and then moves on. For one brief moment, they have the opportunity and responsibility. A lot of what the people coming behind can do depends on how those in front leave things. Not all at-risk kids are involved in sin. They may just fail to realize that they have an impact on the group that is behind them.

Seniors go through this. Either the seniors will make a significant contribution to the leadership of the group, or they will make some excuse for not being around anymore. It is part of life. Most of the inactive seniors do not realize the opportunity they are missing in helping others. They forget that they have benefited from the efforts of people who are older than they are. Although this type of at-risk is normal, I do not believe it is healthy.

The young people will perceive that the group has changed when they change as individual. I always have some fourteen or fifteen-year-old approach me with "The whole youth group has changed" or "We're just not as close as we used to be ... ." A fifteen-year-old has just lived through a period in her life when the most exciting thing in the world was conflict. She and her group of three friends spend all their time on the phone with each other and at each other's houses. Suddenly they decide to quit wasting all their time talking about boys and start talking to them. They end up spending time with Joe Handsome rather than the conflict queens. Do they feel as close to their friends as they did? NO. Has their relationship with all their peers changed? YES. Is there anything wrong? NO.

Look for transition problems when they move from junior high to senior high. Look for ambivalence in your juniors and seniors. Recognize this as a phase that all of us will have to live through about every three years or so. Do not minimize it when the kids go through it, but do understand it and be patient. When a senior says, "No one was there," what they mean is that it was a room full of insignificant underclassmen and non-human adults. We need to remind them that we are not changing, but they are.

I borrowed the term "at-risk" from the field of secular education and adapted it for our purposes to discuss "spiritually at-risk." Students who are at-risk spiritually are lacking in seven vital areas. To borrow from H. Stephen Glenn and Jane Nelsen, I have attempted to list these and identify certain deficiencies present in many congregations. These common errors contribute to making our young people susceptible to being at-risk.

**Deficient Area
Contributing Factor(s)**

- Perceptions of Personal Capabilities
- Perceptions of Personal Significance
- Lack of ability to read and comprehend Scripture without adult assistance.
- Young people are directed and not guided.
- Closed-ended questions predominate in Bible classes.
- Young people are not given responsibility for tasks or projects. Adults micromanage so that no one experiences failure. (But they do not experience success either when we do all the work.)
- Young people are not included in programs such as service projects, evangelism, and benevolence (Carol Dweck). Dweck, Carol. *Mindset: The New Psychology of Success.* New York: Random House, 2006.
- Perceptions of Personal Power
- Intrapersonal Skills
- As we take away personal significance, we also remove consequences for inadequate preparation and poor choices.
- Decisions are made for them and not by them: curriculum, schedules, service projects, etc.
- Lack of forum to talk about personal understanding. Often activities are not "de-briefed." Opportunities for personal and group insights are lost when we do not explore the "What," "So What," and "Now What" of experiences.
- Fixed mindset, not growth mindset (Dweck).
- Interpersonal Skills
- Problem-solving Skills
- Activities and doctrine do not focus on the relationship aspect of church. This is not the social aspect, but the relationships and implied responsibilities that each

member has to the body. We are not teaching how to get along with each other.
- Judgmental Skills
- We focus more on rules than values.
- We teach facts, not concepts.
- Spirituality is not taught as having relevance to the everyday human condition.

In addition to the observations about what creates the "at-risk" profile, here is an adaptation to help deal with an at-risk student:

Tips for Motivating the At-Risk Student

1. Teach those at-risk one concept at a time. Concepts build on concepts that lead to a major idea by the end of the quarter. (For the Bible teacher, always have one concept, simple and direct, for the at-risk in your class, and repeat it at several classes.)
2. Find out what gets the students excited when they first come to your class. Reference "Point of Ignition" as found in *The Talent Code* by Daniel Coyle.
3. Get the student to start talking by asking questions about their interests, and then start asking them questions that will lead to a concept. Get them to start investigating. Create an interest (Spirituality must be relevant to the human condition.) If the Bible lesson cannot relate to the real world of the at-risk student, we will lose them.
4. Praise often and try to reward effort rather than success. At-risk students in secular schools need to succeed every two to three days. Success here is defined as someone noticing my effort rather than my results. Find "success" in your at-risk Bible student during each class.

5. In school, they say to use thin books and give small amounts of work at a time. Students need appropriate amounts and levels of instructional material. A child from a non-religious background needs easy-to-comprehend lessons. A modern translation is a must in this instance.
6. Decorate the room with modern pictures (sports, media, etc.). It may take some creativity but can be done. An example could be a poster of the "Big Guy" with his famous "I'll be back." Your added caption may be, "Jesus said the same thing two thousand years ago. ... Will you be ready?"
7. Allow the student to express self through drawings.
8. Sing songs. Youth group singing is vital to the survival of everyone. It creates a bond but also gives the "fringe" student something he or she can take home. They may not sing with the group but will hum their favorite song in their mind away from the group.
9. At-risk students do not bring homework back. This means your at-risk Bible students will not bring workbooks back. Use class time wisely. It is the only Bible many of these kids will get.
10. Hide exams within the lesson done in class. I do not give exams in Bible class but do check to see if comprehension is taking place through open-ended questions or discussion opportunities. Just because a young person cannot make the Bible Bowl cut does not mean he or she has not learned or grown. Facts are important, but conceptualization is more important. Fixed mindset kids do great at Bible Bowl but are usually lousy in discussion; they are not sure that the answer is "right," and they do not want to lose their identity as "smart" by making a blunder.
11. Get out from behind the desk. Stay close to the

students. Walk up and down the class. Be accessible. Sit in a circle.

12. Go to the student so that they can ask questions quietly without ever having to raise their hand or feel dumb by asking out loud. For the Bible teacher, this may mean a follow-up after class. A phone call or a visit that asks, "Did you get the point in today's lesson?" or "Is there anything from our class that I need to clear up for you?" can go a long way. We often assume biblical literacy on the part of our students. They may not "all remember the story of Daniel in the lion's den." These are awesome teachable moments.

13. Praise success often, from the beginning. When you ask for daily Bible readers do not be afraid to count down. "How many read six out of seven days? Five? How about four. ... " If the student reads one day, praise the effort. If they are not reading, ask about prayer. Find a success to celebrate.

14. Praise physical appearance. Tell them how good they look. Notice new shoes, changes in hair, earrings, tattoos, etc. (We tell them we care if we notice the little things).

15. Use the words "I love you" often with the class. At-risk students may not hear these words anywhere else but near you.

16. Americans have been conditioned not to touch, and we must still be careful (never hug a child without his or her permission), but this is a need for the at-risk student. Shake hands, high-five, or pat the student on the shoulder. If they seem to draw away, this is because they may not know how to accept it. Or it may be a trigger to a trauma. Ask what is okay to do. "So you aren't a hugger? How about a fist bump?" They will learn to like the attention when they get used to it.

17. Be open and friendly. Make students feel comfortable. Teachers and leaders want love, respect, and appreciation—but they must dish it out first before they will get it from students. Convince them that you care.
18. Be yourself. Stop trying to be the "teacher," "Mr. Minister," etc. Have a good self-concept and be a role model. Let students see you laugh at yourself. Relationships with children must be built around real feelings and playfulness.
19. At-risk students need logic and order. Be sure they see what it does for them and not for you. They need internal motivation. Do not teach rules; teach concepts and values. Show them how God's plan makes sense.
20. Find the strengths in the students and point them out often.
21. Have the at-risk student teach something to another student, even if you must use a young child. Allow them to help you with younger ages so they feel like they are learning something.
22. Change language to help the at-risk student. Eliminate the words "difficulty" or "trouble" and replace them with the word "opportunity." Use the word "challenge" and not "problem." Focus on what can happen instead of what cannot or will not happen.
23. Give the students an object that is small but visible to remind them of their personal strengths. I use very small rapid links like the ones used to splice chains together. Every student is a link in our chain. Each one brings some kind of strength to our group. This reminder in their pocket may keep them going.
24. Have students record their successes. They can go back and read them if they feel a failure. Remind them of the battles that they have won.
25. Never give up on an at-risk student. This is what they expect to happen. If you give up, then they have

conquered you! (If this is the position in the secular world, at school, what should our position be?)

Discussion Questions

1. What did you find most shocking in this chapter?
2. What did you find most helpful in this chapter?
3. Discuss or list five suggestions from the chapter that you are going to start doing to help at-risk young people.

Bibliography

Coil, Daniel. *The Talent Code*. New York: Bantam, 2009.

Dweck, Carol S. *Mindset: The New Psychology of Success*. New York: Random House, 2006.

Glenn, H. Stephen and Jane Nelsen. *Raising Self-Reliant Children in a Self-Indulgent World*. 2nd ed. Albuquerque: Harmony, 2000.

Chapter 54
Training Teens to Lead
J. D. Schwartz

Christians Are Called to Lead

If you pay much attention to New Testament language and watch Jesus interact with His 12 apostles, you quickly realize that Jesus has an expectation for His disciples to impact the people around them and the culture in which they live—Matthew 5:1–20. In other words, we are called to lead others to Jesus. In Matthew 28:18–20, Jesus commissions His followers to "go," "make disciples," "baptize," and "teach." In Acts 17:6, Paul, Silas, and Timothy are so effective in their work that they are referred to as those who have "turned the world upside down." Paul calls us "ambassadors for Christ" in 2 Corinthians 5:20. These are just a few of the passages in the New Testament that allude to the impact of Christians in the world. The beauty of the concept of New Testament leadership is the individuality and diversity in which it can be manifested and applied. Take a look at 1 Corinthians 12, Romans 12, and Ephesians 4, and you will see that impact and leadership begins within the church.

So, what is leadership? Leadership can be obvious and displayed in an upfront and vocal manner, and this is the most accepted and usual ideal for leadership. But leadership can also be quiet and "behind the scenes" and is no less significant as such. In many ways, leadership on display in one's life is relative to the God-given gifts and passions that are inherent in his/her person. So long as one is willing to assert his/her God-given ability and passion for kingdom work, then he/she is a leader in the kingdom.

One phrase I use with teens on a regular basis when teaching the subject of leadership is "everyone is a leader to someone." In other words, every Christian has a direct impact on someone— older, younger, male, female, within the church, and especially those outside of the church. Christians are watched, studied, and followed. So, the question then is this, "How can we effectively and intentionally train the teens in our churches and youth ministries to be impactful leaders in His kingdom and in the way we interact with all those with which we come in contact?"

The Culture for Teen Leadership

Training begins with culture. Before we really jump into this, let me throw out a disclaimer: There is no perfect equation or solution for building teen leaders in His kingdom. There will always be ideas and programs that can be used to help encourage and equip teen leadership, and most of those will be completely different from one church to another because of the passions, focuses, and strengths of the respective congregation and her leadership. In other words, kingdom leadership is not about a program. It is a culture that perpetuates activity and growth in the hearts and minds of individuals when presented with opportunity.

I have found that culture within youth ministry is extremely significant in dictating the organization and direction of a ministry that develops kingdom workers. A carefully thought-out and defined culture becomes the foundation for everything you do to move your teens into kingdom activity. It focuses on your ministry's mission; it helps determine the types of programs you will introduce and elevate to achieve that mission; it communicates expectations and activity for those involved. All of this is guided by God's Word and His desire for His people to be active in work and service. Do you have a mission statement for your ministry that provides focus, determines programming, and communicates expectations? If not, I would challenge you to sit down with your ministry leaders—elders, deacons, parents, and teens (especially the teens)—and ask them to help you determine some group goals and passions that will lead to a more focused and embedded culture for your ministry.

As you begin building the culture that produces kingdom workers, there are some foundational building blocks that you need to be mindful of. These include the activity and example of the youth worker(s), and programming principles that will lead to your ministry's effectiveness, along with the encouragement and opportunities for growth and leadership.

The Youth Worker

What are you doing as the youth worker to model what you are asking your teens to be and do? There has already been a very effective chapter dedicated to the youth minister as a leader, so we will not revisit all of that again. However, we must at least reiterate the significance of the role of the youth worker as a leader and example to the teens. Paul said, "Be imitators of me, as I am of Christ" (1 Cor 11:1). To ask teens to step out as leaders, the youth worker must be willing to step out in the same manner. In my experience, kingdom work, especially in dealing with people, is often speckled with situations that are uncomfortable. Serving people is often messy and uncomfortable. But if we ask our teens to lead in the kingdom, they must see our willingness to do the same ... no matter what—evangelism/outreach, service, benevolence, and labor-intensive work.

Programming Principles

Do you have a purpose in the things you are doing to uphold your ministry's mission and produce kingdom workers? Some misconceptions about youth ministry tend to lean towards the lack of spiritual depth in our ministries, the lack of organization, and the desire to be separated from the rest of the congregation. Who needs spiritual depth, when you can pack the house with pizza (if you grew up in the 90's) or Chick-fil-A (for the Millennials and Gen Z) and games? Why does a youth minister always have to be thought of as the guy in flip-flops and a t-shirt who never gets anything accomplished? Why would anyone think it to be a good idea for our teens and children to be disconnected from the rest of the church? If we are going to produce teen leaders and life-long kingdom workers, we must actively work to change the perceived purpose of youth ministry.

Spiritual Depth and Biblical Teaching

For teens to be spiritual leaders and kingdom workers, they need to know how to be pleasing to God. Being pleasing to God comes only from an understanding of who Jesus is and His invitation for us to be heirs and workers in His kingdom. Be diligent in teaching the Bible, and base everything you do on the foundation of His Word—both in principle, theology, and application. Do not underestimate teens's ability to read and comprehend God's Word or their attention span in doing so. Challenge them to dig deeper and to know more. In turn, they will grow in their desire to learn more, love more, and live more as an active kingdom worker.

Intentional Organization and Opportunity

Teens need to be encouraged—sometimes gently pushed—and given opportunities to lead. Sometimes, they need someone to "tap them on the shoulder" with an opportunity and word of encouragement toward an opportunity in leadership. Are you actively "shoulder-tapping" teens in your ministry? What types of things do you do in your ministry that offer that encouragement and opportunity? Remember, there is no perfect program. As a matter of fact, some teens will respond to some opportunities/programs whereas other teens will respond to other opportunities/programs. That is okay! God did not give us all the ability to speak or sing. He made some to be the mouth and some to be the hands (cf. 1 Cor 12:18–20). Be kind and patient in your encouragement.

A couple of years ago, I began offering our teens a spiritual gifts "test" (more like an evaluation) that is intended to help an individual identify his/her spiritual gifts. I do this at the beginning of the calendar year, along with the reminder of our mission statement that comes from Romans 12—"Lifting up the Lord in worship and service, while lifting up others in love." Our teens produced this statement out of the desire to fulfill their active places in God's kingdom. All you need to do is search the internet for a spiritual gifts test—you will most likely want to change the wording in some of the findings to reflect Scripture more accurately. I like to give a different version of the "test" each year for the sake of variety. It is a blessing to see the light bulb come on in a teen's mind of what he/she is already good at or might be good at that is also useful and blesses the church.

You cannot stop with the test though. For the rest of the year, you will need to work to offer and encourage opportunities for your teens to use their spiritual gifts.

Here's a broad list of some of these areas along with some of the things that can be done:

Public Leading:

- *Lads 2 Leaders*—(or a similar style of program designed to encourage different styles/tasks for leadership in the church)
- *Intergenerational Worship*—Include your teens in the congregational setting Bible class teaching

- *Nursing Home and Smaller Church Worship*—Take your teens to other places for exposure to more worship-leading opportunities

Grief and Loss:

- *Encourage teens to attend funerals and join in comfort*
- *Funeral singing*—Depending on the family and funeral home, small group singing may be preferred.

Evangelism and Outreach:

- *Mission trip opportunities*
- *1-on-1 Bible study training*

Active and Continuous Community Outreach:

- *Bus Ministry*—Our "Into-the-City" ministry has challenged our teens to put their Bible class knowledge and faith into evangelistic action and has become a driving force in our student ministry. On Wednesday nights during the school year, from 6:00–8:00 pm, we bus children from government housing neighborhoods to our building. We typically have 25–40 children and teens but sometimes have more. Some of our teens ride the buses to assist with pick-up and drop-off, and this has become a neat time for our teens to develop deeper friendships with the bus riders. During our time with the children, our teens, along with a team of adults, join in the processes of teaching, singing, praying, doing crafts, and mentoring. We have been doing this since 2017 and are seeing first-hand God's Word and grace in action. We currently have 4 teens (that may not seem like a lot, but this is a slow and patient ministry) who began riding the bus on Wednesdays and are now joining us on Sundays

and in other youth functions on a consistent basis. This ministry has also opened doors to the following ministry opportunities in our community that require our teens' action and involvement.
- *Community Housing Needs*
- *School Breakfast/Lunch Distribution in the Summer* — Schools in your area may be using federal subsidies to distribute meals to children in the summer.
- *Elementary School Grade Adoption*—Some administrations welcome partnerships to benefit their classrooms.

Student Ministry Leadership:

- *Ministry Ideas and Planning for Events*
- *Student Accountability and Encouragement*—Involve your teens in the mentoring and involvement process with their peers.

This is by no means an exhaustive list of opportunities, and chances are, you will find ways to be even more creative in these areas. The purpose is not to point out specific programs, but a variety of opportunities that encourage and engage teens in Kingdom work according to their passions and strengths.

Intergenerational Faith Sharing and Growth

To be blunt, a youth ministry should NEVER separate its teens from the rest of the church. While it is understandable to have programs that are relevant and beneficial to teens in ways that are different, it should ALWAYS be the goal to connect teens with adults in any given program. In Titus 2:1–8, Paul challenges the church to be active in the generational passing of active faith. The "older" men and women are obligated to teach the "younger" men and women in ways of life and service. I am not just talking about chaperones. ... I'm talking about active and engaged mentors. Fuller

Youth Institute has done the research and sites a 5:1 adult-to-teen ratio needed for the success of a teen growing up to become a faithful and active kingdom worker (https://fulleryouthinstitute.org/stickyfaith, home page). What are you doing to actively attach the "older" in your congregation to those who are "younger" in your congregation? This can be accomplished in a variety of ways, but it must be done. Teens need mentors who model and teach kingdom activity. They need to know they are valued. They need to know they are loved. They need prayers, encouragement, and comfort from a variety and host of faithful adults.

Teens also need to be mentors who model and teach kingdom activity. It's a powerful practice to empower teens with the ability to mentor those who are younger. Not all teens will embrace this. They may not like the idea; they may not be spiritually mature. But those who do will make a lasting impact on a younger teen/child as they themselves grow in their faith-walk.

Lead On

Everyone is a leader to someone, and there is no more significance to this fact than in God's kingdom. Build a culture in your ministry that empowers, encourages, and cultivates leadership and kingdom work. Then, rejoice as God uses the teens in your ministry to "turn the world upside down" (cf. Acts 17:6).

Discussion Questions

1. Why does God place so much importance on Kingdom work and Christian impact?
2. What are some ways, ministries, or opportunities *in which* you have been encouraged to step out as a Kingdom worker?
3. Of the three programming principles discussed, which do you think the churches of Christ have been most

effective at accomplishing? Which of these could we do better? Why? [For further discussion of this question, look at this article referred by Dr. Kirk Brothers: Fraze, David W., and Tyler S. Greenway. "Growing Young in the Churches of Christ: Exploratory Analysis Across Churches Within a Denomination and Denominational Comparisons." Pages 9–30 in *The Journal of Youth Ministry*. (Association of Youth Ministry Educators. Vol. 2.20, Fall 2022.)]
4. In what ways have you seen mentoring be most beneficial?

Bibliography

Powell, Kara, Griffin, Brad M. and Crawford, Cheryl A. *Sticky Faith, Youth Worker Edition: Practical Ideas to Nurture Long-Term Faith in Teenagers.* Grand Rapids: Zondervan, 2011.

Lawrence, Rick. *Jesus-Centered Youth Ministry.* Loveland: Group Publishing, 2014.

Powell, Kara, Mulder, Jake, and Griffin, Brad. *Growing Young: Six Essential Strategies to Help Young People Discover and Love Your Church.* Grand Rapids: Baker Books, 2016.

Rainer, Thom S. and Geiger, Eric. *Simple Church.* Nashville: B&H Publishing Group, 2011.

Chapter 55
Introducing Teens to Missions
Austin Fowler

Are We Mission-Minded?

When you look at the life of Paul, there is no doubt that he was mission-minded. He traveled all over the Middle East, Europe, and Asia Minor to preach the saving message of Jesus Christ. While that was his mission, he had a secondary mission, and that was to train young evangelists including Timothy and Titus, to leave behind to help new congregations to be firmly established and grow (Titus 1:5). I truly believe that if we want congregations of the Lord's church to grow, we need to train the next generation (2 Tim 2:2). Over the last several decades, the Church of Christ has declined. There was a time in the last century when we were one of the fastest-growing religious groups. Why was that? Part of the reason was that we focused on evangelism and missions. Today, we have a generation that does not know how to do home Bible studies because they have never seen their parents do one. We need to change that culture. We can change that culture by introducing our teens to mission work, domestical and foreign.

When we teach our teens in Bible classes, we focus on the hot topic issues (i.e., drugs, alcohol, sex, etc.) or the fundamental issues (instrumental music, baptism for salvation, etc.). But have we ever done a class on missions or evangelism with our teens? I am confident that, for the most part, we have failed on this issue. If we want to introduce them to the mission, we need to teach, train, practice, and be the leading example for them to follow in evangelism. While most of this chapter deals with foreign mission work, we must also introduce them to domestic and local missions. If we forget to do the mission at home, we will not be able to send missionaries to other countries, or they might have to come here to teach us how to do tasks.

This chapter is a "how to" section on conducting a mission trip in a foreign country. There are three keys to making sure you run a successful campaign. The first key is to focus on **souls**. The whole purpose of going is to teach the loss of the community that you will help spread the gospel, not to be on vacation. The second key is **safety**. Remember, you have the lives of teenagers in your hands. Security needs to be a priority on this trip. Parents have entrusted you with their children's lives. A third key is **setup**. This third key is, in my opinion, the primary key for all three. If you have proper setup and preparation for the campaign, everyone will have the right mindset on souls and you will have measures in place to ensure the safety of all team members. Let me dive deeper into some items to consider when taking teens on a mission trip.

Coordination (Setup)

Remember, setup and preparation are the primary keys to success. Before you take teens to another country, you must go over and scout the area yourself. Ideally, I would like to go down six months before the scheduled trip. This will allow you to have time to review and finalize everything for your upcoming mission trip for your team. One of the biggest things you can do is have a key contact person in the country you are working. They need to speak both English and the primary language of the country they are working in. They can help you in preparing for the campaign. This person will be your right-hand man during the week you are doing the mission. Remember, take care of this brother when you have the opportunity by covering his expenses, taking him to eat, and verbal praise.

Pre-Campaign Trip

I have created a checklist for everything I do in the country during the "pre-campaign in-country" trip. Here is the list:

- *Hotels*
  - Will you have two different hotels? You will have one for the place where the campaign will be located. But will you need one that you use for the first and last night because of travel and flights getting in late?
  - Do not just go to one hotel but go to multiple to get the best price.
  - While you are visiting the hotels, get the following information:
    - The price
    - The contact information for the hotel manager.
    - Learn how many different kinds of rooms they have (i.e., singles, doubles, triples, and quads)
  - Do they have Wi-Fi?
  - Do they have breakfast provided?
  - Do they have security?
  - Note: Go to several of the different hotels in the area. Take pictures of the rooms and write down all the information you possibly can so when you come home to make the decision, you have notes that will help jog your memory of everything you saw on your trip.

- *Buses*
    - How many buses do you need? (Remember: You will have your people, as well as possibly translators and local preachers, that might be a part of the campaign).
        - Get the contact info for the bus company.
        - Get the price in writing.

- *Food*
    - Remember, you are working with teens who love Zaxby's and Chick-fil-A and they are very picky eaters.
    - Will you have the locals prepare food? Prepare a menu so the campaigner can know what to expect.
    - Are there restaurants to eat at in town? Is there a mall with a food court?
    - Does the hotel have a restaurant to go back to for meals?

- *CongregationalNeeds*
    - It is essential that while on your trip, you spend time with the leadership/men of the congregation. During this meeting, you can learn a lot about them, their needs, and how you can help them the most during the campaign.
    - Note: The church building might be small. They might need some things to accommodate the locals, visitors, and your groups.
        - Do we need to rent a facility to have more room?
        - Do we need to rent chairs?
        - Do we need to rent a PA system?
        - Do we need to rent bathrooms?

- *CongregationalPlanning*
    - VBS
        - Can we go into the schools to do VBS?
        - How many times a day do you want to do VBS?

- Typically, in the past, we did three a day—one in the morning, one in the afternoon, and one in the evening during the preaching. The one in the morning or afternoon could be at a local school.
- What kind of classrooms/facilities do they have for a VBS at the church building?
  ◦ Gospel Meeting
- Who are the speakers going to be?
- What is the theme going to be?
- Get one of the local brothers to Create flyers and get them printed in the country so they can start advertising for the campaign.

• *Translators*
  • Will you need translators?
  • How many translators do you need?
  • Do you have any translators that are coming from the United States with your group?

Pre-Campaign—US Prep

While many plans are involved in the pre-campaign in-country trip, just as much preparation is needed when you come home from that trip; here is a checklist for that side preparation:

• Things to Order:
  ◦ Team T-shirt—We have always ordered two per person in the past. One for the day you travel to the country and the other for when you travel home. This helps to keep up with all your team members while going through security at the airport.
  ◦ Lanyards & Name Tags—You can get these from Christian Universities.
  ◦ Luggage Tags —This is optional. Getting your group's luggage off the conveyor belt can be helpful. You can get a group to start

pulling them as you see the luggage tag for your group and put them in a group.
- Bibles—We always order paperback Bibles and use the Reina-Valera 1960 translation.
- Songbooks—This is based on the needs of the congregation. Some congregations already have them.
- Tracks—There are some great Bible-study tracks that have been translated into Spanish. You will need these to hand out during the door-knocking portion of the campaign.
- Additional Bible study material.

- Things to Do:
  - Create Hotel Room Assignments—By laying this out, it will help you decide who will room together and how many rooms you will need.
  - Door Knocking Teams—Remember, you are training these teens on how to do mission work. The ideal team includes an elder, preacher, Bible class teacher, or deacon as the team leader. You also need a teen on each team who is able to learn how to do Bible Studies. Remind team leaders of their responsibility to demonstrate how to lead a Bible study and, later on in the week, to allow the teen to lead part of or all of a Bible study.
  - Copy of Passports—This is important to have. I would suggest leaving one copy in the church office. Then you need to take three extra copies as the team leader. One for each hotel is helpful because hotels often want this info when you check-in. Having these copies will save you time and make hotel check-in run smoother. Have one extra copy in case of an emergency (many campaigns will have the team members put a copy of their passport in each piece of luggage).
  - VBS—Get a VBS coordinator who will handle all the VBS work during the trip. A part of your shared team expenses will be material for VBS. Allow them to decide what to teach and to have the freedom to run it. Remember, get your teens involved in the

preparation and delivery of VBS. They need to learn how to set it up and run it so they can help with it when they get to their home congregations.

• Extra Things to Pack:
  ◦ Medicine—It is always good to have extra medication in emergencies.
  ◦ Hand Sanitizer

With proper setup, the trip can go much more smoothly. Obstacles are a part of mission work. When you set up correctly, you try to remove as many obstacles as possible to make sure your team can have an enjoyable trip but they can also get as much work done as possible.

Coach

I have been a coach in multiple sports for the last several years. You can take athletes and enhance their skills to make them better athletes. It is an incredible journey and, of course, a rewarding one. Coaching takes a lot of time and preparation to help your athletes perform under the Friday night lights. A typical week for the coaching staff is to meet on Sunday afternoons between church services to watch the film and create a game plan. Monday after school, we sit down with the players, watch the film, go over it, and instruct them on the game plan we created on Sunday. We go over the new plays and changes in the scheme based on our opponent. We all teach in a classroom. Then we go out to the field and practice until Thursday. We go over and over the plays until we reach perfection. Finally, Friday arrives to put into play what we prepared for all week. The same is true when it comes to evangelism. We preach and teach that we need to be evangelistic and to introduce our friends and neighbors to Jesus, but I think that teens do not do it because they do not know how. This would be like a coach going into a football game on Friday without properly training the players Monday through Thursday. Teens need to be guided and instructed in the ways of evangelism. For foreign campaigns, there needs to be coaching for the mission trip to go well. I want to give three ways in which we can coach our teens and introduce them to the mission.

The First Thing We Need to Do Is Instruct (Film Room Work)

Instruction takes place before the campaign in a classroom setting with the adults who will be with the teens in the campaign. We need to show them different Bible study materials they can use on the mission trip. Here are a few that I suggest: *Back to the Bible, Does It Matter,* and *Open Bible Study.* These are very easy to use and teach them how to do it. Instruct them on how to handle different Bible study questions that might arise in a study. We need to prepare our teams to do home Bible studies, and it would be best if you taught them different cultural features they might experience on the trip. For example, in Latin America, you do not flush toilet paper down the toilet due to the plumbing. Another example is not to drink water, have ice in your drink, or eat anything that might be washed in water (i.e., lettuce). During this time, it is vital to go over the rules for the trip. It is important to stress that the rules are in place to keep them safe and to have a successful trip.

The Next Step Is to Allow Time to Practice (Practice During the Week)

Break the teens into groups in the classroom and practice going through the Bible study methods. Allow them time to practice implementing the strategies you taught in your classroom. The old saying, "Practice makes perfect," is accurate regarding evangelism. The only way to get better at evangelism is by doing it and practicing it on people. Doing it in small groups with people they know will allow them to build their confidence to do it in real life.

The Last Step Is to Provide Time to Do (This Is the Game)

Of course, we love high school football because of what happens under the "Friday Night Lights." With the film room and practice work, the team will be ready to play. Hopefully, this analogy has helped you see the importance of doing it in evangelism. We must get our teens out in the mission field to do what we have taught them. This can be done through foreign and domestic mission works in the United States. We need to invest the time to teach them how to do tasks and be evangelists so they can be productive and fruitful in their journey.

Concerns/Communication

Many of the teens you are taking on the mission trip will have concerned parents. One way to help with the concerns is by getting the parents to go with you. You cannot make this trip without adults taking the journey with you. Why not include parents? There will be some that will send their child without going personally. The question is how you ensure their children's safety in a foreign country. The first thing is to tell the parents everything you can about the trip. Communication is the key to their concern. Let me give you three ways to communicate effectively and efficiently with the parents. I use the Remind App. You are probably already familiar with this program if you are a youth minister. It is a mass messaging system to help communicate to whoever signs up with it (it was designed for the education system to communicate with students in classes). I encourage you to share information before your trip through this app. You can send out encouraging messages, things to pray for, updates about the trip, and whatever else you want to communicate.

Of course, you are going to another country where you may not have cell phone service (though carriers such as Verizon and AT&T have coverage in most Latin American countries and other places in the world). Many of these parents will want to know their child is safe and hear about their day. Most of the hotels I have stayed in have Wi-Fi. They can communicate with them when they return to the hotel to let them know they are safe for the evening. WhatsApp is widely used in Latin America and is easily downloaded to a phone. This can be helpful for communication with the group or parents (as a separate group) during your trip.

Cost

Of course, the cost and budget are two of the big questions concerning leading a mission trip. My mentor, Spencer Broome, was the master of introducing teens to mission work and taught me how to do this. He created a spreadsheet with every expense for the mission trip. I would be happy to share this with you. The budget calculates every single cost you can have on a campaign on one Excel spreadsheet (hotels, buses, translator expenses, materials, etc.). The spreadsheet totals all expenses and divides the amount by the total number of team members. Keep in mind that people do drop out due to different circumstances. We always subtract two people from the number signed up to determine the average cost. This allows you some wiggle room in case people drop and if something is higher than budgeted. The key to any campaign's cost is ensuring you stay within budget. This keeps elders and congregations happy! Remember that this is God's money we are dealing with.

The next key item is fundraising. Roughly speaking, the campaign will cost team members about $2,000 to $2,500. It is anywhere from $700 to $1,000 for a plane ticket and $1,000 to $1,200 for shared team expenses. You then add $250 for food while on the trip. The question is, how do you pay for all of this? I highly discourage congregations from paying for the whole bill. Some teens need to have "skin in the game." Doing this will allow teens to be more bought in and have more respect for the mission because they are invested.

I suggest giving them advice on how to raise funds from family members and friends. Make sure they have enough details about the trip, what will be accomplished for God's kingdom, and how funds will be managed so they can share the info with potential supporters. Some supporters will fill more comfortable sending the funds to the church on their behalf rather than just handing the teen a check. Setting up a way for donors to do this can be helpful.

Conclusion

Please feel free to contact me if you have any questions concerning mission work. I have plenty of resources to help you prepare for the trip. I will gladly share anything I have with you to help your mission trip go well. You can contact me by email at austin@house-tohouse.com. May God bless you as you strive to fulfill the great commission and teach the next generation about mission work.

Discussion Questions

1. Share some reasons why congregations often do not take the time to show teens how to evangelize.
2. What is something in this chapter that you had never considered before when planning a mission trip, and how did the discussion help you?
3. Share other ideas, besides those mentioned in this chapter, for how to communicate with campaigners, parents, elders, etc. as you carry out a mission campaign.
4. What is one thing not discussed in this chapter that you think would be good to consider or prepare for when planning a mission trip with teens?

Chapter 56
Technology in Ministry
Jason Helton

Introduction

Technology is our toolbox for communication, teaching, and ministry. How you incorporate technology is something you need to really think about and consider as you grow in ministry. Our aim is to use tech to become more effective in our outreach. In other words, we are high tech so we can have high reach. Technology should make us more effective in engaging and ministering to people. It is easy to get caught up in the thrill of buying gear and trying to be like other people we see online, but that is not what we are called to do. It is important for us to have a clear purpose when we use technology to enhance our ministry. To help us do that, let us break this chapter into two sections: communication and teaching.

Technology for Communication

Technology has always been a vehicle for more effective communication. Alexander Graham Bell paved the way for modern communication when he designed the first telephone. Before that Johannes

Gutenberg invented the printing press which changed society forever. Today, there are new apps and platforms created every year (or day, or week, or month...) that impact how culture communicates.

When it comes to communicating in ministry, it is impossible to do too much. There will always be people that do not read an email, post, or message. But that should not stop you from trying to communicate well. When it comes to communicating with parents, understand that you will still get questions even if you post the most complete and detailed information humanly possible. It is important to understand that your information is one piece of a thousand pieces of information they take in every day.

With that said, I would recommend you try to create a central and consistent source of information exchange. If you send a weekly email, schedule it for the same time each week. Your click rate will increase with consistency, not volume. Fewer emails with more consistent timing will yield better communication. Use social media to communicate and share ideas but do not rely on this as your main source of information. When possible, use your teens to create content that will engage their peers. But keep in mind social media is often most popular for its entertainment value, not substance.

You should also have one other source of real-time communication (text or some type of mobile messaging is encouraged). This method of communication is used to update and remind parents in real time. Whether you use GroupMe or something like the Remind App[1], you should have a way to directly message your parents so they can know about details relating to trips and events. You should also limit these messages. They are reserved for very important or timely alerts like when you plan to be back at the building from a trip. If you send multiple text messages a day, people will begin to block or mute your messages and you will defeat your own purpose. Be wise but consistent in how you message. Post regularly and in visible places how parents can connect to these sources of information.

Using social media in your ministry is worth considering. Most teens follow their friends and accounts that entertain them. If you are looking to adopt a new social media platform because your students are on it, first ask them why they follow certain accounts. Follow similar accounts and see how they use that platform. Often older generations will try to recreate the popular trends on social media as a way to connect and show their relevance to teens. This does not always end successfully. My encouragement to you is to find one or two platforms that most of your students are on and use those platforms to communicate with them and encourage them. Do not try to be something that you are not. If you have interns, use them to help you with your social media engagement. Ask them to create content for the ministry while they are working with you. They do not have to be the only ones that learn during the summer. You can benefit greatly from what they can show you. Plus, this will help you keep up with changing trends.

For platforms like Instagram, consider creating a business profile. Switching to a business profile gives you access to things like analytics that will help you know more about your audience. For instance, a business profile will show you trends like what time of day your followers are active, what kind of demographics your audience is made up of, and so much more. If this information is not relevant for your ministry, consider using it for your congregation's main account. It will be a huge help when trying to promote events and other content.

Another aspect of communication is what your students will tell you via social media. People, especially teens, will reveal more in an online video or chat than they would ever consider revealing in a one-on-one conversation with a youth minister or parent. For this reason, it can be helpful for a youth minister to have a presence on social media. But, this can be a challenge. Being consumed by social media is also a real challenge for adults as well as teens. Familiarize yourself with what those dangers are and set boundaries for yourself to ensure that you do not become driven by temptations like lust, pride, jealousy, or gossip. Again, this can be a fine line so it is important to keep in mind the words of the Apostle Paul in Galatians 6, "Keep watch on yourself, lest you too be tempted" (Gal 6:1).

Technology for Teaching

Using technology in the classroom can be very helpful. Several years ago, using a PowerPoint presentation became a new and innovative way to capture your audience's attention. Now it is practically standard for elementary and middle schoolers to have to present their class projects using PowerPoint. So how can you leverage technology in the classroom? The first place I would start is by talking to the professional teachers in your congregation. Regularly check in with them to find out what new technologies and methods are being used in the school setting and consider how you can adapt them for your ministry.

An app that I think is great and has proven to be an interactive way for me to engage students (and parents) is called Poll Everywhere[2]. The free version is very helpful in engaging your audience with real-time polls and questions and can be a very good way to encourage participation in class. In large classes, people tend to not speak up as much. This resource allows people to answer questions anonymously and you can see their feedback in real time. There are a lot of ways to use this. I especially like to use it to get feedback from intergenerational audiences.

Another resource that you may not think about is your church website. Church websites can be a great place to post Bible study curriculum and resources. Consider creating a parent's resource section on your youth ministry page. Here you can provide information like what your teenagers are studying in Bible class. It would be a great blessing to parents if they could see the content from their kid's Bible class or the spiritual content you plan to address on a retreat or at church camp. This could become a great way to equip the entire family and not just the teens. Consider making your youth ministry page a hub of information for parents to find all the information they need for youth-related activities.

Podcasts have also become incredibly popular. Could you host a podcast that features teen-friendly guests, or perhaps your teens as guests? YouTube is typically more popular among younger generations than audio podcasts but with a digital camera (or even your camera phone) and an inexpensive microphone, you can produce a high-quality show in minutes! At the time of this writing (2023), a short vertical video is where the platforms are trending. Algorithms favor and promote that style of visual content. How can you leverage that for your ministry? You could conduct funny or interesting interviews with your elders, other ministers, or adults in the congregation. This can be a great way to introduce chaperones, interns, or Bible class teachers.

A great resource to help stay relevant with the constantly changing pop culture is Spotify and Apple Music. These platforms will always have a "what's popular now" or a "trending" section and can give you and parents a general pulse on what is currently popular in music and entertainment. This does not necessarily mean that all your teens are engaged with this content, but it does give you an idea of what they are hearing and what is being promoted in their world. You can reference some of these cultural influencers to draw illustrations for your Bible teaching. Clever teasers posted online can be a way to build intrigue for what you teach in the classroom.

When it comes to taking Bible classes beyond Sundays and Wednesdays, consider apps like Marco Polo[3] that allow you to have a conversation through video messaging. This is a great way to have a small study group or prayer group stay in touch and continue the conversation outside the classroom. Using an app like Marco Polo also allows you time to think through responses to difficult questions while also communicating nuance with body language that often gets lost when communicating through text or email. As more apps come out that promote community and connection, research them to see what might be helpful in increasing your effectiveness as a teacher.

One last suggestion when it comes to using technology in teaching. If you use Bible study software, show that in class. It can be very impactful for you to model how you conduct a Bible study. If your students can see you in real time researching and highlighting passages and terms, then they will not only be better equipped for that specific study, but they will also become better Bible students in the future. Perhaps consider purchasing Bible study software for your seniors when they graduate. There may be special discounts out there for software like Logos[4], Olive Tree[5], and Accordance[6].

Conclusion

One of the greatest blessings you can offer your families is to be a person that is well-researched in digital trends. Often parents are so far removed from the world of social media and tech trends that they need someone they trust to help guide them through this chapter of life. Be familiar with trends and ways to disciple their children as they learn to navigate a very challenging time. Use sites like Urban Dictionary and Bark Technologies to equip parents with knowledge and skills for parenting in a digital age. This may become the single greatest way to minister to your families.

Discussion Questions

1. What are some risks that I should be aware of when it comes to using social media in my ministry?
2. What are some ways that social media can enhance my ministry?
3. What Bible study tools do my teens and families need?
4. How can I leverage our church website to better equip our teenage families?
5. What content do I already have (retreat booklets, class handouts, curriculum, etc.) that I can better format for families to use in their own Bible study?

6. How can I model digital discipleship through my own social media accounts? Am I currently doing that?

Notes

[1] https://www.remind.com/
[2] https://www.polleverywhere.com
[3] https://www.marcopolo.me/
[4] https://www.logos.com
[5] https://www.olivetree.com
[6] https://www.accordancebible.com

Chapter 57
PowerPoint Usage 101
W. Kirk Brothers

Introduction

A cartoon I have seen comes into my mind as I begin this chapter. The cartoon shows a gallows, an executioner, and a condemned man. Instead of a noose hanging from the gallows, there is a screen, and the man is being forced to watch Power-Points. That cartoon is a reminder that many have experienced what some call "death by PowerPoint." There is no denying that in some corners PowerPoint has been overused and poorly used. In spite of that, *PowerPoint* (Microsoft Corporation) has become an effective tool in preaching and when used properly, it can be an outstanding aid. Other programs that can be helpful are *Prezi* and *Keynote. ProPresenter, SongShow Plus, MediaShout.* I have used *Prezi Pro* and have attended a Prezi workshop. I have friends who love using *Keynote*. Having noted that other programs are available, this presentation will focus on *PowerPoint* because it is the program most widely used and available in congregations across the country.

PowerPoint Purposes

Before purchasing the equipment and software necessary to use PowerPoint, you will need to consider why you want to use it. The mere fact that many others use it does not necessarily mean your congregation needs PowerPoint (though very few do not use in it in today's culture).

General Purposes

I have found that projection systems can assist with announcements, singing, focusing people's thoughts during various parts of worship, and in projecting lesson PowerPoints. If your congregation decides to use PowerPoint, you will need the appropriate equipment (software, computer, projector, mounting equipment, etc.), lighting, and set-up to make this work. Bright lighting and large windows can make PowerPoint projection difficult. Some congregations have added curtains to assist in lowering the amount of light coming in from windows. The equipment necessary to project can be expensive. I recommend having an expert in lighting and projection systems assist your congregation with the size projector you will need and the amount of lumens that will be needed. If you have a large auditorium you will need a "long throw" lens. Some congregations use rear-projection systems, and many congregations are moving away from projectors and toward using flatscreens. Limits on screen size can be a problem but there is much better picture quality with flatscreens.

Lesson Purposes

Next, you must decide what your purpose is for using a PowerPoint presentation in your specific sermon or Bible class lesson. How can PowerPoint assist you in connecting God's Word to people's mind, hearts, and lives? The goal of your message is to help your audience in their journey to becoming like Christ by explaining, illustrating, and applying a portion of God's Word. Your PowerPoint is not the goal of the lesson; it merely assists you in teaching God's Word. You must consider what you hope to accomplish by using PowerPoint. I seek to use my PowerPoint to do the following:

1. Show the title of the sermon (on an attractive and thought-provoking slide).
2. Emphasize the key idea of the sermon (what I call the "Biblical Bull's Eye").
3. Highlight the key points.
4. Get the text of Scripture in front of people (this is the greatest benefit for me).
5. Use colors, underlining, and highlighting to emphasize various parts of a passage.
6. Use pictures/graphics/videos as illustrations to help people to remember, focus, understand, and think/reflect.

Highlighting the Text

Some speakers avoid putting the words of the biblical text on their PowerPoint slides. They prefer to cite the passage on the slide so that people can look the verse up in their own Bibles. Some feel that PowerPoint keeps people from using their personal Bibles. I take a different approach. First of all, it is my observation that very few audience members look at their Bibles during the sermon (no matter how often you ask). Also, research shows that few people who claim to be Christians know Scripture well (cf. Christian Smith, *Soul Searching*, Mark McCrindle, *The ABCs of XYZ*, or James Emory White, *Meet Generation Z*). Putting the text of the main passages on the screen assures me that my audience has looked at God's word during the lesson (more than would look at their Bible if I just left it up to them to open their Bibles). I find that some will still look at the verse in their translations even if I put it on the screen.

I also like to use font colors, the glow feature, and underlining to emphasize key elements of passages (such as the five participles in Ephesians 5:15-21). It helps me to highlight what the author is trying to communicate with words and phrases in the text. I have found that this is an opportunity to not only assist people in understanding the text but to encourage people to make notes that can be used in personal study. I encourage people to make notes in the margins of their Bibles (or through adding notes to the text in their Bible apps). In the end, I believe that more personal learning and Bible study is achieved when I put the text on the screen.

The Power of Pictures

Pictures can be very powerful. Pictures inspire people to think. Putting a picture of a jet airplane on the screen while you are telling a story about a jet can tremendously enhance the power of the illustration. I have known of speakers who had nothing but pictures in their PowerPoints. They picked a different picture to go with each idea or illustration in the lesson. This can be very effective. Video images can also add punch to your message and your illustrations.

A Word of Caution

You must be careful not to use too many slides in your presentation. I use 20 to 30 slides in the typical sermon. I tend to use more slides for classes than for sermons. It is important that you do not make the PowerPoint a mere reproduction of your notes. Doing so makes you obsolete. Putting all your notes on the screen also removes any element of surprise in the sermon. Finally, having too many slides can cause your key ideas to get lost in the mass of information. I put all the notes for my sermon in the "Notes" portion of the PowerPoint (which only I can see). The PowerPoint slides should highlight and stress key ideas. If you reproduce everything in the slides, you emphasize nothing.

PowerPoint Preparation

A key factor in preparing a PowerPoint presentation is making sure the fonts are legible. I try to never use anything smaller than a 28 font (and prefer 32 and above). I know of one expert on PowerPoint that never uses anything smaller than a 40 font. Be careful about using fancy fonts. They are often hard to see on a screen. Fonts that look great on your computer will frequently be hard to see when they are projected. Also, remember that you may need to play your PowerPoint on a different computer than the one you created it on (or you may share it with people by email or text). When you travel to speak at different congregations, you may discover that the computers in those congregations do not have all the fonts your computer has. I avoid using custom fonts that have to be manually loaded to my computer. Standard fonts that I use are Arial, Calibri, Cambria, Times New Roman, Tahoma, Veranda, etc. Indeed.com recommends the following fonts for professional presentations: Tahoma, Georgia, Verdana, Palatino, Garamond, Roboto, Gill Sans, Lato, Corbel, and Futura (10-29-23). You can also embed some fonts in your presentations, but some will have copyrights that do not allow this. A simple "embed PowerPoint fonts" search on the web will give you directions on how to do so. You can also save slides as a photo file and then insert it back into the PowerPoint as a picture. This will keep the font that is on the slide. Also, be careful about putting the fonts too close to the edge of the slide. The layout may look fine on your computer, but you may not be able to see the words on the edges when you project the slides onto the screen.

Font Colors

The colors you use for fonts and backgrounds are important as well. The colors you use for the words on the screen need to contrast well with your background colors (black/white, yellow/blue, etc.). Dark backgrounds work best with light-colored words and light backgrounds work best with dark-colored words (do not use dark on dark or light on light). The outlining feature on the new versions of PowerPoint (.pptx extension) allows you to create an outline or a glow effect around the letters in your words. This helps the words to stand out against the background.

Slide Backgrounds

You can vary the background color schemes, change fonts, and add graphics to increase the "eye appeal" of the presentation. You can find background pictures using Google images but you need to be very careful not to use copyrighted material. You can subscribe (for a fee) to PowerPoint background services like *ignitermedia.com*. You can get free pictures from *unsplash.com* and can purchase pictures from sites like *123RF.com*. You can also create your own backgrounds by using your digital camera or smartphone to take pictures that can become backgrounds for your slides. For example, I have discovered that Zoos are great locations to take pictures that can become backgrounds. Zoos put a lot of work into the habitats for the animals and the aesthetics of the park (ponds, lilies, trees, flowers, etc.). This scenery can become a great picture background for a slide. If you will purchase and learn to use programs like *Photoshop* or *Canva*, you can make simple alterations to the pictures you take and create several different types of slides from a single picture. You can also create graphics for advertising youth activities with these programs. It is important to remember that modern digital cameras often take pictures that create very large files. As a result of this, some PowerPoint shows that include several pictures (such as Missions reports) will bog down or freeze up. Thus, you may need to decrease the quality/size of the picture file before inserting it into the show. I usually save a copy of the picture at the original size in case I need it for other applications. I often use

Photoshop or *Photoshop Elements* to adjust my pictures but there are other programs that will do so as well.

Using Videos

Make your presentation suitable for the age of the audience to whom you are showing it (i.e., young people tend to like movement and graphics while older adults often like less movement). You can insert video clips into PowerPoint slides for use in lessons. Movie clips can be purchased from sites like *wingclips.com*. Movie clips can be very helpful but you must be careful. Many congregations feel uncomfortable with video clips being played in the auditorium on a Sunday morning that include sound. Yet, I have found that some of these same churches are ok with a video clip on a Sunday night or in a classroom. I frequently use video clips in classes. When I use them in sermons, I generally turn off the sound (because the instrumental music in movie clips makes people uncomfortable) and just let the video play on the screen over my head while I talk about it. Most people seem to be ok with a clip if there is no sound. I will also use videos I have recorded, such as videos of my honeybees, in presentations. Make sure you talk to your congregation's elders/leadership about this before using any video clips. You also need to be careful about the kinds of movies you show clips from. Do not use clips from movies that are inappropriate for Christians (we should not be watching those anyway). I also tell people that we use filtering software that takes out the inappropriate parts when watching movies at our home (*Vidangel*, *ClearPlay*, etc.).

PowerPoint Presentation

If someone else will be changing your slides for you (and they do not have "dual-screen" capability which allows them to see your current and next slide), print out a handout copy of the entire show and go over it with them (most churches now have dual-screen capability so this is not necessary). PowerPoint will allow you to print multiple slides per page. These can also be used as handouts for the audience. It is good to preview the show under the exact conditions in which it will be shown (which often requires arriving early when guest speaking). Look at it from every corner of the auditorium and make sure it is visible. Remember that presentations never look as good on the screen as they did on your computer (though flatscreen presentations are often pretty close). Testing the show beforehand also helps you to make sure that the fonts you chose transferred when you copied it and that videos function properly.

Pre-Presentation Considerations

When guest speaking, I usually email my PowerPoints ahead of time, so they have plenty of time to upload it to the system. This also gives the elders time to look at any videos I might use. It is also important to find out what slide-size ratio the church uses (4:3, 16:9, 16:10, etc.). If not, it will frequently mess up your slides when they are converted to the new size (even though) they will tell you it is no big deal). You also need to check ahead and learn if the church is going to be inserting the PowerPoint into a program like *ProPresenter*. Many of these programs do not play well with PowerPoint. They often turn each slide into a jpg and remove all animated bulleting you have built into your PowerPoint. Thus, instead of being able to reveal items in a list one at a time, they are revealed all at once. Having all of the items in a list show up at once on a slide can be a little like telling the punchline of the joke before actually telling the joke. If they use these kinds of programs, you will probably need to create a separate slide for each bullet point you have built into the slide. I have found that such presenter programs are good for the person running the control board, but bad for the preacher or teacher. As you can tell, I am not a fan. Just make sure you are prepared for this.

My friend Jason Hart is a youth minister in Arkansas and has also preached for several years. He double majored in Bible and art.

I always hated to speak after him at events because his PowerPoints were so awesome and made mine look lame. He reviewed this chapter and gave me some helpful insight. One thing he noted is that he likes to use widescreen formats (16:9, 16:10, etc.) because he can divide the screen into 1/3s or have an offset of two columns. Jason also shared that due to there being so many different presentation formats, he has started using still slides only (with no animations). If he has multiple points on a slide that he does not want to reveal all at once, he creates several progressive still slides that add the points. This process adds several slides and limits creativity for your animations but overcomes potential issues with the presenter programs.

Remotes and Cheater Screens

Part of pre-testing includes making sure that the remote control works well and that you know how to use it. Each remote is different and you need to know the function of every button on the remote you will be using. Some congregations do not have a remote control, so I always take one with me. I do not want to say, "Next slide please," through my whole sermon. Note whether the congregation has a monitor that you can use to tell if your slides are advancing properly. Not all congregations have a monitor (in today's technological world, I think it is unacceptable to not have a "cheater screen" the preacher can see from the pulpit or a podium, but no one asked me). Some have a monitor that is viewable from the pulpit but is not viewable from other locations (such as when you are using a portable stand down closer to the audience in a Bible class). Remember to talk to the audience during your presentation, not to the screen. It is very frustrating when a speaker stares at the screen while delivering a lesson. Make sure you know your presentation well enough that you can maintain eye contact.

I prefer to have someone else advance my slides when preaching at my home congregation where I preach on a regular basis. It allows me to have my eyes and hands-free to maintain contact with my audience. It often takes time to train a person to advance the slides for you and to listen for your cues. I generally tell the person changing my slides to change the slide when I mention anything on the next slide. Shawn Butterfield of the Graymere congregation in Columbia, TN is one of the best I know at doing this. He might be able to give some pointers to the person who does it at your congregation. When teaching a Bible class, I like to change the slides myself. If you plan to control the changing of the slides yourself, you will want it to be as seamless as possible. Practice advancing your slides while you practice delivering your sermon. I have found that I can usually train someone at my home congregation to advance the slide for me, but I have found that when traveling, the person running the projection booth usually cannot keep up. They will say that they can but frequently struggle to do so. Thus, when traveling, I usually advance my own slides. You need to be prepared for both possibilities.

What If I Need Notes?

If you need notes of your slides to look at during your lesson, you might try a couple of things that I do. First of all, I used to print handouts of my slide show with six slides per page. Next, I would cut the pages down to a size that fits in my Bible. I would then paperclip the reduced handout pages into my Bible. If I use notes in my sermons, I typically want them in my Bible. I do not like to take pieces of paper into the pulpit. I now preach almost exclusively from my iPad. I put a copy of my PowerPoint in the *PowerPoint* app on my pad and my phone (emergency backup). I usually remove all bulleting and videos from the copy in my iPad because I do not need them. The *Keynote* app will display Power-Points, but it usually adjusts your fonts and layout. I also put a backup of my PowerPoint in a folder in my Google Drive. This allows me to access it in an emergency if I need to while traveling. More and more churches are also making it possible to run your slideshow directly from your laptop or pad.

Conclusion

Jesus regularly used visuals and the best teaching methods of His day to proclaim the Word of God. He could, for example, have merely told His audience to be humble learners. Instead, He placed a small boy in front of the audience to give a visual representation of His message. We are doing no differently when we use a PowerPoint. As long as it does not violate Scripture, we owe it to God to use the best of technology to help people understand God's message for humanity. The Devil has been using technology long enough to deliver his message. It is time we started doing more to use it for God's glory. PowerPoint presentations are one way to do so.

Discussion Questions

1. Discuss whether you think it is best to include the full text of the passages in your PowerPoint slides or whether it is best just to give the reference and let the students look at the passage in their own Bibles (or both).
2. What are the top mistakes you have seen people make when using PowerPoint?
3. What are some ways that PowerPoints have helped you through the years? (best practices)
4. Talk to the young people in your youth group about what they like and do not like in PowerPoints.

Bibliography

Editorial Team. Popular PowerPoint Fonts for Professional Presentations. uk.indeed.com, 8-16-23, accessed 10-23-29.

McCrindle, Mark. *The ABCs of XYZ: Understanding the Global Generations*. 3rd ed. Bella Vista, Australia: McCrindle Research Pty Ltd, 2014.

Smith, Christian. *Soul Searching*. New York: Oxford Press, 2005.

White, James Emory. *Meet Generation Z*. Grand Rapids: Baker Books, 2017.

Sample PowerPoint Slides (Jason Hart)

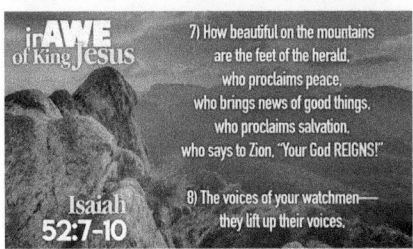

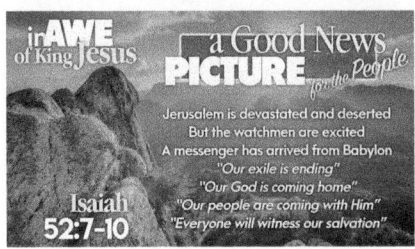

632   In Christ's Image

Chapter 58
Equipping Parents for Digital Parenting
Chad Landman

Introduction

> The digital age is upon us. In the span of less than three decades, we have redefined the way that humans communicate, entertain, inform, research, create and connect—and what we know now is only a hint of what is to come.[1]

Albert Mohler wrote those words a little over ten years ago, and he was as correct then as he is now. For the past eight years or so, I have been blessed to travel around this country talking with parents in churches about how to be the best digital parents they can be. I list some helpful tools and give out a lot of information, but digital parenting, as I have found, is more about the mindset of the parent rather than the actual tools, apps, and services we might use to keep our children safe.

The Digital Age

Mohler was correct. Thirty years ago, seems like ancient history compared to now but think about the fact that in 1993 we were just starting to see personal computers in homes. The internet would not hit it big for another couple of years. Facebook was still over a decade off (Feb. 2, 2024, marked the 20th anniversary). YouTube, Twitter, and Instagram were not even conceived of yet.

Fast-forward to just 2010 and you see how much things had changed. The iPhone, released in 2007, changed the way we communicate, let alone how we perceive the mobile internet. Other companies followed suit, and now we have a sea of black glass rectangles that we stare at for hours a day. And all of this happened in just the span of the last 15 years. Television and radio took 10 times as long for it to become so heavily adopted.[2] The iPhone is so ubiquitous now that we cannot imagine life without it.

Now, think about your kids. Whether they are 4, 14, or 24, they have grown up in an entirely different world than you did. Haydn Shaw referred to Generation Z as the "internet-in-your-pocket" generation.[3] James Emory White notes, "The speed by which this technological revolution has taken place is stunning and makes it difficult for older generations to realize the radically different world into which Generation Z has been born."[4] Today's young people will never know the world without Netflix or YouTube. They will never have to run home to record something on the VCR because they forgot to tape it. They will never understand not being able to listen to any music they want in any genre and whenever they want. This generation of kids has a lot more pressure and things to deal with than we ever did. These digital devices are wonderful for productivity, communication, and entertainment—but they also come along with peer pressure and other dangers that no generation before them has ever had to deal with.

Helping Families Manage the Digital Age

We are all connected by social networks and 24-hour news, yet we are farther apart than ever. The church is the only thing on this earth—the church that Jesus built and died and was resurrected for—that can provide that true connection. So, as we look at digital parenting, let us think briefly about how you as a minister can help equip your families for the digital world by talking about and implementing these ideas.

Talk Often About the Importance of Truth

Truth has always been important, but never as important as it is now. What we see on our screens needs to be always be tested. Paul told the Thessalonian church to "test everything; hold fast what is good" (1 Thess 5:21). He said this in relation to prophecies that were being promoted but had no truth behind them. Does that sound familiar? Our kids, growing up in this digital world, need to first be taught the truth; about us, the church, our world, and everything in between. Do not let the primary influencer of your child be a screen. Romans 12:2 declares, "Do not be conformed to this world, but be transformed by the renewing of your mind." That verse literally means "do not let the world squeeze you into its own mold."[5] Parents are the ones molding children, the ones who every day have a constant influence on them. They will be products of their environments and build physical, spiritual, and emotional homes a lot like the ones they are growing up in.

Stop Blaming Technology and Start Looking at Our Parenting

There is no substitute for your good, godly parenting. Period. Digital parenting is less about the technology and more about the parenting behind that technology. The Bible says, "Train up a child in the way he should go; even when he is old he will not depart from it" (Prov 22:6). We must guide our children in godly ways, or they will grow up and not follow His ways, on a screen or otherwise. If we place too much importance on grades or sports and not on Christ, we should not be blaming "the technology" when our kids turn out to have no love for the Lord.

Have a Plan

I cannot overemphasize this enough. A failure to plan is a plan to fail. I highly doubt that any of the parents you will deal with in your congregation are not saving for their kids' college or their own retirement. The plan is to have enough money when your kids are ready for school or you are done working, right? So why would we not have a plan for our child's digital development? My son is on the Autism Spectrum, and we have what is called an IEP, or Individualized Education Plan for him at school. In digital parenting, we need to have a DPP (Digital Parenting Plan) for every child, because as you know, every child is different. You and your child need to talk in-depth about when your child will get a phone, when and what social media they will be allowed to have, what rules will be in place, and what disciplinary measures will be taken when they violate those rules (and they will).

Fight Fire with Fire

You may be thinking, "What do I mean by 'fight fire with fire?'" Well, the very thing you are trying to do with digital parenting is protect your children, and you need not look further than your own device. YouTube and Google can be powerful tools to help you figure out issues in dealing with all sorts of situations. Knowledge is power, and information is readily available. In this day and age, none of us should say, "Well I did not know that." No excuses. If you messed up your taxes this year, who would be to blame for that? You would. This is because all the knowledge is out there and accessible to do your taxes and there are even qualified people you can pay to do your taxes for you. So, there is no excuse there, and there will not be an excuse when your child makes a mistake with their technology.

Some of the tools available now are outstanding and fairly easy to implement. If you have iOS (Apple) devices, then start with ScreenTime for little ones. You can use Google's Digital Well Being app for Android devices. Then you can move into more specific use-case apps. These can include OurPact or Qustodio, both of which are available on Android and Apple operating systems. These apps guide you through the setup process of being able to monitor your child's app usage, social media, text messaging, and several other things. For older teens who are driving, Life360 is an excellent way to keep track of their active lives. The app will monitor where they are, will alert you when they arrive or leave a place of your choosing, and will even tell you how fast they are driving down the highway.

Realize That They Are Just Kids

It is important to remember that your kids are going to make mistakes... because they are kids. Remember what Moses wrote in Genesis 37:2 about Joseph? "Joseph, being seventeen years old..." I find that really funny. We know Moses was probably marking history and not making a joke, but you see how he prefaced the story of how foolishly Joseph behaved and got himself thrown in a pit and sold into slavery? It is as if he was saying, "No seventeen-year-old has made great decisions. Exhibit A is Joseph." We cannot expect our children to be perfect, and we cannot expect them to know right versus wrong unless we teach them and help them to learn from their mistakes.

Conclusion

I truly believe that this next generation of kids will be the greatest generation that the church has ever seen—IF we guide them the proper way. As parents and ministers, we need to be constantly thinking about ways that we can help our kids navigate the digital world so that they can grow up to become responsible digital citizens —and not just that—but holy members of God's kingdom as well.

Discussion Questions

1. What do you think is the number one problem facing young people and technology today?
2. What are some ways you can brainstorm on how to help parents who are facing a delicate situation (Example: a teen found sharing inappropriate photos)?
3. Research one parental control app (there are a bunch). What are the apps weaknesses and strengths? Why would or would not this app be useful to parents to use for their children's protection?

Notes

[1] Mohler, Albert. *The Christian Leader in the Digital Age.* albertmohler.com, Feb 26, 2013.

[2] Horace Dediu; Comin and Hobijn (2004); OurWorldInData.org/technological-change.

[3] Haydn Shaw, *Sticking Points* (Carol Stream, IL: Tyndale House, 2020), 123.

[4] James Emory White, *Meet Generation Z* (Grand Rapids: Baker Books, 2017), 42.

[5] Cf. "do not let yourselves be molded" in *Linguistic & Exegetical Key to the Greek New Testament* by Cleon Rogers Jr and Cleon Rogers III. (Accordance Software, 2020).

Remaining Strong in Youth Ministry

Chapter 59
What I Have Learned in Youth Ministry
Chase Surrell

Introduction

I am grateful for the opportunity to share some of the important lessons I have learned from my many experiences in youth ministry (20 years as of the writing of this book). I must admit after a long period in youth ministry there are still days where I am reminded that I do not have everything figured out. The dynamics of youth ministry are continually changing. Technology continues to move forward, impacting youth ministry. The issues our youth are confronted with have changed over time. As one group of students moves on and another group joins the youth program, you will quickly learn what worked with one group might not work with the other. Each year you may have to reorganize and evaluate what the next year will look like given these changes in your youth program. As I have navigated through the different seasons and changes in ministry, I have made my share of mistakes. I hope to share with you some important lessons I have learned along the way so you will not make the same mistakes I made.

Make Sure You Grow

As I reflect on my years in youth ministry setting aside a time for personal Bible study was challenging. I am sure that some of you may find this confession shocking. You may be thinking to yourself, "How can a youth minister not make time for Bible study?" Events and activities do not plan themselves. There is a great deal of time and energy that goes into organizing an event. Also, there is the important responsibility of teaching multiple Bible classes during the week. The curriculum plan, class lessons, and visual aids we construct take time. Some congregations may ask the youth minister to work alongside the minister and be involved in other ministry tasks. Going with a minister to visit members is valuable and important, but it also takes up time. Some youth ministers may be asked to work with several ages and not just teenagers. At one congregation I was asked to work with the college age down through 3rd grade. Just take a moment and reflect on that age gap. I oversaw youth events, devotionals, and some of the classes for all those ages. There were several times in my ministry I felt like there just were not enough hours in the day. It was easy to prepare and study for other people's spiritual growth, but somehow my spiritual growth got pushed to the side. Preparing a lesson for class is not a substitute for challenging Bible study.

In your ministry, you are going to have a difficult time helping teens to grow spiritually if you are on empty. Even in the busyness, you must find moments for prayer and Bible study. If you do not make personal Bible study a priority in your life, then you most likely will not make time for it. When you do not make time for personal Bible study your ministry will be impacted, and your spiritual growth will be impacted. Tim Elmore tells a story that motivated me to contemplate how important it is to feed myself spiritually. There was a chief baker who created a new recipe for breads, bagels, pastries, and cinnamon rolls. Soon, word gets out about this bagel shop. Crowds start forming lines each day, waiting for the new sweets to come from this baker's marvelous kitchen.

The baker does not have enough help and ends up trying to serve all the customers himself. He is scurrying back and forth, busy with all the requests of the people. The baker is oblivious to what is happening to him. His exhaustion is quickly becoming burnout. As you watch him over a few weeks you see a change. The man is getting thin. . .very thin. It almost seems like he is shriveling up. What's up with that? With continued observation, the problem becomes obvious. The man never stops to eat. The irony is, he is busy serving bread for everyone else, but never stops long enough to feed himself. With food all around him, he is starving (Elmore 2010, 5). Does this story sound familiar? In youth ministry, we can be just like the baker. We can spend so much time feeding others spiritually that we forget to feed ourselves spiritually. The lack of spiritual nourishment leads to burnout, shallow Bible classes with no thought-provoking content, and missed opportunities for deeper discussions with students. Make sure that you keep moving forward in your spiritual growth.

Relationships Are Key

After being in youth ministry for a long period of time I have learned that relationships are vital. I am sure many of you already know this and understand that we need to be very intentional to build and grow relationships within your ministry. I wish someone had told me how to build relationships when I was younger. Be sure you learn about your teens and find out what their interests are. Ask your teens what they like to do. Go to their school activities and support them. Celebrate with them when they have success. Walk with them and support them when they face challenges. Take opportunities to have meaningful conversations with them. When we take the time to build those relationships with our teens two significant things will happen. First, as they get to know you, they begin to feel more comfortable around you. When students feel comfortable around you, they begin to trust you. You need your students to trust you if you want them to confide in you. If teens do not know you or trust you then they will not come to you for help. Secondly, when you grow and build relationships with your teens, they will be willing to listen to your words of guidance. There is an old saying, often attributed to Theodore Roosevelt, that I have heard many times, "People don't care how much you know, till they know how much you care." When you spend time with your teens and invest in their lives, it lets them know you care. When you need to have those hard conversations with your teens, they will be more open to hearing what you have to say. You may never know the impact you have on a teenager just because of the personal relationship you have with him or her.

In addition to developing relationships with our teens, it is vital that we focus on developing other relationships to help our ministry thrive. First, do not forget to focus on building relationships with parents. Remember parents are not the enemy; they are allies. You need their help, and you cannot do everything yourself. For your ministry to succeed you need their support. It is important that you spend time getting to know the parents of the teens and start building up their trust in you. When trust is built between the youth minister and parents there is so much more that can be done for God's kingdom. Communicate with them regularly, and let them know how they can play a role in the ministry program.

Secondly, it is important to build good relationships with the elders. In 1 Timothy 3:1, Paul writes "The saying is trustworthy: If anyone aspires to the office of overseer, he desires a noble task." It is important to respect your elders and the leadership positions they hold. Over my ministry career, I have had good leaders and some leaders who are good people. In my experience, I have also seen good men in leadership positions who just do not understand how ministry works. Likewise, I have seen youth ministers who do not fully understand all the elements that go into church leadership. Be patient and understanding with your leadership. Support them, and encourage them. Remember you need an eldership that will love and support you in your ministry. I learned very quickly that elderships do not like being surprised. Be open and honest with them about what is taking place in your ministry. It is vital that you keep an open line of communication with the leadership. I wish I had done this in my early years of ministry. Someone might be thinking the question, "Well what if they will not listen?" The reality is sometimes your leadership will listen to your input and accept it and sometimes they will not. As youth ministers, we must realize we are not always going to have things happen the way we want them to happen. You must work through these times, and keep striving to do your best.

Thirdly, it is important that we build relationships with other youth ministers. During the early parts of my youth ministry career, I was blessed to have two youth ministers who worked close to me. These two men had been in the youth ministry field for some time and had a lot of wisdom to share. Often, I would go to them for advice on how to deal with issues. They would encourage me to look at the situation in a different way. When I was discouraged, they would pick me up. And in return, I would do the same for them. The three of us grew a strong bond and were often seen together. I am so thankful to these two men who took me under their wing and mentored me. Even now I am fortunate to have several youth ministers that work close by. Once a month we try to meet and enjoy a meal together. We pray for each other's ministries. We talk about the successes and the frustrations we are experiencing. We lean on each other for support and help. You need a support system in ministry.

Goals and Communication are Important

Another confession I wish to share is in my early years of youth ministry, I was guilty of putting events on a calendar just to keep the youth group busy. I guess you could say we were busy without a purpose. One way to address this issue is to set goals for your youth program. Setting goals will give you a clear direction for your ministry. This will help your students keep focus on what you hope to accomplish. Your goals will help structure your calendar. Instead of just having events so that you can be active, now you can plan with purpose and make sure the events and programs accomplish your goals. Setting goals will allow you to evaluate the progress of your youth program. You need something you can look at to see if you are on track or if you are weak in certain areas of your youth program. Once you have established goals for your youth program, be sure to communicate them to your youth, parents, leadership, and volunteers. Having goals for youth program will be of little value if you are not communicating them to others.

I could share with you several examples of where I failed to be an effective communicator. When you do not communicate effectively it will negatively impact your planning, frustrate your parents, and cause confusion with your leadership. It is not a fun experience when the elders call you in for a meeting and let you know they need more information about the events of your youth program. Most problems can be avoided if you communicate and let people know what is going on. Be sure to communicate your information early and often. It is wise to use every communication tool you have at your disposal and share information in different ways. If most of your parents are on social media, then go meet them where they are and create a private group on social media. You can create a text group and send messages. I would suggest you create a youth events calendar and distribute it to your parents and teens. Work with your church secretary and get important information in the church bulletin. Effective communication may take more time and effort, but it is worth it to have everyone on the same page.

Make Time for Your Family

As I have continued in youth ministry my family dynamic has changed. I am now a husband and a father. In the early stages of my youth ministry career, I had more time to dedicate to youth events and more time to be involved in the community. After I became a husband and a father, I soon learned I could not devote the same amount of time to youth ministry as I did when I was single. I had to learn the important practice of balance. Creating balance is difficult in youth ministry. Youth ministry is not like a normal job. As my dear friend Jerry Elder always says, "You don't have a job, you have a ministry." We do not have a place where you can go and punch a time clock. We are on the clock all the time. Therefore, we must be intentional to create time for our families. Scheduling family time will likely look different for each family. Make sure you communicate with your spouse and children to create a plan that works best for you. Another reason it is hard to create balance in youth ministry is because of unrealistic expectations. Over my time in ministry, I have been asked to do a lot of jobs other people did not want to do. I have been asked to oversee ministries that did not follow under the umbrella of youth ministry. It is okay for you to say, "No!" Learn to set healthy boundaries, and learn to say "No." You cannot be involved in every activity or ministry in your congregation. Do not cheat your family of their time. You cannot turn back the clock and get those hours back. Remember if you are a husband and father, you have obligations to fulfill. Ephesians 6:4 states, "Fathers, do not provoke your children to anger, but bring them up in the discipline and instruction of the Lord." Your obligation as a father is to teach your children about Jesus and help them get to heaven. Ephesians 5:25 states "Husbands, love your wives, as Christ loved the church and gave himself up for her." Your obligation as a husband is to love your wife and help her get to heaven. Do not neglect your family.

Conclusion

To be transparent, when I first started youth ministry, I would have never dreamed of being in youth ministry for many years. When people ask me how long I plan to stay in youth ministry my answer is, "I don't know." I feel like spiritual development is crucial during the teenage years. I have a passion for youth ministry, and youth ministry is where I want to serve. I hope the lessons I shared will help you in your ministry. When I was younger, I thought being a youth minister would be fun. The truth of the matter is leadership is hard. As a leader, you will have hard conversations with families —families that you built relationships with and care about. As a leader, you will have to handle and process frustration and hurt. As a leader, you will receive criticism. Just remember that not all criticism is bad, and you will not make everyone happy. There will be peaks and valleys in your ministry. Be sure not to let the low moments defeat you. Even in the low times, stay committed to your ministry. In the low moments take care of yourself spiritually and find someone you can talk to. The being you better be talking to the most in those low moments is the Lord. Whatever you face in your ministry, do not let it pull you away from your relationship with the Lord.

Discussion Questions

1. What are some things that inhibit you from focusing on your personal relationship with God?
2. What are some habits or resources that have helped you to strengthen your personal relationship with God?
3. Brainstorm ideas for building better relationships with parents and elders.
4. What are some good ministry habits you have seen in someone else?
5. What did you find most helpful in this chapter?

Bibliography

Elmore, Tim. *Habitudes Book #1: The Art of Self-Leadership*. Poet Gardener Publishing, 2010.

Chapter 60
Don't Quit
Dale Jenkins

Introduction

Paul told young Timothy to "fulfill your ministry" (2 Tim 4:5). Darby renders that phrase, "fill up the full measure of thy ministry." And while every Christian is to be a minister, those who, like Paul and Timothy, have chosen the ministry of teaching God's word seem to have a unique responsibility. The visual to Paul's statement is of a cup filled to the top, and then a little more added to it so that it is overflowing. What a beautiful and lifelong mission, but a challenge, nonetheless.

You have read this fantastic book about ministry to young people and their families. You have the tools, the training, the heritage, and the background. You have in your possession probably the most comprehensive handbook that has ever been put together in churches of Christ for those who have an interest or who are trying to work well with young people. It should be on the top of your desk, and it should be referenced often. But the fact is that neither tools, training, heritage, skills, nor natural talent ensure the effectiveness of the mission to fill to the full your ministry. Ministry is a unique field.

Give Me Two

Give me two people, one with all the training our schools offer and the other a dairy farmer who loves kids and practices consistency. The one without the skills impacts hundreds of kids. The skilled one got his feelings hurt and quit.

Two more guys. One's talent virtually runs in his veins, and the other is awkward and rather goofy. The one with the massive talent cannot work with parents or leaders and jumps out of ministry in no time, disquieted that people cannot see that his way is best. The goofy guy learns to say, "I could be wrong," trusts his elders' wisdom, and knows that parents are, well, parents and grows his group tremendously.

Two more guys. One is cool to the max. He has mad gaming skills, an excellent eye for design, and is uber-creative. The other, well, he is not. His eye for design is outdated, he does not play video games, and he uses dated "already been tried" programs. But he outworks the guy who rests on his own coolness and continues impacting lives for many generations.

The above are all real examples. I have noticed that hard work trumps coolness, respect for authority trumps creativity, patient dedication wins out over a flashy presence, and love for teens trumps talent. The guys who are most effective for the longest time may have talent, creativity, and connection skills, or they may not. But every one of them has dedication, consistency, and faithfulness in their work.

This is absolutely essential because this work is not easy, and the obstacles are ever-changing. It is not like putting gizmos on sprockets—the same thing every day. It's not factory work where you clock in at eight and clock out at 5. It's not counseling where you leave your clients in a file cabinet at the end of the day. It's not accounting where all the columns line up, and you close the books out each day or year. It's not firefighting where you put the fire out, and it's over. Yet there is a monotony to it as you must be consistent, there is a factory nature to it as you will be called into account for the hours you work, there is counseling as you get into the messy lives of others, there is accounting as you will be responsible for balancing a budget, and there will be fires to put out. But the fires will probably reignite, the numbers will rarely balance out, the counseled persons will not stay in the file cabinet, the hours are rarely 40 hours a week, and every day, the planned schedule will have to be flexible.

Sticktoitiveness

"Stick-to-it-iveness" is not a word, but it should be. See, there will be plenty of times to walk away, pursue something different, or throw in the towel and quit. There will be the parent who you can never please, the teen who seems to personify evil, the elder whom you feel is working against you, the deacon who wants everything done right so badly they makes your life miserable at times, the calendar that refuses to be tamed, and the push between "church work" and family time. And none of that gets to the personal insecurities, the self-doubt, the sin you struggle with, the challenges of the text, the guilt that you sacrifice either time in ministry for family or family time for ministry, the loneliness many ministers feel, the knowledge that with your skills and education, you could support your family better financially while working more reasonable hours in some other work.

The list of reasons to quit is endless, and I would never minimize it. Yet, I want to remind you that you signed up for this. You signed up for unjust criticism, for the unnecessary undervaluing, the untenable hours, the unfair expectations, and the misunderstanding of what you do. This is not just a current thing that is new to ministers, a cultural thing that is unique to American youth ministers, or a congregational thing that only you and your community deal with. Paul said it this way, "Everyone who wants to live as God desires, in Christ Jesus, will be persecuted" (2 Tim 3:12, NCV). Or better yet, consider Jesus's own words: "Remember the word that I said to you: 'A servant is not greater than his master. If they persecuted me, they will also persecute you'" (John 15:20). And we must never forget, "In the world, you will have tribulation. But take heart; I have overcome the world" (John 16:33). It is in those times when ministry life seems to be closing in on you, and you think door-to-door vacuum sales would be a better option than this that you need to take heart in Peter's assertion,

> For this is a gracious thing, when, mindful of God, one endures sorrows while suffering unjustly. For what credit is it if, when you sin and are beaten for it, you endure? But if when you do good and suffer for it you endure, this is a gracious thing in the sight of God. For to this you have been called, because Christ also suffered for you, leaving you an example, so that you might follow in his steps (1 Pet 2:19-21).

These Things Do Not Help

You are going to be tempted to quit. So what do we do about it? First, here are three things we are tempted to do that probably will not help.

Moving Is Not Necessarily Going to Make It Better

While sometimes we may need to move for a fresh start, it most often is just a band-aid. But, while moving physically to another location does not really help the feeling you need to quit—moving on emotionally **is** essential. In fact, in our book, *Biblical Keys to Effective Ministry* we say that "there is a direct parallel to how long it takes you to get over a hurt and your long-term effectiveness in ministry." Yet, moving on does not completely solve the quitting problem because by the time you move on, another matter that may make you quit will undoubtedly arise.

Moaning Will Not Make It Better

Yes, you do need people in your life to whom you can unload and lean on when the going gets tough. But there is a difference between mourning and moaning. While moaning may make you feel better for a moment, in the long term, it will zap the joy from your ministry.

Malice Is Not Going to Make It Better

Malice, along with its brothers, revenge, unforgiveness, and bitterness, always hurts the one it is contained in more than the one it is released on. It never brings the satisfaction that we might believe it would, and it leaks into other parts of our lives and causes us to be less like Jesus rather than more like Him.

These Things Do Help

So, what will help you when you think of quitting? While there may be many options, I want to suggest a few that I find helpful. When you are at your end and ready to quit, there are some things you might remember and do.

Remember Why You Got into This

I imagine you did not get into this to get rich, you did not get into this to feel rested all the time, you did not get into this thinking everyone would love you, and you did not get into this believing it would be a cushy job with a bunch of lavish perks. You can feel free to add to this little list.

When the church at Ephesus had left their first love, before the Lord came to unchurch them (i.e., remove their candlestick), He gave them a remedy. "Remember therefore from where you have fallen; repent, and do the works you did at first" (Rev 2:5). So, I suggest you do what He said. Go back. Go back and remember. Go back and redo the old stuff that you got into this for. Go back to where you started. A love for Jesus, for His people, and His young people. Remember the excitement and joy that took you into ministering to young people.

Love the Good Things in Your Ministry

You got into this to do good, not to do paperwork! Sometimes all the administrative stuff that comes with the role can weigh us down. I'm not suggesting you ignore things like records if your leadership expects them, but I am suggesting you not make those the focus of your ministry. I am unsure where I first heard it, but someone said: "We do the things we do not want to do to get to do the things we love." I've known plenty of leaders who require meticulous and sometimes taxing records to be turned in (sometimes that is because we or someone before us is/was irresponsible). I have also known ministers who, upon learning of this paperwork, have focused so much on the paperwork they forgot why they got into this work in the first place. So, do more good things than paperwork. Load your ministry with good things! Maybe your issue is not paperwork; perhaps your issue is difficult people. If your focus becomes those difficult people, your work will only become more complex. Do not focus your lens on the problematic people; instead, "do more good things." I have known ministers who get so myopic on a challenging individual that they let that person steal the joy of their ministry. What I have noticed over and over is that when a minister has someone "out to get them," there are multiple others who want to support them, but the minister starts focusing on the few instead of the many.

Learn to Value Your Ministry

Youth ministry is ministry. The significance of youth ministry is often undervalued. This undervaluing may be because many of our first youth ministers took those roles to work with an experienced minister so they could learn what they were doing. And that was not bad. But it made youth work look like a bike with training wheels (or a stepping stone to what they really wanted to do in ministry). Then there will be those who believe your job is "just playing with the kids" and that you are nothing more than a big kid yourself. The reality is that church leaders typically will pay you about 25–40% less than the pulpit minister. Even preachers are prone to not seeing the seriousness of your ministry. But just because others do not value what you do, does not mean you should. Youth ministry IS real ministry. It is down in the trenches where young people are making the most serious decisions of life and making choices that will affect the rest of their lives. Youth ministry is where most of the young people who "grow up in church" determine to become Christians. Youth ministry is where opinions on the validity of the church will be solidified. Youth ministry is where most often, decisions about becoming a minister are determined. Paul told Timothy to "let no one despise your youth" (1 Tim 4:12). I would suggest you should not despise it or your work with youth either. What you do is of uber importance to the Lord, the Lord's People, and the Lord's Work.

Recognize that You Are Not Alone

Youth ministry may sometimes feel isolating. To stay in this, you must surround yourself with positive influences who will build you up. Way too many ministers have ministry friends who only talk negatively about the church, about our commitment to God's authority, about elders, and about ministry. It would help if you found other ministers, both younger and older than you, who will encourage you. But that is not all: Remember, there are people in your congregation, even the young people you influence, who want to stand beside you and hold you up. Remember also that the Lord, who cannot lie, has promised, "I will never leave you or forsake you" (Heb 13:5).

Conclusion

It is not a sin to step away from paid ministry. Sometimes it would be a sin not to. But think it through long and hard. Strive to grow and learn from those things that are discouraging to you and might make you think about quitting. The Lord and His church need you. YOU are valuable and vital, as is your work. So, please, don't quit.

Discussion Questions

1. What are some healthy things you have done when you get discouraged?
2. What are some things YOU are responsible for that lead to frustration, and what can you do to avoid those things?
3. Are there specific times/seasons of discouragement for you? What can you do during those times to keep going?
4. What characteristics are needed in the people who help keep you going?

Bibliography

Darby, John Nelson. *The Holy Scriptures: A New Translation from the Original Languages*. Public domain. 1890.

New Century Version. Nashville: Thomas Nelson Publishers. 1983, 1987.

Appendix 1—Camp Medical Release Form

_____ CAMP STAFF
HEALTH HISTORY AND MEDICAL RECORD

The information on this form will be provided to any health care providers in case of an emergency. This information will not be used to discriminate against a participant on the basis of any disability.

Name of Physician_____ Phone ( ) -

Medical/Hospital Insurance_____
　　　　　　　　　　　Carrier　　　　　　　　　　　Policy or Group #

Check all that apply

____ Allergy to a medicine, food, plant, or insect toxin. Explain _____

Is participant allergic to the following drugs: ____ Penicillin ____ Sulfa Drugs ____ Tetracycline ____ Aspirin

List allergies to other drugs or allergens: _____

____ Any condition that may require special care, diet or restriction of activities for medical reasons?
　　　Explain _____

____ Asthma ____ Heart Trouble ____ Nose Bleeds ____ Diabetes ____ Convulsions ____ Fainting Spells

Do you wear? ____ Dentures ____ Contact Lens ____ Other (Explain) _____

Is any medication, including medication for behavior modification, being taken at the present time? ___ Yes ___ No
If yes, explain _____

Date of most recent examination ___/___/___

Are you aware of any current health problems? ___ Yes ___ No If yes, explain _____

Is there any disease, accident, illness or past/present history related to the following? (If yes, please give dates and full details.)

	No Yes Year		No Yes Year		No Yes Year
Serious Illness/Injury	___ ___ ___	Appendicitis	___ ___ ___	Rheumatic Fever	___ ___ ___
Surgery	___ ___ ___	Kidney Infection	___ ___ ___	Stomach	___ ___ ___
Ears, Eyes	___ ___ ___	Teeth, Tonsils	___ ___ ___	Blood	___ ___ ___
Back, Limbs, Joints	___ ___ ___				

Immunizations	Last Yr. Given	Immunizations	Last Yr. Given	Have Had	
Tetanus		Measles		Measles	
Diphtheria		Mumps		Mumps	
Polio		Rubella		Rubella	
Hepatitis (A, B, or C)		Varicella (Chicken Pox)		Chicken Pox	
(circle one/any)				Tuberculosis	

Emergency Medical Release
In consideration of my participation in the Horizons, I provide the following release. I understand that a health problem or a medical emergency may develop that necessitates the administration of medical care, hospitalization or surgery. In the event of illness or injury, I hereby authorize _____ and its representative(s) or agent(s)) to secure any necessary treatment, including the administration of anesthetics and surgery. I further give permission to _____ and its representative(s) or agent(s) to provide this medical history form to health care personnel. I authorize my physician, health care provider or any hospital to provide reasonable and necessary medical treatment or supplies. Either the original permission or a photostatic copy thereof is valid as an authorization. I recognize that _____ sickness and accident insurance does not provide full coverage for participants in this activity or event. I accept responsibility for payments of those medical costs incurred for injuries or illnesses that are not covered by _____ insurance. I have read this Release and Assumption of Risk Agreement and signed it on behalf of myself, my heirs, assigns and anyone entitled to act upon my behalf.

*Signed_____ Date_____
　　　　　Staff Member's Signature　　　　　　Month, Day, Year

Appendix 2—Youth Ministry Protocol List

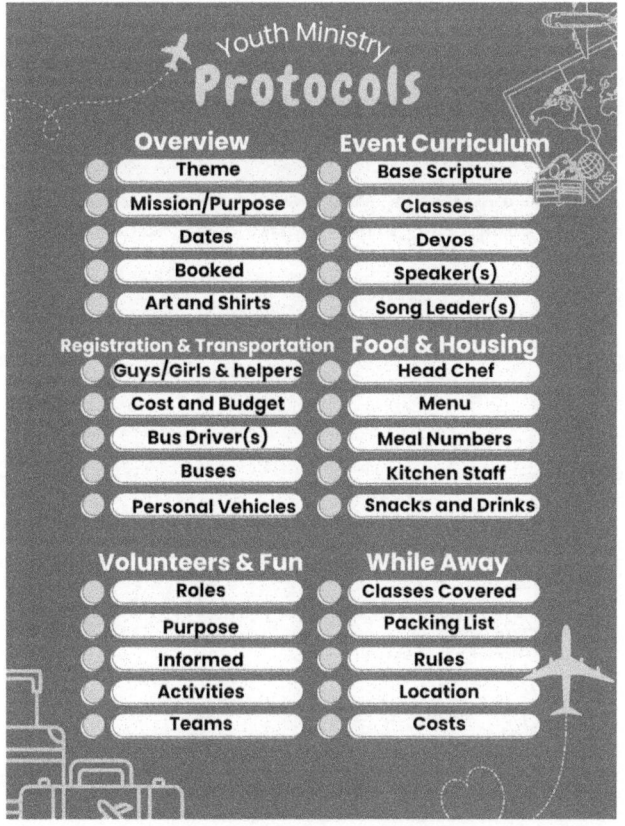

Appendix 3—Curriculum Development—Student Learning Objectives handout

Curriculum Development - Student Learning Goals/Objectives
Kirk Brothers

Mission Statement for Education Program: (Create a mission statement for your youth education department, should include purpose of program and philosophy of education)

Student Learning Goals: List what you think teens should know, believe, value, do or be able to do when they graduate from High School (and your youth program).

KNOWLEDGE	BELIEFS	ATTITUDES/VALUES	ACTIONS/ABILITIES

Student Learning Objectives (one-sentence statements of what kids should gain from being in your Bible classes in junior high and high school):
1.
2.
3.
4.
5.

Contributors

Jordan Abrams — Youth Minister, Madison Church of Christ (Madison, AL)

Jody Apple — Evangelist, Gold City Church of Christ (Dahlonega, GA); Student Minister

Josh Austin — Preaching Minister, Church of Christ at Salt River (Mesa, AZ); Raised on Navajo Reservation

Dr. Bill Bagents — Professor of Ministry, Counseling, and Biblical Studies, Heritage Christian University; author and associate editor with Heritage Christian University Press

Jarrod Bailey — (deceased) Former Campus Minister, University of Tennessee at Martin

Joey Barrier — Director of the Center for Missions Training and Information; Adjunct Instructor, HCU

Billy Bearden — Preaching Minister, Foote Street Church of Christ (Corinth, MS)

Lori Boyd — Women's Minister; Author; Speaker; High School Teacher at Middle Tennessee Christian School (Murfreesboro, TN)

Dr. Kirk Brothers — President and Professor, HCU; Missionary, Latin American Missions; Academic Director, Bible School of the Americas

Contributors

Kyle Butt — Author, Debater, and Speaker, Apologetics Press

Ben Coleman — Family and Education Minister, Bartlett Woods Church of Christ (Arlington, TN); Adjunct Professor, Freed-Hardeman University

Hector Cruz — Preaching Minister, Iglesia de Cristo de Church Street (Lewisburg, TN)

Dr. Nathan Daily — Vice President of Academic Affairs and Professor, HCU

Larry Davenport — Young Families Minister, Jackson Heights Church of Christ (Florence, AL); Executive Director, Challenge Youth Conference

Michael Deese — Youth Minister, Hartselle Church of Christ (Hartselle, AL)

Luke Dockery — Youth and Family Minister, Cloverdale Church of Christ (Searcy, AR); Adjunct Professor of Youth Ministry, Harding University

Justo Dorantes — Preaching Minister, Iglesia de Cristo, Beltline (Decatur, AL)

Craig Evans — Preaching Minister, Mt. Juliet Church of Christ (Mt. Juliet, TN)

Austin Fowler — Project Coordinator, *House to House Heart to Heart*; Missionary, Latin American Missions

Dr. Ryan Fraser — Professor, Freed-Hardeman University; Preaching Minister and Elder, Bethel Springs Church of Christ (Bethel Springs, TN); Licensed Clinical Pastoral Therapist

Tim Frizzell — Family Minister, Crieve Hall Church of Christ (Nashville, TN)

Dr. Ed Gallagher — Professor, HCU; Associate Minister and Educational Director, Sherrod Avenue Church of Christ (Florence, AL)

Ryan Gallagher — Preaching Minister, Hamilton Church of Christ (Hamilton, AL)

Jesus Gallardo — Hispanic Minister

Jeremy Gargis — Youth Minister, Pulaski Street Church of Christ (Lawrenceburg, TN)

Justin Guin — Associate and Youth Minister, Double Springs Church of Christ (Double Springs, AL); Adjunct Instructor, HCU. He and Tiffany have three children, with their oldest being diagnosed with Autism Spectrum Disorder.

Tiffany Guin — Special Education Teacher, Double Springs Middle School (Double Springs, AL); M.S. in Special Education.

Dr. James C. Guy — Professor, Faulkner University.

Ben Hayes — Preaching Minister, Highland Park Church of Christ (Muscle Shoals, AL); Licensed Counselor

Jason Helton — Media Outreach Minister, Madison Church of Christ (Madison, AL)

Matt Heupel — Preaching Minister, Woodlawn Church of Christ (Florence, AL)

Jeremy Hinote — Associate Clinical Director, LifeStance Health; Licensed Counselor (Augusta, GA)

Carter Hoover — Youth Minister, Centerville Church of Christ (Centerville, TN)

Beto Huamani — Preaching Minister, Iglesia de Cristo (Madison, AL)

Dale Jenkins — Cofounder of The Jenkins Institute; Board Member, HCU

Philip Jenkins — Youth Minister, Mt. Juliet Church of Christ (Mt. Juliet, TN)

Jeff Johnson — Evangelist and Elder, Conyers Church of Christ (Conyers, GA)

Lonnie Jones — Licensed Counselor; Consultant; Speaker (Huntsville, AL)

Patrick Kershaw — Youth Minister, Killen Church of Christ (Killen, AL)

Andrew Kingsley — College Minister, University Church of Christ (Montgomery, AL)

Dr. Brandon Lanciloti — Certified Public Accountant; Associate Professor and Assistant Dean of the College of Business, Freed-Hardeman University

Chad Landman — Education Minister, Graymere Church of Christ (Columbia, TN)

Bryan LeMasters — Discipleship Minister, Mt. Juliet Church of Christ (Mt. Juliet, TN)

Thad Looser — Children's Minister, Tuscumbia Church of Christ (Tuscumbia, AL)

Colt Mahana — Assistant Dean to Spiritual Life and Chapel Services, Faulkner University

Dr. Jim Martin — Retired Vice President, Harding School of Theology

Zack Martin — Instructor of Historical Theology, HCU

Bill McDonald — Retired Funeral Director, McDonald Funeral Home (Centerville, TN)

Blaine McKinney — Communications Minister, Mt. Juliet Church of Christ (Mt. Juliet, TN)

Chuck Morris — Preaching Minister, Spring Meadows (Spring Hill, TN), Former Adjunct Youth Ministry Professor at Freed-Hardeman University

Justin Morton — Preaching Minister, Walter Hill Church of Christ (Murfreesboro, TN)

Lauren Moss — Children's Ministry Coordinator, Mt. Juliet Church of Christ (Mt. Juliet, TN)

Will Myhan — Student Minister, Highland Park Church of Christ (Muscle Shoals, AL)

Jeremy Pate — Youth Publications Coordinator, Apologetics Press

Dr. Andrew Phillips — Preaching Minister, Graymere Church of Christ (Columbia, TN); Adjunct Professor, HCU

Jon David Schwartz — Youth Minister, Graymere Church of Christ (Columbia, TN)

Dr. Will Sharp — Campus Minister, Central Church of Christ (Tuscaloosa, AL)

Dr. Rosemary Snodgrass — Licensed Counselor, Retired Professor, HCU

Paul Spurlin — Connections Minister, Piedmont Road Church of Christ (Marietta, GA); President and CEO, Ministry League

Chase Surrell — Youth Minister, Great Oaks Church of Christ (Memphis, TN)

Reed Swindle — Preaching Minister, Waterview Church of Christ (Richardson, TX)

Dewayne Tapscott — Preaching Minister, Southwest Church of Christ (Huntsville, AL) and Piney Grove Church of Christ (Winfield, AL)

Richard Turner — Youth Minister, Madison Church of Christ (Madison, AL)

Dr. Steve Wages — Professor and Director of Cloverdale Center for Youth and Family, Faulkner University

Rob Whitacre — Director, *House to House/Heart to Heart* School of Evangelism

Heritage Christian Leadership Institute Series

Corrupt Communication: Myths That Target Church Leaders
by Bill Bagents and Laura S. Bagents (2022)

Counseling for Church Leaders: A Practical Guide
by Bill Bagents and Rosemary Snodgrass (2021)

In Christ's Image: A Guide to Youth and Family Ministry
edited by W. Kirk Brothers (2024)

Lead Like the Lord: Lesson in Leadership from Jesus
by W. Kirk Brothers (2021)

Liderando Como Jesús: Lecciones de liderazgo de Jesús
by W. Kirk Brothers (2024)

CYPRESS

To see the full catalog of Heritage Christian University Press and its imprint, Cypress Publications, visit www.hcu.edu/publications

www.ingramcontent.com/pod-product-compliance
Ingram Content Group UK Ltd.
Pitfield, Milton Keynes, MK11 3LW, UK
UKHW021249180426
11946UKWH00003B/46